NATIVE
PEOPLES
AND
CULTURES
OF
CANADA

ALAN D. McMILLAN

NATIVE
PEOPLES
A N D
CULTURES
O F
CANADA

AN ANTHROPOLOGICAL OVERVIEW

SECOND EDITION — REVISED AND ENLARGED

DOUGLAS & McINTYRE • **VANCOUVER/TORONTO**

97 98 99   5 4 3

Douglas & McIntyre Ltd.
1615 Venables Street
Vancouver, B.C. V5L 2H1

The publisher gratefully acknowledges the assistance of the Canada Council and of the British Columbia Ministry of Tourism, Small Business and Culture for its publishing programs.

Canadian Cataloguing in Publication Data

McMillan, Alan D. (Alan Daniel), 1945–

Native peoples and cultures of Canada

Bibliography: p.
Includes index.
ISBN 1-55054-150-1

1. Indians of North America—Canada—History. 2. Inuit—Canada—History*
3. Métis—History.* I. Title.
E78.C2M24 1988   971'.00497   C88-091141-7

Maps by Brian McMillan
Editing by Brian Scrivener
Front cover art and page 185, Eagle (band) design
    by Reg Davidson, courtesy of Potlatch Arts Ltd.
Typeset by Fiona MacGregor
Printed and bound in Canada by Best Book Manufacturers, Inc.

CONTENTS

PHOTOGRAPH CREDITS

All photographs are credited in the captions. Some institutions are identified by
their initials:

CMC: Canadian Museum of Civilization
NAC: National Archives of Canada
PABC: Provincial Archives of British Columbia
RBCM: Royal British Columbia Museum
ROM: Royal Ontario Museum

Preface to the First Edition

In the past few decades, Canada's First Nations have increasingly entered public consciousness. Movement of large numbers of them into urban centres has made them much more visible, and frequent reporting in the media of such contentious issues as land claims, treaty grievances and fishing rights has kept native issues in the public mind. Articulate native spokesmen received extensive media attention during the recent constitutional debates, in which they presented their demands for a new relationship with government. However, the historical and cultural bases for native claims and grievances are still not well understood by the general public, leading to such commonly heard questions as: "Just what is it that natives want?" and "Why should they have special rights in Canada?" Most Canadians are not hostile to native aspirations but lack the knowledge of traditional native cultures and the modern situation that would allow them to assess the issues.

The stimulus for this book is the lack of an up-to-date overview on Canadian natives, past and present. Diamond Jenness's *The Indians of Canada*, originally published in 1932, is still the classic work on the subject. It provides an excellent summary of traditional native ways of life. However, Jenness was writing at a time when native populations were plummeting, primarily due to diseases introduced by Europeans, and survivors were frequently demoralized and abandoning native customs. Jenness concluded that natives were doomed to extinction, through either dying out or being absorbed into Euro-Canadian culture. Throughout, he laments the passing of the Canadian native. His comments on the people of the Pacific coast are typical:

Their old world has fallen into ruins, and, helpless in the face of a cat-astrophe they cannot understand, they vainly seek refuge in its shat-tered foundations. The end of this century, it seems safe to predict, will see very few survivors. (p. 350)

Fortunately, despite the conditions that Jenness observed, his gloomy predictions were in error. In the following years native populations increased dramatically. Despite all pressures, native people in many areas have maintained or revived their languages, ceremonies, art and other aspects of their culture. Native political leaders have emerged to press vigor-ously for new recognition of native rights and values. This resurgence of native identity affects all aspects of contemporary native affairs.

Also since Jenness's writing, the various sub-fields of anthropology have made great advances in the study of native cultures. Archaeologists have painstakingly sifted through the soil of village and camp sites across Canada, recovering evidence of how people lived long before Europeans reached these shores. Ethnohistorians, working with archival documents, have cast new light on the early years of contact and resultant native cultur-al changes. Linguists and native elders have collaborated to record and pre-serve native languages, many of which border on extinction. Ethnographers living in native communities have documented surviving traditional prac-tices as well as new adaptations to changing conditions. Present research continues to expand our knowledge of native cultures and how they have changed through time. In addition, an increasing number of native writers has enriched the available literature with published works ranging from tra-ditional histories and myths to autobiographies and political statements.

This book draws together data from a number of approaches to provide a broad historical perspective. It attempts to provide an overview of native Canadian life from earliest prehistory to modern issues. No book, however, could fully do justice to the cultural heritage of any group, let alone cover an entire nation, and much of the rich and dynamic quality of human lives is lost when committed to paper.

Personal experiences, including travel throughout Canada and research with several native bands in British Columbia, have helped shape this book. Primarily, however, it stems from teaching an anthropology course dealing with Canadian native cultures at Douglas College. Over the years my approach to teaching the course has evolved into that taken in the present volume. It is with the hope that this approach will be useful to a wider audience that this book is offered.

In writing a book of this nature, one incurs more intellectual debts than could ever be acknowledged. Many anthropologists, historians, native writ-ers and others have stimulated my thoughts and supplied the information that I have incorporated into this book. To others, who provided me with photographs, unpublished reports, specific information and advice, I am even more directly indebted. These people are too numerous to be listed here, but that does not make my gratitude for their contributions any less. Dr. Knut Fladmark and Dr. David Burley of Simon Fraser University and Jacqueline Gresko of Douglas College offered helpful comments on various chapters of the manuscript. My brother, Brian D. McMillan, prepared the maps and most of the drawings in this book. My editor, Brian Scrivener, and the folks at Douglas & McIntyre, particularly Saeko Usukawa and Barbara Hodgson, kept the project running smoothly and forced me to be concise, curbing my tendency to compile a massive tome. Finally, I am grateful to my wife and sons for their tolerance of my absences and preoccupied state throughout the preparation of this book.

Preface to the Second Edition

Much has happened since the first appearance of this book in 1988. The Oka crisis of 1990 riveted public attention on native grievances. The Marshall inquiry in Nova Scotia and the Aboriginal Justice Inquiry in Manitoba, among other legal hearings, provided stinging indictments of the treatment of aboriginal people in the Canadian criminal justice system. The failure of the Meech Lake Constitutional Accord in 1990 showed that aboriginal people must be recognized as a political force in Canada. By 1992, aboriginal organizations were full participants with the federal and provincial governments in drafting the Charlottetown Accord. Any future attempts to shape Canada's future must address the concerns of aboriginal people.

Slightly over one million people reported having aboriginal origins, either as their only ancestry or in combination with other origins, in the 1991 census. This represents an increase of 41 percent from the 1986 census. Although aboriginal populations are growing rapidly, such a huge increase clearly also represents greater awareness and pride, resulting in more people identifying with their aboriginal heritage. This is not an isolated Canadian phenomenon; the greater cultural awareness and struggle for political control by aboriginal peoples around the world was recognized by the United Nations declaration of 1993 as the International Year of the Indigenous Peoples.

As in the first edition, I continue to be indebted to a wide range of academic and aboriginal authorities, some of whom provided me with information, suggestions and other assistance, while others I know only from their published works. Most of the acknowledgments in the first edition still apply. Once again Brian Scrivener edited the volume. The maps, including several prepared for this edition, are by Brian D. McMillan. As always, I owe a debt of gratitude to my wife and sons for their support.

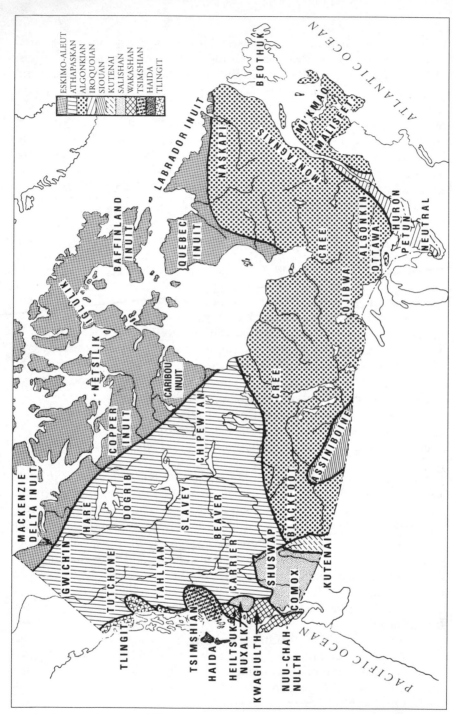

Native language families of Canada, showing approximate locations at time of European contact.

CHAPTER 1 *Introduction: Canada's First Nations*

Over a million Canadians today claim at least partial descent from the original occupants of this country. Aboriginal populations continue to increase, and interest in their culture and heritage, by natives and non-natives alike, continues to grow. Yet the terms "aboriginal" and "native" do not indicate a common or shared culture, but only descent from the various First Nations in North America prior to the arrival of Europeans. Indeed, a great variety in ways of life, histories and languages has characterized the aboriginal peoples of Canada. Three categories of aboriginal people are specified in Canada's constitution: Indian, Inuit and Métis.

"Indians" form the most heterogeneous of the three categories, with a wide range of separate languages and cultures across Canada. This name is, of course, a misnomer, being derived from Christopher Columbus's mistaken belief that he had reached India. The term "Amerindian" (for American Indian) is preferred by some scholars, but has not had widespread acceptance. Some aboriginal people consider the term "Indian" offensive, while others prefer it as a self-designation. It is often required by the legal context, referring to the constitution or the Indian Act. Legal distinctions divide this group into those recognized as "Indian" by the federal government, a status enjoyed by over 550,000 Canadians, and those who are denied this recognition, the so-called "non-status Indians."

The Inuit of the Canadian Arctic have a separate origin and history, representing a later movement of people into Canada. They are closely related to native populations in Alaska and Greenland. In Canada, the former designation "Eskimo" has been almost totally replaced with the singular "Inuk" and the plural "Inuit." These terms, meaning "person" and "people," are

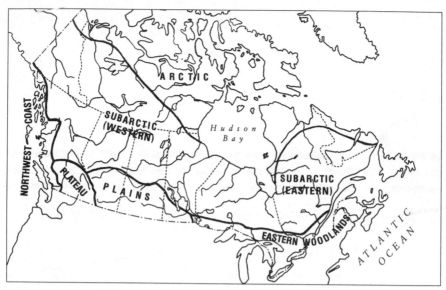

Native culture areas of Canada

how the aboriginal occupants of Arctic Canada refer to themselves in their own language (Inuktitut). This is a relatively homogeneous ethnic category, with a common origin and single language across the entire Canadian Arctic.

Unlike Indians and Inuit, the Métis emerged only in historic times, during the fur trade period. They are a product of the unions between male fur traders, most commonly of French-Canadian origin, and native women, particularly Cree. The resultant population of mixed ancestry forged a common identity on the Canadian Plains during the nineteenth century. This shared identity and lifestyle led to aspirations for the creation of a "Métis Nation" in the Canadian west. Such aspirations were crushed when Métis provisional governments under the leadership of Louis Riel were suppressed by military forces, first in Manitoba in 1870, and then, decisively, in Saskatchewan in 1885. The federal government, which assumed that the Métis would be assimilated into the general population, took no responsibility for their administration and refused them recognition as aboriginal people.

The Métis, of course, did not disappear. Small communities survived, a largely forgotten minority, across the prairie provinces and in parts of the Northwest Territories and the Yukon. Only in latter years have the Métis re-emerged in Canadian consciousness. Particularly important was the 1982 recognition in the constitution of the Métis as one of the "aboriginal peoples of Canada." Public attention was also focused on the Métis during

1985, when a number of conferences and other events marked the centennial of the ill-fated Métis uprising in Saskatchewan.

These three groups can be collectively referred to as "natives," "native people" or "aboriginal peoples." The term favoured by many native Canadians today is "First Nations," with its implication of many separate, formerly sovereign entities. This term, however, applies primarily to status Indians, whose national organization is known as the Assembly of First Nations. Some authorities express concern over the widespread use of such collective terms as "native" and "aboriginal," as these mask major cultural and legal distinctions between the groups.

CULTURE AREAS

Culture areas are broad geographic units within which cultures tend to be similar. Such similarity stems primarily from the fact that all occupants of the area based their economies on the same essential resources, such as bison on the Plains and salmon on the Northwest Coast, as well as from the cultural borrowing which took place between adjacent groups. This provides a convenient means of classification, allowing anthropologists to speak in general of "the Plains tribes" or "the cultures of the Northwest Coast." Such concepts, however, mask considerable internal variability and ignore broad ties of trade and religious thought that linked aboriginal peoples across the continent.

Six native culture areas exist in Canada, although none are contained exclusively in this country. The Arctic, the tundra land of Canada's far north, and the Subarctic, the vast land of northern forests, cover most of the country. The latter is usually divided into Eastern and Western, based on the division between its Algonkian and Athapaskan occupants. Coastal British Columbia encompasses much of the Northwest Coast culture area. Only the northern portions of the Plateau, Plains and Eastern Woodlands fall within Canada.

Culture areas have to be understood as somewhat artificial divisions, imposed for descriptive and analytical convenience. They do not necessarily correspond to native identity. The Cree who moved onto the Plains from their Subarctic homeland early in the historic period did not cease to be Cree, although they did adopt certain traits useful in their new surroundings.

ABORIGINAL LANGUAGES

The exact number of aboriginal languages spoken in Canada at European contact is unknown. Some disappeared early in the historic period, without ever being recorded. Others exist in a wide range of dialects, confusing

Canadian native people. Top left: *Gwich'in, Old Crow, Yukon, 1946.* CMC 100582
Top right: *Kwagiulth, Quatsino Sound, B.C., ca. 1912.* CMC 86135
Bottom left: *Sarcee, near Calgary, Alberta, 1921.* CMC 53311
Bottom right: *Copper Inuit, Bernard Harbour, N.W.T., ca. 1916.* CMC 36915

attempts at linguistic classification. Distinguishing between two closely related languages and two dialects of the same language is a somewhat subjective task, further complicated by the passage of time and loss of traditional knowledge of the language. Approximately 53 distinct aboriginal languages survive in Canada.

Language families each consist of a number of separate but related languages. Eleven native language families exist in Canada, with differences between them as great as those between English and Arabic. They range from large families containing many separate languages to language isolates with no close relatives. Linguistic diversity is greatest in the west, with six families occurring only in British Columbia.

The eleven language families are listed below, roughly in order of size. The first number following each language family is the estimated population in Canada today. Except for the Inuit, this is based on Department of Indian Affairs and Northern Development population figures, listed by band, for the end of 1993. The second figure is the number reported in the 1991 census for people in Canada speaking a language within that family. Comparison with surveys done in the 1980s suggests modest growth for most aboriginal languages. The most pronounced growth was in the Algonkian family (particularly Cree and Ojibwa) and in Inuktitut (Eskimo-Aleut family). The only languages to show marked decline in use were those in the Iroquoian and Tsimshian families. This may primarily reflect problems with census data, as not all reserve communities fully participated in the census process. The Aboriginal Peoples Survey which followed the 1991 census gives a higher estimate of Tsimshian-speakers (about 3000). In general, the Survey reported that 36 percent of native adults could carry on a conversation in their aboriginal language.

ALGONKIAN (365,000 / 150,755). By far the largest and most widespread language family in Canada, this contains such well-known individual languages as Cree, spoken from northern Quebec to the Rockies, and Ojibwa, spoken from southern Ontario to Saskatchewan. Other Algonkian languages include Mi'kmaq and Maliseet in the Maritime provinces, Innu (Montagnais-Naskapi) in northern Quebec and Labrador, and Blackfoot in Alberta. The now-extinct Beothuk of Newfoundland may have spoken an Algonkian language; however, lack of information leads some linguists to give it separate status as a twelfth language family.

ATHAPASKAN (50,700 / 21,815). Northern Athapaskan languages are spoken from interior Alaska to Hudson Bay. Athapaskans occupy the western Subarctic, with several groups in the Plateau and Plains. Individual Athapaskan languages include Gwich'in, Hare, Dogrib, Han, Tutchone, Chipewyan, Slavey, Beaver, Kaska, Sekani, Tahltan, Carrier, Chilcotin and Sarcee.

IROQUOIAN (47,500 / 730). The languages of the original Canadian Iroquoians, such as the Huron and the Neutral, are now extinct. All Iroquoian languages spoken today in southern Ontario and Quebec are those of the famous "Six Nations" or "League of the Iroquois," originally from northern New York state. Mohawk is the dominant language among Canadian Iroquoians, while others (Cayuga, Oneida, Onondaga, Seneca and Tuscarora) are endangered.

SALISHAN (41,500 / 3345). Languages in this family are spoken throughout southern coastal British Columbia, both on the mainland and on eastern Vancouver Island, with Nuxalk (Bella Coola) an isolated example on the central coast. They are also the dominant languages of the adjacent Plateau, in southern interior British Columbia. Coastal languages include Nuxalk, Comox, Sechelt, Squamish, Halkomelem and Straits, while those in the Plateau consist of Lillooet, Thompson, Shuswap and Okanagan.

ESKIMO-ALEUT (33,000 / 26,805). Several Eskimo-Aleut languages are spoken in Alaska and Siberia. However, all Canadian Inuit speak dialects of a single language, known as Inuktitut. An even larger number of Inuktitut speakers exists in Greenland.

TSIMSHIAN (16,000 / 495). Several closely related Tsimshian languages are spoken on the northern mainland coast of British Columbia. The Nisga'a in the Nass River valley and the Gitksan along the Skeena River speak distinct dialects of one Tsimshian language. The Coastal Tsimshian of the lower Skeena and offshore islands and the Southern Tsimshian of the outer islands to the south speak dialects of a second language.

WAKASHAN (15,200 / 3840). The northern Wakashans, occupying the central mainland coast of British Columbia and the northern portion of Vancouver Island, are usually referred to as the Kwakiutl. In the north are the Haisla and Heiltsuk, while the southern groups are collectively termed the Kwagiulth or Kwakwaka'wakw. The southern Wakashans, along the west coast of Vancouver Island, were historically called the Nootka, although today they prefer to be known as the Nuu-chah-nulth.

SIOUAN (13,000 / 4540). This consists of a single language, Dakota, spoken in the southern portions of the three prairie provinces. Dialects of this language are spoken by both the indigenous Assiniboine and the Dakota proper, who are nineteenth-century arrivals into Saskatchewan and Manitoba.

HAIDA (3200 / 220). The Haida occupy the Queen Charlotte Islands, off the northern coast of British Columbia. Their language is an isolate. Although it has been suggested that the Haida language, along with Tlingit, may be distantly related to the Athapaskan family, such connections are highly speculative.

TLINGIT (850 / 155). Most Tlingit speakers live on the southeastern Alaskan archipelago. Their distribution, however, extends into extreme northwestern British Columbia and the southern Yukon.

KUTENAI (750 / 170). This small language group is restricted to southeastern British Columbia. The Kutenai (or Kootenay) language has fascinated linguists as it has no close relatives. Inconclusive attempts have been made to link it to Algonkian and Salishan, but it remains a linguistic isolate.

Language distributions are not static; they continually change over time with movements of people. This process was greatly accelerated in the early historic period, when new pressures, such as the introduction of firearms, disrupted traditional relationships between groups. The Cree and Ojibwa spread far to the west in response to new opportunities and pressures of the historic fur trade. Accordingly, a map of language distributions, such as the one in this book, represents only one late stage in a dynamic process of human migrations.

Only three aboriginal languages (Cree, Ojibwa and Inuktitut) are considered to have excellent chances for survival. All others are endangered, with several facing possible extinction. Although some languages are likely to slip into oblivion with the death of the present generation of elders, determined efforts are being made to halt or reverse the process. Federal educational policy, which once used the schools as instruments of assimilation, punishing children for speaking their own languages, now strongly supports preservation of native languages through the schools. Native communities across the country are experimenting with language and cultural programs, and a substantial percentage of native children now receive some form of native language instruction.

ANTHROPOLOGISTS AND CANADIAN NATIVES

"Indians have been cursed above all other people in history. Indians have anthropologists." (Vine Deloria, Jr. in *Custer Died For Your Sins*)

The above quotation from an American Dakota author illustrates the tension often felt between native groups and anthropologists. Many natives have charged that anthropologists, as members of a colonizing race, are involved in exploitation, removing what they need (information, stories, songs) but providing little or no benefit to the native people they study.

Anthropologists and Canadian natives.
Top left: *Franz Boas (upper right) with George Hunt and his family, Fort Rupert, ca. 1894.* Courtesy American Philosophical Society, Philadelphia
Top right: *Marius Barbeau transcribing songs from a phonograph.* CMC J4840
Bottom left: *Diamond Jenness in the Arctic, 1913-16.* CMC 50806
Bottom right: *Anthropologist T. F. McIlwraith on left with group of Nuxalk, all in ceremonial dance costumes, at Bella Coola, 1922.* CMC 56872

The additional role of many nineteenth- and early twentieth-century anthropologists as collectors of artifacts, transporting the remaining treasures of native communities to distant museums, added greatly to this perception. Today, however, much anthropological research is applied work, done in cooperation with native communities. This ranges from linguists preparing instructional materials for teaching native languages, to archaeologists and ethnohistorians gathering data to be used in legal battles over aboriginal land claims. Government administration and public policy have become fields of study for some anthropologists, who act as advocates on aboriginal issues. Mutual benefit is a requirement for most modern First Nations research.

Anthropology is literally "the study of humans." In North America, however, most research has focused on aboriginal peoples. Sub-fields of anthropology have emerged to study different aspects of native cultures: the ethnographer to collect details of traditional culture from elderly informants, the linguist to study and record the language and the archaeologist to push their history back in time through study of ancient remains. While in earlier times one anthropologist might have been involved in all of these lines of research, today most are more specialized in their approach.

Ethnography, the descriptive recording of specific cultures, is the popular image of the anthropologist, as a researcher observing and recording the way of life of a different society. Early ethnographers in North America attempted to integrate themselves into the culture in order to understand and record the people's lifestyle and beliefs. Later, as the traditional culture became increasingly changed by Euro-Canadian influences, ethnographers began to rely more heavily on knowledgeable native informants for aspects of culture no longer being practiced.

The heyday of ethnography in Canada was the last two decades of the nineteenth century and the first few decades of the twentieth. This was the brief period between the emergence of anthropology as a separate discipline, with field work being done by trained professionals, and the disappearance of much of traditional native lifeways. Although these observers were able to gather great quantities of information on many native groups, they were far too late for others. For example, the Huron and other Canadian Iroquoians, so important in Canada's early history, had been extinct or dispersed for centuries before the emergence of ethnographers. Other groups, while still surviving, had gone through extensive cultural change. The Mi'kmaq, for example, had been in contact with Europeans for almost 400 years before being studied early in the twentieth century. In more remote regions, however, such as the central Canadian Arctic, relatively complete ethnographic data on traditional cultures could be obtained well into this century.

One of the earliest and most important of ethnographers working in Canada was Franz Boas (1858-1942). Trained in his native Germany as a geographer, Boas joined a scientific expedition to the Canadian Arctic in 1883-84. His account of the Inuit of Baffin Island, published as *The Central Eskimo* in 1888, was his first major contribution to ethnography. He then turned his attention to the cultures of the Northwest Coast and in 1886 began field research that continued throughout the rest of his life. Boas was an indefatigable field-worker and a prolific writer, who was concerned with fully documenting native life by amassing great quantities of descriptive information on groups all along the Northwest Coast and into the interior of British Columbia. Most of his writing was on the Kwagiulth, particularly the group at Fort Rupert on northern Vancouver Island. His volumes of descriptive data, produced in collaboration with George Hunt, a native resident of Fort Rupert, make the Kwagiulth among the best documented aboriginal peoples in Canada. Boas and Hunt also published volumes of myths and other oral traditions in *Kwakwala*, the language of the Kwagiulth people. By the end of his life, Boas had become the dominant figure in American anthropology, leaving the field stamped with his insistence on rigorous empirical data collection.

Boas also coordinated the Jesup North Pacific Expedition, a massive research and publication project dealing with aboriginal peoples on both sides of Bering Strait. The Jesup series included important volumes by Boas and Hunt but also by other researchers supported and encouraged by Boas. One of the most important was James Teit, a rancher in southern interior British Columbia, who wrote, in good Boasian fashion, major ethnographies on the Interior Salish.

Perhaps the most distinguished Canadian ethnographer was Diamond Jenness (1886-1969). Born in New Zealand and educated at Oxford, he came to Canada to participate in the Canadian Arctic Expedition of 1913-18. His study of the Copper Inuit of the central Arctic resulted in the major ethnographic source for these people, *The Life of the Copper Eskimos* (1922). Jenness also did field work among the Coast Salish, the Carrier and Sekani of the western Subarctic, the Sarcee of the Plains and the Ojibwa of the Eastern Woodlands. In addition, he made contributions in linguistics, physical anthropology and archaeology. His knowledge of native groups across Canada is clearly shown in his best-known work, *The Indians of Canada* (1932).

Another prominent Canadian ethnographer, a contemporary and associate of Jenness, was Marius Barbeau (1883-1969). Born in Quebec, he eventually studied at Oxford, where he became intrigued by the new field of anthropology. Barbeau was fascinated by the native cultures of the Northwest Coast, particularly the Tsimshian, and began extensive research among them. He was greatly aided in this work by William Beynon, a local resident of Tsimshian descent, who gathered much of the data. Barbeau is best known for his writings on art, such as *Totem Poles* (1950), which records these monuments along the entire west coast of Canada. However, his greatest interest was in the myths and stories, as well as the music. Taking a phonograph into the field, he recorded hundreds of songs and legends.

Many other anthropological pioneers made important contributions. In the East, Frank Speck's study of the Naskapi is an ethnographic classic, as is Wilson and Ruth Wallis's account of the Mi'kmaq; Ruth Landes and Frances Densmore provide the major studies of the Ojibwa. On the Plains, important ethnographic research includes that of Clark Wissler on the Blackfoot, Robert Lowie on the Assiniboine, David Mandelbaum on the Plains Cree and Wilson Wallis on the Canadian Dakota. Many researchers have contributed to our knowledge of Northwest Coast cultures, but particularly important ethnographic works include John Swanton's description of the Haida, Homer Barnett's study of the Coast Salish, Philip Drucker's account of the Nuu-chah-nulth and Tom McIlwraith's work among the Nuxalk. In the Arctic, such pioneers as Knud Rasmussen, Kaj Birket-Smith and Therkel Mathiassen should be acknowledged.

However, credit for the knowledge gathered and published by these researchers belongs largely to their native informants. These people were the repositories of the traditions of their cultures, and we are greatly indebted to them for sharing their knowledge with anthropologists. Furthermore, many clearly went well beyond the passive role implied by the term "informant" and could better be described as colleagues and collaborators. Certainly George Hunt played that role with Franz Boas, as did William Beynon with Marius Barbeau.

Although the major period of traditional Canadian ethnography has passed, some modern researchers are turning to documenting native life in its present complex situation. Good examples come from the writings of anthropologist Hugh Brody. *In The People's Land* (1975), dealing with the Inuit of the eastern Arctic, and *Maps and Dreams* (1981), on the Beaver of northeastern British Columbia, Brody documents the modern realities of native life. These include the nature of relationships with Euro-Canadians, the persistent struggle to maintain native identity and beliefs, and the constant threat to native lands and the animals upon which their cultures depend. These and similar studies offer insights into how native cultures are adapting to new conditions, and they provide a context for understanding modern native grievances.

Ethnohistory, a mixture of anthropology and history, looks at native cultures through written documents. Source material includes the journals and correspondence of explorers, fur traders, missionaries, early settlers and government administrators. Ethnohistorians use techniques of historical research to study native cultures at the time of European contact and subsequent changes. As ethnohistory is restricted to writings left by Europeans, a considerable time lag exists from east to west, corresponding to the rate of European exploration. Thus, almost two and a half centuries separate the early observations of Jacques Cartier on the St. Lawrence Iroquoians in 1535 and those of Captain James Cook on the Nuu-chah-nulth of western Vancouver Island in 1778.

One outstanding example of ethnohistoric documentation is the insight into Huron life provided by the *Jesuit Relations*. From their bases in Huronia from about 1634 to 1650, Jesuit priests sent back voluminous correspondence, describing their work and the people they were attempting to convert, to their superiors in Quebec. There the documents were compiled and sent to Paris, where they were published, providing colourful descriptions of this new land and its people for European readers. As the Huron were dispersed and their culture largely destroyed by 1650, our knowledge of them comes almost entirely from the writings of a few early observers, supplemented by archaeological research.

As vital as this ethnohistoric documentation is, it also has weaknesses and limitations. The explorers, missionaries and government agents who left these records were not trained observers, nor could they be totally objective about practices they were attempting to eradicate. In addition, their accounts of native life are often woefully incomplete, or based on very brief periods of observation. Even the important description of Nuu-chah-nulth life provided by Cook was based upon a stay among them of slightly less than one month, an insufficient time, as Cook himself lamented, to gather data on many aspects of their culture.

Linguistics includes the scientific study of the nature and structure of languages, the evolution of languages over time, including tracing historical relationships between languages, and the interrelationship between language and thought. In early work with Canadian natives linguists were conscious of the declining use of many native languages and the increasing diminution of traditional knowledge, so dedicated much of their efforts to recording songs, myths and other oral traditions in the native languages. As native languages include many phonemes (the smallest units of sound in a language) not found in English, attempts to write native languages using the English alphabet proved unsatisfactory. Accordingly, linguists devised a number of different orthographies (writing systems) to record native languages, using a combination of symbols and English letters to represent all phonemes used. While many such orthographies are now in use across Canada, the International Phonetic Alphabet provides a common standard.

Much earlier, around 1840, a system of syllabics for writing Cree was invented by James Evans, a missionary at Norway House in Manitoba. Syllabic writing differs from that using an alphabet by having one character for the whole syllable (minimally, a consonant and vowel combination). Once established for the Cree, it spread to the neighbouring Ojibwa and Montagnais and later was adapted for writing Inuktitut and several Athapaskan languages. It is still in widespread use.

Another major task of linguistic analysis is to trace historical relationships between languages. Classification of closely related languages into language families indicates a common origin. Where individual languages today are located at some distance from all others in the family (such as Sarcee on the Plains), we can trace past population movements. In addition, controversial attempts have been made to link various language families into larger linguistic units, suggesting a common origin in the remote past.

One of the most distinguished linguists to work on such problems was Edward Sapir (1884-1939), who pioneered studies of language and culture and of the psychology of culture. During a period of residence in Canada he conducted field work on a number of native languages, most extensively with the Nuu-chah-nulth of western Vancouver Island. He not only collected data on the structure of the language but also amassed a large body of myths, stories and accounts of traditional life. Sapir is also well known for his attempts to classify native language families into a small number of "super-stocks," sharing remote common ancestry. For example, he classified the Wakashan and Salishan languages together in a group termed "Mosan" and lumped Mosan into one large super stock with Kutenai and Algonkian. Such suggestions of distant past relationships are provocative but cannot be conclusively demonstrated and are regarded with suspicion by most linguists. However, the American linguist Joseph Greenberg has recently proposed a controversial classification which would place all the above languages and many others in a single category, as is discussed in the next chapter.

Today, much linguistic work is applied, rather than purely academic. Linguists work with native bands across Canada, developing writing systems and assisting in preparing materials for native language instruction. This important role may do much to counter Deloria's claim that anthropology is essentially extractive and exploitative.

Physical (or biological) anthropology, unlike the other sub-fields which study cultural (or learned) behaviour, deals with inherited human physical characteristics. Although largely a biological study, such cultural factors as marriage rules and dietary practices affect biology and must be taken into account. Physical anthropologists study variation in human populations, the environmental and hereditary bases of that diversity, and the evolution of humanity to modern form. Both living and skeletal populations provide information.

Studies of physical characteristics of living populations have a long history in Canada. Boas, for example, included measurement of physical attributes (such as height and head shape) in his studies of Northwest Coast populations. More recently, researchers have investigated such topics as physiological adaptations to cold climate shown by native groups in the Canadian north and how social practices such as marriage patterns help shape the genetic profiles of human populations.

The physical anthropologist often works with the archaeologist to exam-

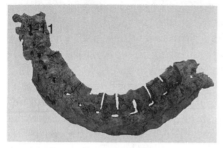

The practice of shaping the head by binding during infancy is evident on the adult male skull (top left) *and the woman* (right), *both Kwagiulth from northern Vancouver Island.* Left, courtesy J.S. Cybulski, CMC; right, NAC PA29860 □ Bottom left: *Many ancient diseases leave their mark on the human skeleton. This collapsed and fused spine, perhaps a result of ankylosing spondylitis or "Marie-Strumpell disease," afflicted a*

ine human skeletal remains recovered through excavation. A wide range of burial practices occurred in native Canada, from single interments to large communal burial pits, as well as placing the dead in caves, in trees or on scaffolds. While burial practices are studied through the context in which skeletal remains were found, the physical anthropologist can also investigate many details through study of bones in the lab. The general morphology, such as height and body build, can be reconstructed. Some insight into diet can be obtained through recent techniques in the analysis of human bone. Many cultural practices also can be seen in skeletal remains. One good example, practiced along the coast of British Columbia, is the intentional flattening of the forehead through binding during infancy, producing a shape consistent with cultural ideals of beauty and status. Evidence of disease, injury or violent death also may be present on the skeleton, giving insights into hazards of life at that time. The prevalence of warfare among the late prehistoric Iroquois is clearly shown in skeletal remains by a high incidence of violent death. Finally, physical anthropologists can study the demography (vital statistics) of past populations, determining age and sex composition of the population, average life expectancy and rate of infant mortality.

Skeletal recovery can pose problems of ethics. Many native people oppose any disturbance of their dead. Nevertheless, human skeletal remains are occasionally exposed by construction projects, by erosion, and during archaeological research. Agreements between First Nations and anthropologists are required for any research on such remains. The potential for conflict over this issue is well illustrated by past events. In 1976, the discovery of a largely intact historic Neutral Indian cemetery in southern Ontario, disturbed by a housing development, forced archaeologists to act quickly to salvage what information remained. As the Neutral have been extinct for centuries, no consultation took place with native bands. When news of the discovery became known, the Union of Ontario Indians was so incensed that they had the archaeologist in charge placed under citizen's arrest for failing to comply with the Cemeteries Act. Work on the site was abruptly halted while legal, moral and political issues were debated. In a similar vein, demonstrations by irate Saskatchewan natives forced the removal of displays containing human burials from the Museum of Natural History in Regina.

In contrast, examples exist of cooperation for mutual benefit. The Hesquiat, a Nuu-chah-nulth group on western Vancouver Island, contacted archaeologists at the Royal British Columbia Museum when they became alarmed at the increasing vandalism and theft occurring at their traditional burial caves. This led to a project to record and remove all contents of the burial caves, which later expanded to a more extensive archaeological program on other sites in the area, as well as linguistic and ethnographic research with the Hesquiat elders. Although professional researchers provided the expertise, all decisions on the direction of the project were made by the Hesquiat. The success of this project led to several others on the Northwest Coast, where archaeologists and physical anthropologists, in collaboration with the First Nations involved, studied and removed human skeletal remains which were being disturbed. After completion of the analyses, all human remains were returned to the First Nations for reburial.

Many museums in Canada and the United States have now adopted policies of turning over to native groups, when requested, all skeletal materials removed from their traditional territory. Some physical anthropologists, however, strongly oppose reburial since it eliminates the possibility of future analyses, when new techniques may be available. This issue continues to be a potential source of conflict.

Archaeology is the study of past human behaviour through material remains. Archaeologists attempt to understand the ways of life of societies that existed in the past, to document cultural change that occurred over time and to develop explanations of how and why such change occurred. Archaeology provides the only approach to the study of cultures that existed long before written records. With the exception of the last few centuries,

Top: *Excavation at the Pender Island site, a large shell midden in southwestern B.C.* Photo by author.
Bottom: *Recording rock paintings in northern Saskatchewan by tracing onto a transparent overlay.* Photo by Zenon Pohorecky, courtesy Tim Jones

the lengthy heritage of native people in Canada can be studied only through material remains that have survived the passage of time. Archaeologists can also study historic native cultures, providing information lacking in the written records. What we know about the Huron and Neutral peoples of southern Ontario, for example, comes from both ethno-historic and archaeological research.

The term "prehistory" is applied to the period prior to written records. Some native people today find it offensive that their heritage is divided into "prehistoric" and "historic," based on the arrival of intruders with their writing systems. As a result, many historians have abandoned use of the term. Archaeologists, however, find it useful to maintain this distinction between the time known from written records and the time primarily reconstructed from ancient material culture. This terminology, however, must not be used to deny aboriginal peoples a history.

Although archaeological sites such as pictographs (red ochre paintings on rock surfaces), petroglyphs (carvings into rock surfaces) and fish traps can be studied only through remains on the surface, other site types, such as ancient villages, contain buried deposits that can be excavated. Modern archaeologists are conscious that excavation is a destructive data-gathering technique, and that maximum information must be recovered. Information used to reconstruct the way of life of the people who lived on the site comes not only from artifacts they made but also from traces of their houses or shelters, other features such as cooking or storage pits, and from bones of animals they ate. Modern archaeologists, often in collaboration with specialists from other disciplines, bring a variety of new scientific techniques to the excavation and analysis of archaeological sites.

There are limitations to the reconstruction of past ways of life through archaeological techniques. As archaeologists are dependent upon material remains of past cultures, obvious biases exist favouring those past behaviours that left most evidence. Other important components of past cultures, such as kinship patterns and political systems, leave fewer material traces. Also, not all elements of material culture survive to be recovered archaeologically. While stone and ceramic objects survive under virtually all conditions, organic materials fare much more poorly. Bone and antler preserve only in non-acidic soils, such as the shell middens on both coasts, while wood, bark, hide and sinew preserve only under exceptional circumstances. In areas of poor preservation, archaeologists are faced with attempting to reconstruct the past using only a small portion of the material culture.

Conditions favouring exceptional preservation of organic materials do exist in Canada. Waterlogging will preserve wood and bark indefinitely, but not hide, flesh or sinew. Several waterlogged sites excavated along the British Columbia coast have yielded objects of wood and bark that would not normally be preserved, such as baskets, fish hooks and line, and cordage. These sites are particularly important on the Northwest Coast, where wood and bark were the dominant raw materials. In addition, at some Arctic sites, where remains have been kept continually frozen, almost no decomposition of organic materials has taken place. Excavation of a late prehistoric Inuit house ruin, resulting in thawing of centuries-old whale oil and food refuse, can be an unforgettable experience! In contrast, the majority of sites in the vast Subarctic contain only tools of stone, perhaps augmented in areas near the Great Lakes by equally imperishable objects such as ceramic sherds or implements of native copper.

Certain discoveries in physics have had major applications in archaeological research. By far the most important has been radiocarbon (or carbon 14) dating. The invention of this technique in 1949 allowed actual dates to be assigned to archaeological discoveries. Atmospheric carbon dioxide contains, in addition to the stable form of carbon (^{12}C), a minute fraction of a radioactive isotope (^{14}C). All living plants and animals contain the same ratio of ^{14}C to ^{12}C as is found in the atmosphere. On the death of the organism, no further radiocarbon is incorporated and the radioactive isotope already present continues to decay at a constant rate. The rate of decay is measured in terms of the "half-life," the length of time in which one half of the radioactive isotope will have disappeared, which in the case of ^{14}C is about 5730 years. The amount of ^{14}C still present in the organism's remains can be measured and compared with the known rate of decay to calculate the time elapsed since death. Samples submitted for radiocarbon dating have to be organic substances, such as wood, bone, shell, seeds or charcoal. These are carefully collected and their exact positions in the site noted, since the age estimates derived from these samples provide the basis for site chronology. A later refinement of the technique, known as AMS (for "accelerator mass spectrometry"), allows very small samples, such as a tiny sliver of bone from an ancient artifact, to be analyzed. Although radiocarbon dating has a number of limitations, the period prior to European arrival in Canada is dated almost entirely by this method.

A major concern of Canadian archaeologists today involves heritage conservation. Native archaeological sites and other heritage remains are being destroyed at an alarming rate, forcing a shift in Canadian archaeology from a purely academic research orientation to an applied management concern. Urban and industrial construction, highways, flooding of large areas for hydroelectric developments and plowing for agriculture all take a huge toll on archaeological resources. Even in remote areas like the Canadian north, which had formerly been spared such disruptions, heritage sites are being threatened by southern demands for development of the north's energy supplies. A conservation and management ethic has linked archaeologists, First Nations groups and environmentalists in attempts to protect Canada's cultural and natural heritage.

Many recent archaeological field projects in Canada have been conducted in consultation or cooperation with local First Nations. Archaeology can be useful to such groups in providing information and objects for native education programs, and in documenting traditional use of the land for legal claims based on aboriginal title. For these reasons, many bands across the country, from the Nuu-chah-nulth of Vancouver Island to the Mi'kmaq of southern Newfoundland, have hired archaeologists, funded archaeological projects or solicited archaeological expertise from various institutions.

Archaeologists, however, may hold quite a different concept of the past than do the First Nations with whom they work. Archaeologists, trained in the European scientific tradition and concerned with collecting empirical data, have tended to discount native traditions about their past as unscientific folklore. Aboriginal people, on the other hand, may perceive their past through surviving oral histories, retold from generation to generation, providing their own explanations for features of the landscape and origins of the people. Such oral accounts document a rich and lengthy history, full of momentous events, migrations and battles, struggles and victories, heroes and sages. Myths tell of powerful transformers, whose ancient actions resulted in the present appearance of the land and the animals. The myths also stress the fundamental unity of humans, animals and supernatural beings, a concept foreign to most Euro-Canadians. Archaeologists have much to learn from these traditions, since scientific reconstructions of the past based on material remains lack much of the richness and human dimension of the oral histories. Both systems of knowledge make important contributions to understanding the aboriginal past.

CHAPTER 2 *The Earliest Arrivals*

Among the most intriguing and controversial of all issues dealing with the First Nations of Canada are questions of origins. When did people first enter what is now Canada? How and when did they move south, all the way to the very tip of South America? What relationship, if any, exists with later native cultures? Unfortunately, the first small groups of hunters, with a simple technology, roaming over vast areas of land, left few traces that survive to the present. Decades of archaeological research have failed to resolve these issues, and new discoveries still spark spirited debate.

One basic point of agreement among anthropologists is that native North Americans originated outside of the Americas. Unlike in the Old World, in the Americas there have been no fossil discoveries of pre-modern humans, such as Neanderthal or *Homo erectus*, so it would appear that humans first entered North America as biologically modern populations (*Homo sapiens sapiens*). The questions are: "From where?" and "When?"

The first question once attracted fanciful speculation. Early writers, unwilling to see in North American natives a people not recognized in the Bible, associated their origins with such historically known seafaring groups as the Egyptians and Phoenicians, or with the "lost tribes" of Israel. An even wilder speculation was that these people were the descendants of those who fled the "lost continent" of Atlantis before it sank into the ocean. Such ideas have not completely died out. However, several early writers recognized a physical similarity between aboriginal peoples of the Americas and Asiatic populations and assumed that an early migration of Asiatic hunters had taken place. Later, with the beginning of anthropological research, the Asiatic origin of North American natives, across what is today Bering Strait, became evident.

Some native people today feel offended by this anthropological belief of migration from Asia. They feel that this demeans their unique status as aboriginal peoples, making them simply the earliest immigrants in a nation of immigrants. Further, such views may conflict with their own religious beliefs and perceptions of their past. Oral traditions often place native groups in their ancestral territory from "the beginning of time." This point is clearly expressed in the "Declaration of the First Nations," prepared by the Assembly of First Nations, which states:

> We the Original Peoples of this Land know the Creator put us here . . . The Creator gave us our spiritual beliefs, our Languages, our culture, and a place on Mother Earth . . . We have maintained our freedom, our Languages, and our traditions from time immemorial.

Basic agreement exists, however, that the First Nations have an ancient heritage in Canada; from the perspective of our own brief lives the thousands of years documented by archaeologists and "time immemorial" are essentially the same.

The second question, concerning the timing of the initial arrival into the Americas, is particularly contentious. Advocates of an early arrival maintain that this occurred at least 30,000 years ago and possibly even earlier (a few speculate as early as 100,000 or more years ago). At the other end of the argument, the conservative view is that there is no convincing evidence for human presence in North America prior to about 11,500 years ago, when the distinctive projectile points of big game hunters known to archaeologists as "Paleo-Indians" first appeared.

In the Beginning: Version One

Sky-woman (known in Huron as Aataentsic), one of the supernatural people who dwell on the upper surface of the visible sky, slipped through a hole and fell into the darkness below. The great turtle, swimming in the primordial sea, observed her descent and commanded the other ocean creatures to bring up mud from the bottom to pile on his back. In this way the earth was formed and still moves about on the back of the turtle. Aataentsic landed gently on this newly formed land and, as she was pregnant when she fell, soon give birth to a daughter. The daughter grew quickly and, becoming pregnant by the spirit of the turtle, gave birth to twin boys, representing good and evil. Iouskeha, the good twin, was born in the normal fashion, while Tawiscaron, the evil-minded, violently burst forth from his mother's body, killing her in the process. It was Iouskeha who made the world suitable for humans by creating lakes and rivers, making corn grow, and releasing the animals from a great cave so that people could hunt them. Tawiscaron, who became the favourite of his grandmother, sought to undo such good deeds. In violent combat between

---

the brothers Tawiscaron was forced to flee. As blood from his injuries dropped on the ground it became the flint which humans use for their arrowpoints and other tools. Iouskeha continues to assist humans, while the spiteful grandmother, Aataentsic, who decreed that all people must die, opposes him. Among the Huron, Iouskeha was identified with the sun and Aataentsic with the moon.

Creation story of the Huron and other Iroquoians

In the Beginning: Version Two

At the beginning of time there was only a vast open sky over a vast open ocean. A single reef lay in this expanse of ocean, with all the supernatural beings crowded on it. Raven, unable to find a place, managed to pierce the sky with his beak and climb into the sky world. There he found a village of large houses. Noting that the village chief had a new grandson, Raven slipped into the house at night and took the infant's place. Eventually he was detected and tossed out of the sky world into the waters below. As Raven floated on the water he heard a voice inviting him into his grandfather's house. He crawled down a kelp stem which he discovered was really a carved post in front of a large house. He was welcomed by a man with the aspect of a sea-gull and given two stones, one black and one speckled. From one pebble Raven created the Queen Charlotte Islands; the other became the mainland. Later a great flood covered the land. When the waters finally receded from a large reef, Foam-Woman, the powerful supernatural figure from which the Haida Raven families are descended, was sitting on it. Various actions of Raven put the world into its present form. It was Raven who brought daylight to a world shrouded in darkness by stealing the sun from a wealthy chief who kept it hidden in a large box.

A version of one of the Haida origin myths

In the Beginning: Version Three

The hunters came quietly over the low rise. They had been following the small family of mammoths all day, and now the shaggy beasts lay directly ahead. Squinting into the glare of the sun off the snow which still covered much of the land on this late spring day, the hunters selected the smallest and weakest animal as their prey. Each of the fur-clad hunters carried a spear, with a sharp tip chipped from stone, with which they would try to dispatch the animal after separating it from the main group. Later, as they butchered the carcass which would feed their entire group for many days, they decided to continue following the herds in the direction of the rising sun. Little could they have known that anthropologists would later call this land Beringia and that they were in the process of colonizing a continent.

Initial entry into North America as often imagined by anthropologists

BERINGIA AND THE
GEOLOGICAL EVIDENCE

For several periods during the Wisconsinan, the final glaciation of the Pleistocene era, most of Canada was deeply buried under huge ice sheets. Glacial conditions were not static, however, but were marked by continual advances and retreats of ice fronts as temperatures fluctuated.

During times of maximum glacial extent a vast amount of the earth's water supply would have been locked up as ice, resulting in a worldwide drop in sea levels by as much as 100 metres. This would have exposed large areas of continental shelf, joining a number of Asian islands to the adjacent mainland. One of the most dramatic effects would have been the emergence of a land surface more than 1000 kilometres wide joining Asia and North America in the area now covered by the shallow waters of the Bering Sea. Although commonly called the "Bering Strait Land Bridge," an inappropriate term for such a large land mass, scientists know this huge sweep of unglaciated land, stretching from Siberia to interior Alaska and into the Yukon, as "Beringia."

The cold, dry steppe and tundra environment provided habitat for herds of large game animals. Mammoth, horse, bison, caribou and musk-oxen occupying Beringia probably provided incentive for a gradual eastern movement of human hunters. As these early nomads followed the game herds into new lands they would have brought with them skills essential to survival in harsh northern conditions, such as the ability to make warm tailored clothing of hide and fur, to construct shelters adequate to withstand extreme cold and to employ group hunting techniques to prey on such large and formidable beasts as the woolly mammoth. It is also possible that some groups were adapted to hunting sea mammals along Beringia's southern coast. Beyond a few basic assumptions, we can say little about the way of life of these shadowy early North Americans.

Geological evidence provides some clues as to when this arrival may have occurred, but dating is far from precise and considerable disagreement exists. The Late Wisconsinan (roughly 25,000 to 10,000 years ago) was a period of cold climate and extensive glaciation, resulting in the exposure of Beringia for much or all of its duration. Most authorities would place human arrival in the Americas during this period. Earlier glacial advances would have also resulted in the exposure of Beringia, but the lack of archaeological sites of this age in Siberia, as well as North America, suggests that human entry to the Americas had not yet occurred. A few archaeologists argue that such sites simply have not been found or recognized yet, pointing to much older remains from northern China as proof that human populations had adapted very early to cold northern climates.

Many archaeologists reject the assumption that humans could have reached North America only when Beringia was fully exposed. At its nar-

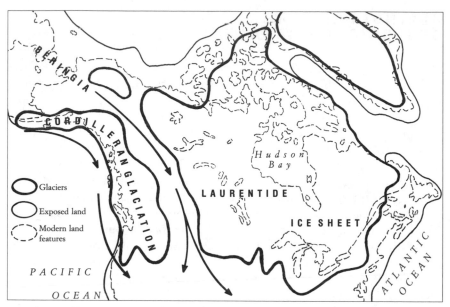

North America near the end of the Wisconsinan glaciation, showing both the "ice-free corridor" and "coastal" possible migration routes for human entry.

rowest Bering Strait is only 90 kilometres wide today, and this width is broken by several islands. On a clear day land can always be seen. Crossing the Strait, either on the winter ice or using some form of watercraft, would have been relatively simple. By comparison, Australia was first populated over 40,000 years ago, despite being separated from Asia by a deep strait. The construction of watercraft would certainly have been within the technological abilities of people at that time.

Another major problem to be resolved concerning early human arrivals is the nature of their southward migration. What route or routes did they take from eastern Beringia to south of the ice sheets, and ultimately throughout North and South America? If the initial spread was during the glacial conditions of the Late Wisconsinan, massive ice sheets might have presented formidable obstacles to southward movement. Hunters could have crossed the unglaciated steppeland of eastern Beringia into what is now the Yukon, but their routes beyond are uncertain. Two major hypotheses concerning southern movement have been advanced.

The traditional viewpoint centres on what has been termed the "ice-free corridor," extending along the eastern slope of the Rocky Mountains. In this view, initial peopling of North America was by way of this unglaciated strip of land between the Cordilleran glacier over the Rockies and the huge Laurentide glacier covering much of northeastern North America. Rather than a single unbroken ice mass existing over most of Canada throughout the Late Wisconsinan, geological studies suggest that coalescence of the ice sheets occurred for only a relatively brief period of extreme glaciation. Many archaeologists have seized upon this geological evidence to provide a logical route out of Beringia for early North American populations, even though there are no archaeological discoveries in the corridor route of sufficient age to support this view. Also, critics of this hypothesis have pointed out that the corridor would have provided extremely inhospitable conditions for human survival: a cold climate, harsh winds and a landscape of rubble, large lakes and turbulent meltwater rivers.

The alternative migration hypothesis involves a coastal route, an idea most vigorously advocated by Canadian archaeologist Knut Fladmark. He points out that most researchers have focused on an interior hunting way of life for early arrivals and ignored the possibility of a coastal adaptation by people possessing some form of watercraft. Although the rugged British Columbia coastline today presents major obstacles to travel, during the Late Wisconsinan lowered sea levels would have exposed large areas of low-lying coastal plain. "Refugia," coastal areas which remained unglaciated, would have provided locations suitable for human habitation. A geological core sample taken from the ocean bottom north of Vancouver Island at a depth of 95 metres yielded evidence of an ancient soil still containing rootlets. Dating of these plant remains revealed that this had been dry land about 10,500 years ago. Scientists now maintain that large areas of the continental shelf were exposed at this time, including several large islands off the central British Columbian coast, which would have greatly facilitated any early migration southward from Beringia. Fishing and hunting sea mammals could have provided a relatively secure food supply for early coastal travelers. However, as people moving by watercraft would leave little evidence of their passing and archaeological sites along the shore would now be submerged, this hypothesis lacks any archaeological support. Several archaeologists are now calling for underwater research as the only possibility for providing the required evidence.

The two hypotheses are not necessarily incompatible, since it is quite possible that there were several distinct movements into North America. The arrival at various times of separate populations with very different cultural adaptations would help to explain the diversity among prehistoric and historic native groups.

EVIDENCE FROM LINGUISTICS AND GENETICS

In recent years the debate over the earliest arrivals in North America has moved from the purely archaeological domain to one which involves linguists, physical anthropologists, geneticists and molecular biologists. By studying modern native populations, these specialists hope to determine historical and evolutionary relationships which have a bearing on the nature, number and timing of migrations into North America.

Central to much of the debate is Joseph Greenberg's controversial argument in linguistics. Greenberg has outraged many of his more conservative colleagues by maintaining that the great linguistic diversity of the Americas can be reduced to three large families, indicating three separate waves of migration from Asia. One of these, on which all researchers would agree, is Eskimo-Aleut. More contentious is his Na-Dene category, comprising all Athapaskan languages plus Tlingit and (more distantly) Haida. Greenberg considers all other aboriginal languages of North and South America to have shared a common origin, and places them in his third category, termed Amerind. It is this huge grouping which has drawn most fire from opponents. Rather than doing detailed comparisons of several languages, as is the traditional procedure in historical linguistics, Greenberg uses a technique of mass comparisons, looking for similarities across a large number of languages simultaneously in order to determine the broad pattern of relationships. In Greenberg's scenario, the ancestors of the Amerind stock entered North America first. He favours a relatively late date, perhaps about 12,000 years ago, which fits well with the view held by many archaeologists. The Na-Dene migration came next, finally followed by the Eskimo-Aleut. Some writers have claimed three different routes for these migrations—the Amerinds traveling down the corridor, the Na-Dene down the coast before expanding inland and the Eskimo-Aleut across the northern reaches of the Arctic.

This model, while sharply focusing debate, remains highly controversial. The majority of linguists disagree both with the methods Greenberg used and with the conclusions he reached. Belief in many separate language families requires an assumption of either multiple migrations into North America or an early arrival with subsequent extensive divergence over time. Both require much greater time depth than Greenberg's views.

The three-migration model has received support from fields other than linguistics. Christie Turner, a physical anthropologist who studies teeth, has conducted a detailed analysis of dental traits based on the remains of thousands of individuals. Teeth have numerous variables which are evolutionarily conservative and are primarily genetically determined, minimizing the effects of environment and other variables. He concludes that all aboriginal peoples of North and South America, along with those in Siberia, Mongolia and north China, share a dental pattern he terms Sinodont. The American Sinodonts are further divided into three groups, corresponding closely to the three defined by Greenberg on linguistic grounds. Turner also interprets this as evidence for three separate migrations into North America, with the Amerinds arriving first. His estimate for the timing of this initial arrival, based on the rate of dental change, is similar to Greenberg's, and he associates these early migrants with the Paleo-Indian archaeological remains. One point of disagreement, however, concerns the Na-Dene migration, which Turner considers to be the most recent.

Genetics also has made a contribution to this study. In an article with Greenberg and Turner, Stephen Zegura reviewed a range of genetic traits and concluded that they could be interpreted as supporting a threefold division. He stressed, however, that different conclusions could be drawn and that genetic evidence could only play a supporting role for inferences drawn from the linguistic and dental data.

Other researchers have turned to the study of mitochondrial DNA (mtDNA), the DNA in the cell outside the nucleus. As mtDNA is transmitted only through the mother, it avoids the genetic shuffling each generation that nuclear DNA undergoes. It also has a relatively rapid mutation rate, resulting in genetic differences between populations emerging more quickly. One major study of global mtDNA diversity independently supported the three divisions of aboriginal peoples in the Americas, roughly corresponding to Greenberg's linguistic stocks, and again concluded that Amerind was the oldest. Attempts to date the genetic divergence of various groups, however, have been inconclusive. Several Amerind populations tested, such as the Nuu-chah-nulth of Vancouver Island, show such a high level of mtDNA diversity that researchers had to conclude that this diversity originated in Asia and that the first migrants to the Americas were genetically diverse.

One interesting implication of the genetic studies, also suggested by dental data, is the close similarity of Na-Dene and Eskimo-Aleut stocks. The Athapaskans and other Na-Dene must have shared a more recent common ancestor with Eskimoan peoples than did the Amerinds. A possible explanation is that the Amerinds were the first group to spread south of the ice sheets, while the Athapaskans are the descendants of groups which remained in Beringia until more recent times.

ARCHAEOLOGICAL EVIDENCE FOR EARLY ARRIVAL

Advocates of early arrival base their claim on sites which, for varying reasons, other archaeologists consider unacceptable or lacking in definitive proof. In some cases the dates are questionable; in others the sites are indisputably ancient but lack acceptable evidence of human presence. The best example of the latter is Calico Hills in central California, which has been seen by some as providing evidence for very early human arrival in North America. The geological deposits are clearly ancient, sufficiently so that proof of human presence would indicate that North America was occupied well before the evolution of biologically modern people. The excavators point to a large sample of flaked stone "tools" as proof of early human presence, but the majority of archaeologists are highly skeptical about these claims for human workmanship and feel that geological forces are far more likely to have been responsible for the flaking. Other sites and surface locations have also stimulated claims for great antiquity, but in the absence of conclusive evidence most archaeologists remain unconvinced.

The case for early human arrival in North America has been greatly weakened by recent re-dating of two supposedly early Canadian sites. By far the most important is Old Crow, in the northern Yukon. Named for a nearby Athapaskan village, Old Crow is actually not an archaeological site but a series of localities along the Old Crow River where fossil animal bones and other materials have been redeposited in huge gravel beds by glacial meltwater. As a result, none of the materials included in the gravels is in original context and the materials cannot be securely dated. Among the fossil bones researchers discovered several which had been modified by humans, including the limb bone of a caribou, cut at one end to a spatulate form and incised with a series of notches to produce a convex "toothed" scraping edge. It was not only immediately recognizable as an artifact but could be readily identified as a flesher, a type of tool in common use among the historic natives of the area for scraping flesh from hides. Radiocarbon dating gave an age of 27,000 years. Unmodified bones of mammoths found in the same deposits yielded similar age estimates.

This dramatic early date sparked a flurry of activity in the Old Crow area. Later expeditions produced a few additional artifacts, such as several antler wedges, considered equivalent in age to the flesher. Many fossil bones collected appeared to have been broken by humans, perhaps in order to extract marrow. Also, some mammoth bones and tusk fragments appeared to have been flaked, and several researchers began to consider evidence for human presence to extend back at least 60,000 years. The date for the flesher, at least, seemed certain and native North Americans were credited in much of the general literature with a minimum antiquity of 30,000 years, based at least partially on Old Crow data.

Some doubts, however, still persisted. The flesher is an artifact type known only from very late periods. Bones of various ages could be mixed in the redeposited gravels. The radiocarbon date was based on apatite (the mineral component of bone) rather than collagen (the organic component), a technique now considered unreliable. Finally, in 1985, a small sliver of the original artifact was tested by a new radiocarbon process. The result was, as some had begun to suspect, that the original date was wildly erroneous. In fact, the flesher is only about 1300 years old, a figure that removes it altogether from the debate on human arrival. Tests on other tools provided similar dates.

The second supposedly early Canadian site to have been recently re-dated is Taber, in southern Alberta. The original discovery consisted of the incomplete skeleton of a human infant, collected from apparent Pleistocene deposits by a geological field crew. Based on analysis of the strata, a date of at least 32,000 years and possibly as much as 60,000 years was presented. However, the imprecision of dating by geological correlation concerned many archaeologists. Finally, in 1981 the bones were subjected to the same radiocarbon technique as the Old Crow flesher and were determined to be about 4000 years old. Thus Taber also disappears as a candidate for evidence of early human arrival in North America.

A similar situation exists in California, where a series of supposedly early human skeletal remains were dated by a technique termed racemization, based on change over time in amino acids in bone. A number of racemization dates were published in the 1970s, suggesting that humans were present in North America at least 50,000 years ago. However, when these were also recently subjected to the new radiocarbon dating process they were all shown to belong to relatively recent times.

While the ranks of sites with claims for dates in excess of 12,000 years have been thinned, there are still serious contenders. One of the best examples is Meadowcroft Rockshelter in western Pennsylvania. Flaked stone tools from the lowest cultural level are associated with radiocarbon dates of between 12,800 and 16,000 years. The usual archaeological requirements of definite tools, in clear stratigraphic association, dated through a series of radiocarbon samples, would appear to have been met. However, even Meadowcroft has its detractors. Specific criticisms are that radiocarbon samples may have been contaminated by the presence of nearby coal deposits (which would add ancient carbon to the samples, making them too old), and that floral and faunal remains from the lowest levels are more consistent with a temperate post-glacial environment than with the late Wisconsinan. These criticisms have been rebutted by the investigators, but "proof" acceptable to all remains elusive.

A final example of evidence for early native presence in Canada comes from two small cave sites in northern Yukon, known collectively as Bluefish Caves. A meagre sample of stone tools, including microblades and waste flakes from tool manufacture, was found with the bones of horse and other late Pleistocene animals in deposits dated between about 15,000 and 10,000 years ago. Unfortunately, the complex nature of the deposits makes it impossible to clearly place the stone tools within the radiocarbon age span. As limited as this information is, it indicates that humans were living at the eastern edge of Beringia during the late Pleistocene.

THE PALEO-INDIANS IN CANADA

The first discovery indicating that humans hunted across North America at a time when the huge beasts of the late Pleistocene were still available as prey came in 1926, near the small town of Folsom, New Mexico. There archaeologists unearthed stone tools in the same level as bones of a species

Early Paleo-Indian projectile points with associated prey species. Left, *Clovis point with mammoth;* right, *Folsom point with giant bison*

of giant bison. Continued work on the site exposed a number of projectile points of a distinctive type, one of which was lodged between two bison ribs. This provided clear evidence that human hunters preyed on these large animals before their extinction at the close of the Pleistocene. Such conclusions were further strengthened in the 1930s, when excavations in Colorado and New Mexico yielded stone projectile points of a somewhat different type associated with the remains of several mammoths. Although this was several decades before the development of radiocarbon dating techniques, it was clear that these aboriginal sites were of considerable age.

The term "Paleo-Indian" has been coined to identify these early hunters of large, now-extinct herd animals ("Pleistocene megafauna" in common archaeological terms). As most of the archaeological discoveries have been at places where animals were killed, we know the Paleo-Indians primarily through the distinctive projectile points they employed to bring down their prey, as well as other stone tools used to skin and butcher the animals. The projectile points were hafted on thrusting spears or on short spears that were hurled with a spear thrower. However, only the points remain for study today. Variations in projectile point styles have led to the definition of several Paleo-Indian "cultures," the best known of which are Clovis, Folsom and Plano.

The earliest well-known archaeological culture in North America is Clovis. Its traces are widespread east of the Rockies, with Clovis or Clovis-like points found from Alberta to Nova Scotia and south to northern Mexico. Its heartland, though, seems to have been across the Great Plains and the American Southwest. Radiocarbon dates for Clovis sites tend to cluster in the brief period between 11,200 and 10,900 years ago.

Archaeologists in the past tended to view the Clovis people as specialized hunters of large game, particularly mammoth. This was a bias induced by the highly visible and spectacular nature of several excavated mammoth kill sites. Actually, such kills were probably relatively rare and the Clovis people likely had a more generalized hunting and gathering economy. The known mammoth kill sites, however, indicate that these people had developed communal hunting techniques to prey on such large and formidable herd animals.

The distinctive Clovis point, along with Folsom, is described as a "fluted" point. After carefully flaking the object almost to its final form, the aboriginal craftsman, with deft blows to the base, removed long flakes from each side. The resultant channel on the lower surface of each side was almost certainly to facilitate hafting to a wooden shaft. "Fluting" is a very distinctive feature associated with the earliest Paleo-Indian cultures.

The Clovis culture figures prominently in many arguments concerning early human arrival in North America. Proponents of the "late arrival" school of thought see the Clovis people or their immediate ancestors as the first native North Americans. In this view, the Clovis hunters arrived at the end of the Pleistocene into a landscape teeming with mammoth, mastodon, giant bison, ground sloth, and the American horse and camel. The extinction of all of these animals by the end of the Pleistocene has frequently been attributed to the activities of human hunters. This "Pleistocene extinctions" or "prehistoric overkill" hypothesis has been proposed by a number of writers but put in fullest form by Paul Martin. In Martin's scenario, small groups of hunters traversed the corridor between the Cordilleran and Laurentide glaciers, arriving near what is today Edmonton around 11,500 years ago. From there they spread explosively to the south, into an unpopulated and biologically rich environment. As the human "front" advanced, population densities became sufficiently large to overkill much of their prey. The "front" then moved on, leaving behind a lower population density. In this way, according to Martin, humans swept across this new land, reaching the tip of South America in only 1000 years and leaving numerous animal extinctions in their wake.

The "prehistoric overkill" hypothesis has been criticized on a number of grounds. The changing climate at the end of the Pleistocene might also have spelled doom for those species highly adapted to glacial conditions. Also, the extinctions did not all occur at once. Horses and camels appear to have preceded the mammoth into oblivion, while the giant bison survived for centuries longer. However, the evidence of Clovis points with mammoth kills and the extinction of the mammoth by the end of the Clovis period makes it likely that Clovis hunters contributed to their demise.

The second early Paleo-Indian culture is termed Folsom, after the location of its original discovery. Folsom points, smaller and more delicate than Clovis, are characterized by extreme fluting, extending over most of the surface of each face. They have a more restricted distribution than Clovis but are found from the southern Canadian prairies to Texas. Radiocarbon dates indicate an age of from 11,000 to 10,000 years ago. By this time the mammoth was extinct, and Folsom people seem to have been relatively specialized hunters of giant bison (*Bison antiquus*). Folsom hunters appear to have been the first to develop the technique of driving bison into natural traps where they could more easily be killed, and most of our knowledge of these people comes from such kill sites.

Although Clovis and Folsom seem to have centred on the Great Plains, fluted points in a variety of styles have been found throughout eastern North America to the Atlantic coast. While some resemble Clovis, others are quite distinct. Since faunal remains are less frequently preserved in these eastern sites we know far less about their subsistence, but it would appear that Paleo-Indian hunters were widespread in North America south of the late Pleistocene glaciers.

Much of Canada would have been covered by glacial ice during the early Paleo-Indian period. However, as the glaciers retreated to the north, human hunters pushed into the newly available land. Numerous surface discoveries of fluted points along the margins of glacial lakes attest to their presence, though only two widely separated sites in Canada have yielded fluted points in their original context and have been radiocarbon dated.

One such site is Debert, in central Nova Scotia. Excavation in the 1960s yielded a large collection of stone tools, including over a hundred fluted points. Several closely resemble the classic Clovis form. Although no faunal remains are preserved in the acidic soils of this region, reconstructions of the past environment led the excavator to suggest that caribou was most likely the major prey animal. Recent blood residue tests on several scraping implements from Debert also suggest the presence of caribou. Radiocarbon dates indicate that Debert was occupied about 10,600 years ago, a time when glacial ice was only a short distance away.

A small excavation at the nearby Belmont site in 1990 yielded an assemblage of stone tools nearly identical to those from Debert. In addition, surface discoveries of Clovis-like fluted points have now been made in all three Maritimes provinces.

Fluted points and other stone tools resembling those from Debert were also excavated at the Vail site, in northwestern Maine near the Quebec border. Once again, faunal remains were not preserved but the major prey animal is believed to have been caribou. These sites show that Paleo-Indian hunters were moving into this area shortly after deglaciation and that a shared way of life was widespread across the northeast in this early period.

Two Canadian fluted point discoveries, showing site locations. Left, *Charlie Lake Cave, British Columbia;* right, *Debert, Nova Scotia*

The other early dated Canadian site is Charlie Lake Cave, in northeastern British Columbia. Located between two sandstone outcrops, the site probably once faced out over glacial Lake Peace. Excavation in 1983 revealed a long history of human use. Found at the lowest level was a small sample of stone artifacts, including a short, extensively resharpened fluted point and the bones of a number of bison of larger than modern form, some still bearing marks of ancient butchering. Radiocarbon dates for this level indicate an age of 10,500 years.

Although Charlie Lake Cave is located within the region of the "ice-free corridor," it is at least a millennium too late to represent initial entry and more likely indicates settlement from the south after final deglaciation. Sites of similar age include Vermilion Lakes and Sibbald Creek, both in southwestern Alberta. The former has yielded radiocarbon dates equivalent to Charlie Lake Cave but without diagnostic artifacts for this time period, while the latter contained several fragmentary fluted points, similar to the one from Charlie Lake Cave, but without an associated date. Surface discoveries of similar small fluted points have been made throughout much of the corridor, from southwestern Alberta to the Yukon.

Other fluted points have been reported from undated sites or surface discoveries across much of southern Canada, from the Rockies to the Maritimes. They have been found particularly frequently in southern Ontario, where one study suggested an age of 10,700 to 10,400 years ago, based on the known chronology of the ancient shorelines on which they were found.

Later Paleo-Indian cultures, collectively referred to as "Plano," are characterized by a variety of styles of unfluted projectile points. As the last of the megafauna disappeared, Plano hunters preyed on more modern species. On the plains a gradual decrease in bison size took place, from the giant

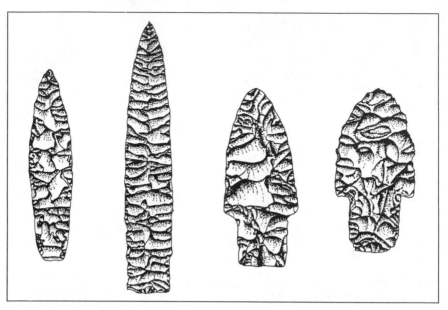

Examples of Plano points. All are surface finds from Saskatchewan. Left to right: *Agate Basin, Eden, Scottsbluff, Alberta*

bison of the Folsom period, to a medium-sized form (*Bison occidentalis*) associated with early Plano sites, and finally to the modern form (*Bison bison*) by late Plano times. Communal hunting techniques for taking large numbers of bison, such as driving them over "jumps" or into narrow canyons, appear to have been well developed.

In Canada, Plano points are widespread. While concentrated on the Great Plains, they are also found in western and southern Ontario, east as far as the Gaspé peninsula of Quebec (with only rare examples from the Maritimes), and north to northeastern B.C. and southern regions of the Yukon and Northwest Territories. Common variants of Plano on the Canadian Plains include the related Eden and Scottsbluff points, with their fine "ripple" flaking; Alberta points, a broad-stemmed variant characteristic of the northwestern plains; and Agate Basin, an early lancelate point with a wide distribution. To the east, in western Ontario around Thunder Bay, the "Lakehead Complex" has been defined for a number of sites yielding large lancelate projectile points.

Once again, most Canadian examples are either surface discoveries or from excavated sites that did not yield suitable organic material for radiocarbon dating. Some fortunate exceptions, however, do exist. The Fletcher site, a bison kill in southern Alberta associated with Scottsbluff and Alberta points, could not be reliably dated through the original excavation in the 1960s. Recent archaeological work at the site, specifically designed to obtain material for dating, uncovered a layer of seeds directly below the bison bone bed. These were dated at 9300 years ago, leading to an estimate of 9000 years for the bison kill. In southern Saskatchewan, the Heron Eden site has yielded a number of Eden-Scottsbluff points associated with bison bones dating to about 9000 years ago. Similarly, a radiocarbon date of 8000 years has been obtained from the Sinnock site, a Plano bison kill location in southeastern Manitoba. In addition, the Cummins site, one of the Lakehead Complex sites around Thunder Bay, has produced a date of almost 8500 years on fragmentary remains of a cremation burial, with geological evidence suggesting that the site was first occupied a millennium earlier. Based primarily on sites further south, the Plano period is usually considered to have lasted from roughly 10,000 to 7500 years ago.

While Plano hunters stalked the big game herds east of the Rockies, quite different early cultures occupied what is today the coast of British Columbia. Evidence of the earliest arrivals in this region may now be lost to coastal submergence; however, radiocarbon dates as early as 9700 years ago exist from the Namu site on the central coast. Crude stone chopping tools and leaf-shaped projectile points mark these early sites and indicate a generalized coastal way of life. Somewhat later, elements of the microblade technology—small, narrow flakes with straight sharp edges, and the cores from which they were struck-were added to the tool inventories of the northern and central coast. From their Eurasian origins, these distinctive tools can be traced through Siberia and Alaska to the central B.C. coast. The early coastal cultures are discussed in greater detail in Chapter 8.

CHAPTER 3 *The Atlantic Provinces*

The First Nations of Canada's Atlantic coast shared numerous cultural traits, despite considerable environmental differences from north to south. This region consists of Nova Scotia, New Brunswick, Prince Edward Island, the Gaspé peninsula and north shore of the St. Lawrence in Quebec, the island of Newfoundland and southern coastal Labrador. All along the Atlantic coastline native groups relied heavily on the resources of the sea. In the historic period all spoke Algonkian languages, with the possible exception of the Beothuk in Newfoundland, whose early destruction left too little information to be certain of this.

The Maritime provinces plus the Gaspé peninsula can be classified as the northeastern extent of the Eastern Woodlands culture area. Southern regions of New Brunswick and Nova Scotia are covered primarily by deciduous forests of the Eastern Woodlands, while more rugged northern regions, such as Cape Breton Island and the Gaspé, are transitional to more northerly environments. Newfoundland and much of the Labrador coast are Subarctic in nature, characterized by igneous rock outcrops of the Canadian Shield and vast coniferous forests. In the north, the Labrador coast grades into true Arctic. The topography of Atlantic Canada is provided by the highly eroded northern reaches of the Appalachian Mountains.

At the end of the Pleistocene, gradual retreat of the glaciers opened this land to human occupation. The Debert site indicates that Paleo-Indian hunters, with their distinctive fluted spearpoints and other stone tools, had reached Nova Scotia by 10,600 years ago. It appears that several millennia elapsed before human populations felt sufficiently pressured to continue north, making water crossings to Labrador and the island of

Distinctive fluted points, found in all three Maritime provinces, mark the early presence of the Paleo-Indians. Courtesy D. Keenlyside, CMC

Newfoundland. The landscape that greeted these early arrivals would have been quite different from the region today. Lowered sea levels at the end of the Pleistocene would have exposed extensive areas of coast, joining Prince Edward Island to New Brunswick and Nova Scotia in a large region known as Northumbria and allowing the spread of plants, animals and people throughout this area. Rising sea levels gradually drowned much of the land on which early hunters might have lived. As the climate changed, the tundra-like landscape of Paleo-Indian times gave way to a boreal forest of spruce and pine, and later to mixed hardwood forests that characterized the area historically. Human populations also changed, becoming increasingly adapted to the abundant maritime resources of the Atlantic coast.

THE MARITIME ARCHAIC

The people of this early tradition relied extensively on maritime resources. Their diet included a wide variety of fish, sea mammals (including walrus and several species of seal), and an array of sea birds. Numerous shared traits, from the coast of Labrador to Maine, have led many archaeologists to place cultures of the entire region within the Maritime Archaic. Others, however, while recognizing the similarity in burial practices and aspects of technology along the Atlantic coast, feel that differences between the Maritimes and Newfoundland are too great to comprise a single culture. Based on a few well-known sites in Newfoundland and Labrador, the Maritime Archaic is tentatively dated at 7500 to 3000 years ago.

Changing sea levels have obscured the archaeological picture in the Maritimes. After deglaciation, large areas once open to human occupation were submerged by rising seas. In fact, Maritimes archaeologists refer to the "Great Hiatus" between 10,000 and 5000 years ago, a period lacking any evidence of human presence. Many important Maritime Archaic sites have certainly been lost to the rising waters. Coastal submergence was largely complete by about 5000 years ago, although sea levels continue to rise slowly and even relatively recent sites are being actively eroded into the sea. In contrast, the coastline north of the Gulf of St. Lawrence is slowly emerging relative to the sea, and sites from early periods may be located at some distance inland. As a result, it is not surprising that the major Maritime Archaic discoveries have been made in Newfoundland and Labrador.

Many Maritime Archaic sites have been recorded along the Atlantic coast, but two are particularly well known. Both are burial sites, revealing the early importance of burial ceremonialism as far north as Labrador. The array of artifact types left with the dead gives a dramatic view of the religious beliefs and subsistence practices of these early coastal dwellers.

The earliest of these sites is L'Anse Amour, located on the southern Labrador coast. This low burial mound, capped by about 300 boulders, was located and excavated by Canadian archaeologists James Tuck and Robert McGhee. Slightly less than two metres below the top of the mound, in a large burial pit dug into the sand, was the skeleton of a child of about twelve years of age, lying face down with a large flat rock on his back. The sand surrounding the skeleton was stained red with ochre, and on each side of the body were concentrations of charcoal, showing where fires had been built on the bottom of the original pit. Charcoal from one of the fires, submitted for radiocarbon dating, indicated that this remarkable burial had taken place about 7500 years ago. This provides our earliest firm date for the Maritime Archaic.

Particularly significant are the many objects left with this unfortunate youth. An ivory walrus tusk, certainly a valuable trade item, was placed by the face. Around the head were piles of knives or spearpoints of chipped stone and polished bone, a decorated bone pendant and a whistle or flute of bird bone. Near the waist were two graphite pebbles and a small concentration of ochre (the two can be mixed to form a metallic red pigment), along with a small antler pestle, possibly for grinding the pigments. One harpoon head of caribou antler is of the toggling type; that is, after being driven into the animal, it holds in place by turning sideways (or "toggling"). It may be the oldest such harpoon head yet discovered and indicates, along with the walrus tusk, that a sophisticated technology for hunting sea mammals had developed by this early date.

The abundance of artifacts with the skeleton, the presence of red ochre and the graveside fires, as well as the considerable effort required to dig the pit and pile boulders on top, indicate that this was a special burial. Certainly no hunting community in this environment could afford the labour or materials to make this a common practice. It seems logical that such special treatment would be reserved for a chief, shaman or other person of great importance in the community, so why would this child have merited such an elaborate burial? Why was he buried face down, with a heavy rock on his back? What was the nature of the rituals that took place there? We may never be able to answer such questions. However, L'Anse Amour shows us that elaborate burial ceremonies took place on these northern shores in very early time periods.

The second important burial site is Port au Choix, located on the western shore of Newfoundland's Great Northern Peninsula, a short distance from L'Anse Amour across the Strait of Belle Isle. Construction activities at this small fishing village exposed a mass of human bones and artifacts covered in red ochre, leading to an archaeological excavation directed by James Tuck. The fine sand of the ancient beach in which the interments were made is extremely alkaline, allowing excellent preservation of bone. Skeletal remains of more than one hundred individuals were excavated, along with numerous burial objects. The site appears to have been a cemetery, in use from about 3900 to 3200 years ago. The significance of this discovery was recognized by its declaration as a National Historic Park, the first such status given to a precontact native site.

The excavated human remains include both sexes and all ages, from infants to individuals over sixty years of age. Most of the adults were buried in a flexed position; that is, the knees were drawn up to the chest and the hands were near the face. Often skeletons were incomplete or were simply bundles of bones, indicating that they had been placed there after the flesh had decayed. This may indicate that these were people who had died during the winter and could not be buried until the ground thawed. This would suggest that Port au Choix was a special location, and that groups away hunting caribou during the winter would transport their dead back to the coast. The presence of red ochre in all the graves and the abundant grave offerings indicates the importance of burial ceremonies.

Many of the objects placed with the dead were functional. Harpoon heads, both barbed and toggling, along with harpoon foreshafts of whalebone, show the importance of sea mammal hunting. A number of large "bayonet" points, ground to shape from slate or bone, were probably once mounted on lances to kill land or sea mammals. Smaller barbed antler and bone points were probably parts of fish spears. Bone implements used in preparing animal hides, such as scraping tools, awls and needles, are well represented. Although wood was not preserved, many grave inclusions are woodworking tools: stone axes and gouges, small knives made from beaver incisors and several large adzes of walrus ivory.

Other burial goods might be classified as decorative items or, with considerable caution, objects of magico-religious significance. Shell beads, perhaps originally sewn to clothing, appear in large quantities. Bone and antler combs, pendants and pins were carved to represent birds' heads. Bear and wolf teeth, seal claws and the bills of such birds as loons and the great auk may have been worn as decorations or as amulets to aid the hunter.

Similarly, numerous white quartz pebbles, as well as crystals of quartz, calcite and amethyst, may have had both decorative and magical functions. Various unusually shaped stones, some slightly altered to resemble birds or animals, may have had special meaning. Particularly striking are two large stone objects apparently representing killer whales. To people who were hunters of sea mammals, the killer whale, the ultimate predator of the sea, must have seemed an animal worthy of respect and possibly fear.

Evidence of Archaic period burial ceremonialism had long been known from sites to the south of L'Anse Amour and Port au Choix. However, the acidic soil at these sites, which are distributed from Maine to Newfoundland, had destroyed all organic remains. These could be described as "boneless cemeteries," where only the grave inclusions made of stone have survived the passage of time. The common occurrence of red ochre, however, indicates that burial ceremonialism was practiced and gives rise to the popular term the "Red Paint People."

Perhaps the most important of such sites in the Maritime provinces is Cow Point, located in south-central New Brunswick. Archaeologists disagree over whether to classify this site as Maritime Archaic or to include it with the Laurentian Archaic, which extends into New Brunswick from the St. Lawrence valley of southern Ontario and Quebec. Excavation in 1970 revealed about sixty oval red ochre stains marking where burials had once been. While only stone objects have been preserved in the acidic soil, many show careful craftsmanship. Particularly distinctive are long slender points, or "bayonets," reminiscent of those from Port au Choix, made of polished slate. They range from smaller utilitarian examples to very long and slender implements, decorated with incised designs, which possibly were made specifically as grave offerings. Polished stone gouges, used as woodworking tools, were also found at this cemetery. Radiocarbon dates indicate that this site was in use about 3800 years ago, about the same time as Port au Choix.

The dramatic nature of these burials and the elaborate grave offerings found with them have attracted most archaeological attention. However, the Maritime Archaic people are also known from sites reflecting everyday life. Once again, rising sea levels in the Maritime provinces have obliterated the majority of such sites, so that most information comes from Newfoundland and Labrador. For example, the Beaches site in northeastern Newfoundland has yielded numerous stone tools, most of which were chipped to shape. The finely made ground stone tools characteristic of the cemetery sites are much rarer but do occur. This site even yielded a fragmentary ground slate point with an incised design similar to those found at Cow Point.

On the central Labrador coast at Hamilton Inlet, Smithsonian Institution archaeologist William Fitzhugh has documented a series of Maritime Archaic complexes dating from about 6000 to 3700 years ago. The most recent and best known is the Rattlers Bight complex, with occupation sites characterized by abundant chipped stone tools, a smaller number of tools ground from stone, and evidence of domestic architecture in the form of large rectangular house remains. Also found at the Rattlers Bight site was a cemetery, identified by the typical red ochre stains of Maritime Archaic burials. Although no bone was preserved, abundant grave offerings of stone were found: both chipped and ground points, gouges and imported materials such as mica and native copper. Interestingly, the chipped stone tools were exclusively of an easily flaked translucent gray stone termed "Ramah chert," which has its origin in outcrops near Saglek Bay in northern Labrador.

The Ramah chert quarries may have been the stimulus for the spread of the Maritime Archaic far up the Labrador coast, reaching Saglek Bay, well north of the tree line, by 5000 years ago. Such northern outposts of this culture are characterized by abundant tools flaked from this distinctive stone. This material would have been an important trade commodity. It appears in archaeological sites as far south as the Maritime provinces and Maine, indicating cultural ties linking all of Atlantic Canada in the Archaic period.

From this archaeological evidence, a partial reconstruction of Maritime Archaic economy can be made. Several species of seals were taken, and walrus, originally plentiful as far south as the Gulf of St. Lawrence, were also hunted. A variety of fish species, including the large swordfish taken by more southerly groups, contributed to the diet. In addition, vast numbers of migratory waterfowl were seasonally available. Over 200 bills of the great auk, a large now-extinct flightless sea bird, were found with one burial at Port au Choix. However, most archaeological remains are of species that were available from spring to fall. James Tuck and others have speculated, at least for the groups north of the Gulf of St. Lawrence, that with the first snows of winter the people moved inland to intercept migrating caribou herds. After spending the winter hunting in the interior forests, the Maritime Archaic people would return to the coast in early spring, when seals could be easily taken on the pack ice. Social groups would have been small bands, following a seasonal pattern of movement.

Many other aspects of Maritime Archaic life have left few archaeological traces. Except for the rectangular stone remains in central and northern Labrador, we know little of their housing. Although warm and waterproof clothing was obviously necessary for people living as far north as Labrador, we have little direct evidence. A double row of shell beads over the skull of one of the Port au Choix burials, suggesting the hood of a parka, is a rare example of indirect evidence for clothing styles. However, the practice of elaborate burial ceremonialism, particularly evident at L'Anse Amour and Port au Choix, provides dramatic insight into the beliefs and activities of the Maritime Archaic people.

THE LATER PRECONTACT PERIOD

About 4000 years ago a new group of people appeared in northern Labrador, eventually replacing earlier occupants along the entire coastline south as far as Newfoundland. Physically and culturally dissimilar to their predecessors, these were Arctic people, who reached the Atlantic coast as part of an expansion across Canada's north. They have been termed "Paleo-Eskimos," reflecting their relationship with, but not direct ancestry to, the historic Inuit. The Dorset, the late Paleo-Eskimo variant which reached the island of Newfoundland over 2000 years ago, spread further south than any other Eskimoan group. Typically a coastal people, the Dorset left sites encircling Newfoundland but did not penetrate far inland.

The abundance of sea mammals allowed the Dorset to settle in fairly large villages. At one such site, near Port au Choix, more than thirty-five rectangular depressions mark where houses once stood. Each house had sod walls, with timber rafters supporting a roof covered with sod, and was dug slightly into the ground. At another site in northern Newfoundland, the Dorset people quarried a soapstone cliff to carve their distinctive bowls and rectangular lamps. Burial remains from several small caves indicate a physical type similar to the historic Inuit of the Arctic, and quite distinct from the Indian populations of Atlantic Canada.

Across the Arctic, the Dorset were gradually replaced by more recent arrivals, the Thule, the direct ancestors of the historic Inuit. The Thule settled only as far south as northern Labrador, and the reasons for the Dorset disappearance from the Atlantic coast, after an occupation of about a millennium, are unknown. The Dorset way of life is discussed further in Chapter 10.

The Woodland (or Ceramic) period began in the Maritime provinces about 2500 years ago with the introduction of finely made pottery, probably as a result of contacts with southern cultures. This early pottery is well made and carefully decorated with patterns pressed into the lip and neck of the pot. Occasionally the entire body is decorated by paddling with a cord-wrapped stick. Such pots allowed cooking directly over a fire, as opposed to indirect techniques like boiling with red-hot stones that had to be used with vessels of wood or bark. However, pottery containers are heavy and fragile, and they are far less suited to a mobile lifestyle than those of bark, hide or wood. It is not surprising that pottery declines in quantity and quality over time, and is largely abandoned altogether prior to European contact.

In coastal regions shell middens mark many Woodland sites. As people began to rely on clams and other shellfish for part of their diet, discarded shells accumulated adjacent to their habitations. Since the shell deposits helped to neutralize the acidic soil, these sites also contain a range of bone and antler tools, in addition to the more commonly found implements of

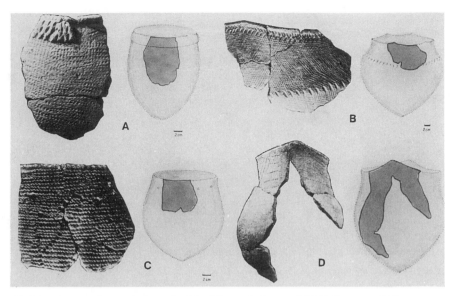

Prehistoric ceramic vessels from the Maritimes, dating ca. 100 B.C. to AD. *300.*
Courtesy D. Keenlyside, CMC

stone and sherds of pottery. Once again, however, coastal erosion has removed much of the archaeological evidence, even from this late period.

While most early Woodland sites document everyday life, one remarkable discovery in northeastern New Brunswick indicates that these people were in contact with religious ideas and ceremonial practices from far to the south. Excavation in the mid-1970s of the Augustine Mound, long an important location to the Mi'kmaq of the Red Bank Indian reserve on which it is situated, revealed that the low mound, about 11 metres in diameter, had been raised over a large central burial pit and ten smaller pits. The latter contained both cremated burials and "secondary burials"—disarticulated remains brought from an earlier location for ceremonial reburial. Radiocarbon dates from one of the pits place the construction of the mound at about 2300 years ago. Stone artifacts interred with the dead include large finely flaked points and knives, gorgets (flat polished stone objects, perforated for wearing at the throat or on the chest) and pipes. Many wealth goods were made of raw materials not available locally. The most numerous of these were thousands of rolled beads and other implements of native copper, a raw material obtained from the western Great Lakes region. The presence of copper in the mound altered the chemical composition of the soil, resulting in excellent preservation of organic materials, such as fragments of woven fabrics, matting and basketry—an unprecedented situation in eastern Canada.

A recently excavated mound near Halifax, known as the Skora site, is the

Excavation at the Augustine Mound, New Brunswick. Courtesy D. Keenlyside, CMC

only other known example from the Maritimes. Evidence from this site shows that the dead were cremated, then their remains, along with associated artifacts, were placed in burial pits dug into a hilltop, prior to the construction of the mound. Radiocarbon dates show that this site was being used at the same time as the Augustine Mound.

The practice of mound burial and the associated artifacts indicate affiliation with the Adena culture far to the south, centred in the Ohio River valley. Do these sites indicate a migration of mound-building peoples far to the northeast of their homeland? Or do they represent trade contacts and religious influences from the south on indigenous peoples? What fate befell these people in the Maritimes? Unfortunately, archaeology cannot answer these questions, and these mounds remain a fascinating puzzle in Maritimes prehistory.

In the late precontact period, developments in the Maritimes led directly to the Mi'kmaq and Maliseet cultures of historic times. Archaeological sites are frequently located along coastal saltwater lagoons or sheltered tidal estuaries, where fish, shellfish and waterfowl abounded. Most coastal shell middens date to this late period. Although found in all three Maritime provinces, they are particularly common in coastal Nova Scotia and southern New Brunswick, with major concentrations in areas such as Passamaquoddy Bay. Large fish weirs were constructed near some sites, particularly those on estuaries where spawning species such as salmon and eels could be taken. Bones of seals and walrus preserved in midden sites indicate that sea mammals were also hunted. No direct evidence exists for the style of watercraft in use, but the presence of bark-working tools in the middens suggests that canoes and houses were covered with this material, as was the case in historic times. Artifacts from the Oxbow site, a seasonal salmon fishing location along a tributary of the Miramichi River in New Brunswick, provide evidence of evolving Mi'kmaq culture over the last 2500 years.

Returning to the north, Newfoundland and Labrador entered what has been termed the "Recent Indian" period somewhat after 2000 years ago. All that remains of these people are meagre archaeological traces, consisting primarily of chipped stone tools such as projectile points and scrapers. In central Labrador, where these remains are referred to as the "Point Revenge Complex," the most common raw material is Ramah chert, showing continued contact with the north. Rocks forming oval tent rings with central hearths hint at the style of housing, and one Point Revenge site yielded the remains of a collapsed wooden tent frame. In Newfoundland, several late prehistoric complexes exist, with similar tools made from locally available stone. Tiny arrowpoints dating from the last few centuries before contact with Europeans identify the "Little Passage Complex." These Little Passage remains can almost certainly be identified with people who became the historic Beothuks, but the situation of the Point Revenge people is more problematical. Although it has been suggested that they were the ancestors of the historic Innu of the region, it is more likely that they became extinct very early in the historic period.

Although the presence of Beothuk culture can be seen in late precontact archaeological remains in Newfoundland, the Beothuks' origin is uncertain. The ancestors of the Beothuks, in one view, were relatively late arrivals from the mainland. If this is the case, they probably spoke a language in the Central Algonkian stock and were closely related to the Innu. A competing view, stressing lengthy cultural continuity, has been argued by James Tuck, who points to archaeological evidence that Paleo-Eskimos and Indians might have been contemporaneous in Newfoundland and southern Labrador. If so, it could be argued that Beothuk culture was the result of a long *in situ* development, possibly extending back as far as the Maritime Archaic.

These "Recent Indian" groups may have been the first native Canadians to encounter Europeans. Norse colonists, after establishing settlements in Greenland in the late tenth century, continued to explore to the south and west. These voyages, described in the Norse sagas, took them along the Canadian east coast and into contact with aboriginal peoples: both Eskimoan (Dorset and Thule) cultures in the north, and Indian (Point Revenge and ancestral Beothuk) peoples further south. The Norse made no distinction, referring to them all as Skraelings (or "savages"). Archaeological evidence of an attempt at colonization comes from the L'Anse aux Meadows site in northern Newfoundland, where remains of sod-walled houses indicate a Norse settlement of about A.D. 1000. Interaction with the natives of the area was hostile, and Norse attempts to occupy the land seem to have been frustrated by the native defence of their territory, forestalling

European colonization for another five centuries.

Throughout this long period, the native cultures of Atlantic Canada were dependent, at least during most of the year, upon the sea. This coastal adaptation continued into the historic period with the Mi'kmaq, Maliseet and Beothuk. In Labrador, however, the historic Innu led a way of life that was more dependent upon hunting in the interior. They are discussed with the other Subarctic Algonkians in Chapter 5.

THE BEOTHUK

The Beothuk were the first aboriginal Canadians to come into continuous contact with Europeans. Their ultimate extinction at the hands of these arrivals is a tragic chapter in Canada's history.

The Beothuk were the original "Red Indians," a term later mistakenly applied to all other North American native peoples. The term refers not to skin pigmentation but to their practice of smearing red paint, made from powdered ochre mixed with oil or grease, over the body and hair, as well as on clothing and utensils. Although the use of paint made from red ochre is common throughout aboriginal America, no other group used it as extensively as the Beothuk. As well as its decorative and possibly religious function, liberally smearing the body with this greasy paint may have provided some protection from the cold and from the hordes of biting insects that plague animals and humans in this environment. Its almost obsessive use throughout Beothuk culture, however, argues for a more deeply rooted meaning. Beothuk burials, where the corpse and all objects interred with the dead were covered with red ochre, suggest a ceremonial or religious association and link Beothuk beliefs and practices with those of the much earlier Maritime Archaic period. The striking appearance of these people is evident from an early seventeenth-century description:

> they are of a reasonable stature, of an ordinary middle size, they goe bare-headed, wearing their hair somewhat long but round: they have no beards; behind they haue a great locke of haire platted with feathers, like a hawke's lure, with a feather in it standing upright by the crowne of the head and a small lock platted before, a short gown made of stags' skins, the furre inner-most, that raune down to the middle of their legges, with sleeues to the middle of their arme, and a beuer skin about their necke, was all their apparell, saue that one of them had shooes and mittens, so that all went bare-legged and most bare-foote. They are full-eyed, of a blacke colour; the colour of their hair was divers, some blacke, some browne, and some yellow, and their faces something flat and broad, red with oker, as all their apparell is, and the rest of their body.
>
> (Howley 1915:17)

Most of our knowledge of the Beothuk comes from eighteenth- and early nineteenth-century descriptions. By this time, European and Mi'kmaq encroachments had reduced Beothuk territory to its historically known core along Red Indian Lake and the Exploits River of central Newfoundland. The decline in population and loss of most coastal resources meant that only an impoverished remnant of Beothuk culture was observed. The full extent of their lives prior to explorer John Cabot's arrival at Newfoundland in 1497 remains largely unknown.

Population estimates for the Beothuks at the time of European contact vary considerably, from a low of about 500 to several thousand. Beothuk social groups were small bands of closely related families even prior to their historic reduction in numbers.

For much of the year the Beothuk were a coastal people who lived by fishing, collecting shellfish and hunting both land and sea mammals. Men ventured out in their bark canoes to harpoon seals and even the occasional small whale. Collecting birds' eggs was an important activity, for which expeditions were made as far as Funk Island, a trip of about 65 kilometres across the rough waters of the North Atlantic. The eggs were hard-boiled for later use or, according to one early description, mixed with seal or caribou fat and sun-dried to form a staple food. A sketch by Shanawdithit, the last of the Beothuks, shows the storage of such traditional foods as dried meat, dried salmon, pieces of seal fat on the skin and long strings of dried lobster tails.

The Beothuk spent autumn and winter in the interior, where the economy centred almost entirely on caribou. They built long "deer fences" of felled trees, branches and posts to channel the caribou herds to where hunters waited with spears or bows and arrows. Enough meat had to be taken and preserved by freezing or smoking to last through the long winter. Historic descriptions of the Beothuk as primarily interior hunters, however, reflect only their final declining years when they had been largely excluded from important coastal resources.

Most of the year the Beothuks preferred to travel by water, using birchbark canoes on inland lakes and rivers as well as along the coast. The shape of Beothuk canoes was distinctive, with sharply pointed prow and stern and a high peak at midlength. For ocean travel they had to be ballasted with large rocks for stability, and for interior portaging several early writers have claimed that they could be flattened by removal of the thwarts. The Beothuks were confident seamen, venturing far from land in these frail craft. In winter, travel through the interior was on foot, using snowshoes and pulling heavy loads on sleds.

Beothuk dwellings were conical structures of poles covered with birchbark, referred to as *mamateeks*. Winter mamateeks might have several layers of bark, separated by dried moss to provide insulation. Earth banked against the lower portion of the structure also helped keep out the winter

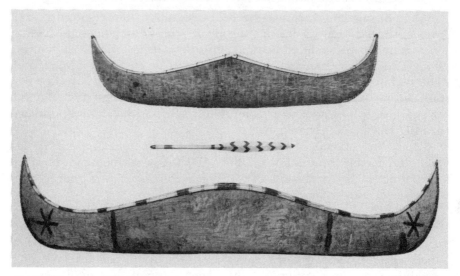

Beothuk canoe models. CMC 67232

cold. A distinctive feature was the presence of sleeping hollows in the ground around the central fireplace.

Many surviving material objects of Beothuk culture were recovered in the nineteenth century from burial sites. The body, wrapped in birchbark and covered in red ochre, was left in a wooden box placed on a scaffold or in a crevice in the rocks. Objects placed with the dead include wooden dolls, models of birchbark canoes and distinctive bone pendants incised with geometric designs which might once have been sewn to clothing.

The documentary evidence for Beothuk culture is so impoverished that we have to turn to archaeological research for additional information. A good example is the Boyd's Cove site in northeastern Newfoundland, occupied by the Beothuk from about A.D. 1650 to 1720 and excavated by Memorial University archaeologists in the 1980s. Eleven circular depressions on the site's surface show that the Beothuk had constructed their houses, which were apparently occupied from early spring until fall, over shallow pits. The site's occupants feasted primarily on caribou and harbour seal, although other mammals, birds, fish and shellfish also were part of their diet. Considering the date of occupation, these people possessed relatively few European goods. The major exception is a large number of nails, which the Beothuk were hammering out and shaping into arrowpoints. Objects of aboriginal manufacture include tiny chipped stone arrowpoints and several distinctive bone pendants with incised designs, showing that these were used as ornaments by living Beothuks and not just placed in graves.

The final years of Beothuk culture must have been ones of great deprivation. Increasingly cut off from the coast by English and French settlement, the Beothuk were forced to rely on the limited resources of the interior. Unlike elsewhere in Canada, where initial relations centred on the fur trade, the Beothuk did not have direct access to items of European manufacture. Instead they resorted to theft from the unoccupied fishing stations. The hostility this created led to retaliatory raids on Beothuk encampments, resulting in considerable loss of life. With populations plummeting due to introduced diseases and hostile encounters with newcomers, they must have found it difficult even to carry out the traditional caribou hunt. In addition, the Mi'kmaq were crossing over to Newfoundland from the mainland, attracted by access to furs for trade. The Beothuk were increasingly pushed into the centre of the island, where the impoverished remnants of the group, plagued by tuberculosis and malnutrition, are described in the early nineteenth-century accounts. As Newfoundland historian Frederick Rowe points out in his book *Extinction*, this tragic story certainly does not need the dramatic exaggerations of huge massacres and wanton hunting of Beothuks for "sport" which have been presented by some writers.

Details on the final years of the Beothuk come from nineteenth-century captives. In bungling attempts to establish communications, English colonists took a number of Beothuk prisoners, the most famous being Demasduit (better known to history as Mary March, after the month of her capture in 1819) and Shanawdithit, captured in 1823. Although a few individuals may have fled the island and mixed with neighbouring groups, Shanawdithit is considered to have been the last of the Beothuk. Her death of tuberculosis in 1829 marks the date of their extinction.

THE MI'KMAQ AND MALISEET

Traditional Mi'kmaq (the spelling adopted by the Mi'kmaq Grand Council; "Micmac" has been the more common term) territory consists of the Gaspé peninsula of Quebec, northern and eastern New Brunswick, and all of Nova Scotia and Prince Edward Island, expanding historically to include southern Newfoundland. Closely related to them are the neighbouring Maliseet (or Malecite) along the St. John River of western New Brunswick and extending just into Quebec. Speaking the same language as the Maliseet are the Passamaquoddy, today residents of Maine, whose historic territory extends a short distance into southwestern New Brunswick around Passamaquoddy Bay. Although all these groups were similar, the Mi'kmaq were more of a coastal people while the Maliseet placed greater emphasis on interior resources and historically cultivated small plots of corn. Early descriptions of native life refer mainly to the Mi'kmaq, since the Maliseet and Passamaquoddy were further removed from areas of early European exploration and settlement.

Most of our knowledge of the Mi'kmaq comes from ethnohistory. Several seventeenth-century writers left extensive observations on native life. Although incomplete and frequently contradictory, a picture of Mi'kmaq culture emerges that can be supplemented with later ethnographic data. However, these seventeenth-century accounts describe people who had been familiar with Europeans and their trade goods for over a century.

Early in the seventeenth century the Mi'kmaq population was estimated at about 3500, while the Maliseet numbered about 1000. Both groups, however, had already suffered considerable decline in numbers due to epidemic diseases that inevitably followed European contact. Also, French trade in alcohol and new food items detrimentally affected native health. Early observer Nicolas Denys praised the traditional diet of meat, animal fat and fish, which allowed the natives to "live long and multiply much," and commented on the poorer health and greater susceptibility to disease caused by the change in diet.

The size of social groups varied with the seasons. Winter camps were typically small groups of several related families, while in the summer more abundant resources allowed bands of several hundred individuals to form. Each had a chief, referred to as a *sagamore*, who held limited power over the group. While inheritance by the eldest son appears to have been common, ability and personality were paramount considerations. The sagamore's duties were primarily to provide leadership and advice, allowing a great deal of independence. The role of the sagamore in the early seventeenth century is described by the Jesuit Father Biard:

> All the young people of the family are at his table and in his retinue; it is also his duty to provide dogs for the chase, canoes for transportation, provisions and reserves for bad weather and expeditions. The young people flatter him, hunt, and serve their apprenticeship under him, not being allowed to have anything before they are married . . . all that the young men capture belongs to the Sagamore; but the married ones give him only a part, and if these leave him, as they often do for the sake of the chase and supplies, returning afterwards, they pay their dues and homage in skins and like gifts.
>
> (Thwaites, *Jesuit Relations* 3:87-89)

That this authority was limited is made clear by the observations of Father LeClercq:

> The most prominent chief is followed by several young warriors and by several hunters, who act as his escort, and who fall in under arms when this ruler wishes particular distinction upon some special occasion. But, in fact, all his power and authority are based only upon the good will of those of his nation, who execute his orders just in so far as it pleases them.
>
> (LeClercq 1910:234)

The Mi'kmaq, while lacking overall political unification, perceived themselves as a common people and paid nominal allegiance to a "Grand Chief," traditionally located at the Mi'kmaq "head district" of Cape Breton Island. One of the duties of this Grand Chief was to call council meetings of Mi'kmaq leaders to discuss issues of common concern. The famed seventeenth-century sagamore Membertou held this role, combining abilities as political leader, warrior and shaman to strengthen his power among the Mi'kmaq.

Mi'kmaq economic life shifted with the seasons as people moved between coast and interior to take advantage of various resources. The annual cycle was described by Father Biard at Port Royal in 1616:

> in January they have the seal hunting . . . In the month of February and until the middle of March, is the great hunt for Beavers, otters, moose, bears (which are very good), and for the caribou . . . If the weather is then favorable, they live in great abundance, and are as haughty as Princes and Kings, but if it is against them, they are greatly to be pitied and often die of starvation . . . In the middle of March, fish begin to spawn, and to come up from the sea into certain streams, often so abundantly that everything swarms with them . . . Among these fish the smelt is the first . . . after the smelt comes the herring at the end of April; at the same time bustards [Canada geese] . . . sturgeon, and salmon, and the great search through the Islets for [waterfowl] eggs . . . From the month of May up to the middle of September, they are free from all anxiety about their food; for the cod are upon the coast, and all kinds of fish and shellfish . . . our savages in the middle of September withdraw from the sea, beyond the reach of the tide, to the little rivers, where the eels spawn, of which they lay in a supply . . . In October and November comes the second hunt for elks [moose] and beavers; and then in December comes a fish called by them ponamo [tomcod], which spawns under the ice.
>
> (Thwaites, *Jesuit Relations* 3:79-83)

Although the coast, rivers and forests all played a part in the Mi'kmaq economy, as much as 90 percent of their diet came from the sea. Fish were taken by hook and line, harpoon, or in weirs and traps. Spearing fish by torchlight was described by Nicolas Denys, who stated that 150 to 200 salmon could be taken in a single night by this method. Shellfish and lobsters were collected, and sea mammals, including the occasional small whale, were harpooned from canoes. And, as mentioned by Biard, waterfowl and their eggs were available in great quantities during seasonal migrations.

Hunting in the interior occupied far less time and provided far less of the diet, but it was a more prestigious activity than fishing. Every young man aspired to become a great hunter. They hunted animals with bow and arrow, or took them with snares set across game paths. Dogs were used in the hunt but on occasion could themselves become the main dish at a feast. Meat was prepared by roasting or by boiling with red-hot stones in large

Mi'kmaq fishing camp, Restigouche. NAC C16436

wooden troughs carved from fallen trees (later these were replaced by copper kettles, which were highly desired trade items since they could be carried by the Mi'kmaq on their travels). Hunting was a precarious activity, and, as mentioned by Biard, people might starve if poor weather affected the hunt.

Transportation also varied with the seasons. The lightweight birchbark canoe was indispensable to Mi'kmaq life. Father Biard described these canoes as "so capacious that a single one of them will hold an entire household of five or six persons, with all their dogs, sacks, skins, kettles, and other heavy baggage" (Thwaites, *Jesuit Relations* 3:83). The use of sails, apparently adopted by the Mi'kmaq in the seventeenth century from European examples, greatly increased the speed of coastal travel. Equally indispensable were snowshoes, allowing winter travel and hunting over deep drifts. The Mi'kmaq also had both the sled and the toboggan (the latter owing its English name to the Mi'kmaq word *taba'gan*).

Mi'kmaq housing reflected the need for seasonal mobility. Bark-covered "wigwams" are described by Father LeClercq as being "so light and portable that our Indians roll them up like a piece of paper, and carry them thus upon their backs wherever it pleases them, very much like the tortoises which carry their own houses" (LeClercq 1910:100). The houses varied in size and floor plan, as described by Nicolas Denys:

> If the family is a large one they make it long enough for two fires; otherwise they make it round, just like military tents, with only this difference that in

place of canvas they are of barks of Birch. These are so well fitted that it never rains into their wigwams. The round kind holds ten to twelve persons, the long twice as many. The fires are made in the middle of the round kind, and at the two ends of the long sort.

(Denys 1908:405-406)

Father LeClercq also described brightly coloured designs painted by women on the bark coverings. Inside, the floor was covered with fir branches, with hides placed over these for beds. While most seventeenth-century descriptions give favourable impressions of Mi'kmaq habitations, references are also made to the constant smoke in the dwellings, the stench of fish and animals being prepared and the danger of severe burns from sleeping too near the fire on a cold winter night.

The basic item of clothing for men was the loincloth. In colder weather, a loose robe of furs or hide, worn with leggings and moccasins, was added. Women wore a similar robe. According to Denys (1908:407), "the girls were very modest . . . always clothed with a well-dressed Moose skin which descended below the knees." This clothing was decorated by painting or with dyed porcupine quills, and people further enhanced their appearance by oiling their hair and painting their faces. By the eighteenth century, however, fur and hide had almost totally given way to cloth, decorated in a distinctive Mi'kmaq style with beads, ribbons and embroidery. The women's traditional high-peaked caps, of beaded and embroidered dark blue cloth, belong to this later period.

Many raw materials were employed for utensils. Birchbark was particularly important as it was readily available, light in weight and relatively waterproof and rot resistant. Boxes, bowls and baskets of this material were ideally suited to migratory people. Even in the seventeenth century these were decorated with porcupine quills, and later these developed into the elaborately quilled birchbark baskets for which the Mi'kmaq are known. Although most traditional Mi'kmaq implements of wood, stone and bone were replaced by metal tools in the historic period, basket making not only continued but expanded into a major craft for sale to Europeans.

In religious beliefs the Mi'kmaq shared with other Algonkians the concept of a supreme being. Several early sources state that the Mi'kmaq identified this creator as the sun, to which they prayed twice daily. Lesser deities included some that were human in form but were immortal and had supernatural powers. By far the most prominent of these among both the Mi'kmaq and Maliseet was the culture hero named Glooscap. Many myths tell how he transformed the animals into their present shapes and how distinctive features of the landscape resulted from his activities. After teaching humans how to make tools and weapons, he departed, promising to return in times of need. At the lowest level of the pantheon were supernatural races, ranging from giants to the forest-dwelling "little people."

Left: *Ornately decorated nineteenth-century Mi'kmaq coat.* CMC 77-6557
Right: *This Mi'kmaq woman and her son display traditional nineteenth-century costumes. Taken in Halifax, ca. 1863-74.*
Public Archives of Nova Scotia, Halifax

Shamans were individuals with power to intercede directly with the realm of the supernatural. Shamanic powers included curing the sick, predicting the future and providing supernatural aid in warfare and the hunt. Healing rituals were particularly dramatic, involving dancing and singing around the patient to exorcise the malevolent force and blowing on the afflicted part of the body to drive out the disease. Some individuals became so successful and received so many goods for their services that they became full-time religious practitioners. However, shamans were also feared, for they had the power to cause disease and injury as well as to cure.

Important in Mi'kmaq social life were feasts held on numerous occasions. Marriages and funerals required feasting, but LeClercq writes that there were also "feasts of health, of farewell, of hunting, of peace, of war, of thanks." To ensure hunting success, they held an "eat-all" feast, during which those present gorged themselves until they consumed every scrap of available food—certainly providing an inducement to do well on the next hunt. Feasts included lengthy speeches, by which family traditions and genealogies were maintained. Songs and dances paid tribute to the host. Such social occasions also provided an opportunity to play *waltes*, a favourite gambling game played by flipping bone dice in a wooden bowl.

Mi'kmaq basket, decorated with porcupine quills. CMC J3332

Warfare was also important among the Mi'kmaq and Maliseet, providing one route to prestige for a young man. Raids were conducted against other Algonkian groups, such as the Montagnais. However, the most bitter hostilities were with the Iroquois, particularly the Mohawk. Many well-known features of Iroquoian warfare, such as taking scalps and torturing captives, were also practiced by the Mi'kmaq.

The Mi'kmaq seem to have achieved an admirable adaptation to their environment, and the seventeenth-century observers, while very much products of their own European backgrounds, all indicate a grudging admiration of native lifeways. Although privation did exist, particularly in the lean months of February and March, for much of the year plentiful food could be obtained with little effort. Warfare might cause hardships, but it also provided a path to glory and political advancement. As befitting a migratory people, their material wants were few. However, this way of life was to change dramatically with increased European contact.

HISTORIC CHANGES

Contact with European fishermen likely occurred shortly after Columbus crossed the Atlantic Ocean. Such encounters would have been fleeting, and as the fishermen were generally illiterate we have almost no record of this period. However, when Jacques Cartier sailed by Chaleur Bay in 1534, the Mi'kmaq loudly hailed the ship and waved furs on sticks to signal their eagerness to trade, suggesting that such relationships had been established for some time. Cartier reports that the natives were so eager for European knives and other iron goods that they traded the furs off their backs and had to return naked to their camp.

Intensive French colonization began early in the seventeenth century, and the Mi'kmaq and Maliseet became loyal allies of the French and partners with them in the fur trade. This was a period of increasing acculturation, despite strong Mi'kmaq feelings of self-worth and their skepticism of claims that France was the superior nation when the French seemed so eager to leave it to voyage to Mi'kmaq lands. The introduction of European trade items, particularly those of metal and cloth, meant loss of much of the aboriginal material culture. The need to obtain furs for trade meant changes in traditional economic patterns, and acceptance of European foods, generally inferior to those in the traditional diet, was detrimental to native health. Alcohol was also introduced by traders, with devastating results. Epidemics continued to reduce the native population, contributing to demoralization and loss of faith in the shamans, who were incapable of dealing with these new afflictions. From the beginning of French settlement, conversion of the natives to Christianity was a goal enthusiastically pursued by the priests.

The alliance of the Mi'kmaq and Maliseet with the French inevitably drew them into conflict with the English and their Iroquois allies. Territorial squabbles between these two European nations came to a temporary halt with the treaty of Utrecht in 1713, by the terms of which French possessions in Atlantic Canada were reduced to Île St. Jean (Prince Edward Island) and Île Royale (Cape Breton Island). Shortly afterwards the French began construction of the fortress of Louisbourg on the latter. From this base, the French encouraged the Mi'kmaq to continue hostilities against the English. Mi'kmaq raids on English ships and settlements escalated the warfare and led to an English campaign of attempted genocide against the Mi'kmaq, even importing a group of Mohawk on the assumption that they would be more efficient in killing other Indians. After establishment of the English settlement of Halifax, the new governor placed a bounty on Mi'kmaq scalps. Hostilities continued until French power in Atlantic Canada came to an end shortly after the fall of Louisbourg in 1758, forcing the natives to make peace with the English.

Pressures of continuous warfare, particularly with the Iroquois, brought about formation of the Wabanaki Confederacy, an alliance of northeastern Algonkians. Although these groups had earlier been allied against the Iroquois and the English, organization into a confederacy probably dates to the middle of the eighteenth century. The confederacy centred on the Penobscot of Maine, with the Mi'kmaq and Maliseet being "younger brothers." This confederacy was in turn allied with the Ottawa and with the Catholicized Mohawk in Quebec, bringing together the major French allies for council meetings. Election of chiefs and use of wampum were Iroquoian traits incorporated into Algonkian cultures through this confederacy.

Historically, the Mi'kmaq were also well established in Newfoundland. There is some possibility that they first reached this island prior to European contact, as the Newfoundland Mi'kmaq maintain today, although there is no evidence of this. Historic records show their presence by the early 1600s. It was after 1760, however, when the English replaced the French on Cape Breton Island, that large numbers of Mi'kmaq sought new lands on southern and western Newfoundland. The search for new hunting grounds in order to obtain furs for trade was a major incentive. According to anthropologist Frank Speck's informants, in early times the crossing of Cabot Strait from Cape Breton Island was done by canoe at night, when the sea was calmer, and canoeists might be guided by a light from the cliffs of southern Newfoundland, kindled by experienced men who had gone ahead of the main body. In later times, the Mi'kmaq were using shallops, small European sailing vessels, to make this dangerous crossing. Relations with the Beothuk appear to have been unfriendly, causing this group to gradually withdraw from the southern portion of the island. After the Beothuk extinction, the Mi'kmaq remain as the only native inhabitants of the island of Newfoundland.

The late eighteenth and early nineteenth centuries were difficult times for the Mi'kmaq and Maliseet. Increased numbers of English settlers poured into the area, particularly after the American War of Independence, displacing natives from the most desirable locations. Decline of the fur trade and loss of traditional lands for hunting and fishing reduced many to starvation, and epidemic outbreaks of disease continued to take a dreadful toll.

After confederation, when the crown colonies of Nova Scotia, New Brunswick and Prince Edward Island became provinces of Canada, administrative responsibility for natives shifted to the federal government in Ottawa. The new nation, however, was looking westward for its future, so was preoccupied with subjugating the Plains Indians and opening the west to white settlers. The Mi'kmaq and Maliseet, reduced in numbers and already dispossessed from most of their land, received little attention. Maritimes natives were left to eke out a living by various forms of labour and craft production through this long period of neglect.

THE MI'KMAQ AND MALISEET TODAY

Over 21,000 Mi'kmaq today live in Canada's five easternmost provinces. They are divided into 28 bands, the largest being Restigouche (now known as Listuguj Mi'gmaq First Nation) in Quebec, Eskasoni and Shubenacadie in Nova Scotia and Big Cove in New Brunswick. The Maliseet population of about 4700 people is divided into seven bands, the largest and best-known of which is Tobique in New Brunswick

The Mi'kmaq of Newfoundland have had a long struggle for recognition as Canadian Indians. Isolated on the island's south coast, the Mi'kmaq at the Conne River settlement, after a lengthy battle with the provincial and federal governments, were finally legally established in 1984 as the Miawpukek Indian band. A few years later their community lands were registered as a reserve under the federal system. This band now has a population of about 1200 people. Other Newfoundlanders of Mi'kmaq origin, particularly on the west coast, are still seeking such recognition.

One other group of northeastern Algonkians extends into Canada today. The Abenaki speak a language closely related to Mi'kmaq and Maliseet and were allied to them in the Wabanaki Confederacy. During the historic wars, their ties to the French led many to leave their New England homeland, settling in Quebec as early as the late seventeenth century. Today there are two Abenaki bands in Quebec, with a total population of about 1750. However, the Abenaki language is all but extinct in Canada and few traits distinguish their reserves from surrounding French-speaking villages. Despite this, native handicrafts continue to be an important source of income and maintenance of cultural identity is a vital concern.

One of the pressing problems confronting Mi'kmaq and Maliseet band councils today is providing a livelihood for reserve residents. Many men find work in the lumber industry. Fishing and lobster trapping have been important occupations on some reserves, although the general decline in the Atlantic fishery has brought tough economic times to native and non-native communities alike. Basketry manufacture, from the finely quilled tourist baskets to more utilitarian splint baskets, is still an important source of income for many. In recent years band councils, aided by new federal funding programs, have introduced a number of band-run enterprises, such as an oyster farm at Eskasoni and a sawmill at Shubenacadie, to employ band members. Unemployment rates, however, remain high.

One consequence of the lack of employment has been the migration of many Mi'kmaq and Maliseet to large urban centres in the American northeast, particularly Boston. Like the Mohawk before them, the Mi'kmaq discovered in "high steel" construction work an occupation that was well-paying and psychologically satisfying. While some moved permanently to the city, many remain transients, returning to the reserve at frequent intervals. The Mi'kmaq population in Boston is substantially larger than many reserve communities in their homeland.

Increasing political awareness led to formation of the Union of Nova Scotia Indians and the Union of New Brunswick Indians. Land claims were among the most important issues, and extensive research has been conducted into both the general claim of non-treaty groups and the specific loss of lands assigned as reserves. One gain from this research came when the federal government was forced to return a large area removed from the Big Cove reserve in 1879.

The Mi'kmaq in Newfoundland are also pressing for settlement of claims to the land. In 1981 the Federation of Newfoundland Indians and the Mi'kmaq at Conne River launched a comprehensive land claim to the southwestern third of the island. Their claim was rejected, at least partially because of their supposed "recent" arrival in Newfoundland. Occupancy since "time immemorial," however, had never been a requirement of earlier agreements, such as the treaties on the prairies. Brian Peckford, then premier of Newfoundland, dismissed the Mi'kmaq as just one of several immigrant groups, like the Irish or the English. The Mi'kmaq at Conne River are now preparing to take their case for aboriginal land rights to court, while the Federation of Newfoundland Indians, which represents those individuals not legally recognized as Indians, continues to fight for "status" for its members and recognition of their rights to the land.

After almost five centuries of contact, Mi'kmaq and Maliseet life has undergone extensive acculturation. Intermarriage with Caucasians has been common since the seventeenth century, and many reserve communities differ little from their non-Indian neighbours. The vast majority of natives maintain the Catholic faith, a legacy of their past loyalty to the French. The Mi'kmaq language is still widely used in many reserve communities, although there is a declining knowledge of the language among younger people. Despite this, the Mi'kmaq and Maliseet have maintained their separate identity, and their culture today integrates traditional native values with those of the larger society that surrounds them.

CHAPTER 4 *The Iroquoians of the Eastern Woodlands*

The Iroquois feature prominently in Canadian history. Events of the early historic period have left them indelibly stamped in the public mind as warriors, yet they were also accomplished statesmen and diplomats. The political alliance known as the League of the Iroquois is one of their enduring achievements.

The terms "Iroquois" and "Iroquoian" are distinct. The former is usually restricted to the groups that allied as the League of the Iroquois. The original five nations of the league (the Seneca, Cayuga, Onondaga, Oneida and Mohawk) were later joined by the Tuscarora from the south, forming the historic Six Nations. Although the homeland of the league was in New York state, today all six groups are found in Canada. The term Iroquoian refers to all the languages in the family, including those of the now-extinct Huron, Petun, Neutral and St. Lawrence Iroquoians, who were the early historic occupants of southern Ontario and Quebec. All the peoples speaking Iroquoian languages shared a common cultural pattern, differing only in minor aspects, which can also be referred to by the general term Iroquoian.

Northern Iroquoian Nations occupied a large block of land around the eastern Great Lakes. Far to the south, the Cherokee and Tuscarora also spoke Iroquoian languages. In Canada, the Iroquoians occupied southern Ontario and adjacent Quebec, from Georgian Bay south to Lake Erie and Lake Ontario, and east along the St. Lawrence River past modern-day Quebec City. This is the Lower Great Lakes-St. Lawrence Lowlands, richly covered with predominantly hardwood forests, with soils and climate capable of supporting native agriculture. In this environment developed the only agricultural societies in aboriginal Canada. Their farming economy and denser population distinguished them from their Algonkian neighbours of the boreal forests to the north.

Throughout the area the ethnographic pattern was one of relatively sedentary village life. Corn, beans and squash, grown in fields near the villages, were the primary staples. Hunting (particularly for deer), fishing and gathering wild plant foods also contributed to the diet. Villages were clusters of bark-covered longhouses, each sheltering several families, and were generally surrounded by palisades for defence. Desirable village locations were those with good soils and a creek or stream for fresh water, but away from any navigable rivers to avoid being surprised by canoes bearing enemy warriors.

BEFORE WRITTEN RECORDS

Initial occupation of the area occurred shortly after the retreat of the glaciers. Stone projectile points from the Paleo-Indian period, including early fluted forms, have been found at several locations and suggest that humans were present by perhaps as early as 11,000 years ago. All, however, are surface finds and cannot be securely dated.

The prehistoric developments that led to the Iroquoian cultures are complex and the archaeological record is incomplete. Considerable controversy exists over interpretation of various discoveries. A simplified overview is presented here, based on the writings of Canadian Museum of Civilization archaeologist J.V. Wright, in which prehistory after the Paleo-Indians is divided into three broad periods: the Archaic, the Initial Woodland and the Terminal Woodland. Even after this sequence comes to an end with the early historic period, much of our knowledge continues to come from archaeological research. While we are fortunate to have extensive early descriptions of Huron life, the neighbouring Iroquoians were poorly documented, so we are forced to rely on what can be recovered from the ground.

The **Archaic** period (*ca.* 6000 B.C. to 1000 B.C.) began across eastern North America as the late glacial conditions in which the Paleo-Indians existed gradually gave way to environments resembling those of today. A variety of hunting, fishing and collecting activities, depending on the availability and abundance of local resources, supported Archaic cultures, which were consequently more diversified than their Paleo-Indian predecessors. The major Archaic culture in southern Ontario and Quebec is referred to as Laurentian. Discarded food remains from Laurentian sites show that these people lived primarily by hunting, with deer, elk, bear and beaver as the most common prey. Fishing also provided a large part of the diet. Wild plant foods leave far less evidence in the archaeological record, but clearly such activities as berry picking and nut gathering would have been important seasonal sources of food.

Typical Laurentian artifacts include a variety of stone tools, both chipped and ground to shape. Projectile points once armed spears, which were hurled with a spear thrower. Distinctively shaped weights of polished stone were attached to the spear throwers to increase their propulsive force. Polished stone gouges appear to have been efficient woodworking tools. In addition, Laurentian sites contain relatively abundant implements of native copper, including projectile points, knives, fish hooks, awls, pendants and beads. The raw material for these objects came from the copper deposits of western Lake Superior, indicating that trade was well established in southern Ontario by the Archaic period.

Many of the Laurentian artifacts come from burial sites, which provide glimpses into the religious beliefs of these people. Burial ceremonialism is indicated by the sprinkling of red ochre over the body and by the placement of objects in the grave. Over time these grave goods become more lavish and abundant. Exotic goods placed with the dead include copper ornaments, beads of shell from the Atlantic coast, pendants of conch shell from the Gulf of Mexico and tools of stone from various distant locations. Extensive trade networks were required to maintain these burial practices.

The dark side of Laurentian life is also reflected in human remains. Violent death is indicated by the occasional occurrence of projectile points lodged in bones or the chest cavity, skull fractures and decapitation. Warfare, that common feature of later Iroquoian life, seems to have been well established in this area as early as the Archaic.

No abrupt change in native lifeways marks the introduction of the **Initial Woodland** period (*ca.* 1000 B.C. to A.D. 900). Instead, the way of life appears to have been a continuation of the Archaic, with one major addition—pottery. While ceramic vessels may not have drastically changed native life, they are of great importance to the archaeologist. The broken sherds are abundant and virtually indestructible. Stylistic variations in form and decoration allow archaeologists to isolate cultural groups and time periods. Woodland pottery is decorated before firing, often by pressing a cord-wrapped stick or a notched implement into the still-damp clay.

Another feature of the Initial Woodland is the elaboration of burial ceremonialism, including construction of burial mounds. Religious concepts expressed in mortuary rites appear to have entered from the south, particularly from the Adena and Hopewell cultures of the Ohio River Valley, with their large burial mounds containing abundant wealth goods placed with the dead. However, burial mounds are not particularly common in the Canadian Iroquoian area, being restricted to the southern margins of Ontario.

One of the earliest and most widely distributed of the Initial Woodland cultures is termed Point Peninsula. Sites assigned to this culture are found throughout southern Quebec and in southern Ontario north of Toronto. Such sites are known for their distinctive pottery, decorated using a notched

Serpent Mound on Rice Lake, Ontario.
Photo by author

or toothed implement and in later periods with the addition of a collar. Soapstone pipes also make their appearance here. Southern ideas and goods entering Point Peninsula culture are evident from the burial mound sites.

Perhaps the most famous of these sites is Serpent Mound, located on a point overlooking Rice Lake, near Peterborough, Ontario. The largest mound has a sinuous elongated shape about 60 metres in length and up to 2 metres high. While commonly known as Serpent Mound, whether it was actually intended to represent a serpent is uncertain. Eight smaller mounds cluster around it. Excavation has revealed numerous burials, both complete and fragmentary. High-status individuals were apparently interred in sub-mound pits, while others were scattered throughout the mound fill. Associated objects were relatively few but included cut wolf and bear jaws, fossils, and beads of shell, copper and silver. Extensive trade networks are indicated by the fact that the copper is from western Lake Superior (a distance of about 1000 km), the silver is from deposits in northern Ontario (about 370 km) and conch shell had to come from the Gulf of Mexico (about 1500 km). Radiocarbon dates indicate that this site was used over several centuries, from about A.D. 100 to 300. The decline in use of burial mounds and exotic grave goods after this period coincides with the beginning of Hopewell collapse further south.

Co-existing with Point Peninsula was another Initial Woodland culture termed Saugeen, distributed throughout southwestern Ontario. Most excavated sites are along rapids, at creek or river mouths, or in other good fishing locations. Fish bones, particularly sturgeon, pickerel and drum, dominate food remains from these sites, which represent seasonal villages where large populations could gather. Evidence of substantial rectangular houses can be recognized by the pattern of small circular stains (termed "post moulds") which mark where posts once stood. Saugeen pottery style is generally similar to that of Point Peninsula, although specific differences can be recognized. Although they do not seem to have constructed burial mounds, Saugeen people did participate in the general pattern of Hopewellian burial rites. Excavation of a small cemetery at the Donaldson site, on the Saugeen

River near its mouth on Lake Huron, revealed such Hopewell-related objects placed with the dead as two copper panpipe covers, a stone ear-spool, three sheets of cut mica and a modified timber wolf jaw.

In the final centuries of the Initial Woodland, Saugeen was replaced in southernmost Ontario by the Princess Point culture. New and distinct pottery styles identify the archaeological remains, although it is difficult to say whether this means the arrival of new people or simply new ideas on how to decorate pots. In this final stage corn agriculture was introduced to southern Ontario. From crops domesticated in Mexico thousands of years earlier, agriculture gradually spread northward as new strains became adapted to cooler climates. This set the stage for a population explosion and the full development of Iroquoian cultures in the Terminal Woodland.

The **Terminal Woodland** period (A.D. 900 to the historic era) saw the emergence of cultures directly ancestral to historic Iroquoians. Two separate but related traditions exist. In southern Ontario, the Terminal Woodland developments leading to the historic Huron, Petun and Neutral cultures are referred to as the Ontario Iroquois Tradition. In the St. Lawrence River valley of southern Quebec and adjacent Ontario, a separate development leads to the St. Lawrence Iroquoians.

In its early centuries, the Ontario Iroquois Tradition was separated into two geographic branches. The southern branch, with sites to the north of Lake Erie, is termed Glen Meyer, while to the north, from Lake Ontario to Georgian Bay, was Pickering. Although differing in various features such as pottery styles, these two regional branches developed in similar ways. They may, in fact, represent a continuum of cultural variation, rather than two distinct regional cultures. The economy was based on corn agriculture, supplemented by fishing and hunting. Small triangular stone arrowpoints show that the bow and arrow were in use by this time. Dwellings were longhouses, clustered into small villages which were frequently palisaded for defence. Pottery and tools of stone and bone were similar to later Iroquoian types. Burial practices included secondary burials (where the disarticulated bones of an individual who had been given an earlier interim burial in a shallow grave or on a scaffold were gathered and buried in a bundle) and small ossuaries (pits containing bundles of disarticulated bones from a number of individuals).

Around A.D. 1300 the Pickering branch appears to have expanded across southern Ontario. Wright attributes this to conquest, with the Glen Meyer people being dispersed and partially absorbed. There is no compelling evidence of widespread warfare, however, causing some archaeologists to be skeptical of this hypothesis. Whatever the cause, the following period was one of fairly homogenous culture across southern Ontario. During this time ossuary burial became common, with some pits containing the remains of hundreds of people. Numerous pipes of pottery and stone, some embellished with effigies of humans or animals, mark the introduction of

Reconstruction of a Glen Meyer village (ca. A.D. 1000), based on archaeological evidence, near London, Ontario. Photo by author

the tobacco smoking habit. From this common cultural base, the separate historic Iroquoian cultures emerged.

In the final centuries before European contact, two branches of Iroquoian culture developed in southern Ontario. The most northerly led to the historic Huron and Petun, while the other led to the Neutral of southernmost Ontario and their close kin the Erie in adjacent New York. The importance of agriculture is greatly expanded in this late period with the introduction of beans and squash, since corn and beans together provide a nutritionally complete diet. As a result, hunting played a lesser role in the economy than in earlier periods. This enhanced economy allowed a sharp increase in population, reflected in the increased size and number of villages and ossuaries. Warfare was evidently widespread, and cut and burned human bones in village debris suggest that cannibalism was practiced, as was the case for captured warriors in historic times. All the basic features of historic Ontario Iroquoian cultures as they become known in the early seventeenth century are present in these late prehistoric sites.

The Draper site, located about 35 kilometres northeast of Toronto, is a large precontact Huron village which was almost totally uncovered by a series of excavations through the 1970s. When the site was occupied around A.D. 1500, populations seem to have been clustering into larger villages, presumably for protection. Segments of the palisade were repeatedly torn down to make room for village expansions. The site eventually grew from a small cluster of seven longhouses to a large village, surrounded by up to four rows of palisades, containing at least thirty-seven houses sheltering nearly 2000 people.

Intensive hostilities in these final years before European arrival led to abandonment of many areas and contraction of territories to those known historically. The Huron withdrew from the lands north of Lake Ontario to cluster in their historic homeland around Georgian Bay. Similarly the Neutral abandoned much of southwestern Ontario, clustering around the western end of Lake Ontario and the Niagara Peninsula.

Along the St. Lawrence River valley, similar developments were occurring throughout the Terminal Woodland period. Although the late prehistoric cultures in this area resembled those in southern Ontario, differences did exist. Pots and pipes were particularly finely made and differ stylistically from those of their western kin. Bone was particularly important as a raw material for making tools. Rather than placing their dead in ossuaries, they buried them in flexed positions throughout the villages. Abundant remains of broken and charred human bones, as well as ornaments and tools made from human bone, indicate cannibalism was comparatively common. Judging from historic information, victims were usually males captured in warfare. Large villages of longhouses, frequently palisaded for defence, were similar to those in southern Ontario and those described in early historic accounts.

THE ST. LAWRENCE IROQUOIANS

Our earliest historic descriptions of Canadian Iroquoians come from the voyages of Jacques Cartier. On his first voyage, in 1534, Cartier encountered a fishing party from the village of Stadacona off the Gaspé peninsula and took two of them, sons of the headman Donnacona, back to France. They served as guides for Cartier's larger expedition of 1535, leading him up the St. Lawrence River to Stadacona (located where Quebec City now stands), where he spent the winter. Both groups endured illnesses that winter. The natives provided medicine made from fronds of white cedar for the Europeans' scurvy, while the French could do nothing to alleviate the natives' suffering from diseases they had brought. Cartier also antagonized the Stadaconans by traveling upriver to Hochelaga (the site of modern Montreal) against their wishes and by kidnapping ten natives, including Donnacona and his two sons, when he returned to France in 1536. All except a young girl died there before Cartier returned to Stadacona during his third voyage, in 1541.

Cartier's descriptions of Stadacona are disappointingly brief. Stadacona was the largest of a cluster of about seven villages, all located on the north shore of the St. Lawrence. The south side may have remained uninhabited because of attacks by a hostile people known as the Toudaman, who were probably the Mi'kmaq or Maliseet. The French appear to have been unimpressed with these villages, which suggests that they were small. Unlike

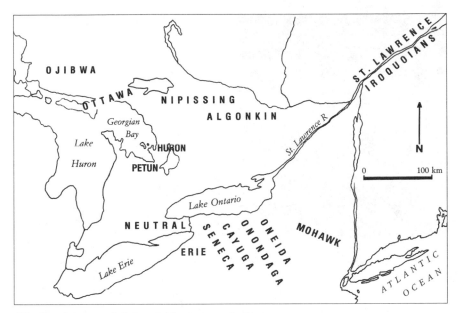

The Iroquoians and their neighbours at early European contact.

most Iroquoian villages, they were not protected by palisades.

Fortunately, Cartier left a fuller description of Hochelaga. On 3 October 1535, Cartier and his men marched through forests and corn fields to the village, read the Gospel to the natives, and climbed Mount Royal to survey the surrounding land. From Mount Royal Cartier could see the St. Lawrence River and noted the turbulent waters of the Lachine rapids that barred further travel upriver. The village itself was located well away from navigable water, presumably for defence, and was surrounded by vast fields of corn. A triple row of palisades, with ladders leading to platforms where defenders could stand during an attack, encircled about fifty bark-covered longhouses. This would indicate a population equivalent to the large Huron villages to the west described by the French a century later. Unfortunately, Hochelaga stands in the clear light of recorded history for only this one day. Cartier did not return to Hochelaga on his later trip up the St. Lawrence, and by the time other explorers reached the area nothing remained of this important Iroquoian village.

Reminders that vestiges of the native past lie beneath the concrete, glass and pavement of modern Montreal occasionally come to light. A good example is the Dawson site, located south of Sherbrooke St. opposite McGill University. Construction in the late nineteenth century disturbed large quantities of Iroquoian pottery, other artifacts and human skeletons. Since then archaeologists have debated whether those are the remains of Hochelaga. Although the question cannot be answered, the Dawson site

St. Lawrence Iroquoian pottery vessel.
CMC K75-1073

appears to be too small to fit Cartier's description and may have been a separate Hochelagan village.

The economy of the Hochelagans and Stadaconans clearly differed. The Hochelagans were typical Iroquoians, relying on crops of corn, beans and squash, supplemented by hunting and fishing. The Stadaconans, while also agriculturalists, lived in a marginal environment for growing corn and had to rely more heavily on hunting and fishing. During winter, men traveled far inland in hunting parties. In summer, fishing and catching eels were important. Large groups of Stadaconans also traveled downriver to the mouth of the St. Lawrence to fish for mackerel and hunt sea mammals such as seals and small whales. It was one of these groups that Cartier encountered in 1534.

The term "St. Lawrence Iroquoians" is something of a catch-all phrase. It is unlikely that they were a single political group, despite the Hochelagan claim to rule all the tribes further downstream. It is not even clear from French accounts whether the villages around Stadacona formed a single tribe or were politically autonomous. Present practice is to refer to the two clusters described by Cartier as Stadaconans and Hochelagans, and to recognize considerable differences between them. In fact, recent archaeological research suggests that there were at least three distinct clusters of Iroquoian villages on the St. Lawrence.

We do not even know if the two groups spoke the same language. Our only information comes from word lists collected from Cartier's Stadaconan captives. Linguistic analysis has indicated that this was a distinct Iroquoian language which cannot be assigned to Huron or any of the Five Nations Iroquois languages as was once thought. It is from this language that Canada takes its name, from a word meaning "village" which was extended to refer to all the lands around Stadacona.

After Cartier's final departure, the St. Lawrence Iroquoians disappear from history. Our next historic records come from Samuel de Champlain, who arrived on the St. Lawrence in 1603. By this time the Stadaconans and Hochelagans had vanished, leaving a no-man's-land traveled only by war parties of Algonkians and Five Nations Iroquois, locked in bitter conflict over this vital waterway.

What fate befell the St. Lawrence Iroquoians? Epidemic diseases, beginning as early as their first encounter with Cartier, may have decreased their numbers. Crop failures may also have played a role, since the lower St. Lawrence River valley was a precarious environment for native agriculture. However, their most probable fate was annihilation through warfare. As early as 1535 the Stadaconans were trying to prevent Cartier from proceeding upriver in order to have a monopoly on French trade goods. Desire to obtain access to European goods or to gain control of the trade would have provided motivation for warfare. The identity of the aggressors is also unknown. J.V. Wright has made a convincing argument that the St. Lawrence Iroquoians were destroyed in warfare with the Huron. He points to the presence of typical St. Lawrence Iroquoian pottery in late Huron sites as evidence that female captives were adopted into Huron society and continued to make pots in their accustomed fashion. Adult males, on the other hand, were killed, explaining the relative lack of St. Lawrence Iroquoian-style pipes, which were a male craft. Others, however, have seen the presence of St. Lawrence pottery in late Huron sites as indicating a refugee population, fleeing destruction in their homeland at the hands of the Five Nations Iroquois, particularly the Mohawk. Whether aggressors or hosts, the Huron had less than a century before they were to suffer the same fate.

THE HURON AND PETUN

These closely related neighbouring groups emerged from the same late prehistoric cultural stratum. Although they were politically separate, they spoke the same language, differed little in customs and were distinguished primarily by the extent of Petun cultivation and trade of tobacco (for which they were known as the "Tobacco Nation"). While closely allied during the seventeenth century, the Jesuits recorded that they had "formerly waged cruel wars against one another."

The Huron and Petun are primarily known through ethnohistoric documents. Recorded history covers only the first half of the seventeenth century, from European arrival to the destruction of the Huron, Petun and Neutral at the hands of the Iroquois. Yet for this brief period we do have extensive written records, particularly for the Huron. The combination of colonial policy, a lucrative fur trade and missionary zeal drew the French into Huron country in the early seventeenth century. Three major written sources provide most of our knowledge. Samuel de Champlain traveled

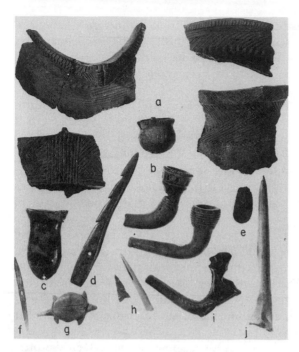

Typical Huron-Petun artifacts: (a) pottery rim fragments; (b) small pot, possibly made by a child; (c) stone pipe bowl; (d) antler harpoon; (e) stone scraper; (f) netting needle; (g) stone turtle amulet; (h) stone and bone arrowheads; (i) pottery pipes; (j) dagger made from human bone.
CMC 73-7763

through Huronia in 1615-1616 and left a detailed account of his experiences. Champlain's request to the Recollet order, a branch of the Franciscans, resulted in the missionary work of Gabriel Sagard, who laboured among the Hurons from 1623 to 1624 and recorded his observations of Huron life. The third and most extensive source of information is the *Jesuit Relations*, which chronicle the work of the Jesuit missionaries among the Huron from 1634 to 1650. These voluminous accounts provide a wealth of information on the Huron (and to a lesser extent on the Petun and other neighbouring groups). Further details can now be obtained only through archaeology.

The name "Huron" was applied by the French from an old term for "boar's head" (suggested by the bristly hair styles of the Iroquoians), which had come to have the more general meaning of "ruffian" or "knave." The Huron referred to themselves as *Wendat,* meaning "Islanders" or "Dwellers on a Peninsula," because their homeland was surrounded by water on three sides. This term survived as *Wyandot,* applied to the descendants of Huron-Petun refugees from the Iroquois wars. Similarly, the term 'Petun' comes from a word used by the French for tobacco. A native word for the group is variously written as Tionontati or Khionontateronon, meaning "People of the Hills."

By the early seventeenth century, Huronia, the Huron homeland, was restricted to the region between Georgian Bay and Lake Simcoe. Its fertile soils lay immediately south of the rocky Canadian Shield. Much of Huronia was open land, since people had cleared and then abandoned their agricultural fields. Sagard describes it as "full of fine hills, open fields, very beautiful broad meadows bearing much excellent hay." Early estimates of Huron villages range between eighteen and twenty-five, of which perhaps six would have been large fortified villages containing numerous longhouses. The total population was estimated to be between 20,000 and 30,000. Epidemic diseases quickly reduced their numbers to about 9000 by 1640.

The Petun were located to the southwest of the Huron. Trails linked the Petun and Huron villages, each requiring about a day's journey. The Petun also maintained close ties with Algonkian groups such as the Ottawa to the west, with whom they traded. Champlain mentions eight villages in 1616, while the Jesuits list nine in 1639. Little information exists on the size of the population, although 8000 may be a reasonable estimate. Again, epidemic diseases caused the population to drop to about 3000 by 1640.

Both the Huron and Petun were confederacies of separate tribes. Of the five groups that made up the Huron, the Attignawantan ("Bear Nation") was by far the largest, occupying the western portion of Huronia, including all of the Penetanguishene Peninsula. The others were the Arendarhonon ("Rock Nation"), Attigneenongnahac (usually interpreted as "Cord Nation"), Tahontaenrat (possibly meaning "Deer Nation") and Ataronchronon (possibly "Nation Beyond the Silted Lake"). The latter group did not appear in the initial Jesuit lists, and it is possible that they were merely a division of the Attignawantan. The Attignawantan and the Attigneenongnahac were the original occupants of Huronia, the others arriving, probably from near Lake Ontario, only a short time before the Jesuits. The Petun were divided into two groups, which the Jesuits called the "Nation of the Wolves" and the "Nation of the Deer."

Village locations were carefully chosen. The primary requirements were access to fresh water and arable soils, available firewood and a location which could be defended. Only larger villages and those on the frontier were strongly fortified, the inhabitants of smaller centres fleeing to these strongholds in times of danger. Palisades, constructed from long slender poles twisted into the ground, encircled the village, frequently in several rows. Large sheets of bark strengthened the palisades, and ladders provided access to walkways where the defenders could stand. Sagard provides details:

> [they] are fortified by strong wooden palisades in three rows, interlaced into one another and reinforced within by large thick pieces of bark to a height of eight or nine feet, and at the bottom there are great trunks of trees placed lengthwise . . . Then above these palisades there are galleries or watch-towers . . . and these they stock with stones in war-time to hurl upon the enemy, and water to put out the fire that might be laid against their palisades.
>
> (Sagard 1939:91-92)

Within the palisades the longhouses were arranged in seemingly random fashion but were usually a short distance apart due to the constant threat of fire. Large villages contained up to 100 longhouses, sheltering 1500 to 2000 people. Champlain, however, estimated 200 "fairly large lodges" at the important village of Cahiague, a figure which has been questioned by some writers. Due to the exhaustion of soils and firewood supplies, villages had to be moved every ten to fifteen years, and at such times the larger villages might split into two.

The longhouse was the basic unit of Iroquoian life. Large sheets of cedar, elm or ash bark were woven between arched poles to form a long structure with a vaulted roof and rounded ends. Each sheltered a number of families. Lengths varied widely according to the number of occupants, and shorter structures could be lengthened to accommodate new inhabitants. Both Champlain and Sagard describe the longhouses as being 25 to 30 fathoms long (roughly 45 to 55 metres) and 6 wide (about 11 metres), although sizes varied considerably. A central corridor running the length of the longhouse contained the hearths. Each hearth was shared by two families, living across the corridor from each other. Raised benches or sleeping platforms extended along each side of the house. According to Champlain and Sagard, however, these platforms were used for sleeping only in the summer, while winter cold forced the family to sleep on the floor near the fire. Food and firewood were stored in enclosed porches at each end and under the sleeping platforms. Fish and corn hung drying from the roof of the house. Personal belongings were also hung from the roof or were buried in storage pits dug into the house floor. Despite openings in the roof, smoke from the fires filled the houses and caused serious eye problems. Although the Huron no doubt appreciated the warmth and social interaction of their homes, the Jesuits described them as "a miniature picture of Hell," complaining of noise and lack of privacy, choking smoke, the stench of urine and rotting fish, unrestrained rampages of dogs and small children, and infestations of fleas, flies and mice.

The diet of the Huron and Petun was overwhelmingly composed of agricultural produce. Corn, along with beans, squash and pumpkins, made up at least three quarters of all their food. Corn kernels were dried and pounded into flour in a hollowed-out tree trunk, using a long wooden pole. While ingenious ways were devised to prepare corn, most were variations on a theme. The everyday meal was a corn soup (*sagamite*), often varied by adding pieces of fish, meat or squash. Small fish might be tossed whole into the pot, removed after boiling a short while and mashed, then returned to the pot without removing bones, scales or entrails. For feasts a thick corn soup might be served with some fat or oil on top. A bread of corn meal, often mixed with deer fat or dried fruit to provide flavour, was baked under ashes. "Stinking corn," prepared by placing small ears of corn in a stagnant pond to ferment for several months before eating, was a delicacy to the

Reconstruction of a Huron village, Midland, Ontario. Photo by author

Huron but revolted their Jesuit guests. Responsibility for raising crops and cooking food fell on the women, who also collected a wide variety of wild plants, such as nuts and berries, which were of little importance except to add flavour to a bland diet.

Hunting and fishing, the responsibility of the men, played a lesser role in the diet. Fishing could be carried out through much of the year, although the spring and late fall spawning runs were peak periods. In the fall men made fishing expeditions to the many islands of Georgian Bay, to catch whitefish, trout and sturgeon, most commonly in nets. Inland, weirs might be constructed along creeks and streams to block the fish run so that the fish could be speared or netted. Champlain described fish weirs along the full length of the narrows between Lake Simcoe and Lake Couchiching.

Hunting was of less importance than fishing in the diet, but was essential to obtain hides for clothing. Deer were the principal game animals, although bear and beaver were also sought. Huronia's dense population meant that game animals were scarce, forcing hunters to set out on lengthy expeditions to the south or east. Deer were frequently taken by the communal drive, in which a line of hunters forced the deer between long converging fences of brush into an enclosure where they were speared or shot with arrows. Deer could also be driven into lakes and killed from canoes. Although dogs were used in the hunt, they might also wind up in the stewpot for a feast, and Champlain and Sagard report that tame bears were raised from cubs for the same purpose.

Their political structure included two types of chiefs. Civil chiefs were concerned with affairs of state and organized feasts, dances, games and funeral ceremonies, while war chiefs were concerned exclusively with military matters. In theory each clan segment had both a civil and a war chief, so that several of each would exist within larger villages. Succession to these positions was by a combination of inheritance and personal abilities, such as wisdom, speaking skills and bravery. Village affairs were conducted by two councils, one composed of war chiefs and senior warriors, the other of civil chiefs and older adult males. All matters were supposedly decided by consensus, with everyone present being given an opportunity to express his views. In practice, according to the Jesuits, the chiefs and elders made the decisions, owing to their higher social standing and powers of oratory. While no individual was bound by any decision, failure to comply would leave one open to criticism or ridicule.

Councils involving the entire Huron confederacy were held at least once a year. This brought together civil chiefs from throughout Huronia to reaffirm their friendship and discuss matters of common concern. The Attignawantan, by virtue of their numbers, seem to have dominated confederacy meetings. Again, no decisions were binding on individual members, and the difficulty in establishing decisive common action was a weakness when faced with the Iroquois onslaught.

Marriages were relatively casually contracted. Residence tended to be matrilocal (that is, the man moved into the household of his wife), although it seems clear that this was the ideal rather than an inevitable rule. Where this ideal was followed, longhouses were occupied by a group of related adult women and their spouses and children. Divorce was frequent and simple, requiring only that the husband move out of the wife's house. Once the couple had children, however, marital breakdown was less common. Descent was matrilineal, all children belonging to the clan of their mother. Young men could not inherit their father's property or position but looked to their mother's brothers. In old age a man counted more on his sister's children than on his own for his support.

Communication between Huron and Petun villages was by foot over a network of narrow trails. Even to the Neutral and beyond, most travel was overland. Because winter was a difficult time for travel, despite the use of both snowshoes and toboggans, the Iroquoians rarely set out on major trips during this season. Travel by canoe seems to have been restricted to fishing expeditions, long-distance trade and crossing Lake Ontario to attack the Iroquois. The forests of Huronia provided birchbark, allowing the Huron to build lighter and more efficient canoes than the Iroquois and Neutral, who had to use the inferior elm bark. However, Huron canoes were not as well made as those of their Algonkian neighbours, nor did they play as large a role in their culture.

Clothing was made from deer hides and beaver pelts obtained by hunting or through trade with the Algonkians. In warm weather men wore only a breechcloth of deerskin and a pair of moccasins. Women added only a skirt, leaving their upper bodies bare. In winter both sexes also wore a cloak, long sleeves and leggings, held in place by leather thongs. Despite this clothing, some people are known to have frozen to death while attempting to travel between villages. Clothing could be decorated by painting or with a trim of dyed porcupine quills. Both men and women wore necklaces and bracelets of shell beads, and suspended shell beads from their ears. Considerable attention was lavished on the hair. Women wore a single tress that hung down the back and was tied with a leather thong, while men cut theirs in a variety of styles. Some shaved the sides of their head, while others cut their hair in ridges, or cut one side and allowed the other to grow long. Both sexes rubbed oil or grease on their hair and bodies, and for special occasions painted their faces and bodies as well. Tattooing, while rare among the Huron, was apparently common among the Petun, depicting, according to Sagard, snakes, lizards, squirrels and other animals.

Religious and mythological beliefs, along with the associated feasts and dances, integrated Huron society. Certain old men were repositories of traditions and myths, which were publicly recited at feasts. In the Huron world, all things, whether animate or inanimate, had a soul or spirit. The more powerful of these were called *oki*. This term was also extended to unusual individuals, such as shamans, witches, fierce warriors or even lunatics. The most important spirit was the sky, which determined weather, wind, waves and other natural forces affecting human life. Lesser spirits were associated with prominent features of the landscape. While some were friendly and could be approached for assistance, others were malevolent, seeking to kill and devour humans, and had to be placated with tobacco and other offerings. Fish and animals also had spirits, requiring care not to offend them. Their bones must never be thrown into the fire or to the dogs or else their souls would be angered and the living animals would no longer allow themselves to be taken.

Every Huron had a soul, and these souls had desires which could be communicated through dreams. Failure to fulfill the dream and satisfy the soul could result in illness or death. If the dream was of an object it had to be identified and obtained, the owner being obliged to make a gift of it. If the dream was of a feast or ceremony, every effort had to be made to recreate it in real life. Dreams were sometimes ambiguous, requiring a shaman to interpret the soul's demands. Occasionally dreams were overtly sexual in nature. A person might request a ceremony for his or her recovery in which the young people of the village danced naked. In another ceremony, which according to Sagard was mainly for older women, pairs of young people were invited to the patient's lodge for a night of sexual intercourse in her presence. Such acts violated normal prohibitions on expressing sexuality, which shows the role of dreams in transgressing cultural restrictions.

In addition to denying the soul's desires, illness could be caused by natural factors or by witchcraft. The former was treated with medicinal plants, while the latter required a shaman to aid in removing the spell. If the witch could be identified he or she might be killed. Some shamans also had the power to control the weather or predict future events.

Feasts, dances and games brought together the social groups which made up Huron society. Feasts were held for a variety of occasions and were an important mechanism for gaining status. Great quantities of food were distributed, although the host was expected to eat little or nothing. Dances were usually performed to cure illness or celebrate a victory. Such social gatherings also provided opportunities for games. Lacrosse was the most popular, often played between teams from different villages. It was a rough sport, played by young men, and frequently resulted in injuries. A gambling game, in which marked fruit stones were tossed like dice in a wooden bowl, was passionately played and bets were heavy, some men losing all that they owned. Games also served a curing function and could fulfill soul desires expressed in dreams. When epidemic diseases were spreading among the Huron, the shamans decided that the whole country was sick and that lacrosse should be played to cure it.

When a Huron died the surrounding villages were notified, so that they could attend the funeral several days later. A feast was held, and gifts were presented to the grieving relatives. The body was placed on a scaffold in the village cemetery, accompanied by offerings. Some individuals, such as those killed in battle or who had drowned, were buried in the ground and shrines raised over their graves. For all except those who had died violently, these arrangements were temporary, and the individual was not considered to have had final burial until the next Feast of the Dead.

The Feast of the Dead was the most important ceremony in Huron society. It was held every ten to twelve years, or whenever a large village shifted location. At this time people from a number of neighbouring villages would gather from their cemeteries the remains of all who had died since the last such ceremony and prepare them for reburial in a common grave. Sagard described the preparation of the corpses by their female relatives.

> The women who have to bring the bones of their relatives go to the cemeteries for them, and if the flesh is not entirely destroyed they clean it off and take away the bones. These they wash and wrap up in fine new beaver-skins, and with glass beads and wampum necklaces, which the relations and friends contribute and bring . . . And putting them into a new bag they carry them on their backs, and also adorn the top of the bag with many little ornaments, with necklaces, bracelets, and other decorations.
>
> (Sagard 1939: 211-212)

After honouring these remains with a feast in their own village, the Huron set out for the Feast of the Dead, the women carrying the bundles of bones. They met at a location where a large circular pit had been dug and a platform, from which the bags of bones and grave goods could be suspended, had been built. The pit was lined with beaver robes, and large offerings such as kettles were placed at the bottom. After several days of ceremonies and a final farewell to the deceased, each family threw the bones of their dead and the grave goods being offered into the burial pit. Several men went into the pit with long poles to arrange the bones, the effect being to mix together the bones of numerous individuals. At last the pit was filled and covered over, presents were distributed, and a final feast was held. Everyone could then return to their villages, secure in the knowledge that their dead relatives had been laid to final rest, and strengthened as a tribe by this shared ceremony. One excavated ossuary contained the remains of approximately 1000 individuals.

Warfare among the Iroquoians, prior to changes brought about by the fur trade, was primarily motivated by a desire to avenge previous deaths and acquire personal prestige. Summer was the time for military expeditions, usually organized by the war chiefs at the request of families which had suffered losses at the hands of the enemy, usually the Iroquois. Groups of several hundred men might set out to attack an Iroquois village. More commonly, they might split into small groups, hiding along paths and in fields, hoping to surprise the enemy. Major weapons were a wooden club and the bow and arrow. Warriors wore armour of wooden slats covering much of the body and carried a shield. The goal of these military campaigns was to capture or kill as many of the enemy as possible. Prisoners, along with heads or scalps as trophies of those killed, were taken back to the Huron villages.

Captives were distributed among those who had participated in the raid, and a decision was made on their fate. Some, particularly women and children, were adopted by the family to which they had been given, usually to replace members lost in previous warfare. They eventually became full members of this society, and the few adult males adopted in this manner might eventually find themselves in battle against their former kin. More commonly adult males were tortured to death. This was a public spectacle, participated in by all members of the village, who competed in acts of cruelty. The victim's suffering might be prolonged over several days. After death finally came, his body was cut into pieces, which were cooked in a kettle and served at a feast. If he had been a particularly brave warrior his flesh and heart were eagerly consumed by young men, who believed that they could thus acquire his courage.

Contact with the French in the early seventeenth century brought about great changes in Huron life and eventually led to their destruction. Initially, relations between these two nations centred on trade. The exchange of beaver pelts and other furs for iron tools and other European goods was so profitable for both sides that the beaver were soon nearly exterminated within Huronia, forcing the Huron to trade with the Algonkians to the north for furs. As the principal trading partners of the French, the Huron held a strategic position, blocking the Petun and others from direct access to trade. Large quantities of furs, obtained from the Algonkians in exchange for corn and European goods, were taken by the Huron to French settlements on the St. Lawrence each year. However, such trips were dangerous and attacks by the Iroquois became increasingly common.

As well as fur trade wealth, the French were seeking salvation for the natives' souls. First the Recollets, then the Jesuits, attempted conversion of the Huron to Christianity. It was the Jesuits who made the most sustained effort and had the greatest effect. After establishment of their central mission, Sainte-Marie, in 1639 the Jesuits had a permanent base among the Huron and were able to achieve a large number of conversions. This weakened the Huron by dividing them into Christian and traditional factions.

Also arriving with the French were European diseases, to which the Iroquoians had no immunity. Smallpox and measles took a huge toll, greatly weakening the Huron confederacy. The smallpox epidemic of 1639 was particularly devastating. Diseases aided the proselytizing of the Jesuits as many Huron accepted baptism as a curing ritual; however, others became antagonistic to the Jesuits when they noticed that most of those who were baptized soon died.

The fur trade also altered the pattern of Iroquoian warfare, from blood feuds spurred by revenge to wars of extermination. The Iroquois, trading first with the Dutch and later with the English, desired access to the rich beaver country to the north from which they were blocked by the Huron. The Iroquois soon had a major advantage in firearms, since the Jesuits forbade any French trade in muskets to the Huron except for trusted Christian converts. The western Iroquois, particularly the Seneca, began raiding far into Huron territory in large, well-organized armies bent on destruction of entire villages. In the east, the Mohawk made any Huron attempts to get their furs to Quebec a very risky venture.

The Huron seem to have been unable to deal with this looming threat, and they became increasingly uncertain about their future. Thousands flocked to the fortifications of Sainte-Marie, greatly increasing the number of Christian converts. In 1648 the Iroquois launched determined attacks, destroying a number of eastern Huron villages. That winter an army of over a thousand men, mainly Seneca and Mohawk, secretly spent the winter camped north of Lake Ontario, so that they could surprise the Huron before the snows were gone in the spring. The Huron were unable to withstand this onslaught, which destroyed the villages around Sainte-Marie. The Jesuit Fathers Brébeuf and Lalemant were captured by the Iroquois and tortured to death according to Iroquoian custom. The surviving Huron decided that their situation was hopeless and abandoned their villages, putting them to the torch so that they could not be used by the Iroquois.

Many refugees perished of starvation or at the hands of marauding Iroquois war parties. Others, particularly the Attignawantan, sought refuge among the Petun, only to share their fate when the Iroquois turned on the Petun and destroyed their villages by the end of 1649. Some fled to the Neutral, who dropped their neutrality after the Huron defeat and subjected these fugitives to a harsh captivity. Many of both the Huron and Petun were absorbed into Iroquois communities, being adopted by their conquerors as a method of replacing their own populations lost in warfare. The smallest Huron tribe, the Tahontaenrat, along with some of the Arendarhonon, were even allowed to build a separate town in the territory of the Seneca. All eventually lost their own cultural identity and adopted that of their conquerors.

One large group of refugees, predominantly Petun but with some Huron, fled to the upper Great Lakes region and allied with such Algonkian groups as the Ottawa and Potawatomi. They became known as the Wyandot, a corruption of the Huron name for themselves. After a number of moves they settled near Detroit. In the nineteenth century, the American policy of removing Indians to settlements west of the Mississippi forced the Wyandot to Kansas and Oklahoma, where their descendants remain. Their language is now extinct, although it was still spoken in the early twentieth century.

Another large group of Huron fled to Gahendoe (Christian) Island, a short distance from the shores of Huronia in Georgian Bay. After the burning of Sainte-Marie, the Jesuits established a new fortress among these Huron and spent the winter of 1649-1650 there. This was a time of extreme hardship, when provisions ran out early in the winter and fishing through the ice proved unusually unproductive. Bands of Iroquois roamed the shores of Georgian Bay, preventing any attempt to hunt on the mainland. Hunger led people to eat moss and bark, and eventually to cannibalism. Large numbers of Huron died of starvation or contagious diseases over the winter. Others were killed or captured by the Iroquois as they attempted to leave the island. Finally, in June of 1650, the Jesuits and about 300 Huron began the final retreat to Quebec.

After 1650, few if any Huron remained in Huronia. The Iroquois had no interest in permanently settling this territory, traveling through it only on occasional hunting and trading expeditions. Only charred poles remained where the villages had stood, and weeds overgrew the corn fields which had once supported the dense population of now-abandoned Huronia.

Descendants of the Huron who fled with the Jesuits still reside at the Village-des-Hurons, just outside Quebec City. Once known as the Huron of Lorette, they now refer to themselves as the Nation Huronne Wendat. Typical of Quebec villagers in this region, they are Catholic and francophone.

Numbering about 2600 people, this is the only Huron population in Canada today. The Huron language, however, is extinct.

THE NEUTRAL

While similar in culture to the Huron and Petun, the Neutral, along with the Erie across the lake which bears their name, emerged from a slightly divergent prehistoric branch. The Neutral language was similar to Huron, the two groups referring to each other as the Attiwandaronk, meaning "people who speak a slightly different language."

We know far less of Neutral life than we do of Huron. Both the Recollets and the Jesuits made excursions into Neutral territory but were not able to establish permanent bases among them. The Neutral hostility to missionary efforts was noted by the Jesuits, who commented that they were regarded as "sorcerers who carried death and misfortune everywhere." As a result, we are much more dependent upon archaeological research to document Neutral life in the early seventeenth century than we are for Huron life.

The Neutral occupied southeastern Ontario, primarily between the Grand and Niagara rivers, with most of their villages near western Lake Ontario. The climate of this area was slightly more benign than that of Huronia, and the hardwood forests sheltered larger numbers of game animals. About forty Neutral villages existed in the early historic period. Although population estimates vary considerably, somewhere between 30,000 and 40,000 people once occupied Neutral territory, making them the most populous of the northeastern Iroquoians. Smallpox epidemics, however, particularly between 1638-1640, drastically reduced their population.

Like the Huron and Petun, the Neutral were a confederacy of separate tribes. However, we have much less information on the constituent groups. Ethnohistorical and archaeological evidence suggests between five and ten separate tribes made up the Neutral, but we do not have even a full list of their names.

The term "Neutral" was applied by the French to these people for their determination to avoid being dragged into the destructive wars between the Huron and the League of the Iroquois. However, they must certainly not be seen as pacifists. The Neutral were embroiled in long-standing warfare with the "Fire Nation" (the Algonkian-speaking Mascouten, in what is now Michigan). All the cruelties of Iroquoian warfare were practiced by the Neutral, the Jesuits noting that they tortured and burned female prisoners as well as male.

Most elements of Neutral life closely resemble those already described for the Huron. They lived in palisaded villages of longhouses, occupied by people related through the female line. They practiced corn agriculture, supplemented by hunting and fishing. However, game was more abundant in Neutral territory and hunting more important in their diet than in that of the Huron. They were less adept canoemen and did not set out on long journeys by water as did the Huron. Like the Petun but unlike the Huron, the Neutral tattooed their bodies and grew tobacco, which was an important trade commodity.

The Jesuits also noted differences in burial customs. Father Lalemant contrasted Huron and Neutral practices:

> Our Hurons immediately after death carry the bodies to the burying ground and take them away from it only for the feast of the Dead. Those of the Neutral Nation carry the bodies to the burying ground only at the very latest moment possible when decomposition has rendered them insupportable; for this reason, the dead bodies often remain during the entire winter in their cabins; and, having once put them outside upon a scaffold that they may decay, they take away the bones as soon as is possible, and expose them to view, arranged here and there in their cabins, until the feast of the Dead.
>
> (Thwaites, *Jesuit Relations* 21:199)

Although both groups held a Feast of the Dead, involving communal reburial in an ossuary, some differences existed. Excavation of the Grimsby site, an historic Neutral ossuary, indicates that care was taken to maintain the integrity of separate burials, in contrast to the deliberate mixing of disarticulated bones from many individuals in the larger Huron ossuaries.

Several writers have argued that by about 1615 the Neutral had developed politically beyond the level of a tribal confederacy to reach the status of a chiefdom. This was achieved with the rise of a powerful war chief named Tsouharissen, who held political power throughout Neutral territory. Support for this view comes from the writings of Daillon, a Recollet priest, who observed of Tsouharissen in 1627: "This man is the chief of the greatest credit and authority that has ever been in all these nations, because he is not only chief of his town, but of all those of his nation . . . It is unexampled in the other nations to have a chief so absolute. He acquired this honour and power by his courage, and by having been many times at war" (Noble 1985:133). The question of whether this organization under a paramount chief would have continued after Tsouharissen can never be answered. Destruction at the hands of the Iroquois put an end to this political experiment after less than four decades of existence.

Seneca expansion westward began the threat to the Neutral. Even after the Seneca attacked and burned an eastern Neutral town in 1647, the Neutral took no action against them, vainly hoping to stay out of the conflict. However, once the Huron and Petun had fallen, the full force of the League of the Iroquois could be turned against the Neutral. Iroquois attacks in 1650 and 1651 weakened the Neutral resolve and caused a collapse of the confederacy. Those living in villages not yet attacked abandoned their lands and fled. A Jesuit account describes their dispersal:

> Great was the carnage, especially among the old people and the children, who would not have been able to follow the Iroquois to their country. The number of captives was exceedingly large, - especially of young women, whom they reserve, in order to keep up the population of their own villages. This loss was very great, and entailed the complete ruin and desolation of the Neutral nation; the inhabitants of their other villages, which were more distant from the enemy, took fright; abandoned their houses, their property, and their country; and condemned themselves to voluntary exile, to escape still further from the fury and cruelty of the conquerors. Famine pursues these poor fugitives everywhere.
>
> (Thwaites, *Jesuit Relations* 36:177)

Many of the Neutral survived as captives of the Iroquois, particularly the Seneca. Others were scattered as refugee populations or absorbed into other groups. The dispersal of 1651, however, marked the end of the Neutral as a separate cultural or political entity.

THE LEAGUE OF THE IROQUOIS AND THEIR ARRIVAL IN CANADA

The famed League of the Iroquois united five separate nations (from west to east, the Seneca, Cayuga, Onondaga, Oneida and Mohawk) into a single confederacy. The League was established shortly before European contact, during the late fifteenth or early sixteenth century. Legends credit Deganawidah, a supernaturally powerful individual from Huron country to the north, with founding this alliance to promote peace among the five quarreling groups, a task in which he was aided by his Onondaga convert Hiawatha. He established the Great Law of Peace, which still serves as the constitution of the League. The warring factions buried their weapons under the roots of a great white pine, the Tree of Peace, which serves as a symbol of the confederacy. The Iroquois visualized their League in the form of a longhouse, with the Seneca and Mohawk the western and eastern doors, respectively, and the Onondaga the central "keepers of the fire." Accordingly, it became the responsibility of the Onondaga to call and host council meetings of the confederacy. League members refer to themselves as the Haudenosaunee, "the people of the longhouse."

Although the League served as a political and military alliance, considerable autonomy was maintained by its members, who often acted independently. It was the Seneca, for example, who pursued most vigorously the wars with the Huron and Neutral, while the Mohawk harassed the

Algonkian tribes along the St. Lawrence. When the French finally won a truce with the Mohawk, they still found themselves assailed by war parties of Onondaga or Seneca. Over a century later, during the American Revolutionary War, most of the League members were staunch British allies, while the Oneida sided with the Americans.

Later in Iroquois history, long after the destruction of the Huron, Petun and Neutral, an additional member joined the League. This was the Tuscarora, an Iroquoian group whose homeland was in North Carolina. Displacement from their lands by Europeans led to the Tuscarora Wars of 1711-1713. After their defeat, the Tuscarora fled north to take refuge among the Iroquois. Around 1722 they were formally adopted as "little brothers" in the League, after which it was commonly known as the Six Nations.

The League was governed by a council of fifty chiefs (commonly called *sachems*), among whom the principal Onondaga chief held the position of honour. Each new chief assumed the name of his predecessor, thus perpetuating the council list from the League's formation. When a chief died, the senior woman in his clan had the responsibility of choosing his successor from the males eligible for the position. The council attempted to achieve unanimous decisions before any action was taken. If lengthy orations and debate failed to produce a consensus, each group was free to follow its own course.

Ethnohistoric information on the seventeenth-century Iroquois is far less extensive than that on the Huron. However, unlike most northern Iroquoians, the Iroquois have survived into modern times. The ethnohistoric and archaeological data are augmented by invaluable ethnographic studies of the Iroquois done in the nineteenth and early twentieth centuries. These studies, while dealing with the Iroquois after centuries of cultural change, give insights into Iroquoian beliefs and other aspects of their lives not recorded for any other Iroquoian group.

The basic pattern of Iroquois life in the early historic period was the same as that already described for the Ontario Iroquoians. They lived in villages of bark-covered longhouses, each sheltering a number of families which were usually related through the women. Society was divided into clans, membership being transmitted in the female line. They were farmers, growing corn, beans and squash as the basis of the diet, but they also hunted, fished and gathered a variety of wild plant foods. They held a Feast of the Dead but did not practice ossuary burial.

One well-known aspect of historic Iroquois life was the use of wampum. Wampum beads of white and purple shell were woven into belts, which were given as gifts at all major occasions. Any treaties or other agreements, whether with other First Nations or Europeans, required the public presentation of wampum. The Onondaga became the "wampum keepers" of the League, that is, the keepers of their public archives. The use of wampum, however, had no great antiquity, probably originating in the fur trade period. Europeans established wampum "factories" on the Atlantic coast to produce sufficient quantities to trade to the Iroquois for beaver pelts. While it once served as a form of currency among Europeans, it was regarded by the Iroquois only as a valuable commodity which could be traded or publicly given to mark important events.

From the beginnings of European contact, the Iroquois were drawn into war with the French. In an attempt to strengthen the French alliance with native groups along the vital waterway of the St. Lawrence, Champlain turned his military force against their traditional enemies, the Iroquois. In 1609 and 1610 he actively aided the Montagnais and others in raids against the Mohawk, Champlain himself killing several Mohawk war chiefs who had not yet learned the power of European muskets. In order to extend French trade into Huronia, Champlain accompanied the Huron and their Algonkian allies on a raid against an Onondaga town in 1615. Thus French colonial policy intensified traditional warfare and forced the Iroquois to look east for their trade alliance, first with the Dutch, then with the English.

The twin spectres of war and disease greatly weakened the Iroquois in this period. As elsewhere, European explorers and colonists brought with them epidemic diseases to which the natives had no immunity. Early records describe the death and despair that accompanied major outbreaks. In addition, warfare, which was endemic among the Iroquoians from ancient times, was expanded and made more deadly by European alliances and the quest for furs. This stimulated further warfare, as rapidly declining populations sought large numbers of war captives to replace their losses. The Jesuits stated in 1668 that the Oneida were about two-thirds Huron and Algonkian ex-captives, and that the Seneca were really a medley of Huron, Neutral, Erie and other defeated groups, with only a small core of the original Iroquois population.

Major Iroquois movements into Canada came in three waves, each with a different motivation. The first was a result of the persistent missionizing efforts of the Jesuits. Small groups of converts to Catholicism, primarily Mohawk and Oneida, were settled by the Jesuits on the St. Lawrence as early as 1667. During the 1670s, their numbers swelled as many Mohawks moved north to join this colony, the Jesuits being able to boast that more Mohawks lived among them than remained in their homeland. As Catholic converts settled among the French, they were soon drawn into conflict with the League Iroquois who remained hostile to the French. After several moves, they established Kahnawake (meaning "at the rapids," the name of one of the original Mohawk villages). Another group of Mohawks, along with a large number of Algonkians, settled a short distance away at Oka, where the community became known as Kanesatake. While remaining agriculturalists in Iroquoian fashion, the Kanesatake Mohawks also shared with the Algonkians the rich hunting grounds to the north. Both settlements exist today as Mohawk communities near Montreal.

Two additional reserve communities later emerged from this first wave of arrivals. In the middle of the eighteenth century, a group split from Kahnawake and moved upriver to establish a settlement known as Akwesasne ("where the partridge drums" in Mohawk). When the international boundary was drawn later in the century, it cut through the middle of Akwesasne. As a result, the modern reserve, near Cornwall, Ontario, has portions in Ontario, Quebec and New York state. Another small Mohawk community was established in the late nineteenth century, when many people left Kanesatake after disputes over land ownership to found the Gibson reserve near Georgian Bay in ancient Huronia. These people are now known as the Wahta Mohawk.

The second and largest wave of Iroquois arrivals in Canada came after the American Revolutionary War. The Mohawk had been the staunchest British allies, although the Seneca, Cayuga and Onondaga had eventually entered the war on the British side. After the war they were unable to return to their traditional lands in New York state. In reward for their loyalty, one group of Mohawk under John Deserontyon (or Deseronto) was given land on the north side of Lake Ontario at the Bay of Quinte in 1783. This group is known today as the Mohawk of the Bay of Quinte and their reserve as Tyendinaga. In the following year a larger group, under the famed Mohawk war leader Joseph Brant (Thayendanegea), moved into southern Ontario to lands purchased for them along the Grand River, near what is today Brantford. The nearly 2000 Loyalists who arrived with Brant were mainly Mohawk, Cayuga and Onondaga but also included some Seneca, Oneida and Tuscarora, as well as a considerable number of Delaware and other groups who had lost their homelands and sought refuge in the League of the Iroquois. Each established separate tribal villages of log cabins along the Grand River.

The original grant gave the Iroquois all land to a depth of six miles on each side of the Grand River from its mouth to its source. Problems soon developed, however. Brant, an ardent supporter of Iroquois sovereignty, maintained that the land was an unconditional grant as restitution for lands lost in the war, and that the Iroquois could do as they wished with the land, including leasing and selling it to Euro-Canadians. Since hunting was unproductive and native farming insufficient to support them, Brant negotiated numerous land sales to finance a transition to European-style agriculture. This policy brought him into conflict with government officials, who maintained that the land was not alienable and that all such transactions had to be approved by the Crown. The Iroquois rejected what they considered to be government interference in their affairs and continued to lease and sell land. Not until 1841 was the land surrendered to the Crown to be established as an Indian reserve, and by this time only a small portion of the

Eighteenth-century engraving of an Iroquois warrior. NAC C-3164

original land grant remained. This community, containing members of all six Iroquois groups, is today known as the Six Nations of the Grand River.

It was among the Six Nations of the Grand River that the council fire of the League of the Iroquois was rekindled. The fire had been extinguished in their New York homeland during the American Revolutionary War, when no common decision could be reached. The Six Nations in Ontario found themselves with the largest Iroquois population and reinstituted the League in an attempt to establish traditional political patterns in their new land. Once again the council meetings were held by the Onondaga, and all six Iroquois nations, plus some smaller dependent groups, participated as separate units. However, their decisions were now restricted to a single reserve, and the council acted much like a municipal government. Nevertheless, traditions of separate tribal membership remain strong among the Six Nations.

The third movement of Iroquois into Canada came with the arrival of several hundred Oneida in the early 1840s. The years after the American Revolution had not treated the Oneida kindly. Loss of their lands and American policies of relocation resulted in one large group moving to Wisconsin. Another group, wishing to be reunited with the other members of the League, purchased land along the Thames River of southern Ontario, near modern-day London. Soon after their arrival, they were readmitted to the League and sent their chiefs to council meetings of the Six Nations. The people became known as the Oneida of the Thames, recently changing their official name to the Onyota'a:Ka.

In addition to the Iroquois, a number of Algonkian groups moved into southern Ontario from the American northeast during this period of resettlement. Three communities of Delaware now reside in Canada. The first arrived with Joseph Brant in 1784, maintaining a separate Delaware community among the Six Nations. Two other groups, one led by Moravian missionaries, followed in the 1790s, settling on the Thames River near London. The Delaware language, however, is nearly extinct today. Later, mainly between 1835 and 1845, several thousand Potawatomi from the American Great Lakes area entered southern Ontario. Lacking claim to land or treaty rights, most of the Potawatomi settled on reserves of Ojibwa and Ottawa bands along western Lake Huron and Georgian Bay. Only two Canadian bands are legally recognized as Potawatomi today (one of these, on Walpole Island near Windsor, is listed as mixed Ojibwa/Potawatomi), and few Canadian Potawatomi still speak the language. In addition to these movements from the south, various Ojibwa bands, in a process beginning as early as the end of the seventeenth century, were filtering from the north into the ancient territories of the Huron, Petun and Neutral, forcefully displacing any Iroquois occupying this area. When the British settled Joseph Brant's Iroquois loyalists along the Grand River, they had to purchase the land from an Ojibwa group known as the Mississauga.

Their spirit of adventure and the rapid westward expansion of the fur trade lured some Iroquois far to the west. These were predominantly the Quebec Mohawks from Kahnawake, Kanesatake and Akwesasne, who served as voyageurs and trappers in the fur trade, first for the North West Company and later for the Hudson's Bay Company. By the 1790s small groups of Iroquois were scattered across the plains and into the Rockies in the service of the fur trade companies. In one of the largest movements, a group of about 250 Iroquois accompanied a North West Company expedition to Fort Augustus, near modern-day Edmonton, in 1798. Many of the men stayed, marrying local Cree women. This mixed population was eventually established as Michel's Band and assigned a reserve. In 1958, by a majority vote, the members of Michel's Band used a provision of the Indian Act to surrender their Indian status and ceased to exist as an Indian band. Their descendants still live in the area, although few traditions of their partial Iroquois heritage remain.

CANADIAN IROQUOIS IN THE TWENTIETH CENTURY

Eight Iroquoian reserve communities exist today in southern Ontario and Quebec. One is Huron (the Nation Huronne Wendat), five are Mohawk, one is Oneida and the largest, Six Nations, contains all six league members, plus several other groups such as the Delaware. All except the Huron are results of historic movements into Canada. By far the most populous

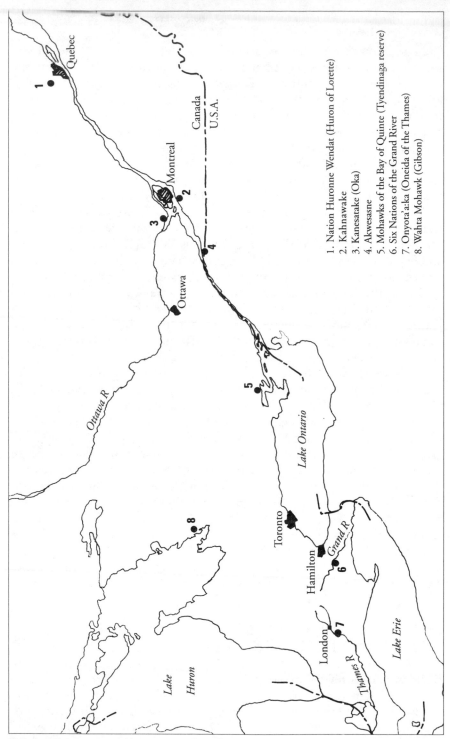

1. Nation Huronne Wendat (Huron of Lorette)
2. Kahnawake
3. Kanesatake (Oka)
4. Akwesasne
5. Mohawks of the Bay of Quinte (Tyendinaga reserve)
6. Six Nations of the Grand River
7. Onyota'a:ka (Oneida of the Thames)
8. Wahta Mohawk (Gibson)

Modern Iroquoian communities in Canada

Indian band in Canada is Six Nations of the Grand River, while Kahnawake, Akwesasne and Mohawk of the Bay of Quinte are the second-, third- and sixth-largest, respectively. Their total population is about 47,500, a figure substantially higher than now exists in their American homeland. The Mohawk are numerically dominant (with about 31,500 of the total), and Mohawk is the only Iroquoian language which is not highly endangered in Canada.

In the modern reserve economy, agriculture has played a declining role. Reserve lands under cultivation today tend to be those leased to non-Indian farmers with the capital to make modern farming viable. Since few opportunities for employment exist on their reserves, most Iroquois commute or relocate to find work in such nearby cities as Montreal, Cornwall, London or Brantford.

One occupation associated with the Iroquois, particularly the Mohawk, is "high steel" construction work. This began in 1886 when many men from Kahnawake were employed in building a new bridge near their reserve. The Mohawk demonstrated such aptitude for this work that their services were sought for other projects, and high steel work continues to be a high-paying and high-status occupation. While most maintain ties with their home reserve and eventually return there, the demands of their work have meant that Mohawk enclaves have developed in New York, Detroit and other large North American cities.

Contemporary Iroquois artists have adapted traditional forms to meet new market demands. This is particularly true on the Six Nations reserve, where the carving of False Face masks and the manufacture of pottery, produced by modern techniques in traditional styles, have been important activities. Handicrafts are also an important source of income for the Huron community in Quebec. Today, however, Iroquois artists are best-known for a recent innovation—the carving of detailed sculptures in soft brown soapstone. Perhaps the best known artist working in this medium is Joe Jacobs, a Cayuga from Six Nations, whose recognition as a major Canadian sculptor has opened the door for a new, distinctly Iroquois art form. Although several younger artists have now turned to abstract and modern themes in their carving, Jacobs and others continue to draw inspiration from Iroquois myths and legends, using their carving skills to make visible the figures from the oral traditions.

In religion, the Mohawk communities stemming from the first wave of arrivals remain primarily Catholic. The Mohawk of the Bay of Quinte, the Oneida of the Thames and the Six Nations communities are largely Protestant. At Six Nations, however, a substantial part of the population follows the Longhouse religion, and this traditional faction has spread in the twentieth century to Akwesasne, Kahnawake, Kanesatake and the Oneida.

The Longhouse religion is based on traditional Iroquois practices and

Left: *Iroquois False Fase mask.* CMC 74-7172 □ Right: *Iroquois False Face dancer with turtle-shell rattle, Six Nations reserve.* CMC J3031

Upper Cayuga longhouse, Six Nations reserve. Photo by author

beliefs. In its most widespread version today, however, it is modified by the revelations of the prophet Handsome Lake, beginning in 1799 among the Seneca in western New York. His visions defined a new moral code, outlawing drunkenness, witchcraft, sexual promiscuity, wife-beating, quarreling and gambling. Social problems besetting the Iroquois were due to evils introduced by whites; these evils must be abandoned and Iroquois ceremonies and values restored. It was an apocalyptic vision, promising destruction of the world by fire if the Iroquois failed to reform. This message was sufficiently compelling that the new religion and moral code quickly spread to the Six Nations reserve.

The restored Iroquois ceremonial life takes place in modern longhouses, which now exist on most Iroquois reserves. The ceremonies are essentially rites of thanksgiving, at which speeches and offerings are made and a feast held for all participants. Important ceremonies include Midwinter (or New Year, the longest of the ceremonies), Seed Planting, Bean (held when the green beans are mature), Green Corn (when the first corn is ripe) and Harvest. Also important are the rites of the medicine societies. Particularly well known are the False Face Society and the Husk Face Society, whose members wear masks as part of their curing rituals. The wooden masks of the False Face Society depict the distorted faces of humanoid beings seen in the forest or in dreams. The Husk Face masks are braided of corn husks and represent agricultural spirits. Both give their wearers extraordinary powers, such as the ability to handle hot coals without being burned, as well as the ability to cure illness. Dreams continue to play an important role in Iroquois religious life, helping to determine the steps one should follow to maintain health and harmony or the ritual which should be carried out to cure an illness.

Iroquois society, particularly at Six Nations, is split into two factions. Those in the conservative or traditional faction participate in the Longhouse religion, uphold the code of Handsome Lake, often speak an Iroquois language, tend to emphasize matrilineal descent and to recognize clan affiliations, and support the council of hereditary chiefs as the only legitimate government. Non-traditionalists belong to a Christian church (usually Anglican or Baptist at Six Nations), tend not to recognize clan distinctions, deal with the federal government through the elected band council and generally speak English as their main or only language. Both groups highly value their Iroquois heritage, but the larger non-traditionalist faction tends to be more acculturated.

A particularly divisive event occurred at Six Nations in 1924. Members of the traditional council, in accordance with their view of Iroquois sovereignty, had followed a policy of non-cooperation with officials of the Canadian government. They had also alienated many of their own people, who viewed them as too conservative and inefficient. Certainly the traditional requirement for unanimity in their deliberations left them unable to reach decisions on many matters. As a result, the hereditary council was locked out of the council house by the Royal Canadian Mounted Police, and an elected council was established in its place. Since then, this has been the only band council recognized by the Canadian government. The hereditary council, however, did not disband but continued to hold regular meetings in the Onondaga longhouse, where this council served as a focus for the discontent of the traditionalist faction. Continued unrest led to an uprising in 1959, when a group of traditionalists seized the council house, reinstating the hereditary council and abolishing the Indian Act, before being suppressed by the RCMP. Today both the elected and hereditary councils continue to exist at Six Nations, as well as at Kahnawake and Akwesasne, and the hereditary chiefs are still seen as the only legitimate government by traditionalists.

The underlying issue concerns Iroquois sovereignty. From the time of Joseph Brant, the Iroquois have maintained that they were a sovereign people, entering Canada as loyal allies of the British Crown, and have rejected the policies of the Canadian government which treat them as dependents. Accordingly, they have strongly opposed the Indian Act, which allows little in the way of autonomous decisions, maintaining that they are a separate nation with their own political constitution. Many of the provisions of the Indian Act, such as the insistence on tracing band membership through the father, run counter to Iroquois practices. In the early 1920s the Six Nations chiefs issued their own passports and sent several of their members to Europe, although they were unsuccessful in their attempt to present their grievance before the League of Nations in Geneva. More recently, when federal voting privileges were extended to all Canadian Indians in 1960, many Iroquois opposed such a move, feeling that their status as a separate nation would be endangered by voting in Canadian elections.

Other contentious issues strengthen the distrust many Iroquois feel for the Canadian government. Particularly galling for the Mohawk of Akwesasne, who live astride the international boundary, is the failure of the Canadian government to recognize the Jay Treaty of 1794. One clause in this treaty, signed between Britain and the new American government, promised "nor shall any Indians passing or repassing with their own proper goods and effects of whatever nature, pay for the same any impost or duty whatever." However, the Supreme Court of Canada has ruled that the Customs Act takes precedence, so that any reserve residents moving their goods north across the border must pay duties. Mohawk protests over this issue have included blocking the busy international bridge crossing the St. Lawrence River from their reserve.

Other specific issues continue to cause discontent. A major example is the loss of Kahnawake lands by flooding during the construction of the St. Lawrence Seaway. The Mohawk protested vigorously but lost their legal battle against expropriation.

Because the Iroquois see themselves as a separate nation within Canada, they have had few common political ties with other Canadian Indians. However, they did form, with a few nearby Algonkian bands, the Association of Iroquois and Allied Indians in 1969 to counter a proposed reorganization of federal Indian administration. For the traditionalists, however, the most important efforts have been to re-establish ties between all Iroquois groups, on each side of the border, in order to recreate the political structure and institutions of the League of the Iroquois and its Great Law of Peace.

TENSION AND VIOLENCE IN MOHAWK COUNTRY: THE EVENTS AT AKWESASNE AND OKA

Violent confrontations troubled all three Quebec Mohawk communities in 1990. The basic issue behind their discontent was that of Mohawk self-determination. The Warrior Society emerged among embittered young Mohawk as a voice for Mohawk Nation sovereignty. A tenuous alliance between the Warrior Society and the traditionalists of the Longhouse often pitted them against the elected band officials.

Akwesasne, with its unique geographic situation, is where many of the tensions first developed. As both an international and a provincial border slice through this community, two federal and three provincial or state governments all claim jurisdiction. The Mohawk position is that they do not recognize these borders. Three separate Mohawk governments also exist on this reserve: the elected Mohawk Council of Akwesasne on the Canadian side, the St. Regis Tribal Council on the American side and the Mohawk Nation Council of traditional chiefs opposed to the elected councils and rejecting the divisions caused by international borders. A total of eight governmental structures claiming some form of overlapping jurisdiction makes Akwesasne an administrative nightmare.

Akwesasne's location makes it ideally suited to moving goods across the international border without detection by Canadian authorities. Cigarettes are the main commodity, but alcohol, drugs and firearms are also part of the trans-border traffic. Canadian cigarettes, shipped to the United States as exports to avoid Canada's high taxes on tobacco products, are transported back across the border at Akwesasne and sold in the row of "smoke shops" lining the highway into Montreal on the Kahnawake reserve. This enterprise was so widespread and lucrative that it forced the Canadian government to lower tobacco taxes to reduce the problem. Although branded as smuggling and considered criminal activities by the government, many Mohawk see such actions as an exercise in Mohawk sovereignty and a right under the Jay Treaty. Large-scale police raids at both Akwesasne and

Kahnawake in 1988 failed to stop this enterprise and had the effect of radi-calizing Mohawk who might otherwise have been moderates. In retaliation, the Kahnawake Mohawk blocked the busy Mercier Bridge into Montreal.

Even more disruptive was the arrival of high-stakes gambling at Akwesasne. A strip of casinos soon existed along the highway on the New York side of the reserve, serving a growing, primarily Canadian, non-Indian clientele. The casinos meant wealth for a few Mohawk and provided oppor-tunities for employment in a community where few other jobs are available. The Warrior Society rose to prominence at this time as the defenders of the casinos from external or internal opposition, maintaining that Mohawk sovereignty was at stake. Other Mohawk, however, resented the undesirable elements they saw moving into their community and opposed the unregu-lated casinos. Early in the struggle the three Mohawk councils reached an agreement that the gambling should stop but lacked the power to enforce this resolution. The people at Akwesasne became increasingly polarized into pro-gambling and anti-gambling factions.

With considerable money at stake, violence soon flared between these factions. The office of the *Akwesasne Notes* editor, who had used this Mohawk newspaper to argue against gambling, was firebombed. Police cars representing the Mohawk Council of Akwesasne, which strongly opposed the casinos, were rammed or shot at. Blockades erected by the anti-gam-bling forces to deter the busloads of casino patrons became sites of increas-ingly violent confrontations with the Warriors and casino employees. The well-armed Warriors, who were not sanctioned by any tribal authority, were denounced by the Mohawk Nation Council of traditional chiefs as a "law-less and terrorist cult." By early 1990 the slide into what has been called the "Mohawk civil war" was well underway. Numerous shootings, beatings and arsons led the Mohawk Council of Akwesasne in April that year to begin evacuation of the Canadian side of the reserve, eventually moving several thousand people to temporary lodgings in Cornwall. On May 1 a gunfire battle resulted in the deaths of two Mohawk, whose bodies were found on the Quebec portion of the reserve. The Canadian and American govern-ments, which had refused to intervene in an "internal matter" on the reserve, were forced into action. Hundreds of officers from the RCMP, the Ontario Provincial Police, the Sûreté du Québec and the New York State Police were dispatched to Akwesasne, quelling the violence and closing the casinos.

At the same time that this was happening, events were leading to a new outbreak of violence involving the Mohawk, this time at Oka, just west of Montreal. This provided an incident which grabbed public attention far more than the situation at Akwesasne. It also offered the Warriors a chance to improve their image, from defenders of gambling and smuggling to defenders of native land rights.

The land dispute at Oka had been brewing for over two centuries. The original eighteenth-century land grant was from the French Crown to the Seminary of St. Sulpice for the settlement and religious instruction of the Mohawk, Algonkin and others under their care. Disputes over land title arose repeatedly in the following centuries. The Sulpicians argued that the native occupants had no legal rights to the land and proceeded to sell off large portions of the original land grant. The Algonkin and some Mohawk moved to other reserve communities as a result of these disputes. Conflict and legal battles over Sulpician land sales continued until 1945, when the federal government purchased the remaining lands. By this time the area was an ethnic checkerboard, with the Mohawk community of Kanesatake occupying small scattered plots of land within and beside the white municipality of Oka. Furthermore, the lands were never legally transferred as an Indian reserve under the Indian Act, continuing the tenuous nature of Mohawk rights to the land they occupied.

The Kanesatake Mohawk tried repeatedly to have their land dispute resolved. In 1961 they attempted, without success, to have their lands formally declared a reserve. In the early 1970s the three Quebec Mohawk communities used the newly established comprehensive claims process to assert aboriginal title over their territories, but were rejected because they could not demonstrate occupancy since "time immemorial." The Kanesatake Mohawk then initiated a specific claim, based on the doctrine of federal "lawful obligation," which was also rejected.

For the residents of Kanesatake the final straw was a proposed expansion of the municipal golf course at Oka into the disputed lands. The existing course, with its clubhouse directly adjacent to an historic Mohawk cemetery, already occupied lands the Mohawk considered theirs. On 11 March 1990 a group of Kanesatake Mohawk set up a barricade in the wooded area slated for development. Armed Warriors from Akwesasne and Kahnawake later joined the local residents at the barricade, setting the stage for the conflict to come.

Early in the morning of 11 July 1990 more than 100 Sûreté du Québec officers, armed with assault rifles, concussion grenades and tear gas, attacked the Mohawk barricades. In the ensuing shoot-out one police officer was killed and the police were forced to retreat. The police then set up roadblocks around Kanesatake, while the Mohawk erected barricades on the highway, using police vehicles abandoned after the failed raid. At the same time the Mohawks at Kahnawake blockaded all approaches through their reserve to the Mercier Bridge, the major traffic artery from the south shore communities to the centre of Montreal. A tense seventy-eight-day standoff was a time of protracted negotiations and intense media coverage. Six Nations Iroquois Confederacy chiefs played a mediating role in the negotiations. In August, the Canadian government sent more than 2000 soldiers to the scene, the first time that Canadian troops had been called out against aboriginal peoples since Riel's North-West Rebellion of 1885.

The Kahnawake blockades were finally dismantled and the Mercier Bridge reopened on September 6, but a small group of Warriors and their supporters held out at Kanesatake until September 26.

These events poisoned relations between the Mohawk and surrounding white communities, leading to some ugly racist riots. Citizens of south shore Montreal communities battled police and burned effigy figures of Mohawk. When women, children and the elderly were evacuated from Kahnawake, police did little to stop the mob that gathered to throw stones and bottles at their vehicles. One elderly Mohawk man suffered a fatal heart attack after this incident.

This was not simply a local outbreak of native discontent. Most of the Warriors at Oka were from the more populous and militant communities of Akwesasne and Kahnawake, viewing this as defence of the Mohawk Nation. One of the Warrior Society leaders (code-named "the General" during the conflict) was a Mi'kmaq from the Eskasoni reserve in Nova Scotia. Also among the final hold-outs were an Ojibwa from Saskatchewan and a Tlingit from British Columbia. First Nations communities in Ontario, the prairie provinces and British Columbia blockaded highways and railways crossing their reserves to show support for the Mohawk at Oka and to press for settlement of their own land grievances.

The incident at Oka is over but the issues are far from resolved. The federal government is committed to the purchase of disputed lands for the Mohawk at Kanesatake. The Warrior Society remains strong at Kahnawake and Akwesasne. The Mohawk continue to assert their right to run their own affairs. A 1992 framework agreement between the federal government and the Mohawk Council of Kahnawake turns jurisdiction for policing, health, social services, education and other cultural matters over to the local community. A Mohawk immersion program in the school is helping to reverse the gradual decline in use of the Mohawk language. A heightened sense of community and Mohawk identity has been one of the legacies of the Oka crisis.

The long troubled "Indian Summer" of 1990 brought native discontent to wide public attention, across Canada and abroad. Canada's treatment of its First Nations was denounced by pro-Mohawk demonstrators in many cities around the world. A South African official publicly rejected Canada's right to criticize other nations for human rights abuses. For a brief period these violent clashes had managed to move First Nations issues to the front of the national agenda.

CHAPTER 5 *The Algonkians of the Eastern Woodlands and Subarctic*

All of northeastern North America, except for the wedge of Iroquoians along the eastern Great Lakes and St. Lawrence River, was the territory of the Algonkian First Nations. In Canada, Algonkian languages are spoken from the Atlantic Ocean to the Rocky Mountains. This chapter deals with those of the upper Great Lakes to Hudson Bay, including subarctic Quebec, Ontario and Manitoba. Although known to history by a bewildering array of regional names, they are classified by modern linguists into Cree and Ojibwa, each with a number of major dialects.

No firm boundary can be drawn between the Eastern Woodlands and Eastern Subarctic culture areas. From the northern shores of the Great Lakes to southeastern Manitoba, there are strong ties to the Eastern Woodlands. Construction of burial mounds and manufacture of pottery are archaeological traits which link this area with Eastern Woodland cultures far to the south. In the early historic period some Algonkian groups practiced marginal corn agriculture or relied on trading with the Huron for agricultural produce. Such Iroquoian rituals as the Feast of the Dead also spread to neighbouring Algonkians. For these reasons, much of the territory occupied by the Ojibwa could be included in the Eastern Woodlands culture area rather than the Subarctic. However, these southern traits are relatively minor embellishments on the basic fabric of Algonkian life shared with their kin to the north.

Linguistic confusion abounds concerning the Algonkians. Much of the problem stems from trying to equate languages and social groups. The Algonkians lived in small independent bands, shifting in territory over time, speaking a continuum of mutually intelligible dialects. Among the best-known groups speaking variants of Ojibwa are the Saulteaux, Ottawa, Nipissing, Mississauga and Algonkin. Only Ottawa and Algonkin, along with Ojibwa, survive today as legal designations for Canadian bands. Similarly in the north, dialects of Cree are spoken from Labrador to the prairie provinces. Closely related are the Innu (Montagnais and Naskapi) in Quebec and Labrador.

Note the distinction between Algonkian and Algonkin. Algonkian (or Algonquian) refers to the entire language family, by far the largest in Canada, while Algonkin (or Algonquin) refers to those groups with their traditional lands centred on the Ottawa valley, along what is today the border between Ontario and Quebec.

Physiographically, the area is dominated by the Canadian Shield, a low, rolling land of forest, rock outcrops and muskeg, with innumerable lakes, ponds and rivers. The climate is continental, characterized by long, extremely cold winters and brief summers. Considerable differences in landforms and resource availability exist from north to south. The more southerly territory of the Ojibwa, in the northern reaches of the mixed forests, provided excellent fishing locations and plentiful wild plant foods such as berries and wild rice. To the north, the boreal forests of the northern Ojibwa and Cree offered fewer plant resources, requiring greater emphasis on hunting. The Algonkians, while sharing many cultural traits, differed considerably throughout the area, each local band making decisions best suited to its environment.

THE TIME BEFORE EUROPEANS

The Canadian Shield environment poses major challenges and limitations to archaeological reconstruction. The highly acidic soils have destroyed all bone and other organic materials, leaving only stone tools to provide glimpses into how people lived in the distant past. While some sites may also contain fragments of pottery vessels and occasional tools of copper, the artifact inventory from most is meagre. Small wandering bands of hunters and fishermen left few material traces of their passing.

The northern regions were still under thick sheets of glacial ice when small groups of hunters first moved into the southern margins. Their presence is shown by surface discoveries of the finely flaked points which identify Plano cultures. Although these discoveries cannot be directly dated, similar late Paleo-Indian tools found elsewhere are as much as 9000 years old. The unique discovery of a late Paleo-Indian cremation burial near Thunder Bay gives some insight into their funerary practices and provides a radiocarbon date of almost 8500 years. In addition, several Plano quarry sites have been investigated, the best known being Sheguiandah, on Manitoulin Island. Here Plano and Archaic peoples obtained fine-grained quartzite which they chipped into their distinctive tools, leaving the ground strewn with waste flakes, broken artifacts and other debris.

The Archaic period, which seems to have developed directly out of late Paleo-Indian, is appropriately termed the **Shield Archaic**. As the glacial sheets retreated northward, archaic peoples eventually occupied the boreal forests of northern Ontario and Quebec. Many Shield Archaic sites are located at narrows on lakes and rivers which provided crossing places for the caribou herds. Fish and caribou would have been the essential resources, although bear, beaver, hare and waterfowl would also have been important. However, lack of bone preservation prohibits precise determination of the aboriginal diet. The sites yield only chipped stone tools, almost all of which can be classified as either scrapers, knives or projectile points, plus the occasional implement of native copper from western Lake Superior. Sites on islands and along waterways suggest that the birchbark canoe was already an essential part of their lives, and it is logical to assume that they also had snowshoes for winter travel. In northern areas, the historic cultures emerged directly from this long-lived cultural pattern.

In southern regions, as among the Iroquoians, the introduction of pottery marks a new stage—the Woodland period. The **Initial Woodland** variant in the central Algonkian area is called the Laurel culture, dated from about 200 B.C. to A.D. 1200. Except for the ceramic technology no great cultural break is evident from the preceding Archaic period. Laurel sites are distributed in Canada from east-central Saskatchewan through the lakes country of central Manitoba to Lake Superior, possibly extending into northeastern Ontario. The heartland appears to be the Rainy River-Lake of the Woods region of westernmost Ontario, as it is there that Laurel sites have their earliest and latest dates and where their most impressive burial monuments are located. In more northerly Ontario, most of subarctic Quebec and in Labrador, however, aboriginal people never adopted the pottery technology which marks this stage.

In addition to pottery sherds and stone tools, which strongly resemble the Archaic forms from which they developed, such native copper implements as knives, chisels and beads are common in many Laurel sites. At Heron Bay, on the north shore of Lake Superior, abundant bone tools and refuse were also found. Wood ash from ancient campfires had neutralized soil acidity, resulting in the preservation of such bone artifacts as harpoon heads, awls, netting needles, beads and beaver-tooth knives, as well as the bones of such food animals as moose and beaver. This still provides only a limited view of their material culture, since nothing remains of the wooden, bark and hide objects that would have made up the larger part of their technology.

The excavation at Heron Bay also yielded important information on long-distance trade connections. Obtained from this site were such exotic goods as obsidian from Wyoming (a distance of about 1850 km), shell from southern Manitoba (740 km) and pottery from the Saugeen culture of southern Ontario (580 km). Native copper from Lake Superior was almost certainly the major trade item being exported. This emphasis on trade along the southern margins of the Shield is shared with Eastern Woodlands groups to the south. In contrast, excavated sites further north in subarctic Ontario and Quebec show little or no evidence of trade.

Excavation at the Ballynacree site in Kenora, which exposed an entire late Laurel village, provides another glimpse into their lives. Patterns of dark-stained post moulds suggest that the village consisted of three oval-shaped houses, sheltering a population of about thirty people. The houses appear to have been large dome-shaped lodges of bent saplings covered with bark, similar to historic Algonkian structures.

Major Eastern Woodlands influences in the southern Algonkian area are particularly evident in the burial mounds, which would have been important centres of Laurel religious life. Burial mounds from this period are found in Ontario between Lake Superior and the Manitoba border. Particularly well known is a cluster of mounds along the Rainy River. One of these, about 35 metres in diameter and 7 metres high, is the largest burial mound in Canada. Excavation at a smaller one of the cluster, the Armstrong Mound, revealed that it was built about a thousand years ago, near the end of the Laurel period. Remains of thirteen individuals were found in this mound. Most were disarticulated bone bundles, liberally covered with red ochre, indicating that skeletal remains had been collected from elsewhere and ceremonially reburied in the mound. The inspiration for mound burials and elaborate mortuary rites clearly lies to the south, in the late Hopewell culture of the central Eastern Woodlands. A Hopewell-style platform pipe was found in the Armstrong Mound.

No sharp distinction exists between Initial and Terminal Woodland, although new pottery styles do occur in some areas. The **Terminal Woodland** period is identified by the development of regional differences out of the relatively uniform Initial Woodland base. As this lasts into the historic period, some sites can be attributed, with reasonable assurance, to known ethnic groups. This allows us to work back in time to reconstruct late precontact life based on what is known of cultures at the time of European arrival.

The late precontact culture found from northern Lake Superior to southeastern Manitoba is termed Blackduck. Its distribution straddles the boundary between the Eastern Woodlands and Subarctic. Blackduck is known primarily by a distinctive pottery style, which may have developed out of Laurel. However, Blackduck pottery is often found mixed with other styles, suggesting that women, who were the potters in historic times, joined their husbands' bands on marriage. If marriage took place over considerable distances, this would result in a number of different styles being produced by a single social group. Easy access to the native copper deposits

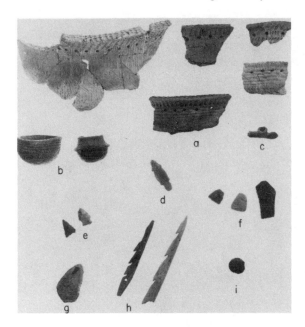

Western Algonkian artifacts: (a) fragments of Blackduck pottery vessels; (b) small pottery vessels made for placement in burial mounds; (c) stone pipe; (d) stone amulet in the form of a beaver; (e) arrowheads; (f) scrapers; (g) knife; (h) antler harpoons; (i) gambling disk made from a pottery fragment. CMC 74-18216

of western Lake Superior is indicated by relatively numerous knives, awls, fish hooks and beads of this material in Blackduck sites. Stone tools, along with those of bone where they are preserved, are similar to those of the earlier Laurel culture. The addition of European trade goods to artifacts of native manufacture ushers in the historic period. Some authorities attribute this complex to the Siouan-speaking Assiniboine, who are known from early historic records to have occupied much of this area prior to Ojibwa expansion. The general similarity with surrounding precontact cultures, however, suggests that these remains were left by Algonkian-speakers.

Blackduck people also constructed burial mounds, although these are smaller than their Laurel precedents. The distribution is much the same, the low Blackduck mounds being interspersed with the larger Laurel mounds along the Rainy River, although Blackduck mounds extend into southern Manitoba. The mounds provide evidence that complex mortuary rites continued into this late period. Bundled bones are found covered in red ochre, and in some cases eye sockets have been filled with clay and shell beads inserted. Small pottery vessels were frequently placed with the dead.

To the northwest, a similar culture has been termed Selkirk. Its distribution is from northwestern Ontario, across the Shield country of Manitoba, into northeastern Saskatchewan. Archaeological sites of this culture contain distinctive fabric-impressed pottery and a limited variety of stone tools. Occasionally, Selkirk and Blackduck pottery types are found at the same site, again suggesting that intermarriage over a considerable distance occurred, with women from several regions being found in any one social

101

Pictographs at Agawa Rock, Lake Superior, showing Mishipisu *(the "horned panther"), serpents and men in canoes.* Photo by author

group. The Selkirk culture is considered to be ancestral Cree in that region. However, not all precontact cultures identified with the Cree made pottery.

Similar pottery styles extend only into the westernmost portions of Quebec, although typical St. Lawrence Iroquoian pottery is found in Algonkian sites along the entire north shore of the St. Lawrence. In interior subarctic Quebec and Labrador the complete absence of pottery technology means that the entire precontact period falls into the Archaic. From work in the Mistassini region of central Quebec, C.A. Martijn and E.S. Rogers divide the entire cultural history into two complexes: the Wenopsk, seen as a regional variant of the Shield Archaic, surviving with little change from around 4000 B.C. to European contact, and the Mistassini, representing the historic Cree Indians of the Mistassini area with their abundance of European trade items. Few outside influences seem to have disturbed this long-lived and stable adaptation.

One fascinating although enigmatic type of archaeological site is the red ochre pictograph. These lively depictions of humans, animals and mythological beings adorn rock faces along the waterways of the western regions, from around the northern Great Lakes to the Shield country of northern Saskatchewan. They are very rare in Quebec and the more northerly Shield country in Ontario. The practice of painting these images on rocks may date to ancient times, but most surviving examples are relatively recent. Some, depicting horses, rifles and other introduced items, are obviously historic. Occasionally, we can recognize familiar figures from Ojibwa mythology, such as Thunderbird and Mishipisu, the "Great Lynx" or "Horned

Ojibwa camp on Lake Huron, a painting by Paul Kane, 1845. ROM

Panther," a dangerous supernatural creature of the turbulent waters. Similar images appear on the bark scrolls which were part of Ojibwa religious life. Although most pictographs cannot be easily identified or interpreted, they give us unparalleled glimpses into the religious beliefs and practices of the late precontact Ojibwa and their neighbours.

THE OJIBWA—OTTAWA—ALGONKIN

The name Ojibwa (variants include Ojibway, Ochipwe and Chippewa) originally came from one group north of modern-day Sault Ste. Marie. The term was later extended to others sharing the same culture and language in the Upper Great Lakes area. From their early historic homeland along the northern shores of Lakes Huron and Superior, with its centre on the major fishery at the rapids of Sault Ste. Marie, the Ojibwa expanded dramatically in the historic period. Some moved to the southeast, into the formerly Iroquoian lands of southern Ontario. Others pushed south into Wisconsin and Minnesota, displacing, often forcefully, the Dakota. The lucrative fur trade lured many far to the north and west, into the Shield country of northern Ontario and Manitoba, in search of new trapping grounds. Some even spread out onto the Plains, becoming the Plains Ojibwa of southern Manitoba and Saskatchewan. This historic spread to different environments meant that major cultural differences emerged among the Ojibwa people.

When Europeans first entered the area there were many similar but politically autonomous groups, who gradually became collectively known as the Ojibwa. A number of names are still in use. The term Saulteaux comes from the French *Saulteurs,* or "people of the rapids," referring to their origins at Sault Ste. Marie. While used as a near-synonym for Ojibwa, it is more commonly applied to western groups, such as those around Lake Winnipeg in Manitoba and Lake of the Woods in Ontario. The American Ojibwa, along with those of southern Ontario, are generally known today as the Chippewa. The Mississauga were originally at the northern end of Lake Huron and on Manitoulin Island, spreading in the historic period into southern Ontario. The Nipissing held the land around Lake Nipissing, to the north of the Huron between the Ojibwa and Algonkin. Although no shared identity existed between the different groups, one is beginning to form today. Many Ojibwa prefer to be referred to as Anishinabe, a term meaning "person" or "first man," and the concept of an Anishinabe Nation has emerged to link the widespread speakers of the Ojibwa language.

The Ottawa (or Odawa) occupied much of the north shore of Georgian Bay and Manitoulin Island, as well as the Bruce Peninsula, where they bordered on the Huron and Petun. Their lifestyle and language were virtually indistinguishable from the neighbouring Ojibwa and the Potawatomi of lower Lake Michigan. Indeed, the three groups shared a tradition of a common origin and remained allied throughout the historic period in a loose confederacy known as the Council of the Three Fires. A number of modern reserve communities in Ontario trace their ancestry to all three groups. The Algonkin (or Algonquin) inhabited the Ottawa valley and adjacent regions in the early historic period. Linguists have classified Ojibwa, Ottawa and Algonkin as a single language with numerous dialects. Thus the term Ojibwa today often includes Ottawa and Algonkin, although these both survive as legal designations for Indian bands.

The numerous politically independent bands that made up the Ojibwa people were linked by intermarriage and common traditions. Each had its own chief and hunting territories. Bands dispersed into family hunting units much of the year, assembling in greater numbers only during late spring and summer. Leadership positions were informal, with chiefs holding power by virtue of their prowess in hunting, warfare or shamanism. No single leader united the Ojibwa people or could speak for more than his small band.

Ojibwa society was divided into clans, each identified by a clan symbol or totem. William Warren, the mid-nineteenth-century half-Ojibwa chronicler of their traditions, stated that they "are divided into several grand families or clans, each of which is known and perpetuated by a symbol of some bird, animal, fish, or reptile which they denominate the Totem or Do-daim (as the Ojibways pronounce it)" (1885:34). Warren lists twenty-one totems, of which the most important were the crane, catfish, bear, marten, wolf and loon. The living totem animals were not worshipped, nor did clan members refrain from killing them for food, although a certain respect had to be

Ojibwa fishermen at the Sault Ste. Marie rapids, a painting by William Armstrong, 1869. NAC C-114501

shown. Clan membership was patrilineal; that is, children inherited their totem animal from their fathers. Persons sharing the same totem were considered to be close kin, and intermarriage was forbidden, even if they came from widely separated bands.

Ojibwa subsistence was based on an annual round of hunting, fishing and plant collecting. Men took great pride in their prowess as hunters and devoted the winter to the hunt for moose, deer, bear and other game. However, by the mid-seventeenth century most of their attention had shifted to beaver due to the demands of the fur trade.

In spring, families returned from their hunting camps to rejoin others at their major fishing sites. Pickerel, pike and suckers could be taken throughout the summer, and the autumn spawning brought whitefish, trout and sturgeon close to shore. Great quantities of fish were netted or speared, and the fisheries served as centres of community life. Particularly good fishing locations attracted large concentrations of people. We know from the writings of the Jesuits that during the mid-seventeenth century up to 2000 individuals might congregate at the rapids of Sault Ste. Marie. A 1670 account indicates that the local "Saulteurs" at the rapids played host to nine other groups, including some visiting Cree from the north.

Plant foods played an important role in the Ojibwa economy. Maple trees were tapped in early spring and the sweet sap collected in buckets. Boiling rendered it down to a coarse maple sugar, which was used as seasoning for a wide range of foods. In summer large stores of berries were collected.

Wild rice (not a true rice but a cereal grass), which grows in the shallow water around the edges of lakes, ripened in late summer. Harvesters worked in groups of two, often a husband and wife. While the man poled the canoe through the beds, the woman bent stalks over the canoe and knocked off kernels with a stick, continuing until the canoe was full. The kernels were then dried in the sun, parched over a slow fire, pounded and winnowed to remove the husk, and stored, providing a staple food for the many Ojibwa fortunate enough to live in these areas.

Agriculture was not practiced by the western Ojibwa, but it had some importance among those groups in contact with the Huron. The Ottawa relied considerably on their crops of corn, beans and squash. The Nipissing and Algonkin, while cultivating small plots of corn around their summer campsites, were unable to depend on horticulture due to poor soil and uncertain weather. As a result, they obtained much of their agricultural food through trading furs and fish to the Huron. A good description of the Nipissing annual round, showing the importance of trade in their economy, was given by the Jesuit Father Lalemant in 1641:

> They seem to have as many abodes as the year has seasons, —in the Spring a part of them remain for fishing, where they consider it the best; a part go away to trade with the tribes which gather on the shore of the North or icy sea . . . In summer, they all gather together . . . on the border of a large lake which bears their name . . . About the middle of Autumn, they begin to approach our Hurons, upon whose lands they generally spend the winter; but, before reaching them, they catch as many fish as possible, which they dry. This is the ordinary money with which they buy their main stock of corn, although they come supplied with all other goods . . . They cultivate a little land near their Summer dwellings; but it is more for pleasure, and that they may have fresh food to eat, than for their support.
>
> (Thwaites, *Jesuit Relations* 21:239-241)

Food was cooked by roasting or boiling. While some of the Ottawa and other southern groups used clay pots for the latter purpose, birchbark vessels were far more widely employed, being more suitable for a highly mobile people. Meat and fish might be cooked with boiled rice or corn and sweetened with berries or maple sugar.

The annual round of movement to the family's hunting and fishing grounds, wild rice fields and maple tree groves required efficient transportation. The birchbark canoe was ideal in this land of rivers and lakes. Large sheets of bark, easily peeled from the birch trees of these northern forests, were sewn with spruce root over a wooden frame. Seams were sealed with spruce or pine gum. Tough, yet lightweight, the canoe could be easily portaged between waterways. In winter, canoes were cached and people traveled on foot, using snowshoes and hauling their belongings on toboggans.

Ojibwa camp on Lake Winnipeg, 1884, showing two types of birchbark lodges.
CMC 594

Housing also reflected the need for mobility, being easily constructed and largely removable. Several styles of dwelling were built, although the principal form was the dome-shaped structure known throughout northeastern North America by the Algonkian term *wigwam*. Saplings were driven into the ground in a circular or elliptical pattern, then bent over and tied together at the top. Sheets of birchbark were used to cover the structure. Sometimes rush mats were used for the sides, but the more durable and water-resistant birchbark was required for the roof. Several layers of bark, separated by moss for insulation, might be used on winter houses. The entryway was covered with a flap of matting or hide, and a hole in the top allowed smoke to escape. In addition to the dome-shaped wigwam, a conical or tipi-shaped structure, also covered with sheets of bark, was common. Most structures sheltered only one family, although several related families might occupy the larger elliptical forms.

Clothing was made from tanned hides of deer or moose, sewn by women using thread of nettle fibre or sinew. Women wore moccasins, leggings and a deerhide dress belted at the waist, while a man's outfit consisted of breech-cloth, hip-high leggings and moccasins. A heavy coat, generally of thick moosehide, was added in winter. Cold weather clothing might also include caps and mittens of beaver or other fur and moccasins lined with rabbit skin. Dyes and porcupine quill embroidery added decoration. When the traders' beads became available, Ojibwa women turned their talents to elaborate beadwork decoration on moccasins, pouches and other elements of their costumes. Care was also taken with the hair, generally worn long and braided by both sexes. Faces were often greased and painted, and the hair might be kept shiny and in place by rubbing in bear grease or deer tallow.

Numerous opportunities existed for social interaction. The naming of a child required a small ceremony and feast. A boy's first kill, even if no larger than a rabbit or bird, required a feast at which all present sampled the meat and praised the boy's efforts. The larger social groups of the summer camps allowed feasting, dancing, lacrosse playing and gambling with bone dice.

These were also good opportunities for young people to look for prospective mates, the preferred marriage partner being a cross-cousin (that is, the offspring of the father's sister or mother's brother, who would belong to a different clan).

On cold and dark winter evenings, as people sat around the fires in their wigwams, a favourite pastime was listening to tales told by the elders. Ojibwa mythology served both to instruct and entertain. The rich oral traditions were filled with supernatural humans and animals, one of the most prominent being the culture hero Nanabush (or Nanabozho). Known as Glooscap among the Mi'kmaq and Wisakedjak among the Cree, this supernatural figure occupied a central place in Ojibwa beliefs. It was Nanabush who put the earth and the animals into their present form, many prominent features of the landscape being attributed to his actions. He served an ambiguous role as both benefactor to humans and a self-indulgent and occasionally obscene trickster.

The most terrifying of these legendary figures was the Windigo, a supernatural giant with an insatiable hunger for human flesh. He haunted the forests during the dark and cold months of winter, retreating to the north when warmer weather arrived. His size and supernatural strength made him a dreaded foe, one that could not be killed by ordinary weapons. Only a powerful shaman could destroy a Windigo. Any unexplained disappearance, such as the failure of a hunter to return from the forest, would be taken to mean that he had fallen prey to the Windigo. This monster was particularly feared as ordinary humans could be transformed into one by conditions of near-starvation, which were not uncommon during the later months of winter. Hunger might turn to a craving for human flesh, causing the individual to commit real or imagined acts of cannibalism, resulting in gradual transformation into the dreaded monster. Anyone suspected of becoming a Windigo could immediately be put to death, and those who, in extremes of hunger, began to lust for human flesh might request their own execution.

Many other powerful supernatural beings inhabited the Ojibwa world. Thunderbirds, who controlled the weather, lived in nests of stones on high mountaintops constantly shrouded in clouds. Lightning flashed from their eyes, and the flapping of their wings caused thunder. The power they could bestow made them particularly sought as guardian spirits. Their mortal enemies and the main targets of their lightning bolts were the generally malevolent denizens of the waters, such as the Great Serpent and Mishipisu, a large and dangerous horned feline.

The Ojibwa world was also filled with lesser spirits. Every animal, bird or plant, as well as some inanimate objects, had a power that could either help or hinder humans. Such a power or supernatural force was called *manitou*. The Jesuit Father Allouez, traveling among the "Outaouacs" (Ottawa) in the mid-1660s, described their beliefs:

The Savages of these regions recognize no sovereign master of Heaven and Earth, but believe there are many spirits—some of whom are beneficent, as the Sun, the Moon, the Lake, Rivers, and Woods; others malevolent, as the adder, the dragon, cold, and storms. And, in general, whatever seems to them either helpful or hurtful they call a Manitou, and pay it . . . worship and veneration.

(Thwaites, *Jesuit Relations* 50:285)

Manitous could be beseeched or placated by offerings of tobacco, or occasionally by sacrificing a dog.

The most sacred force was Kitchi Manitou ("Great Spirit"), often identified as the sun. He was the ultimate source of all power, but was remote and had little to do with everyday human affairs. Although playing a prominent role in recent Ojibwa religious thought, Kitchi Manitou does not appear in the early historic accounts (such as that of Father Allouez) and may be a fusion of introduced Christian concepts and traditional native beliefs.

When young people reached adolescence, they sought the assistance of supernatural beings through a vision quest. Children, particularly boys, would seclude themselves in the forest, refraining from food, drink or sleep until a vision appeared. In this vision their guardian spirit was revealed, and they learned the particular powers they were to receive later in life. Whether they would be successful in hunting, in warfare or in shamanism depended upon the guardian spirit they acquired at this time. Many of the rock paintings, depicting humans, animals and supernatural beings, were created as part of this quest for supernatural power.

The Ojibwa were widely respected for their shamanic powers. Shamans could cure illness, see into the future and provide charms or potions to ensure success in love or on the hunt. One well-known ritual is the Shaking Tent, in which a shaman summoned his spirit helpers to a small lodge by drumming and singing. The sudden violent shaking of the tent and the babble of voices emanating from it announced their arrival to aid the shaman in curing or prophecy. Other shamans used their powers for malevolent purposes. Unexplained illnesses and death were considered the work of evil sorcerers.

While their religious beliefs and practices were shared with the other central Algonkians, the Ojibwa developed a unique formal organization of shamans. This was the famous Midewiwin (literally "mystic doings") or Grand Medicine Society. As well as its primary role in curing illness, the Midewiwin became the main expression of Ojibwa religious concepts. It was a structured hierarchy, with a number of distinct levels, which was open to both men and women. Prolonged periods of instruction into the secret lore and rituals, along with a substantial payment to the officers of the lodge, preceded each initiation to a higher level. Birchbark scrolls incised with pictures were used to teach ritual songs and other lore required for each initiation. Nineteenth-century descriptions indicate that there were four successive levels; however, when Ruth Landes did her ethnographic field work in Ontario and Minnesota in the 1930s, there were eight—the first four called earth grades and the second four called sky grades. Few progressed beyond the lower levels, due to great costs and fear of sorcery involved in the higher levels. Each initiate had a medicine bag, which held the herbal remedies used in curing, and the *migis*, a small white shell which was ceremonially "shot" into new members, infusing them with spirit power. The extensive training of the Midewiwin meant that its members became the repositories of traditional religious knowledge.

The Midewiwin appears to have developed in post-contact times, possibly incorporating elements of Christianity with traditional Ojibwa beliefs. Ethnohistoric accounts of this organization, lacking in the seventeenth-century *Jesuit Relations*, first appear early in the eighteenth century. It appears to have developed as a native response to European pressure—a method of preserving their traditions in the face of extensive culture change. As such it parallels other nativistic movements, such as the Longhouse religion of the Iroquois and the Ghost Dance which emerged much later among Plains tribes.

The Huron Feast of the Dead was practiced by some Ojibwa groups, apparently introduced through the Nipissing, who were major trading partners of the Huron. The Jesuit Father Lalemant described such a ceremony among the Nipissing in 1641, noting that about 2000 people were in attendance, including some Huron and Ojibwa from as far away as the rapids of Sault Ste. Marie. The display and exchange of valuable gifts featured prominently at this gathering. As well as a communal reburial of the dead, the ceremony served the functions of publicly installing new chiefs and renewing alliances between the Algonkian groups and with the Huron. The Feast of the Dead appears to have been a short-lived phenomenon among the Algonkians, disappearing after the dispersal of the Huron and establishment of French missions later in the seventeenth century.

Alliances were essential in organizing war parties, especially against the Ojibwa's hated enemies, the Iroquois and Dakota. War parties set out to avenge previous deaths and to provide young men with opportunities for glory. Warriors armed themselves with bows and arrows, spears, knobbed wooden clubs and moosehide shields. Typical practice was to stealthily approach the enemy camp, then rush in and kill as many of the foe as possible. Scalps were taken, later to be stretched over wooden hoops and placed on poles which were carried during a victory dance.

In the period covered by early historic documents, the eastern Ojibwa were embroiled in warfare with the Iroquois. After dispersing the Huron and Petun, the Iroquois turned their military might against the Algonkin, Nipissing and Ottawa, raiding as far as Sault Ste. Marie and James Bay. The Nipissing and the Ottawa were driven far to the west, not being able to return to their homelands for several decades. They were not simply on the defensive, however, as we know from Jesuit accounts that an alliance of Algonkians ambushed and destroyed a sizable Mohawk and Oneida war party near Sault Ste. Marie in 1662. By the end of the seventeenth century, as Iroquois power waned and beaver became scarce, the Ojibwa embarked on expansion, ultimately to occupy the vast area which they inhabit today.

THE CREE

The term Cree developed as a contraction of Kristinaux, Kiristinon or a host of other variants by which one group speaking this language was known to early French explorers. They were first mentioned in a Jesuit account of 1640, referring to the "Kiristinon, who live on the shores of the North sea [James Bay] whither the Nipisiriniens [Nipissings] go to trade" (Thwaites, *Jesuit Relations* 18:229).

The distribution of Cree speakers at European contact is difficult to determine. However, they seem to have occupied lands surrounding James Bay and along the western shores of Hudson Bay, north almost to the Churchill River. Their territory appears to have extended at least as far as Lake Winnipeg to the west and Lake Nipigon to the south. Seventeenth-century accounts indicate that they frequently visited the northern shores of Lake Superior, and on a number of occasions they were reported to be fishing at Sault Ste. Marie as guests of the Ojibwa.

During the fur trade period, after the Cree obtained early access to firearms through trade on Hudson Bay, their territory was dramatically increased. Lured by profits from furs, the Cree expanded far to the west, eventually occupying southern portions of the Western Subarctic as far as the Peace River of Alberta. Many groups pushed out onto the Plains, allying with the Assiniboine against their enemies and adapting their culture to become Plains warriors and bison hunters. By the early nineteenth century Cree-speakers occupied the largest geographic extent of any Canadian native group, reaching from Labrador to the Rockies.

Although a single language was spoken throughout this vast area, dialectal differences meant that only neighbouring groups could converse with ease. Recent linguistic studies have isolated nine major dialects: Plains Cree (spoken on the plains and the western woodlands), Woods Cree (in the woodlands of central Saskatchewan and Manitoba), West and East Swampy Cree (two dialects spoken in the lowlands to the west of Hudson and James bays), Moose Cree (south of James Bay), East Cree (spoken through a large area of subarctic Quebec east of James Bay), Attikamek or Tête de Boule (in the Upper Saint-Maurice River region of Quebec), and Naskapi and Montagnais (of eastern Quebec and Labrador). Although their language can be classified with Cree, the latter two, better known as Innu today, have maintained a distinct separate identity and are treated separately here.

Throughout their subarctic environment (the Plains Cree are discussed in Chapter 6), the Cree were primarily hunters. Moose, caribou, bear and beaver were the main prey. Failure to take big game meant that smaller but more plentiful animals such as hare became crucial for survival. Geese and other waterfowl were also seasonally important, particularly for the Swampy Cree of the Hudson Bay Lowlands. Snares and deadfall traps were widely used, as were bows and arrows. Fishing, while not as highly valued, was important, allowing larger social groups to assemble at good fishing locations during the summer. Although they picked berries in summer, plant foods played a limited role in their diet.

In general, the environment in which the Cree lived was less bountiful than the Ojibwa lands to the south. Winter conditions were harsh, with extremely cold temperatures, heavy snowfall and short periods of daylight. When strong winds coincided with low temperatures, hunters faced the threat of freezing to death. In summer, while the climate was pleasant, travel was more difficult due to innumerable ponds and bogs, and people were tormented by swarms of mosquitos and blackflies. As well, resources were scarce. Many of the plant foods collected by the Ojibwa did not grow among the Cree, and even good fishing locations were relatively rare. The solitary forest animals hunted by the Cree were scattered thinly across the land, requiring people to live in small social groups which were constantly on the move. Winter starvation was always a possibility, and survival cannibalism, while abhorrent, was not unknown. The spectre of the Windigo was never far from their winter camps.

Cree material culture was similar to that of the Ojibwa. Prior to winter freeze-up the light birchbark canoe was indispensable to travel across their land of waterways, and snowshoes, toboggans and sleds allowed mobility during winter. Housing was the conical wigwam, frequently covered with caribou or moose hides rather than birchbark, which was not common in the northern forests. In some areas winter houses were constructed of sod and earth over closely spaced poles. Clothing, predominantly of tanned caribou or moose hide, was similar to that of the Ojibwa. It was frequently embellished with quillwork, later replaced by beadwork and coloured threads in floral designs. An early Jesuit description of ceremonial finery comes from a 1671 encounter with East Cree men "with painted faces, and adorned with all their costliest ornaments,—such as high head-dresses and porcelain collars, belts, and bracelets" (Thwaites, *Jesuit Relations* 56:173).

Social organization among the Cree existed on several levels: the nuclear family, the hunting group (or local band) and the community (or regional band). Marriages tended to occur at an early age, and one was not considered an adult until married. Cross-cousin marriage was preferred, although far from an inevitable rule. Most marriages were monogamous but a good hunter might take several wives, who were often sisters. Three to five nuclear families, usually related although sometimes linked only by bonds of friendship, made up the hunting group, living and traveling together throughout much of the year. The community was the largest social aggregate, consisting of all those who gathered at one location during the summer months, generally at a favoured fishing locale on the shore of a lake, where breezes kept away annoying insects. Later, trading posts became centres of such gatherings. While not functioning as an economic unit, this larger group provided opportunities for social interaction and for young people to search for spouses. This structure was highly flexible, and any family which was dissatisfied could join relatives in other groups.

In the hunting camps a division of labour based on sex was evident. The primary male role was that of hunter and trapper. Small groups of men worked together, often being away from the base camp for days at a time while they traveled great distances in search of game. They butchered their kills and hauled back meat from the hunt. Men did the heavy work of transporting supplies and setting up camp, and they also manufactured most wooden articles, such as toboggans, sleds and snowshoe frames. Women's tasks were primarily performed in the vicinity of the base camp. They caught fish with set lines and hunted or trapped small game such as hare and ptarmigan. Such food was often essential for survival when the male quest for big game was unsuccessful. Women also performed day-to-day tasks in the camp, such as gathering and splitting firewood, replacing conifer bough flooring, cooking meals, and preparing hides and pelts, as well as engaging in constant manufacture and mending of moccasins, mittens and other apparel. Adolescent daughters aided in these tasks and in the care of younger children.

Hunting involved far more than simply tracking and killing animals. To the Cree, hunting was a religious activity and only through proper ceremonial acts could humans wrest from nature their means of livelihood. A successful kill was not just brought about by the skill of the hunter but was also a "gift" from the animal. Respect had to be shown or the animal would not allow itself to be taken in the future. The bear commanded particular consideration, but caribou, beaver and other animals also had to be respected. The hunter thanked the animal he had killed and offered it tobacco. For larger animals, a feast was held, to which all members of the hunting group were invited. Small portions of meat were placed in the fire as offerings to ensure future successful hunts. Care had to be taken with the bones or the animals would be offended. Bear and beaver skulls might be suspended from trees, while special platforms were built to keep other bones out of reach of camp dogs. Only abundant and less-valued species, such as hare and fish, were fed to the dogs.

Other rituals involved divination, to determine the location of the animals or to predict the outcome of the hunt. Scapulimancy was one such practice. A caribou scapula (shoulder blade) was placed on hot coals, the resultant cracks and scorch marks indicating trails and the location of game. In addition, the Shaking Tent ritual might be employed to summon spirit assistance in directing hunters to the animals they sought.

THE INNU (MONTAGNAIS AND NASKAPI)

The Montagnais (French for "mountaineers," due to the rugged topography of their land) and Naskapi (of uncertain derivation, but thought to be a derogatory term meaning "uncivilized people" applied to the more northerly bands) occupy eastern Quebec and Labrador. The Naskapi inhabit the northern, largely barren-ground environment between Hudson Bay and the central Labrador coast, while the Montagnais dwell in the forested country to the south, extending to the northern shores of the Gulf of St. Lawrence and the lower St. Lawrence River. They differ little in language and culture, major distinctions being ones of adaptation to slightly different environments. Accordingly, they are usually linked with the hyphenated term Montagnais-Naskapi, although they prefer to call themselves Innu (or "person").

In the north, Naskapi subsistence centred on the herds of barren-ground caribou. During autumn migrations, caribou were speared from canoes as they crossed rivers or lakes. In winter, hunters on snowshoes drove caribou into deep snow and shot them with bows and arrows while the animals floundered in the drifts. During summer some Naskapi moved to the Labrador coast to fish, while others remained inland to fish in lakes and rivers and to hunt small game.

The Montagnais had access to a wider range of resources. Moose and woodland caribou were the major game species, although a variety of smaller forest animals were hunted and trapped. Coastal resources along the Gulf of St. Lawrence were also extremely important. Fishing played a prominent role in the diet, and large numbers of eels were taken in weirs during the early autumn. Seals could be hunted by canoe or clubbed on the rocky beaches. Edible roots and berries were present, and maple trees could be tapped for sap. In addition, those in contact with the Huron traded moosehides for corn and tobacco.

Innu social groups varied with the seasons. Winter hunting camps consisted of several, usually related, nuclear families. Successful hunters, those who had "power" over animals, assumed positions of leadership, but this was by example only and no person had authority over another. Group composition was not permanent, and new combinations of families could be formed in successive winters. In summer, small groups emerged from the mosquito-infested woods to gather on the shores of large interior lakes or at the mouths of rivers. These summer camps were the largest social groups, providing the major opportunities for social interaction and festivities.

Above: *Innu camp, Labrador,*
CMC 54584
Left: *Labrador Innu, ca. 1880.*
CMC J-6541

Material culture was similar to that of neighbouring Algonkians. The birchbark canoe, snowshoes and toboggan were all essential to seasonal migration. Housing was usually the conical wigwam, covered with birch-bark among the Montagnais and caribou hide among the Naskapi. Most clothing was made from caribou hide in the general Algonkian pattern, although the Naskapi adopted the tailored coat, occasionally with hood, of the coastal Inuit. These long, caribou-hide coats, almost invariably painted with geometric patterns, are the best-known examples of Naskapi material culture in museum collections.

Innu religion was intensely personal. If individuals respected the animals and "lived the right life," they acquired increasing powers of communica-tion with the spirit world. Those who made a particular effort to acquire spirit power could become shamans, capable of holding the Shaking Tent ritual or interpreting the cracks on scorched animal bones to determine the location of game. Offerings were made to the spirits of animals killed, and their bones, especially skulls of bears and beavers, were carefully placed in trees or on platforms. Successful hunts required a feast, a particularly important one following the kill of caribou, when hunters ritually consumed marrow from the long bones. Following the feast, each hunter played the drum and sang hunting songs given to him by the spirits.

During the period of early historic contact, the Montagnais were embroiled in bitter conflict with the Iroquois. Warfare was also recorded with the Mi'kmaq and the Inuit, but the Iroquois were their most hated foes, with whom they shared such cruelties as the torture of prisoners. These traditional enmities were intensified early in the historic period by trade rivalries along the St. Lawrence. Champlain allied himself with the Montagnais and nearby Algonkians, accompanying them on raids deep into Iroquois territory. One war party assembled at the mouth of the Saguenay River numbered 1000 warriors. By the late seventeenth century, the Montagnais had been greatly weakened by warfare, European diseases, depletion of game and displacement from their lands along the St. Lawrence.

IMPACT OF THE FUR TRADE

With the advent of strangers from across the sea in the early seventeenth century, the Algonkians of the St. Lawrence found themselves drawn into a new pattern of social and economic relations. The insatiable greed of the newcomers for furs, plus the eagerness of more distant natives to obtain cloth and those wondrous European metal goods, meant that the Montagnais, Algonkin, Nipissing and Ottawa were ideally situated as intermediaries in the early fur trade. Iron knives and hatchets, copper kettles and other European items were traded for large quantities of furs, which could be taken down the St. Lawrence River to Quebec and exchanged at great profit. As early as the 1630s one French observer commented that European clothing had largely replaced traditional garb, and that copper kettles were so widely used that cooking vessels of bark were only a memory. The St. Lawrence was a route to riches, and the Algonkians had to contend with an Iroquois bid for its control. To the north, the Cree also entered this trade relationship when the newly formed Hudson's Bay Company began to establish trading posts on the shores of Hudson and James bays after 1670. Groups living far inland began to make annual journeys down to salt water to trade their accumulated furs for coveted European wares.

New opportunities offered by the fur trade led the Ojibwa and Cree to expand westward, seeking new trapping lands for beaver and other furbearers. This process, begun before the end of the seventeenth century, continued through most of the eighteenth. The Ojibwa pushed west to Lake Winnipeg and north far into territory formerly held by the Cree. By the mid-eighteenth century large groups of Ojibwa were making trading trips to Fort Albany, a Hudson's Bay Company post on James Bay. The northern Ojibwa intermingled with the Cree, abandoning such southern traditions as the Midewiwin and totemic clans, and living in small, scattered hunting and fishing bands identical to the Cree. Today a number of northern Ojibwa bands consider themselves to be (and are officially designated as) Cree, while others in northern Ontario and Manitoba are listed as "mixed" Ojibwa-Cree.

Until the late eighteenth century, Hudson's Bay Company employees were content to remain in their coastal "factories" (major trading posts), waiting for natives to arrive with furs. Such posts as York Factory, Fort Albany and Moose Factory on Hudson and James bays drew native traders from great distances inland. Major competition developed from the generally French, Montreal-based trade along the Great Lakes-St. Lawrence River system. Rather than waiting for natives in a few fixed locations, the French spread far into Algonkian lands to pursue trade, often settling among them and taking native wives. The Algonkians quickly realized that this competition could be used to demand greater returns for their furs.

After the defeat of the French, the trade through Montreal was taken over by merchants of English and Highland Scots descent, eventually leading to the establishment of the North West Company. This was a period of intense competition, finally disturbing the Hudson's Bay Company's long complacency in the north and requiring its traders to establish posts inland. These two great rivals pushed westward, struggling for control of the trade, each attempting to establish posts in the most advantageous locations. This period of "taking the trade to the Indians" lasted until 1821, when the North West Company was finally absorbed by its competitor. Although the price of goods rose and many posts were closed with the elimination of this competition, the Hudson's Bay Company continued the fur trade among the northern Algonkians into modern times.

The fur trade had a great impact on native life. Many native implements of stone, bone, wood and hide were quickly replaced by purchased objects of iron, copper and cloth. As a Montagnais chief jokingly stated: "The Beaver does everything perfectly well, it makes kettles, hatchets, swords, knives, bread; and, in short, it makes everything" (Thwaites, *Jesuit Relations* 6:297). Traders' firearms made hunting more efficient but forced hunters to rely on the posts for ammunition. Many native groups began to place greater emphasis on trapping furbearers than on hunting food animals, requiring a shift in diet to European foodstuffs. Such staples as flour, lard, sugar and tea, as well as tobacco, became necessities, tying bands to the trading posts for supplies. Liquor was also widely distributed, with devastating impact, by traders. The overall effect was to destroy native self-sufficiency, making them at least partially dependent upon the traders, and many bands began to establish their summer camps around the posts.

Some social changes were also results of the fur trade. Traders recognized socially prominent men as "captains" who bargained with the traders on behalf of their bands. The "captains" were provided with presents, including food and tobacco, to be distributed among their people. In exchange for this enhanced prestige, the "captains" were to ensure that their groups returned to the same post the following year. This new leadership position, however, was as limited as traditional roles, authority lasting only as long as the trading expedition.

Another trade change in Algonkian culture was the system of land tenure. Early in this century, Frank Speck documented well-defined family hunting territories among the Algonkians and concluded that this was a fundamental feature of Algonkian life which had survived years of cultural change. More recently other anthropologists have recognized this as another adaptation to the fur trade. Since food was shared, access to hunting lands was originally open to all. However, the taking of animals for furs was an individual act for private profit. Accordingly, individuals attempted to keep others from what they regarded as "their" resources. The distinction between food and furs is clear in Eleanor Leacock's study of the Montagnais, in which she states that a man could kill a beaver on another's land if it was needed for food but not to obtain the fur for sale.

The beaver and other furbearers could not continue to withstand such pressures. In traditional hunting, the Algonkians practiced conservation measures, since there was no advantage in having an overabundance of meat. During the fur trade, natives were supplied with firearms and steel traps and were offered an apparently limitless market for furs to purchase the European goods on which they were now dependent. Along the St. Lawrence, beaver were already scarce by the mid-seventeenth century, and by the early nineteenth century they were depleted from all but the most remote regions. With game stocks also largely eliminated, many native groups found themselves hard pressed to avoid starvation. Their plight is described by explorer and fur trader David Thompson at the end of the eighteenth century:

> The Nepissings, the Algonquins and Iroquois Indians having exhausted their own countries, now spread themselves over these countries, and as they destroyed the Beaver, moved forwards to the northward and westward; the Natives, the Nahathaways [Cree], did not in the least molest them . . . For several years all these Indians were rich, the Women and Children, as well as the Men, were covered with silver brooches, Ear Rings, Wampum, Beads and other trinkets. Their mantles were of fine scarlet cloth, and all was finery and

dress. The Canoes of the Furr Traders were loaded with packs of Beaver . . .
Every intelligent Man saw the poverty that would follow the destruction of
the Beaver, but there were no Chiefs to controul it . . . almost the whole of
these extensive countries were denuded of Beaver, the Natives became poor,
and with difficulty procured the first necessities of life . . .

(Thompson 1916:205)

In his controversial book *Keepers of the Game*, American historian Calvin
Martin posed a novel thesis to account for this depletion of fur and game
animals. Traditionally hunting was a "holy occupation," based on respect
and understanding between humans and animals. Spiritual reprisal, which
could take the form of illness, would follow any wanton slaughter of game.
It was the introduction of European diseases, in some areas before
Europeans themselves had arrived, that broke this mutual compact, Martin
argued. Blaming the animals for the illness and death which beset them, the
Indians were no longer bound by traditions of respect and could literally
"make war upon the animals." When equipped with European technology
and lured by European commodities, no taboo remained in place to halt
the Algonkian overkill. Martin's thesis, however, has been strongly challenged by anthropologists. The link between disease and animals is tenuous,
and some historic references clearly indicate that the natives rightly perceived Europeans as the cause of their afflictions. Others point out that, far
from disappearing, native traditions of spiritual relationships with the animals they hunt continue to the present.

THE CENTRAL ALGONKIANS
IN THE MODERN ERA

Like the fur trade period, the modern era did not begin at a single time or
have a common impact throughout the vast Ojibwa-Cree-Innu distribution. It is marked by a decline in hunting and trapping, and a rise in wage
labour and government assistance as the means of support. Such a shift
took place much earlier among the southern Ojibwa than in the north,
where one band of Innu was still living a migratory life until the 1950s,
when they were relocated to the new mining town of Schefferville in an
attempt to integrate them into the modern economy. In general, the result
of this period has been the removal of economic self-sufficiency, making
natives marginal populations in their own lands, and the continual
encroachment on native lands for logging, mining and hydroelectric developments.

In the south, many Ojibwa are located near urban centres, such as
Thunder Bay and Winnipeg, which offer opportunities for employment
and all the amenities of city life. Winnipeg has a very large native popula-

tion, a good portion of which is drawn from nearby Ojibwa ("Saulteaux") reserves. Their lives differ little from those of other urban native Canadians. In reserve communities, commercial fishing, wild rice gathering (particularly around Lake of the Woods) and handicraft production provide income for many.

In more isolated areas to the north, Cree and northern Ojibwa settlements, often on the location of former trading posts, have become larger, more centralized and more permanent. While such communities may be predominantly native, there are invariably Euro-Canadian administrators, teachers, missionaries, merchants and medical personnel. Facilities run by non-natives, such as the church, school and store, have become centres of community life. Band government has shifted from traditional informal leadership to an elected chief and councilors. On many reserves the band government is the major employer, although some individuals work seasonally in construction, logging, tourist guiding, commercial fishing, tree planting or forest fire fighting. Improved health services have decreased infant mortality and stemmed the spread of infectious diseases. Most communities have their own schools, and education levels are rising. As during the fur trade period, the trading posts are central to the community, although they now have become retail stores with a cash economy. The Hudson's Bay Company continues to be the largest trade and retail organization, although most communities now contain smaller independent stores, many of which are run by natives.

Introduced elements of Euro-Canadian culture continue to change native life. High-powered rifles and steel traps have replaced traditional methods of taking game. The birchbark canoe has been replaced by commercially manufactured models, often powered by an outboard motor. Snowmobiles are widely used for winter travel and hunting. Longer distance trips are by airplane or, for those communities with road access, by automobile. Yet the overall impact has been to reduce mobility. Outboard motors, snowmobiles and chainsaws may make life easier but require fuel and parts from the store. Children's education and government welfare and family allowance payments also tend to keep people in the community throughout much of the year.

Nevertheless, in many northern communities a substantial number of families go into the bush to hunt, trap and fish for part of the year. In some areas, such as near James Bay, the number of hunters has remained high, people seeing this not just as a way to obtain food and furs but as a reaffirmation of their traditional beliefs and values. Accordingly, many parents withdraw their children from school in order to educate them in "bush skills" they need to survive as Cree.

Throughout Ontario and Manitoba the Cree and Ojibwa signed treaties with the government. This process began as early as 1850, with the surrender of Ojibwa territory to the north of Lakes Superior and Huron, and continued to 1905, when Treaty No. 9 extinguished native title across northern Ontario. In Quebec and Labrador, however, natives were not required to sign away their lands. The Grand Council of the Cree, the Conseil Attikamek–Montagnais in Quebec and the Innu Nation (formerly the Naskapi-Montagnais Innu Association) in Labrador were formed to demand resolution of the land claims issue.

The matter was brought to a head in 1971, when the Quebec government launched a massive hydroelectric project, involving blocking and diversion of rivers flowing into James Bay. The Cree were threatened with extensive flooding of traditional hunting and trapping areas, requiring relocation of several villages. The Quebec government did not recognize any native claim to the land until a legal injunction obtained by the Cree temporarily halted the huge project. Finally, in 1975 the governments of Canada and Quebec and the Cree and Inuit of the James Bay region signed the first land claims agreement in modern Canadian history. In return for surrender of their claim to the land, the Cree and Inuit received monetary compensation of $225 million to be paid over a twenty-year period, ownership of the lands around their communities and exclusive hunting, fishing and trapping rights over much larger areas. Although stung by charges from other native groups that the deal was a "sellout," the Cree under Chief Billy Diamond maintained that this was the best deal possible under the threat of imminent development and that it ensured the continuation of native lifeways in northern Quebec. The Naskapi of Schefferville signed a similar agreement in 1978. The principle of local self-government for the communities covered by these agreements was consolidated in the Cree-Naskapi (of Quebec) Act in 1984.

The Quebec Cree today run their own school boards and other administrative structures. Settlement money has been used to finance Cree-run industries, including their own airline (Air Creebec) and a partnership with Yamaha to manufacture fibreglass canoes. Cree villages have new houses and schools, electricity and running water.

At the same time, much has been lost. Old village sites and valued fishing locations at river rapids are now flooded under reservoirs or left dry as river water has been diverted. An unforeseen environmental disaster from the flooding of the forests has been the release of an organic form of mercury into the reservoirs. Although the total amount of mercury is small, it is concentrated in fish and poses a significant health hazard for people who rely heavily upon fish in their diet. Even more devastating have been the massive social problems that followed the opening up of their homeland to large numbers of outsiders.

In addition, the Quebec government plans further assaults on the Cree homeland. Proposed additional dam construction would link much of northern Quebec into one huge hydroelectric project. This time, however, the Cree have had decades of experience in dealing with governments and are determined to fight all attempts to further intrude on their lands. Their tactics have included taking their political battle to the northeastern American states, in order to discourage any potential customers for Quebec's energy exports.

The Innu have had to contend with similar pressures on their traditional lands. In addition, Innu hunters in Labrador are now facing another threat to their way of life—low-flying jet bombers on test runs from a nearby NATO training centre. The sudden and deafening noise as the jets appear overhead destroys the peace of the Innu camps and drives away the game. Innu protests in Labrador and St. John's have focused considerable public attention on their plight.

Industrial wastes have polluted the waterways in many areas of the Cree and Ojibwa homeland. One well-known example is the English-Wabigoon River system in northwestern Ontario. Tests on fish taken from the river showed levels of mercury far in excess of those considered safe for human consumption. The Ojibwa of the Grassy Narrows and Whitedog reserves north of Kenora were suddenly confronted with the spectre of mercury poisoning, which can lead to irreversible damage to the brain and nervous system, blindness, paralysis and death. Fish consumption was discouraged by the government, even though the Ojibwa rely heavily on fish in their diet, and the collapse of the commercial and sports fishery put many men out of work.

After a lengthy legal battle, a 1985 settlement awarded the two bands $16.6 million in compensation. As part of the settlement, a mercury disability fund was established to aid band members whose health has been impaired by mercury poisoning. While hailing the settlement as a successful quest for justice, natives are also conscious of the cost: "Whatever money we get from the settlement will never be enough to replace what we lost. In looking back over the years, I realize that my people have lost a lot more than just their livelihood. They lost their pride and their self-determination to be self-sufficient" (Grassy Narrows Chief Arnold Pelly, *Vancouver Sun*, 26 November 1985).

Social problems have beset many Ojibwa, Cree and Innu communities in recent decades. Violence, suicide, family breakdown and alcohol abuse have reached alarming levels in some villages. At Davis Inlet, an Innu community in Labrador, the recent attempted suicides of six gas-sniffing children focused media attention on conditions of poverty and despair. In a study of the Ojibwa at Grassy Narrows, Anastasia Shkilnyk traces the social disintegration to their relocation from the old community, where they were isolated and relatively self-sufficient, to the new reserve, which is unsuited to traditional activities but is linked by road to Kenora and the modern economy. The poisoning of their waterways, loss of jobs and threat to their health were cumulatively devastating. She takes the title of her disturbing book, *A Poison Stronger Than Love*, from a statement by an anonymous resident of Grassy Narrows: "The only thing I know about alcohol is that alcohol is a stronger power than the love of children. It's a poison, and we are a broken people." Such highly publicized cases have alerted many Canadians to the Third World living conditions endured by some First Nations in Canada.

Such problems and frustrations have led to outbreaks of violence. Young natives around Kenora, tiring of the slow pace of negotiations and social and economic discrimination in the town, organized the Ojibway Warriors Society, which was strongly influenced by the militant American Indian Movement (AIM). In July 1974, the Ojibway Warriors militarily occupied Anishinabe Park in Kenora, claiming that the land rightfully belonged to them because it had originally been purchased by Indian Affairs as a camping ground for Indians. For more than four weeks the media barraged the Canadian public with images of armed Indians behind barricades, foreshadowing the Oka crisis in Quebec in 1990. Despite the militant stance, the occupation ended without bloodshed. The Ojibwa were unsuccessful in their specific demand for return of the land, and their general concerns regarding discrimination were lost in local backlash against their actions.

More positively, a major achievement of the past few decades has been the development of a distinctive and widely acclaimed Cree-Ojibwa art style, usually referred to as "Woodlands art." The originator and foremost practitioner is Norval Morrisseau, an Ojibwa from the Lake Nipigon area of northern Ontario. His inspiration came from the legends of his people, and from the images in the rock paintings and on the birchbark scrolls. However, the taboo on depicting legendary figures, except by a shaman in a ritual context, initially brought him into conflict with the elders. His introduction to the Canadian art world in the early 1960s brought wide recognition. Bold and brilliantly coloured, with "x-ray vision" showing internal organs and undulating "power lines" connecting the figures, his style is instantly recognizable. Early contemporaries who helped shape the Woodlands style were Carl Ray, a Cree from Sandy Lake in northern Ontario, and Daphne Odjig, an Ottawa from Manitoulin Island who has developed a very distinctive and personal variant of the Woodlands style. By the 1970s, many young Cree-Ojibwa artists emerged and Woodlands art achieved international acclaim. These vigorous, colourful paintings illustrate the strength of the Algonkian oral traditions and serve as a new vehicle for native identity.

With the largest native populations in Canada, the Cree and Ojibwa are in no danger of disappearing. Nearly 180,000 people are registered as members of Cree bands. This figure includes the Plains Cree but not Cree-speaking Métis or non-status Indians. In addition, there are over 14,000 Innu in Quebec and Labrador. The Ojibwa have a population of about 116,000 in Canada, plus almost as many in the United States. Listed separately in government statistics are about 9500 Algonkin and over 3000 Ottawa

Painting of a moose by Norval Morrisseau. CMC 81-13152

(although all Ottawa bands are mixed with Ojibwa). Their languages are healthy: the 1991 census lists nearly 94,000 Cree-speakers, over 30,000 Ojibwa-speakers and over 8000 Innu able to speak their language. Despite centuries of contact and the adoption of many elements of Euro-Canadian life, the Algonkians have resisted assimilation and are determined that their cultures will survive.

CHAPTER 6 *The Plains*

Few cultures on earth have captured the popular imagination as forcefully as the First Nations of the Plains. Even the word "Indian" tends automatically to conjure up the typical image of the historic natives of the Plains— mounted warriors and bison hunters bedecked in feathers and buckskin. Proud and warlike, their conflicts with other natives and the non-Indian invaders of their homelands have become legendary, inspiring numerous "western" movies and novels. Even natives elsewhere in Canada have felt compelled to don Plains-style headdresses and costumes in order to be identified as "Indians," and Plains dances and ceremonies promote a Pan-Indian identity far beyond their original distribution. Yet, like most stereotypes, this image has only a limited validity. Plains cultures were constantly changing, and the horseback warrior with the feather headdress represents only a very recent and short-lived stage in a long period of cultural evolution.

The Plains environment is the flat, semi-arid grasslands extending across southern portions of the three prairie provinces, from the Rocky Mountains in the west to the woodlands of southeastern Manitoba in the east. Only the northern reaches of this vast land of sun, wind and grass fall within Canada. The climate is continental, with hot, dry summers and long, cold winters. In the east is the tall grass prairie, while the short grass of the "high plains" lies to the west. A broad belt of aspen parklands along the northern edge of the Plains marks a transition to the boreal forest of the Subarctic. The terrain varies from flat and featureless ancient lake bottom to rolling and wooded uplands, such as the Cypress Hills on the Alberta-Saskatchewan border. Deeply incised river valleys provided water, wood and shelter. The western Plains has a more rugged topography, with cliffs and dry coulees providing relief.

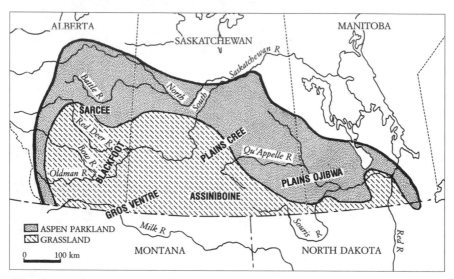

The Plains culture area, showing the division into grassland and aspen parkland and the early nineteenth-century distribution of ethnographic groups.

Vast herds of bison (popularly known as buffalo) provided the basis on which Plains cultures developed. Once existing in such numbers that they darkened the Plains, bison were the staff of life for the Plains nomads until the destruction of the herds in the nineteenth century. Not only did bison provide sustenance, but their hides were indispensable for shelter and clothing, and various implements were fashioned from the bones and horns. Even dried dung served as fuel on the treeless plains. Yet it would be wrong to portray the Plains tribes as solely dependent upon bison. Pronghorn antelope also once existed in great numbers, and mule deer, elk, prairie chicken and other game, as well as a variety of edible plants, helped vary the diet. Eastern groups, as recent arrivals from the Woodlands, also ate fish, but this was considered beneath the dignity of such high plains hunters as the Blackfoot.

In the early historic period, most Plains dwellers spoke Algonkian languages. The powerful Blackfoot Confederacy, composed of the Blackfoot, Blood and Peigan, epitomized the high plains hunters and warriors. Their allies, the Gros Ventre (or Atsina), although extending far into Canada during the early historic period, were eventually pushed south of the border. Their bitter enemies during this time were the recently arrived Plains Cree and Plains Ojibwa. In addition to these Algonkian-speakers, the Athapaskan Sarcee became part of the Blackfoot Confederacy, and the Siouan Assiniboine (or "Stoney") were closely allied and intermingled with the Plains Cree. Another member of the Siouan family, the Dakota, arrived in Canada only at the end of the horse and bison days.

The historic Plains natives were highly nomadic, ranging over great distances to hunt, trade and make war upon their enemies. No clearly defined territorial boundaries existed, and tribal distributions were constantly shifting. New groups surged onto the Plains with the advent of horses and guns, while others were displaced. Plains culture history was dynamic, frustrating attempts to place neat labels on maps or to assign archaeological remains to known ethnic groups.

PLAINS CULTURE PRIOR TO THE WHITE MAN

So engrained is the image of the Plains warrior on horseback that we find it difficult to imagine Plains culture without horses. Yet our ethnographic and historic accounts refer only to the brief florescence which occurred between the introduction of the horse in the mid-eighteenth century and the destruction of the bison herds just over a century later. For many millennia prior to this, humans had successfully wrested their livelihood from the Plains as pedestrian hunters, following bison herds on foot and using dogs to help carry their goods. The vast herds of bison are now gone from the Plains, but traces of those who pursued them—stone tools, campsites, piles of bones left from a successful hunt—remain to tell their stories to the archaeologist.

The arrival from the south of people known as Paleo-Indians (see Chapter 2), with their distinctive fluted chipped-stone spearpoints, marks the beginning of the **Early Prehistoric** period (*ca.* 9500 to 5500 B.C.). Many discoveries of fluted points have been made across all three prairie provinces. Forms include classic Clovis and Folsom points, as well as a small triangular variant. However, none has been found in a datable context. Many were plowed up by farmers or otherwise found on the surface, while a few, such as at the Sibbald Creek site west of Calgary, have been scientifically excavated but lack any clearly associated radiocarbon date. Estimates of age rely on the dating of similar discoveries farther south on the Plains.

Later Paleo-Indian point types, collectively referred to as Plano, are also widely distributed across the northern Plains. These are large, lancelate, unfluted points which are often masterpieces of the flintknapper's art. Projectile point types found on the Canadian Plains include those termed Plainview, Agate Basin, Hell Gap, Alberta and Eden-Scottsbluff. Once again most are surface discoveries; only a few have associated radiocarbon dates. Sites such as Fletcher in southern Alberta and Heron Eden in Saskatchewan show where Plano hunters using Eden-Scottsbluff points carried out mass bison kills about 9000 years ago.

Long before the end of the Early Prehistoric period the spruce forests and large glacial lakes which marked its early stages had been replaced by grasslands. While early Paleo-Indians shared their environment with such Pleistocene fauna as the woolly mammoth and giant bison, by Plano times these had either become extinct or reached near-modern form. Herds of bison allowed Plano cultures to maintain their big-game hunting lifestyle for thousands of years, and set the stage for all later cultural developments on the northern Plains.

The beginning of the **Middle Prehistoric** period (*ca.* 5500 B.C. to A.D. 100) is marked by the appearance of medium-sized notched or stemmed points, presumably to facilitate hafting onto a wooden shaft. Some researchers distinguish the three stages on the assumption of different weapon use: early Prehistoric lancelate points arming thrusting or throwing spears, middle period notched points being used on short spears or darts hurled by an atlatl (spear thrower), and small notched or triangular points of the late stage indicating introduction of the bow and arrow. However, others argue that many Paleo-Indian points armed atlatl darts, and that the change in shape simply provided greater efficiency in hafting.

Projectile point types serve as key indicators for further divisions of Plains prehistory. While much of the material culture changed little over long periods, shifting styles of projectile points have allowed archaeologists to distinguish different phases or "cultures." Whether these actually correspond to different human populations, however, remains debatable.

At the beginning of the Middle Prehistoric period, the Plains entered a long hot and dry spell (the Altithermal or Atlantic period). Grasslands expanded considerably to the north and east at the expense of parklands and forest. Drought and limited water sources would have made survival difficult for both humans and bison. At one time archaeologists posited a "cultural hiatus"—abandonment of the northern Plains as a result of the adverse climate. More recently, evidence has accumulated that makes it unlikely that the northern Plains were ever entirely abandoned; however, human populations were small and few archaeological sites of this age remain. After a period of several millennia, the climate shifted to essentially modern conditions and the grasslands retreated to roughly their present location.

A number of early side-notched point types are collectively classified as the Mummy Cave series. The people who made these points hunted bison, elk and other large game with the use of atlatls and also took bison by means of "jumps," driving them to their deaths over a cliff. Their distinctive projectile points are found at the earliest levels of the famous Head-Smashed-In bison jump in southern Alberta.

Perhaps the best known and most widespread of Middle Prehistoric cultures is Oxbow. Appearing somewhat before 3000 B.C., Oxbow points are found across the plains and parklands of all three prairie provinces, later extending north into the boreal forest. Evidence for use of the hide-covered tipi at this time comes from Oxbow points found with circles of stone

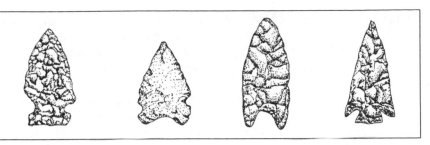

Middle Prehistoric projectile point types. From left to right: *Mummy Cave, Oxbow, McKean, Pelican Lake*

which once held down tipi covers. At the Harder site in Saskatchewan, archaeologist Ian Dyck excavated six to eight round patches of packed earth which he interpreted as evidence for tipis, although stone rings were not present. He estimated that this Oxbow campsite, strewn with stone tools and butchered bison bones, was occupied for a short period by about fifty people.

Insights into Oxbow beliefs and ceremonial practices come from two non-residential sites. At the Majorville medicine wheel (a large ring of stones with central cairn and radiating spokes) on the Bow River of southern Alberta, archaeologists found Oxbow points at the lowest level of the cairn, indicating that the use of these enigmatic monuments goes back to at least this time. Also, excavation at an Oxbow cemetery, the Gray site in Saskatchewan, revealed remains of more than 300 individuals. Although some are primary extended burials, most are incomplete bone bundles, indicating that those who died at some distance from the site were defleshed and their bones taken back for burial. Extensive use of red ochre hints at funerary rituals, as does the placement of such exotic goods as marine shell ornaments and copper beads with some of the dead. Eagle talons and other animal remains possibly once were parts of medicine bundles, suggesting that the historic pattern of Plains religious practices was already in place.

Coexisting with late Oxbow is the McKean phase, divided into three related point styles. Many archaeologists maintain that McKean and Oxbow represent separate prehistoric cultures, with McKean being a more recent arrival from the Great Basin to the south. Some even see the stylistic variants within McKean as indicating distinct ethnic groups, along the line of the historic Plains Cree and Assiniboine. Henry Kelsey stated in 1690 that the Assiniboine could distinguish their arrows (although admittedly looking at more than just the points) from those of the Plains Cree and Blackfoot, even though the Assiniboine and Cree lived and hunted together, and all three groups used the same techniques for taking bison. At the

Cactus Flower site near Medicine Hat, all three McKean point variants were found. A tubular pipe and possible gaming pieces hint at social life, and it appears that these people also lived in tipis. A cremation burial site near Saskatoon suggests that mortuary practices differed from those of the Oxbow culture.

A later phase across the Canadian Plains is termed Pelican Lake, dating roughly 1300 B.C. to A.D. 100. Their finely flaked corner-notched points are considered by many to have developed directly out of McKean. Campsites are frequently large, possibly indicating the larger social groups required for mass bison kills. Remains from the Head-Smashed-In and Old Women's bison jumps in southern Alberta show that the Pelican Lake people were adept at the practice of stampeding bison over cliffs. Burials, often secondary bundles, were placed in pits on hilltops and covered with rock cairns. Ritual practices are indicated by red ochre in the graves and such wealth items as grizzly bear claw necklaces, decorated gorgets of shell from the Gulf of Mexico, dentalium shell beads from the Pacific coast and small pieces of copper from the western Great Lakes.

The **Late Prehistoric** period (*ca.* A.D. 1 to 1740) is marked by the addition of two innovations to the traditional tool-kit of the Plains bison hunters: pottery-making and use of the bow and arrow. In the eastern portion of the Plains, burial mounds with exotic grave goods indicate new ideas arriving from the Eastern Woodlands. It is difficult to make a clear distinction between the Middle and Late Prehistoric periods and some overlap exists. In one commonly used classification, the Besant phase is considered Middle Prehistoric while the largely contemporaneous Avonlea is placed in the Late Prehistoric, based on the assumption of different weapons systems. A purely chronological scheme is employed here, beginning the late period with Besant.

The Besant period is dated from about A.D. 1 to 800. A side-notched atlatl dart head is supplanted toward the end of this phase by a smaller point considered to be an arrowhead. Common use of a brown chalcedony ("Knife River flint") from a quarry in North Dakota indicates trade. Sherds of pottery appear in a few Besant sites but are not abundant; nor would such fragile vessels be particularly useful to Plains nomads. Their campsites, where stone rings indicate use of hide-covered tipis, are widely distributed throughout the northern Plains. Bison kill sites include both jumps and "pounds," where the animals were driven into an enclosure. In addition, the mortuary aspect of Besant is shown in a series of burial mounds in the Missouri Valley of North and South Dakota (sometimes termed the Sonota Complex but considered part of Besant here). Bison skulls and other remains buried in the mounds suggest rituals associated with the hunt, and a number of exotic goods placed with the dead indicate ties to the widespread Hopewell Complex, a mound-building culture of the central Eastern Woodlands with far-reaching trade connections.

Late Prehistoric projectile point types. From left to right: *Besant, Avonlea, Prairie Side-notched, Plains Side-notched*

Coexisting with Besant was the Avonlea phase (*ca.* A.D. 200 to 800). Characterized by small, delicately thin, notched points, this culture is credited with introducing the bow and arrow to the Plains. Broken pieces of pottery frequently occur in Avonlea deposits. Most of our knowledge comes from bison kill sites, and the Avonlea people seem to have brought bison hunting to new levels of efficiency. At some sites, such as Head-Smashed-In in Alberta, they drove bison over cliffs. At others, such as Ramillies in Alberta and Gull Lake in Saskatchewan, they drove bison into corrals or traps, often using natural features of the landscape. Once inside, the trapped animals soon fell prey to the hunters' arrows, and the task of butchering could begin.

The final centuries of prehistory on the northwestern plains of Alberta and Saskatchewan are marked by a series of small, side-notched arrowpoints, at sites which also generally yield a few pottery sherds. They can be grouped into two overlapping stages, termed Prairie Side-notched and Plains Side-notched. In Alberta, this late period is known as the Old Women's phase, after a bison jump which yielded abundant evidence from its upper layers that bison continued to be the mainstay of life. The Old Women's phase extends into the Protohistoric and is considered by many to represent the early Blackfoot and Gros Ventre.

In the northeastern Plains, while small side-notched points also mark the final centuries of prehistory, more attention is focused on the relatively abundant ceramics. The Blackduck pottery style of the Eastern Woodlands (discussed in Chapter 5) spread into the parkland and plains of southern Manitoba. With a more diverse economy than their western contemporaries, people of the Blackduck culture hunted bison and smaller game, fished and collected a variety of plant foods. They also brought with them the practice of burying their dead in mounds. Although most archaeologists associate Blackduck with Algonkians, some argue for attribution to a Siouan group such as the Assiniboine.

Burial mounds of this late period are concentrated in southern Manitoba

Shell gorget from a burial mound in southwestern Manitoba. The raw material and the characteristic "weeping eye" motif suggest an origin far to the southeast. ROM

and adjacent North Dakota, with rare examples extending into eastern Saskatchewan. Manitoba archaeologist Leigh Syms has termed this the Devil's Lake-Sourisford Burial Complex. Burials, in pits under mounds, often contain grave goods. Finely made miniature pots, commonly decorated with spiral designs or with presumably sacred images of Thunderbirds, turtles and broken arrows, are thought to have been manufactured specifically as mortuary offerings. Similar motifs would almost certainly once have embellished tipi coverings, clothing and shields, but the mortuary offerings provide the only remaining evidence. Other objects placed with the dead include engraved shell gorgets, incised stone tablets and tubular stone pipes. Widespread trade networks are indicated by catlinite (red pipestone) from Minnesota, copper from Lake Superior, obsidian from Wyoming and dentalium shell from the Pacific coast. This burial complex appears to have lasted from about A.D. 900 to 1400, with some elements surviving into the historic period.

Ties clearly exist to the Mississippian culture of the lower Mississippi valley, which was undergoing a period of expansion and widespread influence. An incised design on a shell gorget from a southwestern Manitoba mound, depicting a human face with forked lines around the eyes (the "weeping eye" motif), is very similar to common images in Mississippian art. Conch shells for such gorgets must have been traded up the Mississippi River from the Gulf of Mexico. Recently, two similar shell gorgets with incised human faces were discovered in a cave in the Sweetgrass Hills of Montana, near the Alberta border; just to the north the Milk River drains into the Mississippi system. Syms (1977) speculates that the burial complex can be attributed to Siouan peoples who spread from the Eastern Woodlands into the northeastern Plains as part of the late prehistoric Mississippian expansion.

The Mississippian spread northward was made possible by improvements in their agricultural economy, particularly the development of a hardy variety of corn, capable of withstanding cold northern winters. Late prehistoric farming communities emerged along the Middle Missouri area of North and South Dakota, eventually giving rise to such historic peoples as the Mandan and Hidatsa. Crops of corn, beans, squash and sunflowers grown in the river valleys supported substantial village populations. The Canadian Plains, however, were too far north for such economies to thrive. None of the groups historically resident on the Canadian Plains practiced horticulture, although many traded for agricultural produce with the Mandan and other such groups to the south.

Archaeological evidence, however, shows that horticultural economies did exist in late precontact times as far north as southern Manitoba. The clearest picture comes from the Lochport site, on the Red River north of Winnipeg, at the northeastern edge of the Plains. As climatic conditions changed, the occupation at Lochport shifted from Plains bison hunters to Laurel and Blackduck fishermen, with a short-lived horticultural stage from about the thirteenth to fifteenth centuries A.D. Presence of the latter is indicated by distinctive pottery, bison scapula hoes and deep bell-shaped storage pits, all similar to those used by horticultural groups in the Middle Missouri area. Charred kernels of corn found in the storage pits provide the most convincing evidence for precontact horticulture. Similar, although less compelling, evidence comes from several sites in southwestern Manitoba, where Middle Missouri-style ceramics and scapula hoes have been found, but no preserved corn.

Throughout the late prehistoric period, the people of the Plains led a stable existence, following the bison on foot and using dogs as pack animals. Numerous campsites are evidence of their nomadic wanderings, and the variety of bison kill sites exhibits their hunting skills and ingenuity. This way of life, however, was to be rapidly and dramatically altered with the arrival of the horse and other European introductions beginning early in the eighteenth century.

ARCHAEOLOGICAL SITES ON THE PLAINS

Plains nomads left no substantial architecture, no monumental artworks, little in the way of enduring memorials to their presence. Most people who now dwell on the Canadian Plains have little idea of the ancient remains around them. Yet the Plains cultures, over thousands of years of wandering after the bison herds, left the landscape littered with traces of their passing. Even in this land of vast open spaces, however, the archaeological record is continually being diminished.

Bison kill sites are particularly well known. Both major types, jumps and

The cliffs at Head-Smashed-In, a bison kill site in southern Alberta.
Photo by author

pounds, required considerable preparation, including construction of long drive lines of piled rocks, wood or even dry bison dung to funnel the animals to the cliff or enclosure. Good locations were used repeatedly, providing a record of hunting techniques over time.

The Head-Smashed-In bison jump in southern Alberta has gained particular fame since its inclusion on the prestigious list of UNESCO World Heritage Sites. An interpretation centre was funded by the Alberta government and staffed by people from the nearby Blood and Peigan reserves. The bluffs at this location were used repeatedly for nearly 6000 years, from early Middle Prehistoric hunters to the historic Blackfoot tribes. The nearby Old Women's site spans the last 2000 years before European contact. Vast bison bone middens beneath the cliffs of these jumps attest to their efficiency. Artifacts are overwhelmingly projectile points used to finish off the wounded animals and choppers and knives used in butchering. While the jumps were in use and the heavy work of butchering and processing the carcasses was taking place, campsites would be established nearby.

In areas lacking such suitable cliffs, bison were driven into a corral constructed of logs, or a natural enclosure finished with logs or brush. At the Ramillies site, north of Medicine Hat in Alberta, stone drive lines led to a natural depression which had been enlarged and closed off on the downslope by an earthen wall topped with large rocks, a construction style apparently made necessary by the lack of nearby wood.

Various rock feature sites are among the most abundant archaeological remains on the Plains. Cairns, medicine wheels, effigy figures, drive lanes, tipi rings and other arrangements of boulders dot the surface of the Plains wherever they have escaped the plow and other disturbance. While the function of some seems clear, others are more difficult to interpret. Cairns may have served as grave markers, food caches, landmarks or for various unknown purposes. Ranging widely in size, they are found singly, in groups, or in association with other boulder sites. For example, the large British Block Cairn in southeastern Alberta is in the centre of a medicine

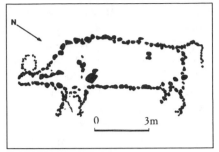

Top left and right: *Human and bison boulder effigy figures, southern Saskatchewan.* Courtesy Saskatchewan Museum of Natural History
Bottom: *Moose Mountain medicine wheel, southeastern Saskatchewan.* Courtesy Saskatchewan Museum of Natural History

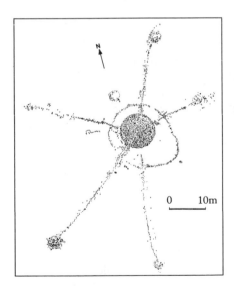

wheel, directly adjacent to a boulder effigy of a man and numerous tipi rings.

Medicine wheels are perhaps the most complex and enigmatic of the boulder sites. They generally consist of a large central cairn or circle, from which lines of stones radiate out like spokes, often with an outer stone circle and outlying cairns. A wide range of shapes, and presumably functions, is evident, leading Alberta archaeologist John Brumley to propose a classification with eight distinct subgroups. These structures are found only in the northwestern Plains, with their greatest concentration in Alberta. Although most are undated, excavation at the Majorville site in Alberta revealed that the large central mound had been built up gradually, beginning about 3000 B.C. Others, however, are relatively recent.

What roles in native life did these unique stone patterns play? Blackfoot informants have reported to several anthropologists that these were memorials to warrior chiefs. As a few were constructed well into this century, specific details could be gathered. All such Blackfoot memorials share a common plan—a stone circle with lines of stones radiating outward. The central circle (perhaps a pre-existing tipi ring) marked the position of the burial lodge where the deceased chief was left, with the radiating spokes being added as signs of respect. Brumley's excavation at a late prehistoric example revealed scattered human skeletal remains inside the central ring.

Other types of medicine wheels clearly served different functions. A major controversy emerged when astronomer John Eddy published his research on the Big Horn Medicine Wheel in northern Wyoming. According to Eddy, the Big Horn wheel, with its large central cairn and smaller cairns on the outer circle, had been constructed for calendric purposes—specifically to mark the position of the summer solstice and the three brightest stars of the midsummer dawn. His search for further examples led him to the Moose Mountain medicine wheel in southeastern Saskatchewan. Although differing in many respects, the pattern of cairns is similar, leading Eddy and others to postulate the same astronomical significance. Astroarchaeological research at other Canadian sites, however, failed to turn up significant alignments, and some researchers have challenged those for Big Horn and Moose Mountain.

Other anthropologists relate the wheels to the primary religious ceremonial of the Plains people, the Sun Dance, which was usually held around the time of the summer solstice. Some wheel types resemble an outline of the Sun Dance lodge—the outer circle being the wall of the lodge, the inner cairn representing the sacred central post and the spokes connecting them representing the rafters. Whether or not medicine wheels were astronomical observatories, they certainly featured in the religious lives of Plains Indians. Discoveries of *iniskim* (a Blackfoot word for small sacred stones, usually fossils, roughly in the shape of bison) and other small items in the central cairn at Majorville suggest that ritual offerings, possibly in the form of medicine bundles, were deposited there.

At other locations, boulders were carefully placed to form effigy figures. Humans and turtles were favourite themes, but Saskatchewan has one well-executed bison outline. Since these were constructed into historic times, some have specific events associated with them. Perhaps the best documented is on the Siksika (Blackfoot) reserve in Alberta, where a spread-eagled human figure lying along a trail of stones commemorates an 1872 duel between a Blood man and a Blackfoot, the stones marking the paths each took and the spot at which the former fell dead.

By far the most common of the boulder arrangements are simple stone circles, usually referred to as tipi rings. It is assumed that they were placed around the edges of the tipi to hold down skin covers. Recognition of this use dates to the mid-nineteenth century, when the explorer Henry Y. Hind referred to "the remains of ancient encampments, where the Plains Crees, in the day of their power and pride, had erected large skin tents, and strengthened them with rings of stones placed around the base" (1971, 1:338). In favourable locations for village sites they may occur in clusters of several hundred. Although some archaeologists have questioned this function, their sheer abundance seems to preclude anything other than domestic use.

Rock art sites, including both petroglyphs (incised designs) and pictographs (paintings), occur in small numbers across the Plains. Petroglyphs are by far the most common, ranging from pictures lightly scratched on cliff faces to deeply pecked and grooved designs on large boulders. Humans and animals predominate, although the most common depiction at the St. Victor petroglyphs in southern Saskatchewan is a variety of animal footprints. The boulder petroglyph "ribstones," most common in Alberta, are covered with a pattern of grooves and pits, presumably representing bison.

The outstanding rock art site on the Canadian Plains is Writing-On-Stone in southern Alberta. The soft sandstone walls of the Milk River Valley provided an excellent surface for native artists to incise (and, much more rarely, paint) scenes of war and the hunt. Although these cliffs were no doubt used over a long period of time, erosion has removed all but the more recent glyphs. Still, several styles can be discerned. The presumably earlier depictions are carefully incised animal and human figures, the latter often hidden behind round shields and associated with a bow tipped with a spearpoint. Possibly these images were created in the final centuries before European contact by individuals attracted to this supernaturally charged area while on vision quests. Other glyphs, often only lightly scratched into the soft cliffs, depict warriors on horseback, occasionally with rifles and long headdresses, and are clearly historic. Several panels show complex battle scenes. These have been interpreted as indicating the arrival of the Blackfoot, who used the convenient cliffs to record their war exploits.

Any unusual landmark could inspire veneration, and small offerings which were left at such locations might be all that would identify them to

Native artists left numerous images in the soft sandstone cliffs at Writing-On-Stone, along the Milk River valley of southern Alberta (top), *including shield-warriors with bows* (bottom left) *and a mounted hunter pursuing an animal* (bottom right). Photos by author

the archaeologist. Huge boulders, often weighing many tons, were carried from the north by Pleistocene glaciers, then dumped on the otherwise featureless prairie when the ice retreated. Such conspicuous objects were "medicine stones," considered sacred by the Plains natives. One boulder in Saskatchewan inspired several Cree legends due to its resemblance to a huge recumbent bison. H.Y. Hind recorded in 1857 that natives were leaving "offerings to Manitou," such as "beads, bits of tobacco, fragments of cloth, and other trifles" at such locations.

THE PROTOHISTORIC–
EARLY HISTORIC PERIOD

The arrival of the horse by the mid-eighteenth century transformed pedestrian hunters into the mounted nomads of popular image. In many locations, when the first European explorers arrived they found horseback warriors already in possession of the Plains. The term protohistoric was coined to cover the brief period of dramatic changes in aboriginal cultures due to European introductions, widely distributed through aboriginal patterns of trade and warfare, before the arrival of Europeans themselves. However, since many early European expeditions briefly traversed the northern Plains, the protohistoric overlaps with the early historic, and the two will be taken together to cover the period from first introduction of the horse to the beginning of continuous European contact slightly more than a century later.

The horse, originally acquired from Spanish settlements in the Southwest, was a feature of southern Plains life as early as 1640. Trade and raiding spread use of the horse to the northern edge of the Plains within a century. While we lack specific information on when most tribes acquired horses, historic records give a reasonably clear picture for the Assiniboine. In 1738, when La Vérendrye accompanied an Assiniboine trading party, they lacked horses. When Anthony Henday traveled with a similar party sixteen years later, they had a few horses for packing goods but not for riding. In 1776, Alexander Henry described considerable numbers of horses among the Assiniboine and their use in mounted warfare. The Blackfoot were well provided with horses at a slightly earlier date; however, northern groups such as the Plains Cree remained "horse poor" well into the nineteenth century.

Within a generation Plains natives had become masters of horsemanship, riding as if the animal had always been a part of their lives. No longer did they need to wait until bison approached the pounds; now hunters on their favourite mounts could ride among the shaggy beasts, selecting the animal to be felled with an arrow. Warriors and hunters ranged more widely across the Plains than had previously been possible, bringing them into greater conflict with other groups. Warfare became continuous, providing young men with opportunities for glory and excitement. Horse raiding was not considered theft but an act of bravery which could be proudly recounted, and it was an important way of obtaining additional mounts. Use of the horse allowed accumulated wealth, since a horse could transport many more personal possessions than was possible with dogs. These new conditions fostered larger social groups and increased interactions with others, resulting in more elaborate political and religious institutions. Plains societies as they are historically known emerged during this brief cultural florescence.

Arriving at about the same time as the horse were the rifle and other European trade goods. These came from the east, brought primarily by the Cree and Assiniboine, who had the strongest ties to the fur traders. As they spread into the Plains, great population dislocations ensued. Smallpox and other European diseases also appeared, with periodic epidemics sweeping across the Plains at least as early as 1781.

The location of the Plains tribes immediately prior to the horse and gun has been the subject of considerable debate. The Blackfoot appear to have the only claim to antiquity on the Canadian Plains, yet historic records show that they were once northeast of their present location, in the parkland along the North Saskatchewan River. The Plains Cree, Plains Ojibwa, Assiniboine and Sarcee all moved onto the Plains in this late period, displacing earlier occupants such as the Gros Ventre.

Other major population movements were taking place to the south as horticulturists abandoned their tedious tasks for the greater excitement of the mounted nomad's lifestyle. Many of the Dakota left their gardens and wild rice plots in Minnesota to move west and adopt all the trappings of early historic Plains culture. Along the Middle Missouri of North and South Dakota, although the Mandan and Hidatsa maintained their horticultural economy and palisaded villages of earth-covered lodges well into the historic period, others found the new attractions of Plains life too compelling. The Crow, for example, emerged during this period as an offshoot of the Hidatsa, moving west onto the high plains as nomadic warriors and hunters. While their new homeland was in Montana and Wyoming, occasional forays took them as far north as southern Alberta and Saskatchewan.

A few earthlodge villagers apparently penetrated this far north. In 1801, Peter Fidler of the Hudson's Bay Company discovered three "Mud Houses" on the South Saskatchewan River. He estimated that they were about twenty years old, and stated that "they are said to have been built by a small war party from the Missouri River, who live in these kinds of habitations." The only major excavated archaeological example is the Blackfoot Crossing Fortified Village (formerly known as the Cluny site), along the Bow River on the modern Siksika reserve. Here a large semicircular trench, ending along the riverbank, encloses eleven small pits and a palisade wall. The artifacts are predominantly pottery sherds of Middle Missouri style and reveal no evidence of agriculture. Despite the great effort required to dig the trench and construct the palisade, the site was apparently occupied only briefly around 1740. Its occupants may have been the Crow or a similar people, in the process of transition from earthlodge villagers to high plains nomads. Remains of several similar, but apparently much later, fortified encampments in southwestern Manitoba have been attributed to the arrival of the Dakota in the 1860s.

THE ETHNOGRAPHIC CULTURES

The horse and bison days were long over by the time ethnographers began their studies of Plains cultures early in this century. The memories of their oldest informants could reach back no further than the mid-nineteenth century. Ethnographic descriptions refer to the few decades prior to the final destruction of the bison herds in the early 1880s, as revealed through the writings of European observers and the "memory culture" of elderly informants who shared their knowledge with early anthropologists.

Throughout their entire history Plains natives relied on the bison, adapting their lives to following the herds. The hunting techniques described in the ethnographic accounts, however, differed somewhat from those employed for thousands of years previously.

Both jumps and pounds continued to be used long after the arrival of the horse. The Blackfoot occasionally drove bison over cliffs, such as at Head-Smashed-In, well into historic times. The Plains Cree and Assiniboine continued to rely heavily on pounds, particularly for the winter hunt. Long drive lines of stone or brush led to a stout corral, which was ringed with people holding hides to make the construction seem more substantial than it actually was. Cree use of a pound was vividly described by H.Y. Hind, who witnessed the scene in 1857:

> In hunting the buffalo they are wild with excitement, but no scene or incident seems to have such a maddening effect upon them as when the buffalo are successfully driven into a pound. Until the herd is brought in by the skilled hunters, the utmost silence is preserved around the fence of the pound: men, women, and children, with pent-up feelings, hold their robes so as to close every orifice through which the terrified animals might endeavour to escape. The herd once in the pound, a scene of diabolical butchery and excitement begins; men, women, and children climb on the fence, and shoot arrows or thrust spears at the bewildered buffalo, with shouts, screams, and yells horrible to hear.
>
> (Hind 1971, 2:142)

Most of the time the Plains tribes preferred to hunt bison from horseback. This eliminated the tedious task of constructing corrals or drive lines and allowed hunters to range widely in search of the herds. Groups of men might attempt to surround the animals or race down upon them in an organized charge. The skill of the hunters in selecting and killing the beasts during a high-speed chase is shown in a 1792 eyewitness account by Peter Fidler:

> Men killed several Cows by running them upon Horseback & shooting them with arrows. They are so expert at this business that they will ride along side

Cree buffalo pound near Fort Carleton, observed by the artist Paul Kane in 1846.
ROM

of the Cow they mean to kill & while at full gallop will shoot an arrow into her heart & kill her upon the spot. Sometimes when they happen to miss their proper aim (which is very seldom) they will ride close up to the Buffalo . . . at full gallop & draw the arrow out & again shoot with it.

(Verbicky-Todd 1984:144)

Bows and arrows were preferred over the traders' guns, which were difficult to load on the gallop and scared the animals with their noise. Arrows were marked, so the hunters could later identify their kills.

The hunter's prize possession was his "buffalo horse," a swift and agile mount which was carefully trained. "Running buffalo" was a dangerous pursuit, and accidents were common in the noise, dust and confusion. The horses had to run alongside bison without stumbling on the uneven terrain or into the gopher holes which pockmarked the prairies. Occasional charges by enraged bulls were an additional menace. Any mistake could result in both horse and rider being gored or trampled.

Successful hunts required group discipline. A large communal hunt could be ruined if a few individuals dispersed the herd while taking provisions for themselves. Warrior societies enforced hunting restrictions. Offenders might be beaten or might have their weapons smashed, their clothes and tipi covers torn, and their dogs and horses killed. Harsh punishments were necessary so that the welfare of all would not be jeopardized by the actions of a few.

Rituals were also important to ensure success on the hunt. The Assiniboine and Plains Cree conducted an elaborate ceremony to dedicate

Assiniboine Indians running buffalo, painted by Paul Kane from his travels in the 1840s. ROM

each newly constructed pound and raised a "medicine pole" in the centre from which offerings were suspended. Singing and prayers were essential to draw the bison near.

Both men and women set to work after a successful hunt. Hides were stripped off carcasses, later to be laboriously transformed by the women into clothing, tipi covers or other useful items. Workers might satisfy their immediate hunger with bits of raw liver or kidney and the sweet fat from the hump. Tongues, a favoured delicacy, might be reserved for the owner of the pound, the ritualist who claimed responsibility for the kills, or for a communal feast. Meat was set aside, marrow extracted from the long bones and sinews saved for later use. One communal hunt could yield a large quantity of meat, and a great feast ensued at which all could gorge themselves.

Meat was prepared in several ways. If it was to be eaten immediately, it was roasted over the fire or boiled in a pit lined with bison hide into which water and hot stones were placed (the name "Stoney" for the Canadian Assiniboine comes from this practice). Some was cut into thin strips and dried for later consumption. It could also be made into pemmican by drying, pounding into a coarse powder and mixing with melted fat; occasionally, dried saskatoon berries were added as well. This mixture was cooled and sewn into bison-hide bags, where it would preserve indefinitely, providing lightweight and nutritious supplies for warriors and hunters setting out on long journeys.

Bison were the mainstay of life, but other animals were hunted. Elk and

Top: *Assiniboines with painted tipi.* NAC C26461
Left: *Inside a Peigan tipi.* NAC C24490

deer were available along the foothills and parklands, and pronghorn antelope existed in huge numbers across the grasslands. Their hides were particularly valued for the manufacture of clothing.

Although there was a strong emphasis on meat, the diet was enriched
with a variety of plant foods. Women worked in the vicinity of the camp,
collecting berries and digging for edible roots. The most important root was
the wild turnip, which was eaten raw, roasted, boiled or pounded into flour
used for thickening soup. Other wild plants were collected for medicinal or
other use.

The only historic example of plant cultivation on the Canadian Plains
was the Blackfoot practice of maintaining small plots of tobacco. Seeds were
placed in the medicine bags of ritualists, who ceremonially planted them in
the spring. Then the small plots were abandoned for the bison hunt, people
returning only to harvest their crop. Other Plains groups smoked the leaves
of several wild plants, in later times mixing these with expensive trade
tobacco.

Essential to the nomadic lifestyle were the tipi and travois. The conical

A Blackfoot couple with horse-drawn travois.
NAC C26182

bison-hide tipi was supported on a framework of poles fastened at the top. The cover, carefully prepared and sewn by the women, required between eight and twenty hides. Flaps at the top helped control smoke from the central fire (although during summer people preferred to do their cooking outdoors). An inside liner provided insulation and protected the occupants from drafts. Clothing, weapons and bags of food were hung from the lodge poles, and sleeping robes were laid out around the walls, serving as couches during the day. The place of honour, reserved for the head of the family, was opposite the door flap. When the camp was set to move, the tipi could be taken down quickly and packed with other possessions on a travois, a framework of poles. Originally designed to be pulled by dogs, the travois was quickly adapted to the horse, allowing larger tipis and more numerous possessions.

The need for mobility was also reflected in social organization. Each tribal group was divided into a number of independent bands, which were the basic social groups throughout most of the year. Band chiefs led by virtue of their wisdom or success in the hunt and required the support and respect of their people. Decisions were made by consensus, the chief hoping to persuade others through oratory and example rather than by direct orders. Good leaders might attract large followings, while those who lacked skill or experienced misfortune might find their band depleted as members drifted away to other camps. In addition to this political leader, each band had a war chief, who assumed control over military matters.

Large tribal gatherings were usually held in midsummer, when bison were concentrated in large herds. A tribal bison hunt might be held, but primary concern was with the major religious ceremony, the Sun Dance, and celebrations of the military societies. These were the integrating mechanisms which drew separate bands into a tribal society. Tribal organization was most fully developed among the Blackfoot and weakest among the mixed bands of Plains Cree, Plains Ojibwa and Assiniboine.

A Peigan warrior. NAC C24487

The image of Plains society portrayed in both popular and academic writing is overwhelmingly a masculine one. Men were the hunters and warriors in a society obsessed with bison and battles. Does this image accurately reflect Plains societies or is it a product created by male observers and male anthropologists? A woman of unquestioned virtue was highly respected and played a central role in several important ceremonies. While much of the women's time was spent in the drudgery of scraping and tanning hides to make clothing and tipi covers, it was the women who owned the hides and tipis. Men, however, were the undisputed heads of their households, expecting the women to perform all menial tasks. Many men took several wives, but this was often requested by the women to ease the burden of household duties. The greater number of women, as a result of male casualties in warfare, encouraged such an arrangement. A troublesome wife could be sent back to her family, and an adulterous one could be killed, beaten or disfigured by having the end of her nose cut off. Several nineteenth-century observers noted that women with mutilated noses were not an uncommon sight in Blackfoot camps.

The tailored hide clothing consisted of shirt, breechcloth, leggings and moccasins for men, and long dresses, leggings and moccasins for women. Bison-hide robes and fur caps were added in winter. Cut fringes and dyed porcupine quill embroidery adorned their finest apparel, along with scalplocks on warrior's shirts and rows of elk teeth on women's dresses. Both sexes greased and painted their faces, both for beauty and in response to visions. Tattooing was practiced by the Plains Cree, the men having their upper bodies tattooed, while women were restricted to lines on the chin. The hair was greased and arranged in a variety of styles, young men in particular spending considerable time on this aspect of their appearance. Eagle feathers were occasionally worn in the hair, and the association with military honours appears to have been traditional. However, the long trailing eagle feather headdresses of the popular stereotype were a very late introduction, entering Canada with the Dakota near the end of the horse and bison days.

Many items of everyday use were embellished with painting. Tipi covers and shields commonly bore depictions of bison or other images suggested in visions. Other items, such as the folded rawhide containers (*parfleches*), were painted with geometric designs. The Plains Cree, Plains Ojibwa and Métis preferred the floral motifs of the Eastern Woodlands over traditional Plains geometric designs, and such patterns, particularly in beadwork, predominated over much of the Plains in this late period.

Warfare was a passion, and the only route to prestige for a young man. The honour of dying in battle was impressed upon boys from an early age. Times of peace were rare, and even then a chief had difficulty restraining young men from setting out on raids. Such expeditions ranged from small groups attempting to steal horses from enemy camps to large war parties organized to take booty (horses, guns, scalps) or revenge. Some groups became embroiled in warfare lasting generations, as each side sought revenge for previous losses. No male prisoners were taken, and each man fought to the death, attempting to inflict as much injury as possible on his foe.

War honours were based on the degree of courage displayed. Warriors attempted to count *coup* on their enemies (from a French word, meaning "a blow"). Greatest honours came from striking an enemy, with the fist, a club or a special *coup* stick. Killing an enemy at a distance was not particularly meritorious; the body had to be actually touched. Taking an enemy's gun or scalping a fallen foe bestowed honour, while stealing a horse was so common that it was considered a lesser achievement. Brave deeds were publicly recounted and often depicted on tipi covers. Such honours were essential if a young man aspired to chieftainship, or if he wished to have the admiration of his comrades and the attention of young women.

Blackfoot men were organized into a series of warrior societies based on age. As they grew older, each group of age-mates advanced through the levels, purchasing the regalia and learning the rituals of each successive society. The Plains Cree, on the other hand, had only a single society, to which entry was gained by a valorous deed. The societies kept order in the camp and on the hunt and guarded against enemy attack. Their rituals strengthened group solidarity and fostered a pride in military prowess. The Blackfoot Brave Dogs, for example, had to demonstrate bravery and contempt for death, never retreating from the enemy in battle. The Blackfoot also had a women's society, where women represented bison in dances to honour the spirits of this essential animal.

Religion permeated everyday life. The universe was filled with supernatural beings, each having the power to help or harm. Manifestations of spiritual power, which could include any unusual object, such as a large rock or a strangely twisted tree, were termed *manitou* among the Algonkians and *wakan* among the Siouan-speakers. Young people sought spiritual power by fasting and praying in secluded locations, hoping a supernatural helper would come to them in a vision. Such helpers might bestow certain powers, give a song or ritual to perform, or details of how to paint the face or tipi, and provided life-long assistance if their instructions were followed. Shamans received their power to cure through such spirit encounters.

Sacred objects, many representing gifts from supernatural encounters, were carefully wrapped in a medicine bundle. Contents might include skins of various animals, eagle feathers, braided sweetgrass used for incense, fossils or other supernaturally charged stones and a variety of other items whose significance was known only to the owner. Particularly important were sacred pipestems contained in bundles. Smoking was a method of communicating with the supernatural, so sacred pipestems were brought out to aid the sick, to settle quarrels or to bless those setting out on war parties. Like a portable shrine, the bundle could be hung outside on a tripod in fine weather. Opening the bundle required elaborate ceremonies, as did its transfer to a new owner, each object being reverently displayed while prayers and songs invoked the spiritual power associated with it.

The most important religious festival of the Plains tribes was the Sun Dance (actually a misnomer since it was not a ritual to the Sun; the Cree called it the "Thirsting Dance"). It was held during the summer, when large encampments assembled. All Plains groups shared the basic ritual, although considerable tribal variation was evident. Among the Blackfoot and Sarcee, it was a virtuous woman who sponsored the ceremony, in response to a vow she took at a time of crisis, as when illness threatened her family. Among the Plains Cree and Ojibwa, it was a man who might pledge to hold a Sun Dance if he returned safely from a war expedition.

Sun Dance ceremonies began with construction of the lodge. While the sponsor fasted, warriors cut down a suitable tree to serve as the sacred central pole, counting coup on it as if it were a fallen foe. Its erection at the camp was a time of celebration. The Plains Cree and Ojibwa constructed a "thunderbird nest" of branches at the top, and all groups hung cloth and other offerings from it. Painted or incised thunderbirds, bison skulls or other vision images might adorn the pole, and an altar with a painted bison skull and sweetgrass incense was placed near its base. Rafters from the central pole rested on the circle of posts and beams that made up the outer wall.

When the leafy branches completing the lodge wall were in place, dances

Blackfoot Sun Dance, ca. 1887. Skewers through the flesh of the dancer's chest are attached by thongs to the central pole, while a shield is suspended by thongs from his back. NAC C49476

could begin. Dancers were those who had made lesser vows, often continuing to perform, without food, water or sleep, for the several days of the ceremony. They danced in place, moving to the rhythm of chanted prayers, blowing on eagle-bone whistles and keeping their gaze fixed on the top of the central pole. This was the time when young men, also in fulfillment of vows, had the muscles of their chests pierced and wooden skewers pushed through. Ropes tied to the skewers were attached to the central pole. The young men danced while leaning back on the ropes until they tore free. Sometimes the muscles of the back were also cut, and heavy bison skulls hung from wooden skewers. Men proudly bore the scars of such ordeals through the rest of their lives. The days of the Sun Dance strengthened people in their shared faith, and the gathering of bands allowed such social activities as visiting friends, courting, gambling and horse racing.

In Plains mythology, a common theme was the trickster/transformer. The Plains Cree brought *Wisakedjak* from their original Subarctic homeland, telling of his actions which put the world in its present order. Among the Blackfoot, *Napi* ("Old Man") was the major legendary figure. While spoken of in respectful terms in some stories, such as those of creation, in others he is seen as foolish or spiteful. The basic Algonkian pattern is evident in myths from the Rocky Mountains to the Atlantic; the Sarcee and Assiniboine had similar stories due to close association with the Algonkians. The myths enlivened the cold winter evenings, as the occupants of the tipi sat around the central fire, listening to elders recount the ancient stories.

When a person died, the body was placed in a tree or on a scaffold. Men of distinction, however, were left in their lodges with their valued possessions. Several of the man's favourite horses might be shot to accompany him into the spirit world. Mourners cut their hair and wore old clothes. A man might leave immediately on a war party, attempting to ease his grief by striking at the enemy without regard for risk to his own life. A woman, in extremes of anguish for the loss of a husband or child, might gash her legs or chop off a finger joint. The Blackfoot believed that the soul of the deceased departed for the Sand Hills, a rather bleak sandy area to the east. There they existed much as they had in life. The hunters continued to pursue bison for their sustenance, this animal being essential to the Plains natives even in death.

THE BLACKFOOT AND THEIR ALLIES

At the height of their power the Blackfoot held a vast area from the North Saskatchewan River to the Missouri River, covering much of modern Alberta and Montana. Most of their territory was the short-grass high plains, although they also hunted in the foothills and eastern margins of the Rocky Mountains. The Blackfoot valued bison far above any other game, referring to its flesh as "real meat." Populous and aggressive, Blackfoot tribes were the major military force of the northwestern Plains.

The Blackfoot Nation comprised three tribes—the Siksika (literally "black feet," from a legend of walking across burned prairie), the Blood or Kainai (meaning "many chiefs") and the Peigan or Pikuni ("scabby robes," from a legend in which the women had not properly prepared the hides). Earliest historic evidence indicates that the Siksika were in the north, along the North Saskatchewan River, while the Blood were along the Red Deer and the Peigan on the Bow. Pressure from the Cree and Assiniboine pushed them south until the Siksika were on the Bow and the Blood and Peigan in southernmost Alberta, the latter extending well into Montana. Although sharing the same language and customs, and frequently intermarrying, they remained three separate tribes, closely allied in warfare despite occasional internal feuds. When all three camped together, they formed their tipis into separate camp circles, each with its own chief. Their common name, Blackfoot, reflects only the fact that the traders reached the northernmost group first, and does not correspond to any native concept of unity.

The term Blackfoot Confederacy usually includes their close allies, the Sarcee. This small Athapaskan tribe originated far to the north, venturing out onto the Plains not long before the fur traders encountered them in the late eighteenth century. Traditions recount a common origin with the Beaver Indians of the Subarctic. In one legend, it was a feud between two chiefs that divided the people. In another, as the original group attempted to cross a frozen river the ice broke; those who had already crossed became

Crowfoot (ca. 1830-90), head chief of the Blackfoot.
NAC PA124101

the Sarcee and those who remained behind were the Beaver. The Sarcee drifted south into the parklands and foothills at the edge of the Plains, eventually allying with the Blackfoot and moving with them onto the high plains of southern Alberta. They intermarried with the Blackfoot and adopted the military societies, religious practices and other customs of their allies, retaining only their separate identity and their Athapaskan language.

Also considered part of the Blackfoot Confederacy were the Gros Ventre or Atsina. Closely related to the Arapaho, Algonkian-speakers inhabiting southern Wyoming and northern Colorado, they split off and moved north onto the Canadian Plains. The early fur traders met them in west-central Saskatchewan, already firmly allied with the Blackfoot. They took the brunt of attacks from the Cree and Assiniboine, eventually being forced south into Montana. A dispute over stolen horses in 1861 broke the alliance, turning them into enemies of the Blackfoot.

Hostile tribes surrounded the Blackfoot Confederacy. In the early eighteenth century, the Blackfoot were on friendly terms with the Assiniboine and Plains Cree, seeking their aid in driving the "Snakes" out of southern Alberta. The Kutenai were also in southern Alberta at this time, eventually being pushed west of the Rocky Mountains by the Blackfoot, although sporadic warfare continued as the Kutenai sought to hunt bison on the Plains. By the beginning of the nineteenth century, as the Cree and Assiniboine pushed west and encroached on Blackfoot lands, they became embroiled in bitter hostilities. Warfare became continual on the western Plains until the reserve period. The last major battle between the Blackfoot and Cree was fought near Fort Whoop-Up (modern Lethbridge, Alberta) in 1870.

The fur trade affected the Blackfoot far less than the Cree and Assiniboine. Since their arid plains had few fur-bearing animals, there was little incentive for traders to establish posts among them. The Blackfoot were not interested in trapping and confined their trade with whites to bison robes and dried meat. Anthony Henday, sent by the Hudson's Bay Company to persuade the western tribes to bring furs to York Factory, was told by the Blackfoot that "it was far off, and they could not live without Buffalo flesh."

As declining bison herds brought the horse and bison days to a close, the Blackfoot were obliged to sign Treaty No. 7 in 1877 and eventually to settle on reserves. The Blackfoot proper, today known as the Siksika Nation, occupy a reserve along the Bow River east of Calgary. The Blood are to the south, on a large reserve along the Belly River, west of Lethbridge. The Peigan, originally the largest of the three tribes, became separated into two groups. The northern Peigan hold a smaller reserve to the west of the Blood, while the southern division occupies the Blackfeet Reservation in northern Montana. The small Sarcee tribe, now officially known as the Tsuu T'ina Nation, received land on the Bow, today adjoining the city of Calgary. The total Canadian Blackfoot population is now about 15,000, while the Sarcee number about 1100.

THE PLAINS CREE AND PLAINS OJIBWA

Much of eastern Canada, from the Great Lakes to Hudson Bay and Labrador, was dominated by the numerous bands of the Cree and Ojibwa people. With the expansion of the fur trade to the west, many moved onto the Plains and adopted a new lifestyle. In 1730, when La Vérendrye traveled through Manitoba, he encountered "Cree of the Mountains, Prairies and Rivers," indicating that some bands were already established on the Plains. The western Ojibwa, termed Saulteaux or Bungi, arrived even later, searching for new lands where furs were plentiful. Eventually, armed with European weapons obtained in trade on Hudson Bay and allied with the Assiniboine, the Cree pushed across the northern Plains to the Rockies. Other groups were displaced in front of them until smallpox and the acquisition of firearms by their enemies finally halted their advance.

The Plains Cree, along with their Assiniboine allies, established themselves as middlemen between the posts on Hudson Bay and the western tribes. Huge profits could be made by taking furs to the posts and bringing back European goods to trade to more distant groups. Later, when the companies established posts across the Plains, the Cree and Ojibwa became major suppliers of pemmican and bison hides. Their close association with the fur trade led to the rise of the Métis, from unions between male fur traders and Cree or Ojibwa women.

Many of the Plains Cree and Ojibwa remained an "edge of the forest" people, preferring the parkland environment along the north and east of

"Kee-a-kee-ka-sa-coo-way," or "Man who gives the War-whoop," a Cree chief painted by Paul Kane, 1848. ROM

the Plains. From the shelter of the woods they could venture out onto the Plains in pursuit of bison. Some bands eventually established themselves as full-time residents of the open prairies.

Despite their Plains lifestyle, these people did not completely abandon their Woodlands heritage. Fish continued to be important in the diet of most groups, although those bands more fully adapted to Plains life began to develop the prairie nomad's scorn of such food. They were regarded as particularly potent conjurers, other tribes seeking their medicines and "love charms." The Plains Ojibwa even maintained the curing rituals of the Midewiwin (see Chapter 5). They introduced floral designs of the Woodlands to the art of the Plains, mixing it with older geometric patterns. The Plains Ojibwa in particular remained a Woodlands people, retaining their religion and folklore almost intact, while adopting what was necessary for a Plains bison-hunting existence and accepting such dramatic rituals as the Sun Dance.

Even before their arrival on the Plains, the Cree were closely allied with the Assiniboine. Their alliance continued on the Plains, with territories overlapping in what is today southern Saskatchewan. They camped together, hunted together and intermarried. Many were bilingual. Some bands became so intermixed that they have been cited as examples of "fused ethnicity"—that is, they were neither Cree nor Assiniboine, but a new hybrid identity. Mid-nineteenth-century accounts describe large camps for bison hunts or the Sun Dance consisting of Assiniboine, Cree, Ojibwa and Métis.

Unlike the Blackfoot, the Plains Cree and Ojibwa lacked a strong tribal organization to tie together their numerous widespread bands. Today they are scattered in small reserves across all three prairie provinces. The Plains Ojibwa tend to be concentrated in Manitoba and eastern Saskatchewan, while the Plains Cree are more numerous in Saskatchewan and Alberta. Cree reserves are frequently shared with the Assiniboine or Ojibwa.

THE ASSINIBOINE AND DAKOTA

The Assiniboine speak a dialect of the Dakota language in the Siouan stock. Originally part of the Yanktonai Dakota in the woodlands of Minnesota, the people who were to become the Assiniboine split off and moved north after a violent internal clash. They first enter historic records as a distinct group in 1640, when they were mentioned in the *Jesuit Relations*.

In the mid-seventeenth century, they were a woodland people, occupying the area around Lake of the Woods and Lake Winnipeg. Already they were involved in the fur trade, supplying furs through Algonkian intermediaries for the French trade on the St. Lawrence. When the Hudson's Bay Company opened its northern posts later in the century, the Assiniboine, along with their Cree allies and trading partners, began long journeys to York Factory on Hudson Bay. As the trade moved west, the Assiniboine spread across the Plains, into Saskatchewan, Alberta and Montana. There they abandoned almost all vestiges of their Woodlands origins, becoming Plains warriors and bison hunters *par excellence*.

With their allies the Plains Cree, the Assiniboine waged continual war against the tribes of the Blackfoot Confederacy to the west. To the south, the bitter enmity with their Dakota relatives simmered for centuries. War parties of Assiniboine, Plains Cree and Plains Ojibwa combined to do battle with these foes.

Several bands of Assiniboine, generally known as the Stoney, pushed west to the Rockies, where they battled the Blackfoot for possession of the foothills and eastern mountain slopes. There they hunted bison on the Plains, elk and other large game in the mountains, and traded at posts such as Rocky Mountain House. They continued to hold this bountiful land, separated from all other Assiniboine and their allies by the hostile Blackfoot, until forced by the Canadian government to join their mortal enemies in ceding their land under Treaty No. 7. Today they occupy several reserves in western Alberta, the largest being at Morley, between Calgary and Banff.

The Sioux or Dakota remaining south of the border after the Assiniboine split also began a movement west onto the Plains. However, not all abandoned their Woodlands heritage. Three large divisions, each containing several major political units, had emerged by historic times. The eastern groups, collectively called the Santee, remained in Minnesota, hunting, fishing, collecting wild rice and growing small plots of corn. From these traditional lands, they continued their age-old wars against the Ojibwa. The central groups, the Yankton and Yanktonai, lived on the edge of the Plains,

hunting bison but also fishing and raising crops. On the west, in South
Dakota, the Teton lived as typical Plains bison hunters and warriors. These
were the people who brought Plains culture to its greatest elaboration, and
who, under such famed nineteenth-century chiefs as Sitting Bull and Crazy
Horse, became among the best known of North American Indians.

The commonly used term "Sioux" comes from a French version of an
Ojibwa word for "snakes" or, metaphorically, "enemies." Their own word
"Dakota" ("allies") has been adopted by most anthropologists to avoid the
pejorative term and to eliminate confusion with the larger Siouan linguistic
stock. However, the language has three dialects and only the Santee called
themselves Dakota. Among the central groups, from whom the Assiniboine
sprung, the dialect replaces "d" with "n"; hence the self-designation
"Nakota." Similarly, the Teton, whose dialect uses an "l", call themselves
"Lakota." Nevertheless, "Dakota" has become the collective term for both
the people and their language.

Dakota hunters and war parties frequently ranged north into Canada.
Alexander Henry's Plains Ojibwa traveling companions warned of constant
danger from the Dakota. He recorded Dakota attacks against the Cree on
the Red River in 1800 and the Plains Ojibwa at Portage la Prairie in 1806.
These clashes were uncomfortably close to the new settlements on the Red
River. However, it was decades later before the Dakota arrived in large
numbers, intending to stay.

The ill-fated Minnesota Uprising of 1862 led to the first large movement
of American Dakota refugees into Canada. After their defeat by American
soldiers, many Santee dispersed from their homeland. Some fled west to the
Tetons, while several thousand drifted northwest into Manitoba. Initially,
they clustered around Fort Garry, joining the Métis in their bison hunt and
trying to avoid hostilities with their traditional enemies, the Plains Ojibwa.
Later, many continued to the northwest, following the declining bison
herds into Saskatchewan, and to the northern edge of the Plains.

The second arrival of Dakota refugees involved the warlike Teton and
their famed chief Sitting Bull. The Teton had signed a treaty with the
American government in 1868 and were given "forever" the land around
their sacred Black Hills in South Dakota. The discovery of gold in the Black
Hills in 1874 meant that forever lasted only six years. Realizing the futility
of further negotiations, the Dakota and Cheyenne prepared for war. In perhaps the most famous battle of all North American Indian wars, the Dakota
annihilated Custer's Seventh Cavalry at Little Big Horn. Realizing that they
could not continue to hold out against American military might, the
Dakota fled north, hoping that the British reputation for justice would
result in fairer treatment. By the end of 1876, nearly three thousand
Dakota were camped around the Cypress Hills and Wood Mountain in
southwestern Saskatchewan, to be joined the following spring by Sitting
Bull and remnants of his victorious army.

The presence of so many warriors on the border caused great consternation. Would the Teton use Canada as a safe base to continue their war with the American military? Would intertribal warfare break out as the Teton competed with their enemies—the Blackfoot, Cree and Assiniboine—for the dwindling bison herds? This explosive situation was defused by the newly formed North West Mounted Police, who maintained order and ascertained that the Teton sought only sanctuary and an opportunity to settle peacefully in this new land.

Such an opportunity was to be denied them. Although the Santee Dakota had been allowed to remain in Canada only a decade before, much had changed in the intervening years. Law and order had been brought to the Canadian west, and the vanishing bison herds would no longer support the lifestyle of nomadic hunters. Denied reserves and rations, the Teton were eventually starved out. Sitting Bull himself held on until 1881, when he reluctantly returned to the United States. Only a few families remained at Wood Mountain, determined to hold on to their new life in Canada.

Since the Canadian government regarded the Dakota as refugees without claim to lands in Canada, they were not included in the treaties signed with other Plains tribes. Eventually, however, they were assigned reserves. Today, ten Dakota bands in Manitoba and Saskatchewan have a total population of about 5500 people. Most are descendants of the Santee who arrived in the 1860s; only the small community at Wood Mountain remains of the Teton presence in Canada. In addition, the Assiniboine, occupying reserves in southern Saskatchewan and Alberta, have a population of about 7500.

THE LATE HISTORIC AND CONTEMPORARY CULTURES

The destruction of the bison herds struck at the very lifeblood of the Plains cultures. Wanton slaughter by non-Indians for meat, hides and sport, plus the huge hunts organized by the Métis, left few animals for the competing Plains tribes. The prairies were systematically cleared for European settlement and agriculture. The final disappearance of the herds by the early 1880s was the death knell for the traditional cultures of the Plains nomads.

Smallpox and other European diseases also took a great toll. Epidemics continued at periodic intervals until late in the nineteenth century. The terrible plague of 1781 is estimated to have killed half of the Blackfoot, and a subsequent epidemic in 1837 wiped out nearly two thirds of those remaining. As late as 1869, a major smallpox epidemic devastated the Plains tribes, nearly exterminating the already-diminished Sarcee.

American whiskey traders arrived to prey upon the weakened and demoralized natives. Fort Whoop-Up, established among the Blackfoot in 1870, was the earliest and most notorious of the whiskey posts. While

American law prohibited trade in alcohol to the natives, there was nothing to restrain traders from moving north of the border. Here they exchanged their foul brew for bison hides, dispensing to the natives a near-lethal concoction of watered-down alcohol mixed with chewing tobacco, molasses, ink, pain-killer and anything else at hand. Drunken brawls and murders soon became commonplace, and natives traded away all they owned to continue drinking. A priest among the Blackfoot in 1874 noted that where "formerly they had been the most opulent Indians in the country . . . now they were clothed in rags, without horses and without guns" (Dempsey 1972:76). The lawlessness surrounding the whiskey trade was one of the reasons behind the formation of the North West Mounted Police in 1873.

This lawlessness had its most brutal outburst in what became known as the Cypress Hills Massacre. In 1873, while a band of Assiniboine were camped near the traders, a party of white wolf-hunters from Montana arrived. Relations between the "wolfers" and natives had long been strained, and this group was seeking revenge for loss of their horses, apparently taken by Cree raiders. Although none of the horses was found in the Assiniboine camp, pent-up hostilities and heavy consumption of rot-gut liquor on both sides led to an eruption of violence. The better-armed wolfers poured volley after volley into the camp, killing men, women and children. The exact number of native deaths is unknown, but estimates range from twenty to forty. Despite the efforts of the Canadian government to bring to justice those responsible for this atrocity, conflicting accounts led to acquittals.

The disappearance of the bison forced Plains natives into a dependent position. European clothing replaced traditional garb of bison hide, and canvas covered their tipis. Metal tools and European firearms had long since replaced items of aboriginal manufacture. With their economy destroyed, destitute bands of natives camped around the posts.

Weakened by diseases and with their traditional way of life becoming unsustainable, the Plains tribes were in no position to resist government offers of assistance in exchange for signing treaties. Between 1871 and 1877, the First Nations of the Canadian Plains ceded by treaty all claims to their lands. The treaties allocated reserves and provided small payments of money and farm equipment. In only a few decades these people had gone from proud and self-sufficient hunters, roaming freely across the Plains, to destitute and dependent groups, confined to small areas of land without any adequate means of support.

The spectre of starvation soon hung over the new reserve settlements. Government policy was to encourage all natives to become self-sufficient farmers, and with this aim equipment and farm instructors were sent to many reserves. Log cabins replaced tipis as many natives began to raise crops of potatoes, turnips, wheat and barley. Not all, however, adopted this new lifestyle, and even those who made the transition to farming suffered crop failures and other reversals. Even in good years the crops could not sustain their population, and government rations of beef and flour were essential to survival. Frequently the rations were inadequate, resulting in widespread hunger and starvation. Weakened by meagre rations and their new life in small smoky cabins, many succumbed to tuberculosis, influenza, whooping cough and other diseases. Once the natives were settled and their traditional life largely destroyed, missionaries and government agents were able to make major efforts to Christianize and acculturate them. Children were taught European ways in the newly created schools and native cere-moniels such as the Sun Dance were suppressed. It appeared to many abo-riginal people that they were about to follow the bison into oblivion.

Outbreaks of violence were surprisingly rare. Tribal enmities and tradi-tional values were still strong, leading young men to seek glory in horse-raiding. Skirmishes between Blackfoot warriors and their Assiniboine or Gros Ventre enemies continued into the reserve period. However, the only uprising against agents of the Canadian government occurred in 1885 with the North-West Rebellion of Louis Riel and the Métis. Several Indian groups, hungry, feeling betrayed by the government and chafing under the restrictions of reserve life, rose up in sympathy. Cree from One Arrow's reserve and Dakota led by White Cap fought beside the Métis at Batoche, while Cree and Assiniboine bands under Big Bear and Poundmaker took up arms to the west. Despite repeated entreaties, the Blackfoot refused to join the rebellion. One Blood chief even offered his band's services to the gov-ernment so that they might fight once more against their age-old enemies. The rebellion was short-lived and failed to win any consideration of native grievances.

Repressive measures were imposed on the reserve communities after 1885. For several decades Plains natives required passes to leave their reserves, and police rounded up all such individuals who were absent with-out permission. Such measures served to isolate bands, restricting common action on their shared grievances and hindering their traditional ceremonial life.

The late religious cults which swept the American Plains were largely ignored in Canada. In their demoralized state American Plains natives wel-comed such messianic movements as the Ghost Dance, which promised return of the bison and disappearance of the whites if the dances were faith-fully performed. The Teton Dakota, starving and resentful over the loss of their beloved Black Hills, abandoned their small farms and danced, turning the new religion into military resistance. The massacre of one Teton group at Wounded Knee, South Dakota, in 1890 put an end to any further native resistance on the Plains. In Canada, the Ghost Dance religion was adopted by only a small number of Dakota in Saskatchewan, and then without the militaristic interpretation of their American kin.

By the end of the century the shift from tipis, horses and bison to log cabins, cattle and gardens was complete. Many bands achieved considerable success in agriculture, despite outdated technology and inadequate areas of suitable land. This success, however, was undermined by government policies, such as the requirement of an agent's permit to sell any produce grown on the reserve. The depression of the 1930s and the trend towards large-scale mechanized farming further discouraged such an economy. Lacking adequate capital to compete, many bands abandoned their agricultural efforts, often leasing land to non-Indian farmers. In the west, the Blackfoot, Sarcee and Stoney were more successful with ranching.

Today, many reserves lack a sufficient economic base. This is particularly true of the relatively small Cree reserves in Saskatchewan, where the only employment possibilities nearby are as casual farm labourers, and such jobs have almost vanished due to increased mechanization. As a result, the rate of migration to the cities is high. Regina and Winnipeg have large native populations, and the search for better economic opportunities continues to draw people to the city. Many maintain strong ties with their reserves and eventually return there, while others settle permanently as urban natives.

The generally larger reserves in western Alberta have offered greater opportunities. Ranching continues to be important to the Blackfoot tribes, the Sarcee and the Stoney. A number of on-reserve industrial and commercial developments have also provided employment for band members. For example, the Blood operate a successful factory constructing prefabricated homes. In addition, revenues from oil and gas have brought relative prosperity to the Stoney.

Native traditions remain strong across the Plains. The sacred rituals of the Sun Dance, after a period of near-disappearance, are again being celebrated on many reserves, and elaborate ceremonies are still required for the opening of medicine bundles. Many modern ceremonies, however, are more secular and social. "Powwows" are a recent phenomenon, offering participants an opportunity to socialize, dance, gamble and reaffirm their Indian identity in a modern context. Such events often feature prizes for the best "Indian dancing" or most elaborate costume. This tends to foster "Pan-Indianism," a general pride in being native, while blurring specific cultural differences between the Plains First Nations.

Rodeos have also offered opportunities for social gatherings and identity for many of the Alberta groups. The Blackfoot, Sarcee and Stoney participate in on-reserve rodeos and in larger events such as the Calgary Stampede. Several world rodeo champions have come from the Blood reserve.

Plains First Nations have participated vigorously in the political battles of the last few decades. Through such provincial organizations as the Indian Association of Alberta, the Federation of Saskatchewan Indian Nations and the Assembly of Manitoba Chiefs, they have battled for settlement of such issues as treaty grievances, restructuring of the Indian Act and the place of aboriginal rights in the constitution.

Many Plains nations have established cultural centres to preserve their languages and heritage. With the exception of Sarcee, their languages are healthy, although Blackfoot and Dakota tend to be spoken only by the older people. Increasingly assuming control of their own educational programs and administration, the First Nations of the Plains are taking a prominent role in the nation-wide drive for greater aboriginal self-determination.

CHAPTER 7 *The Plateau*

The high, generally arid Plateau lies between the Rocky Mountains on the east and the Coast Mountains on the west. Roughly bisected by the international border, the Canadian portion falls within the southern interior of British Columbia. The northern boundary is less clear, the Plateau grading into the forested environment of the Subarctic. Jenness, terming this intermontane region "the Cordillera," considered it to extend far to the north, including the Tahltan and Tagish of northern British Columbia and southern Yukon. Others take the northern boundary to the territory of the Carrier and, occasionally, the Sekani of central British Columbia. Most authorities, however, place these peoples in the Subarctic culture area. The Plateau is considered here to consist of the territories of the Interior Salish, Kutenai and Chilcotin, plus a few bands of southern Carrier who pushed into the northern Plateau in recent times.

The Plateau landscape is diverse, consisting of a series of valleys, plateaus and mountain ranges, generally oriented north-south. Environment varies from sagebrush near-desert in the west to heavily forested mountain slopes in the east. The Fraser River, with its major tributary the Thompson, and the upper reaches of the Columbia River drain the Canadian Plateau. Long, dry, hot summers with cold winters characterize the climate.

The Plateau is also linguistically and culturally diverse. The Canadian portion is dominated by speakers of four Interior Salish languages: Lillooet, Thompson, Okanagan and Shuswap. The Kutenai, who speak a linguistic isolate, are in the mountainous southeast of British Columbia. The Plateau Athapaskans consist of the now-extinct Nicola in the central Canadian Plateau and the Chilcotin and southern Carrier in the north.

161

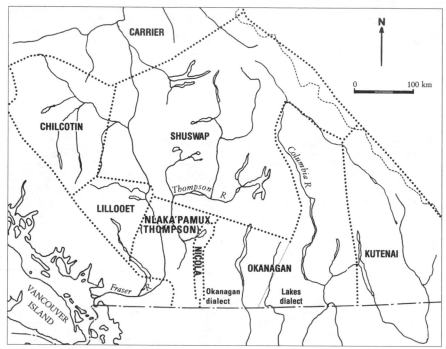

Ethnographic groups in the Canadian Plateau.

Sustained contact with Europeans came late to the Plateau. Nineteenth-century descriptions of Plateau cultures provide only meagre details, and the vast bulk of our knowledge comes from ethnographic research conducted early in the twentieth century, particularly by James Teit. Such information is doubtless affected by the late date at which it was obtained.

Huge runs of salmon annually ascend the rivers, providing the most important food resource throughout much of the Plateau. Vast quantities were caught and dried for later consumption. Not all Plateau groups, however, had access to salmon rivers, and throughout the Plateau other resources were important. People followed the seasons, hunting, fishing and gathering a wide range of foods.

On the east and west were the dynamic Plains and Northwest Coast culture areas, whose influences were strongly felt in the Plateau. An infusion of Plains traits appeared late in the Plateau, after arrival of the horse and full development of the historic Plains cultures. Such traits as feather headdresses, tipis and warriors' societies characterize this late Plains influence, being particularly marked among such eastern groups as the Kutenai. Northwest Coast influences were of longer duration, especially along the Fraser and Thompson Rivers, where a shared salmon-fishing economy resulted in parallel evolution with the coast. Many fine pieces of late precontact art from the Plateau have coastal counterparts, and many elements of the ceremonies and social organization of the ethnographic western Plateau groups mirror those of their coastal neighbours. Rather than being a barrier between coast and interior, the Fraser Canyon seems to have been an area where goods and ideas traveled in both directions.

THE PERIOD BEFORE CONTACT

The earliest occupants of the Plateau entered from the south sometime after glacial retreat freed the land. Exactly when these hunters pursued their prey into what is now interior British Columbia is unknown, nor do we know much about how they lived. Undated surface discoveries of fluted and large stemmed points indicate a way of life generally similar to that of Paleo-Indians on the Plains. Indeed, bison once roamed the valleys of the Plateau in early post-glacial times, as did species more typical of the later Plateau such as deer and elk. The discovery of a cache of large, finely-made Clovis points near Wenatchee, Washington, south of the Okanagan Valley in Canada, shows the early Paleo-Indian presence in the Pacific Northwest.

Several other sites, from somewhat later in this early period, show the arrival of cultures with tool-kits which included microblades, small razor-blade-like slivers of stone that were used as cutting edges in composite tools. Radiocarbon dates from a site on the Thompson River, where a small excavation yielded microblades and broken deer bones, shows that such people were hunting in the Plateau by about 8400 years ago.

Another radiocarbon-dated find from this period is the incomplete skeleton of a young man discovered at Gore Creek, near Kamloops. This unfortunate individual seems to have met his death in a mudslide about 8200 years ago. Detailed study indicates that he had a relatively tall and slender physique, a type often associated with inland hunters, and carbon isotopic analysis of the bone showed that land mammals, not salmon, made up most of his diet. The more specialized salmon-fishing cultures of later periods appear not to have yet arrived on the Plateau.

Middle Prehistoric sites contain a variety of chipped-stone tools. Microblades are common in sites of this period, disappearing from the archaeological record sometime before 4000 years ago. Chipped-stone projectile points go through a series of changes over time, generally paralleling the Plains sequence, from early leaf-shaped and stemmed points to the corner- and basally-notched points characteristic of the Middle Prehistoric Period to the small side-notched arrowheads of late precontact times. Despite these changes, a basic continuity to such historic cultures as the Thompson and Shuswap is assumed. Lack of any major preserved architectural features means that we know relatively little about village sites of the Middle Prehistoric Period.

Top: *Excavation at the Keatley Creek site, a late precontact pit house village near Lillooet, B.C.* Photo by author
Left: *Detailed reconstruction of a Thompson pit-house by the ethnographer James Teit. Archaeological evidence shows that pit-houses had a wide range of construction styles.* CMC 22010

Most archaeological attention in the Plateau has been on the Late Prehistoric period, with its large and highly visible pit-house villages. This style of housing appeared in the Canadian Plateau about 4000 years ago and survived into historic times as the preferred winter home of the Interior Salish and nearby Athapaskans. Pit-houses were earth-covered log structures built over excavated depressions, most commonly circular in form. After abandonment, the houses decayed and collapsed into the pit, leaving obvious depressions ("house pits") which mark the sites today. Late Prehistoric winter villages varied greatly in size, from one or two houses to large concentrations. Over a hundred house pits can still be seen at a few of the larger examples.

Pit-house villages indicate a stable and sedentary way of life. Huge surpluses of salmon, taken in the summer and fall and dried for winter use,

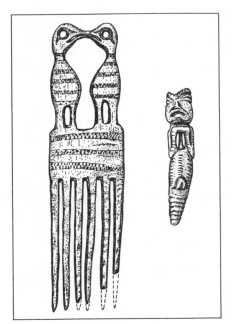

Left: *Small carvings in antler are relatively common in the late precontact period. The comb adorned with birds and the "rattlesnake-woman" figure were found with an infant burial in a pit-house village site near Lillooet, B.C.* Courtesy Arnoud Stryd
Right: *A rattlesnake forms the brow of this small (8.7 cm high) steatite seated human figure bowl, found near Lytton at the confluence of the Fraser and Thompson rivers.* Simon Fraser University Museum of Archaeology and Ethnology, drawing by Barbara Hodgson

were stored in bark-lined cache pits, which today crater the ground around the house depressions. Where preservation of bone is good, these sites contain harpoon points and other fishing gear, and an abundance of salmon bones. Carbon isotopic analysis on human bone also shows the late precontact Plateau peoples were obtaining much of their protein from salmon.

Although both archaeologists and ethnographers have emphasized fishing and hunting in Plateau life, the gathering of wild plant foods was also important. Even where no evidence remains of the plants themselves, there are several indications of their use. Antler handles of digging sticks, used by women to gather edible roots and bulbs, are frequently found. Earth ovens, indicated by depressions which can be large enough to be confused with house pits, provide additional evidence. Today filled with rock, ash and charcoal, these pits once held quantities of edible roots which were gathered from upland areas in the spring. Roasting improved both their taste and storage properties, allowing food to be preserved for the winter months when people remained in their pit-house villages.

Late precontact sites in the western Plateau have yielded examples of fine artwork, many resembling those of equivalent age from the adjacent Northwest Coast. Some utilitarian items, such as digging stick handles, were embellished with geometric designs, while other artworks include finely wrought sculptures of antler and steatite (soapstone). Steatite tobacco pipes, usually trumpet-shaped, often were decorated with carving, and beautifully sculpted steatite bowls took a variety of human and animal forms. One type of carved stone bowl, featuring a seated human figure, is distributed from Vancouver Island on the coast to Shuswap Lake in the central Plateau. Some Northwest Coast examples may have had an interior origin or inspiration, as suggested by depictions of rattlesnakes, indigenous to the dry Plateau but not the coast, on the human's back or brow. Imagery is complex, featuring frogs or toads and lizards as well as rattlesnakes with the humans, suggesting levels of meaning unavailable to us but perhaps associated with shamanism. Ties with the coast can also be seen in a decorated whalebone club, of a type known historically from western Vancouver Island, found at the Chase "burial mound" (actually a natural ridge used as a cemetery in the last few centuries prior to European contact). Among many beautiful art objects placed with the dead at this site was a unique fragmentary wooden mask, possibly preserved by the numerous copper artifacts in the site. Its raised peg-like eyes resemble those on historic masks used by Salish dancers. It would appear that a tradition of wooden sculpture, now lost to decay, once linked late precontact Plateau art with that of the Northwest Coast. Indeed, we have to question whether any sharp distinction between these two areas existed at this time.

The western Plateau was a strategic area for trade. The Fraser Canyon, separating the Plateau from the Northwest Coast, was the major source of the soft steatite used in carving and the very hard translucent green nephrite, which was carefully cut and polished to form adze blades and chisels used in woodworking (although some examples are far too large and carefully wrought for such a utilitarian purpose and may have been valuable display items). The canyon also provided one of the major fisheries in British Columbia, and dried salmon was almost certainly widely traded. Long-distance trade is shown by such imported goods as native copper, coastal shell ornaments and obsidian. Even pieces of turquoise, which must have had an origin far to the south, have been found in the Okanagan. Such wealth items presumably conferred prestige and power, hinting that social distinctions characterized the late precontact communities.

Evidence for late prehistoric cultural complexity is strongest in the west, along the Fraser River, where major salmon runs supported dense populations. This can be seen at several very large late precontact villages near the modern town of Lillooet. At Keatley Creek, the most extensively excavated of these sites, over 120 circular depressions mark where houses stood. Archaeologists estimate a population of 500 to 1000 people at the height of occupation, a village size considerably greater than any historic example.

Several houses exceed 20 metres in diameter, compared to the historic average of 6 to 8 metres. Such huge pit-houses may have been homes of high-ranking chiefs, or possibly ceremonial structures; in either case they would suggest a social organization more complex than what was known historically.

Nearby, at another large village site, burials with wealth goods provide further evidence of social distinctions. A child buried in one of the larger house pits was accompanied by a beautifully carved antler comb, several small sculptures in antler and soft stone, and several hundred dentalium shell beads, a wealth good traded in from the coast. The presence of such items with a child suggests that social distinctions were at least partially inherited.

Brian Hayden, the archaeologist who excavated Keatley Creek, refers to this period of large villages and evidence for social complexity as the "Classic Lillooet" stage, reaching its height about 2000 to 1000 years ago. Following that time, an abrupt and simultaneous abandonment of all the large villages seems to have occurred throughout the region. In searching for an explanation, Hayden, in collaboration with a geographer studying the area, advanced the hypothesis of a catastrophic landslide which blocked the Fraser River about 1000 years ago. Native traditions tell of later slides which prevented the salmon from ascending the river. A massive landslide would have been a calamity, causing cultural collapse in a society highly dependent upon salmon and forcing the people to disperse into small groups. These societies were just regaining similar levels of complexity when the arrival of Europeans and their diseases posed the next great threat to their survival.

Other archaeological efforts have focused on the search to identify Athapaskan migrations. Members of this linguistic stock pushed south from their homeland in the Subarctic, eventually reaching as far south as the American Southwest. There they became such historic peoples as the Navajo and Apache, speaking languages closely related to those of northern British Columbia. In one theory, the logical route for these people in their southward wanderings was through the Plateau, and the now-extinct Nicola might have been remnants of this migration. In the northern Plateau, archaeologists have also attempted to document the arrival of the Chilcotin and southern Carrier, generally conceded to be late arrivals in their historic homelands. Some have seen evidence of their passing in the distribution of microblades or a particular type of projectile point, yet such tools were not unique to a single ethnic group. Archaeologists generally have been frustrated in their efforts to relate precontact stone tools to known ethnic groups, and evidence for Athapaskan migrations on the Plateau remains elusive.

Among the most dramatic of archaeological remains in the Plateau are the rock art sites. Most are pictographs—painted figures in red ochre (a natural pigment mixed with animal fat or salmon eggs to make a bright and

Pictograph sites, such as this one in the Okanagan Valley, are widespread in the Plateau. The rock overhang on the left might once have sheltered an adolescent on his solitary quest for a personal guardian spirit. Under it he painted the image on the right, perhaps depicting his supernatural protector. Photos by author

durable paint). Paintings on boulders or cliff faces abound throughout most of Interior Salish territory. They are less common among the Kutenai and rare in Chilcotin lands. Depicting humans, animals, supernatural creatures and abstract symbols, they range from single figures to large panels with hundreds of painted images. Teit's ethnographic work documents the association of these paintings with the guardian spirit quest, when adolescents sought secluded locations to fast and wait for an encounter with a supernatural protector. Many of the images on the rocks were painted while praying for supernatural aid or represent the guardian spirits obtained. Others are records of dreams, perceived as supernatural messages. Such religious concepts were central to Plateau groups, and the practice of painting these images on rocks may be an ancient one. However, it is unlikely that any still visible are older than a few centuries.

THE INTERIOR SALISH

The international border slices through the centre of the lands occupied by Interior Salish people. Four Salishan languages are spoken on the Canadian Plateau, while others exist to the south.

People speaking the Lillooet language are westernmost. They are divided into the Upper Lillooet (or Stl'atl'imx), on the Fraser River around the modern town of Lillooet, and the Lower or Mt. Currie Lillooet (or Lil'wat) of the Pemberton Valley, which extends into the Coast Mountains. The latter, in particular, were in close contact with coastal groups and were a major source of coastal customs and trade goods entering the Plateau.

The Thompson held the vital Fraser Canyon and mid-Fraser region, as well as lower reaches of the Thompson River before it joins the Fraser. Named for the explorer who "discovered" the river their ancestors lived along for millennia, these people prefer to call themselves the Nlaka'pamux.

The Okanagan occupy the Okanagan Valley of the southern Canadian Plateau, extending well into the state of Washington. Also speaking a dialect of the Okanagan language were the Lakes people to the east, around the Arrow Lakes. They differed somewhat in culture from the Okanagan proper, being more closely related to the Colville Indians to the south, who they joined on their reservation in Washington in the late nineteenth century.

The Shuswap are the northernmost group and occupy by far the largest territory. Their land stretches from the Fraser River on the west to the Rockies on the east, including the North and South Thompson Rivers and Shuswap Lake.

Populations were concentrated along the Fraser and Thompson Rivers, which supported bountiful salmon runs. The Thompson and Upper Lillooet had a particularly high population density, equivalent to anywhere on the Northwest Coast and among the highest in aboriginal Canada. The major Thompson village was at Lytton, at the confluence of the Fraser and Thompson. Here Simon Fraser encountered a community of 1200 people in 1808. The Okanagan, whose rivers lay near the end of the long Columbia drainage system and had poorer salmon runs, had a lower population density. In the eastern Plateau, among the Lakes and eastern bands of Shuswap, population levels were markedly lower.

The Plateau economy was based on a seasonal pattern of movement, with people living and working in small mobile bands from spring to fall. In winter, several bands might join to form a larger, relatively permanent village with more substantial housing. Here they lived primarily on stored foods and held major social and ceremonial activities.

Salmon was the vital Plateau resource, and much of the late summer and fall was spent intercepting the spawning runs. Canyons offered particularly favourable fishing locations, where masses of large silver fish teemed in the eddies, waiting to fight their way up the next rapids or falls in their journey upriver. Here they could be scooped out of the water with large dip-nets, or could be harpooned or speared or caught in traps. People annually congregated at such fishing locations as the Fraser Canyon, building wooden platforms to support themselves along its precipitous walls. The rugged country of the Thompson provided numerous excellent fishing locations, while the Upper Lillooet and many of the Shuswap had access to smaller canyons.

Dip-netting for salmon on the Fraser River near Lillooet. PABC HP68625

The Lakes moved south to Kettle Falls on the Columbia, where one of their favoured fishing techniques was to place a large basketry trap at the base of the falls so that it interfered with the salmon's leap. Those that failed to clear the falls dropped back into the trap, where the confined space prohibited another attempt. This fishery was described by the artist Paul Kane, who visited the falls in 1847:

> The salmon . . . continue to arrive in almost incredible numbers for nearly two months; in fact, there is one continuous body of them, more resembling a flock of birds than anything else in their extraordinary leap up the falls . . . The chief told me that he had taken as many as 1700 salmon, weighing on an average 30 lbs. each, in the course of one day. Probably the daily average taken in the chief's basket is about 400. The chief distributes the fish thus taken during the season amongst his people, everyone, even to the smallest child, getting an equal share.
>
> (Kane 1968:218)

Although fishing was primarily a male activity, women were also extremely busy during salmon runs. Large quantities of salmon had to be preserved for later use. The fish were cut into fillets and hung on drying racks. Plank roofs over the racks prevented the outside from drying too rapidly in the sun, while warm breezes blowing through the canyons slowly dried the fish. Salmon could also be preserved by roasting, then drying and pounding them into a coarse powder ("salmon pemmican"). Dried salmon allowed large sedentary groups to form during the winter and was highly valued as a trade commodity to groups lacking a sufficient supply.

While almost total attention was given to the salmon during annual runs, other fish were also important and could be taken throughout the year. Sturgeon, trout, suckers and other species were caught by a variety of techniques. Some groups even fished with hand lines through the winter ice.

Hunting could also be carried out through much of the year. Men pursued deer, elk, bear, mountain goat and bighorn sheep, as well as smaller prey such as marmot, rabbits and beaver. The bow and arrow was the favoured weapon, though animals were also taken in snares and deadfall traps. Long fences were constructed to lead deer into snares, or into lakes where they could be taken by hunters in canoes. Dogs were frequently used to run down the prey. Some Okanagan are even known to have crossed the Rockies to hunt bison on the Plains.

Gathering of plant foods, largely considered women's work, also contributed greatly to the diet. Fresh green shoots of such plants as fireweed and cow parsnip ("Indian rhubarb") were enjoyed in the spring. Various edible roots and bulbs such as balsamroot, bitterroot and wild onion were dug with sticks of hard wood. They were roasted in earth ovens and preserved for winter use. When berries ripened later in the summer, they were eagerly consumed fresh and pressed into dried cakes to be stored for the winter. Groups of women and children, with perhaps a few men, often established camps in upland areas abundant in roots or berries, enjoying this opportunity to work together and socialize. Major upland valleys, such as Botanie Valley north of Lytton, attracted people from considerable distances, coming to partake of the harvest, but also to visit old friends, gamble and trade.

During the coldest months of winter, people lived in semi-subterranean pit-houses, each sheltering several families. An area of soft sandy soil near a creek was usually chosen, and a circular pit was dug. According to the ethnographer James Teit, this task fell to the women, who used their digging sticks and flat-bladed scrapers. Stout rafters were then set into place to support the roof. The log superstructure was covered with bark, then with earth and sod, providing effective insulation from winter cold. Teit's detailed description best documents pit-house construction, but archaeological and ethnographic evidence indicates that there was a variety of shapes and sizes. A notched log ladder was set in place from the inside of the house to an opening at the top, which served as entrance, smoke-hole and skylight. While people slept at night and during times of danger, the ladder could be set aside and the entrance closed. An elevated platform around the wall served as a sitting and sleeping area. Under the platform and hanging from rafters were baskets and bags containing food and equipment. Although people were warm and secure during winter months, houses must also have been dark and smoky, and occupants were eager to be on the move again in early spring, leaving behind only a few old folks content to remain in their insulated homes. Pit-houses could be re-used in following winters, until the timbers began to rot or, as apparently often happened, they became infested with insects, rodents or rattlesnakes. A few groups did not use the pit-house but remained in mat-covered lodges more typical of summer months, banking them with earth and snow against the winter cold.

Winter villages ranged from a single large pit-house to a cluster of pit-houses sheltering several hundred people. In the middle of winter these might have resembled only large mounds of snow, until one noticed well-worn trails leading to the notched-log ladders and smoke emanating from the entranceways on top. On sunny days, people sat outside on the sloping roofs of their homes to work and socialize with their neighbours. Nearby were small huts, constructed for menstruating women and girls entering puberty, who had to be isolated from activities in the main houses. The village might also have several dome-shaped sweat-lodges, where both men and women ritually purified themselves. Bark-lined cache pits, in which food and other goods were stored, might be lost to sight under dirt and snow, but raised platforms around the houses kept food for more immediate consumption out of the reach of dogs and other animals.

During the rest of the year, people were scattered at their fishing, hunting, root-digging or berry-picking camps. Housing was temporary, as people moved from place to place. The common summer dwelling was a framework of poles covered with mats or bark.

Each winter village (or, in some cases, a small cluster of nearby settlements) was politically autonomous. Positions of village chiefs tended to be hereditary, as the son of a wealthy and influential chief had a great advantage over other possible candidates. However, he had to prove worthy of the position or his leadership would not be recognized. Each village might have several headmen or "chiefs," respected for their wealth, oratory or abilities. Some individuals might rise to prominence through skill in hunting or fishing, or military prowess, and would take leadership for those activities. There were no leadership positions above the level of the winter village or village cluster, and no mechanism existed to link the various communities speaking the same language.

Warfare was far from unknown among the Plateau groups. The Shuswap were embroiled in wars with the Chilcotin, and they occasionally raided the Lillooet for slaves and dried salmon. The Upper Thompson were known as warriors, sending out expeditions against the Lillooet or Shuswap for plunder, adventure or revenge. War parties were led by a war chief and accompanied by a shaman, who used his supernatural power to weaken the enemy. Most war parties were small, although Teit mentions that some Thompson expeditions involved several hundred warriors. Weapons consisted of spears, bows and arrows, knives and war clubs. According to Teit, the Thompson and Upper Lillooet poisoned arrowpoints with rattlesnake venom or the juice of a small yellow flower. Men wore armour of wooden slats or thick hides and carried shields. In times of danger a log stockade was constructed around the camp; Simon Fraser described a "fortification . . . surrounded with palisades eighteen feet high" among the Lillooet in 1808. Although female slaves captured in war were common among the western groups, most were eventually absorbed into the society and their children were not considered slaves.

Peaceful trade relationships also existed among the Plateau groups. Dried salmon, preserved roots and berries, and other foodstuffs were common items of trade. The Lillooet were the chief intermediaries in trade with the coast and it was largely through them that such coastal goods as dentalium and other valuable shells entered the Plateau. In the east, the Lakes traded dried salmon to the Kutenai for bison-hide bags and robes. Major fisheries or root-collecting areas brought large numbers of people together, each bringing regional specialties to these large "trade fairs."

While some groups used dugout canoes of cedar or cottonwood, bark-covered canoes were far more widely distributed. The pointed prow and stern projected under the waterline, leading European observers to refer to them as "sturgeon-nose" canoes. The turbulent rivers of the Plateau, however, largely restricted canoe use to lakes. Most travel was done on foot, the people transporting personal gear and trade goods on their backs or on the backs of dogs. Snowshoes were widely used for winter travel.

Clothing was prepared from tanned animal hides and generally resembled that of Plains tribes. Male attire was a shirt, breechcloth and long leggings, while women wore a long dress and short leggings. Both sexes wore deerhide moccasins. Tanned buckskin clothing was a luxury, however, and lower status individuals had to make do with footgear made of salmon skins. Caps and robes were added in cold weather. Clothing was often beautifully embellished with porcupine or bird quills, dentalium shells or elk teeth, later replaced by elaborate beadwork. Eagle feathers were also much in vogue, being worn in headbands or attached to clothing.

People took considerable care with their appearance. Children of both sexes had their ears pierced, and many also had a hole made in the nasal septum. Inserted in these openings were tubular ornaments of dentalium shell, bird quill or bone, often decorated at each end with pieces of red-headed woodpecker scalp. Necklaces and pendants of dentalium, native copper, grizzly bear claws and other valuables were also worn. Both sexes greased and painted their faces and took care with the hair, oiling it and arranging it in a variety of styles. Tattooing of simple designs on the face was common, though far from universal, for both men and women.

Artwork in wood was much less developed than on the Northwest Coast, although the Thompson and Lillooet carved powerful images of deceased individuals to set up at cemeteries and occasionally decorated the ends of pit-house ladders. More elaborate was the art of weaving, particularly among western groups. Thompson women wove blankets of mountain-goat wool similar to those of their Salish relatives along the lower Fraser, often incorporating complex, brightly coloured geometric patterns. Thompson

Thompson man and woman in beaded buckskin costumes, 1913. CMC 20823, 30987

and Lillooet women also wove beautiful coiled cedar-root baskets, carefully working in cherry bark and other materials to form geometric designs. Used for general carrying and storage purposes, some were woven so tightly that they could hold water. Eastern Plateau groups relied more on well-made birchbark containers.

Numerous supernatural beings inhabited the Salish world. Some had power to aid and protect people, some were dangerous, while others were occasionally glimpsed in the woods or waters but took little interest in human affairs. Young people began early in life to prepare themselves to seek supernatural power. At puberty they set out on solitary vigils, fasting and praying while waiting for a guardian spirit to appear in a vision. While not all who sought such power were successful, those who obtained a vision received supernatural assistance throughout their lives. Some became shamans, gaining power to heal from such spirit encounters. Both men and women could be shamans, healing by extracting the disease-causing object or retrieving the lost soul. Shamans were feared because their supernatural power gave them the ability to inflict illness and death as well as to cure, and some became malevolent sorcerers.

Some ceremonies reaffirmed religious beliefs, while others were purely secular, meant to enliven the long winter months. Throughout the Plateau, aboriginal people honoured the first roots of the season and the earliest berries to ripen with special ceremonies, and many groups also held a "first salmon" rite to welcome the first of the silver masses to ascend the rivers each year. Such ritual observances were essential to ensure continuity of these vital foods. An important winter ceremony, practiced on the Canadian Plateau primarily by the Okanagan, was the Guardian Spirit Dance, following instructions received as part of a vision. The dances were performed in winter, when people were assembled in their pit-house villages; failure to do so would result in sickness and death. A more secular event, also carried out during the winter by western groups, was the "potlatch," clearly borrowed from the Northwest Coast. A chief demonstrated his wealth and enhanced his prestige by lavish public distribution of food and goods, although such events were modest compared to coastal extravagances.

Myths and legends of the Plateau Salish featured the exploits of transformers, the greatest of whom was Coyote. Coyote was sent to "put the world in order," transforming the inhabitants into their present human and animal shapes. It was Coyote who brought the salmon up the rivers to the Plateau people, after breaking dams on the lower Fraser and Columbia, leaving only rugged canyons where they had stood. Not all of his actions were noble, however, and myths often portray him as greedy, deceitful or obscene. Evidence of Coyote's adventures can be seen throughout the Plateau in various rock landmarks, which are imprints of his passage or are people turned to stone in this mythological age.

THE KUTENAI

The bountiful but mountainous environment of the easternmost Plateau, up to the high peaks of the Rocky Mountains, was home to the Kutenai (also spelled Kootenay). The drainage of the Kootenay River, including Kootenay Lake, linked the various Kutenai bands. With the international border cutting through their territory, they now occupy southeastern British Columbia, northern Idaho and northwestern Montana. Although

Top: *a group of Kutenai, showing typical Plains traits, ca. 1914.* PABC
Left: *A Kutenai chief.* CMC 41202

their land teemed with game, and fish and edible plants were plentiful, the Kutenai people were not numerous and population density was low.

The origins of the Kutenai are obscure, posing an intriguing puzzle to anthropologists. Their language casts no light on the problem since it has no close relatives, underscoring the unique nature of these mountain-dwelling people. Nor do their origin myths clarify this issue, since informants provided Harry Turney-High, the major ethnographer of the Kutenai, with conflicting accounts. In one version, the Kutenai have always occupied the rich lands of the eastern Plateau, ever since they "woke up" at their "Big Village" of Tobacco Plains, today astride the British Columbia-

Montana border. Other informants, however, insisted that they originated east of the mountains. Certainly this is where they were first encountered by such European explorers as Alexander Henry and David Thompson, the latter providing the clearest statement that the grasslands of southern Alberta were once Kutenai territory. Informants' statements, historic accounts and the obvious Plains character of Kutenai culture have led many researchers to conclude that the Kutenai were pushed over the mountains in protohistoric times as the Blackfoot moved into southern Alberta. Others maintain that the Kutenai are a Plateau people, venturing out onto the Plains and borrowing much of Plains culture, only after acquisition of the horse in the early eighteenth century.

The Upper Kutenai, higher on the Kootenay River drainage and closest to the Rockies, strongly resembled Indians of the Plains in culture. While deer, elk and caribou were hunted, the preferred prey was bison. Several times a year the Kutenai traversed high mountain passes to hunt on the Plains. Large numbers, including women and children, set out on horseback for the summer and fall hunts, while the mid-winter hunt, which was a much more arduous undertaking owing to deep snow in the passes, was conducted by smaller groups traveling on snowshoes. Once bison herds were located, the shaggy beasts were killed by hunters on horseback, in the fashion of the Plains tribes, during summer and fall, while in winter hunters on snowshoes could overtake the animals as they floundered in deep snow. Turney-High's informants denied that they ever drove bison over cliffs; however, one myth describes such a technique, raising the question of whether this reflects an earlier, pre-horse practice of the Kutenai or late diffusion of the story from Plains groups. While some of the meat was enjoyed fresh, most was dried and pounded into pemmican, which was stored in Plains-style parfleches (rawhide bags) and taken back over the mountains, serving as a staple food until the next hunt.

Their travels onto the Plains brought the Kutenai into conflict with the "enemy people over the mountains," particularly the Blackfoot. As a result, hunts were organized like military campaigns and the Kutenai preferred to travel in large groups, making them less vulnerable to attack. Constant skirmishes did take place, and the Kutenai displayed all the ferocity of Plains warriors, "counting coup" on their enemies and taking scalps from the vanquished. Typical of Plains military organizations, members of the Kutenai Crazy Dogs Society vowed never to retreat in battle.

The Lower Kutenai, farther from the Plains down the Kootenay River and along Kootenay Lake, rarely participated in bison hunts and displayed fewer Plains traits. The animal most important to their economy was the deer, which was hunted in communal drives led by a Deer Chief. Long lines of beaters drove the animals to where archers waited, continuing until enough were killed to supply the entire community with dried venison.

The bountiful Kutenai environment provided many other resources.

Geese, ducks and other birds were abundant. While the Upper Kutenai hunted birds individually, the Lower Kutenai organized communal hunts, under a skilled Duck Chief, to take large numbers of ducks in nets, preserving their flesh as a staple food. Fish of various species, including large sturgeon, were taken by all Kutenai on hooks and with weirs and traps. The importance of fish in the diet seems out of place in the Plains-oriented culture of the Upper Kutenai, but this was a resource no Plateau people could ignore. Similarly, in the use of plant foods the Kutenai resembled the Interior Salish. Women used their digging sticks to collect such foods as bitterroot and camas in the spring, and in summer they gathered large quantities of berries, some of which were dried for winter use.

Although there was a shared common identity of being "Kutenai," each band was politically autonomous. Only when several bands moved together across the mountains would the others accept the leadership of the Tobacco Plains chief. Among the Upper Kutenai, military honours conferred prestige and rights to chiefly status, although there was a tendency for the position to be hereditary. Lower Kutenai chiefs were chosen by a council of elders, selecting the individual with the greatest ability and supernatural strength. Lesser chiefs were men of proven ability at certain tasks, taking charge during such activities as fishing, deer hunting or netting ducks. No class system existed, the only high-status positions among the Upper Kutenai being held by men who had distinguished themselves by "counting coup" against the enemy. The Kutenai, however, held as slaves any women and children captured in battle, but they were not treated harshly and were usually absorbed into the community through marriage or adoption.

For the Plains-oriented Upper Kutenai, the hide-covered tipi was the year-round dwelling, though some informants recalled use of a mat-covered lodge in winter. The Lower Kutenai covered their summer tipis with rush mats or covers sewn from dogbane ("Indian hemp"). In winter, they used the same materials to cover an elongated lodge, sheltering a number of families. The semi-subterranean pit-houses common to the rest of the Plateau were not used by the Kutenai.

Travel along lakes and rivers involved a variety of watercraft, but most common was the "sturgeon-nosed" bark-covered canoe. Mountainous terrain meant that most travel was on foot, using snowshoes in winter and employing the dog as a pack animal. With the introduction of the horse in the eighteenth century, the Kutenai could range much farther afield, making hunting and trading trips far out onto the Plains. Goods were packed in bags on horses; the Plains-style travois was not used.

The tanned hide clothing of the Kutenai conformed to the general Plains-Plateau pattern—shirt, breechcloth, leggings and moccasins for men, and a long dress, leggings and moccasins for women. Robes, hats and mittens were added in cold weather. The Kutenai rarely decorated clothing, instead relying on the whiteness of the hide and lavish use of long fringes for aesthetic appeal. Only in recent times, under influence of such groups as the Plains Cree, was beadwork added. Similarly, Plains-style feather head-dresses appeared only recently among the Kutenai. Hair was worn long and braided, by both sexes, never cut except in mourning. Women parted the hair in the middle, with a plait on each side, while men wore three braids, on each side and down the back. For festive occasions, both sexes painted their faces and adorned their braids with items such as weasel tails.

Kutenai religious concepts resembled those of both the Plains and Plateau. Young people embarked on solitary quests for a supernatural guardian, the spirit power they received aiding them in hunting, warfare or other activities throughout their lives. Some guardian spirits gave the power to cure, making human recipients powerful shamans. Objects indicated in the vision were gathered and placed in a sacred "medicine bundle," in the fashion of the Plains tribes.

Their ceremonies were almost purely Plains in character. Rituals welcoming the earliest salmon, roots and berries, so vital to the Interior Salish, were not practiced by the Kutenai. The major ceremonial, bringing together both Upper and Lower Kutenai, was the Sun Dance. Generally held each year in the spring, the exact time and place were revealed to the Sun Dance Chief in a dream. Members of the Crazy Dogs military society were summoned to take charge of proceedings. Although the Kutenai had their own distinct version, and lacked such Plains embellishments as the self-torture of young men, the Kutenai ritual shared the basic features of the Plains Sun Dance.

Myths of the Kutenai reflect influences from several sources. Some have a strong Plains cast, while others, particularly those featuring Coyote as transformer, are nearly identical to Interior Salish tales. A few, in which the transformer takes the guise of Raven, closely resemble myths of the Northwest Coast. In mythology, as in much of their culture, the Kutenai present an intriguing fusion of ideas from both east and west.

THE PLATEAU ATHAPASKANS

The Athapaskans are one of the great linguistic stocks of aboriginal North America, occupying the entire western Subarctic from Hudson Bay to interior Alaska. At various times in the past, restless wanderings took some populations far from their Subarctic homeland, with these populations eventually settling in new environments and taking on many of the characteristics of their neighbours. This Athapaskan expansion continued in historic times, as groups pushed into the northern Plateau. Chapter 9 deals more fully with the Athapaskan way of life.

When Europeans entered the Plateau, they found a small enclave of Athapaskans, the now-extinct Nicola, along the Nicola and Similkameen

Chilcotin coiled spruce-root basket with designs in cherry bark and grass. RBCM

river valleys of south-central British Columbia. In all but speech they resembled the Interior Salish, living in pit-house villages during the winter and dispersing in summer to small camps of mat-covered shelters. Their economy was the same as other Plateau groups, except that salmon did not ascend their rivers, forcing them to trade for dried salmon with their Salish neighbours. Their presence has been interpreted alternately as remnants of an early Athapaskan migration southward, or as the late arrival of a Chilcotin war party, intermarrying with the Interior Salish and settling among them. Disease, intermarriage and encroachment on their lands by the Thompson, Okanagan and non-native settlers led to their disappearance as a distinct people before the end of the nineteenth century.

At the northern edge of the Plateau were the Chilcotin and southern bands of the widespread Carrier people. These were the southernmost languages in the huge continuous distribution of northern Athapaskans. Chilcotin country lies between the Coast Mountains and the Fraser River, including most of the Chilcotin River drainage and the headwaters of several rivers flowing west to the Pacific. Both archaeological and ethnographic evidence suggest that the Chilcotin were late arrivals in their modern homeland, perhaps moving in from the north only at the beginning of the historic period, attracted by access to European goods through the Nuxalk at Bella Coola and the possibility of establishing themselves as middlemen in trade to the Plateau. They were still expanding their territory in the late nineteenth century, moving eastward to land along the Fraser formerly held by the Shuswap, as were several bands of Carrier. Their traditions recount battles between the Chilcotin and both the Carrier and Shuswap.

In the "memory culture" recorded by ethnographers, the Chilcotin reveal many Plateau traits. They lived a seasonal round of hunting, fishing, digging roots and collecting berries. Since not all Chilcotin had access to salmon, they relied on trade with the Shuswap and Nuxalk for additional supplies. In winter, many lived in Plateau-style pit-houses, though these tended to be smaller than Salish pit-houses, often sheltering only one family. Others preferred to retain more typically Subarctic winter houses of logs or poles, roofed with bark. Women wove beautiful split-root coiled baskets, a trait obviously borrowed from the Salish. Some Chilcotin baskets are masterpieces of the weaver's art, distinguished from the work of other groups by a strengthening hoop of willow beneath the rim and elaborate decoration, often depicting animals, woven over the outer surface. From the Nuxalk over the Coast Mountains they obtained dentalium and abalone shells, eulachon oil and European goods in exchange for cakes of berries, mountain-goat skins and furs. The tubular dentalium shells were highly valued, being commonly worn as nose and ear ornaments, often embellished with tufts of red-headed woodpecker scalp in the Interior Salish fashion. These shells were also traded to the Salish, whose name for the Chilcotin, according to Teit, means "dentalium people."

The influence of the Nuxalk and other coastal groups is evident in Chilcotin social organization. Society was loosely divided into three classes—nobility, commoners and slaves. Some knowledge of a clan system existed, though a child could apparently inherit from either the mother or father. At least some bands developed hereditary chiefs, and such high-ranking men vied for prestige by distributing wealth at potlatches. This complex of traits was very recent among the Chilcotin and only weakly grafted onto an essentially egalitarian society more typical of the Athapaskans.

HISTORIC IMPACT AND CONTEMPORARY CULTURES

Brief encounters with European explorers, acting as agents of the fur trade companies, occurred early in the historic period. Alexander Mackenzie passed through the lands of the northern Shuswap and Chilcotin on his way to the Pacific in 1793. David Thompson was in Kutenai country by 1807 and among the Lakes Okanagan in 1811. Simon Fraser, on his epic journey in 1808 down the river which now bears his name, came into fleeting contact with the Chilcotin, Shuswap, Lillooet and Thompson. Horses, originally a European introduction, had already been present among the Plateau people for generations. Although eastern groups such as the Kutenai were adept horsemen, the horse played only a minor role as a pack animal in the western Plateau. By the time of Simon Fraser's visit, the Salish had also acquired European goods through trade with the coast. Fraser observed copper kettles and a "gun of large size." More seriously, he also noticed several natives suffering from smallpox, this dreaded European-introduced disease reaching the Plateau before Europeans themselves.

In the years following these explorations, the fur trade companies established posts in the Plateau. Natives were drawn into the fur trade, depleting game stocks and becoming dependent upon new goods, such as firearms and metal tools, brought by the traders.

Intensive contact and disruption of native lifeways did not occur until 1858, with the "gold rush" on the Fraser River. An influx of thousands of men seeking quick riches created a mining frontier among the Interior Salish. While the fur traders saw the natives as essential partners, to the miners they were merely obstacles, to be moved or eliminated. Natives were displaced from their traditional village locations and their vital fisheries, and in the lawlessness surrounding this new frontier acts of violence were commonplace.

This population surge led to the proclamation of British Columbia as a crown colony in 1858, encouraging permanent settlement. Natives found themselves in continuing conflict with Europeans, who no longer needed their services but wanted their lands. Increasingly these were usurped by new settlers, who recognized no valid native claims to the land. In addition, greater contact with the new arrivals subjected Plateau natives to new outbreaks of diseases such as smallpox and measles. Particularly devastating was the smallpox epidemic of 1862-1863, which swept across British Columbia, killing about one third of the native population.

Although conditions for aboriginal people in the 1860s were so appalling that colonists feared an "Indian war," outbreaks of violence were minor. The most serious clash came in 1864, as a party of European labourers attempted to construct a wagon road across Chilcotin country. Recognizing how this would affect their land and culture, and blaming the work party for outbreaks of smallpox and harsh treatment of native employees, a band of Chilcotin attacked their camp, killing fourteen of the seventeen men. Shortly after, they attacked a pack train crossing their country, killing several more whites, as well as murdering a settler and looting several homesteads. These actions resulted in the new colonial government sending out a large military force to quell the uprising. After initial failures, the soldiers enticed the Chilcotin into their camp, the natives apparently believing that they had been promised a truce or pardon. They were promptly arrested and taken away for trial, after which five of the leaders were hanged, bringing to an end the so-called "Chilcotin War."

This was a time of considerable movement, as groups adapted to declining populations and loss of lands. The Lakes left Canada altogether in 1870, joining their Colville relatives on a reservation in Washington. The Thompson and Okanagan expanded into the territory of the Nicola, who became extinct. Bands of Carrier pushed south into the heart of former Chilcotin country, left largely vacant as many of the Chilcotin moved east into former Shuswap lands along the Fraser River, which the Shuswap abandoned as their numbers dwindled. Considerable differences exist between the modern reserve distribution and ethnographic territories.

Reserves were assigned to the Plateau groups during the 1870s and 1880s. As each band was a small, separate political unit, reserves tend to be small and scattered. Each band was given traditional village sites but lost all former hunting and gathering areas. Reserves were allocated out of lands traditionally claimed by aboriginal groups; they did not sign treaties or otherwise cede any of the remaining land.

When aboriginal groups were confined to reserves they lost control over important economic resources outside their reserve boundaries. Ranches and settlements soon spread throughout the rest of their traditional lands, driving away game and destroying berry patches and root-digging sites. Many traditional fishing locations at canyons and falls have been flooded by dams. Particularly catastrophic was a landslide caused by blasting for railroad construction in 1913, tumbling millions of tons of rock into the Fraser Canyon and blocking the salmon from reaching their spawning grounds. The Fraser's fish stocks plummeted and have never fully recovered.

Plateau First Nations today are fighting for resolution of several serious grievances. Particularly vexing are restrictions on traditional native fishing practices. While recognizing the need for conservation, natives argue that fishing is part of their aboriginal rights which have never been extinguished, and they resent fishing closures and prohibitions on sale of fish. Several scuffles have broken out between natives and fisheries officials, and the potential for more serious violence exists. Another concern is the intention of the CNR to double-track their railway lines along the Fraser. Remembering the disaster of 1913, native leaders are strongly opposed to this plan, arguing that it will endanger both their ancient heritage sites and fragile salmon spawning areas. Perhaps the major concern, however, involves their land claims, where they seek compensation for loss of traditional lands never surrendered through treaty.

In order to fight these battles, Plateau natives have formed political organizations. The Allied Tribes of British Columbia began among the Interior Salish in 1915. More recently, Plateau natives have been active in such broader organizations as the Union of British Columbia Indian Chiefs. George Manuel, a Shuswap from near Chase, served as president of both this provincial union and the national organization, as well as the founding president of the World Council of Indigenous Peoples. Much political action, however, is at the local level, and related clusters of bands have formed tribal councils to fight land claims and other issues.

A recent highly publicized example is the Stein Valley, within the Nlaka'pamux (Thompson) comprehensive claim area. Plans to log the valley alarmed the Nlaka'pamux and Lillooet, who feared damage to their heritage sites in what had been an important hunting and spirit quest area.

They sought to block any logging of the valley, not just through legal channels but by gathering public support in large "Save the Stein" summer festivals. Such measures have been at least temporarily successful.

Today, as tourists set out for the scenic Fraser Canyon, the beaches of the sunny Okanagan Valley or the mountain splendour of Kootenay National Park, little attention is paid to the small native communities along the way. Many of the 20,000 Interior Salish, as well as the 2500 Chilcotin and 750 Kutenai, still occupy ancestral lands, although divided into numerous bands spread across many small reserves. Some, such as the Okanagan, hold valuable real estate as reserve lands, and leasing to non-Indians for residential and recreational use has made them relatively prosperous. Others are not so fortunate. While little immediately distinguishes these small communities from others around them, native heritage is far from dead, and many bands are attempting to revive traditional customs and ceremonies. When the salmon runs ascend the Fraser, men can still be seen with their dip-nets poised over the turbulent waters, and the observer scanning the valley walls from Lillooet to Lytton or through the Fraser Canyon can still see wooden racks hanging crimson with the flesh of drying salmon, the mainstay of Plateau life for millennia.

CHAPTER 8 *The Northwest Coast*

Coastal rainforest hugs the Pacific shores from southeastern Alaska to northwestern California, including the entire coastline of British Columbia. Frequently shrouded in clouds, the rainy coast bears a lush green mantle of cedar, fir, hemlock and spruce. Along much of the coast, rugged mountains descend precipitously to the sea, requiring native cultures to be well adapted to a maritime way of life. Studded with island archipelagos and cut into by bays and fiords, the convoluted coastline offered protected village locations and access to a great variety of resources. Huge dugout cedar canoes once traversed these waterways, transporting people for feasts and ceremonies between large villages of cedar-plank houses. Coastal culture extended far up the major rivers—the Nass, the Skeena and the Fraser—so that even groups lacking direct access to salt water shared the coastal lifestyle. Despite diversity in language and customs, a shared cultural pattern existed along the entire Northwest Coast.

Salmon and cedar were the essential resources. Salmon annually ascended the rivers in vast quantities, allowing huge food surpluses to be accumulated. The sea provided fish of many species, seals and sea lions, and almost inexhaustible supplies of clams, mussels and other "beach foods." Foods from the land were relatively minor compared to the largesse of the sea. Stands of tall, straight-grained cedar provided a near-perfect medium for the talents of Northwest Coast woodworkers. This material was the basis of elaborate technology and artwork characteristic of the Northwest Coast.

This secure economy supported the densest populations and most complex political organizations in aboriginal Canada. Social distinctions based on birth, dividing the society into nobles, commoners and slaves, are characteristic of all the coastal First Nations. Here developed a sophisticated art

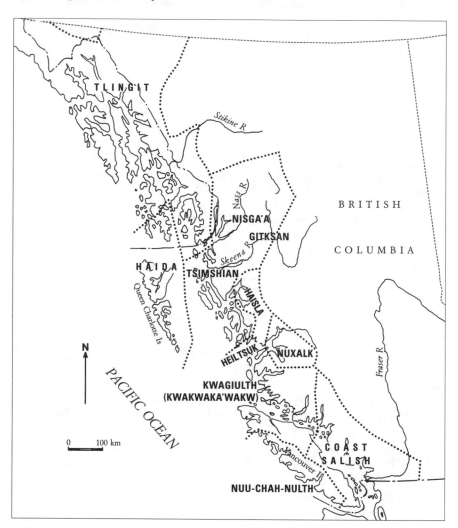

The Northwest Coast.

tradition, considered by many to rank among the world's great artistic achievements. Here also occurred the most elaborate and lavish of Canadian native ceremonials, as chiefs validated and enhanced their status by huge feasts and public distribution of goods, and dancers gave dramatic performances wearing masks and other regalia for which Northwest Coast artists are so justly famed.

The Northwest Coast was also the most linguistically diverse area of aboriginal Canada. At least sixteen languages, from five different linguistic stocks, were once spoken along the British Columbia coast. In the north were the Haida and Tsimshian (the latter divided into at least two languages, with several major dialects), as well as the Tlingit of the Alaskan panhandle, whose distribution extends a short distance into Canada. The central groups belong to the Wakashan stock, consisting of people who historically have been termed Kwakiutl (divided into Haisla, Heiltsuk and Kwagiulth) and Nootka (now known as the Nuu-chah-nulth, speaking two closely related languages). Also on the central coast are the Nuxalk (or Bella Coola), a northern enclave of Salish-speakers. On the southern British Columbia coast are speakers of six related languages, collectively termed Coast Salish. Four of the five stocks occur only on the Northwest Coast, and all five are unique in Canada to British Columbia.

THE TIME BEFORE EUROPEANS

By about 12,000 years ago the glaciers' retreat to the mountain-tops had left the land available for human settlement. In this **Early** period (*ca.* 10,000 to 5500 years ago), the first arrivals encountered a landscape markedly different from that of recent times. As glacial meltwater rushed to the ocean, sea levels rose, resulting in such features as a large saltwater arm reaching far up the valley now drained by the Fraser River. Relieved of the great weight of ice, the land also gradually rebounded. Sea levels fluctuated wildly along the entire coast for thousands of years, presenting great obstacles to our search for remains of this period. Evidence of the earliest arrivals may have been completely obliterated, or can be recovered only by underwater research. Even somewhat later periods have been all but lost through the ravages of time and the restless sea.

Only stone tools remain of the tool-kits possessed by these early cultures, known variously as the Lithic stage, the Pebble Tool tradition or the Old Cordilleran culture. Large, leaf-shaped spearpoints and numerous "pebble tools"—smooth cobbles or pebbles picked up from the beach or riverbank and bashed to remove a few flakes, creating a sharp edge—mark the presence of these earliest occupants. The pebble tools, although appearing crude, could be quickly produced, used for a variety of cutting or chopping tasks, and then discarded. Such tools have been found in deposits dating as

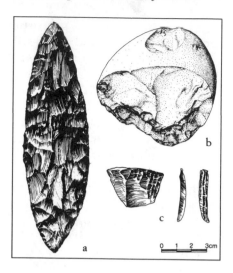

Artifacts from the Early Period on the Northwest Coast. (a) leaf-shaped spear point or knife; (b) pebble tool; (c) microblades and microcore. Courtesy Simon Fraser University Museum of Archaeology and Ethnography, drawings by Barbara Hodgson

far back as 9700 years ago at the Namu site on the central coast. They also occur in abundance at the lowest levels of the 9000-year-old Milliken site in the Fraser Canyon and the deep Glenrose Cannery site on the lower Fraser River. When people began to camp at Glenrose over 8000 years ago, this site was near the mouth of the Fraser, now about 20 kilometres downriver. Although few bones have survived to indicate their diet, these early people seem to have had a less specialized economy than later coast-dwellers, relying on hunting land mammals as well as exploiting the riches of the sea and rivers. At Milliken the discovery of numerous charred pits of the wild cherry, which ripens during the time of the salmon runs in August and September, suggests that even at this early period Northwest Coast peoples were timing seasonal movements to coincide with the appearance of salmon.

Later in this stage a new technology appeared on the northern and central coast, marked by small, thin, parallel-sided flakes, like miniature razor blades, struck from specially shaped cores. Termed microblades, these once were hafted as the cutting or piercing edges of composite tools, whose wooden, antler or bone handles have not been preserved. These distinctive tools had their origins in northern Eurasia, spreading to Alaska by about 11,000 years ago and to the northern Northwest Coast by 9000 years ago. About 8500 years ago they were added to the tool-kit at Namu, on the central British Columbian coast. Sites located on the outer coast indicate that the people who made the microblades used watercraft and relied heavily on the sea for subsistence.

The transformation of these small and relatively unspecialized groups into large, complex societies took place in the **Middle** period (*ca.* 5500 to

1500 years ago). Early in this stage sea levels stabilized at close to their present positions, and environments became essentially modern. Great stands of cedar covered the land, and increased stocks of salmon made their way up the rivers each year. New techniques, both for taking salmon and for preserving most of the catch for later consumption, allowed large communities to form. People also turned to shellfish as an important part of their diet, and it was during this period that huge shell middens appeared. Today visible as layers of crushed clam and mussel shell, with fire-cracked rocks, charcoal and ash, these ancient village sites grew as layer after layer of garbage accumulated. Some, such as the famous Marpole midden in southern Vancouver, once spread over several hectares with deposits up to 5 metres deep, representing the accumulated debris of hundreds of people living seasonally on the site over thousands of years. All along the coastline eroding pieces of clamshell in dark organic soil mark ancient village sites, and many modern reserve communities sit atop layers of garbage discarded by their ancestors millennia ago.

Excavations at these shell middens have yielded a much more plentiful and diverse array of artifacts than appear in the Early period. In part this is due to a much larger population, supported on a more secure economic base. Partly it is due to innovations which appeared during the Middle period, as cultures became increasingly adapted to the rich resources of the rivers and sea. However, it also reflects factors of preservation; earlier cultures might appear more complex if we could see more of their tool-kits than just implements of stone. The shell in the middens neutralizes acids in the soil, preserving artifacts of bone, antler and shell, providing a fuller picture of the peoples' technological ingenuity.

Unfortunately, we still lack objects of many raw materials which were vital to prehistoric artisans. Wood, bark, root and hide are not preserved in shell middens. Only in deposits that have been continuously waterlogged (termed "wet sites" by archaeologists) do objects of wood or plant fibre survive. Under normal conditions, even the more abundant Middle period remains provide only a limited view into the nature of these societies.

The early Middle period, covering the first two millennia, is less well known and appears less complex than the following two millennia. Regional differences are evident, since projectile points and other stone tools chipped to shape are common on the southern coast yet are rare in sites on the Queen Charlotte Islands and the west coast of Vancouver Island. A new technology of shaping stone tools by grinding and polishing was introduced. The earliest art objects also appear. Particularly impressive is a small antler sculpture from the Glenrose site on the Fraser River, depicting a human with what appears to be a beard and an elaborate hairdo drawn into a topknot. It probably once served as the handle of a carving tool, with the hollow at the back holding a beaver tooth as the cutting edge, showing that the practice of decorating functional objects extends far back

Left: *This antler sculpture of a man with his hair drawn into a topknot, from the Glenrose Cannery site on the Fraser River, once served as the handle of a carving tool. Dated at over 4000 years, it is one of the oldest art objects from the Northwest Coast.* Laboratory of Archaeology, Department of Anthropology and Sociology, University of British Columbia
Centre: *Haida woman wearing a labret, 1884.* RBCM
Right: *This small seated-human-figure bowl came from the Marpole site, near the mouth of the Fraser River.* Laboratory of Archaeology, Department of Anthropology and Sociology, University of British Columbia

in time. Labrets ("lip plugs," worn through a slit in the lower lip) also make their appearance. Although historically restricted to high-ranking women on the northern coast, their use seems once to have extended to both sexes and the entire coast. Evidence is lacking, however, for the large cedar-plank houses of later times, as well as for the social ranking characteristic of historic groups. Northwest Coast cultures were clearly developing towards historic forms but had not yet reached that level of complexity.

Full development of Northwest Coast cultures occurred in the final two millennia of the Middle period. In fact, the Locarno Beach and Marpole phases of the Fraser River/Strait of Georgia region are sometimes seen as a "cultural climax," hinting at societies more complex than those known historically in this region.

The Locarno Beach phase dates from roughly 1500 to 500 B.C. Projectile points chipped of basalt, large ground-slate and bone points, and microblades of quartz crystal are among the more common artifacts. Personal

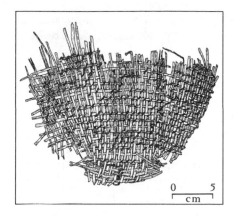

A 3000-year-old basket, recovered from waterlogged deposits on the Musqueam Indian reserve in Vancouver. Drawing by Kathryn Bernick

adornment, possibly indicating status distinctions, is shown by labrets and earspools (pulley-shaped objects believed to have been worn by perforating and stretching the ear lobes). Although earspools were unknown among historic groups, they are found in several precontact cultures; images of humans with such ear ornaments also occur on stone sculptures and a finely carved antler spoon from the Gulf Islands. A man wearing a conical hat similar in shape to historic basketry examples is depicted in a small antler carving from the Locarno Beach site, and several baskctry hats with knobs at the top, historically indicating high status, came from waterlogged deposits of this age on the Olympic Peninsula. A site on the Musqueam Indian reserve in southern Vancouver has also yielded 3000-year-old water-logged basketry, showing that Locarno Beach people were already masters of the weaver's art.

The height of prehistoric achievement on the southern coast came during the Marpole phase (*ca.* 500 B.C. to A.D. 500). Particularly common artifacts are large barbed antler harpoon points, projectile points chipped from basalt or ground from slate, thin ground-slate knives for filleting salmon, and microblades. Mastery of woodworking is indicated by the appearance of the specialized carpenter's tool-kit—antler wedges for splitting straight-grained cedar, carefully polished adze and chisel blades of hard stone for shaping wood, and distinctive hand-mauls, laboriously pecked and ground from hard stone, used as hammers to drive wedges and chisels. Although we have no direct evidence for their houses, large circular stains mark where huge posts once stood, suggesting that villages of plank-covered houses similar to those known historically stood along the waterways of the southern coast 2000 years ago.

The Marpole people also produced artworks and objects of personal adornment. Labrets and earspools were worn, as were long strings of stone and clamshell beads. Occasional discoveries of caches containing thousands of beads may represent accumulation of great wealth, worn on special occasions by high-status individuals. Necklaces of dentalium shell, a wealth item obtained in trade from western Vancouver Island, were also worn, as were a variety of pendants of stone, bone, antler and tooth. Some of these pendants and other small objects are miniature masterpieces of artistic achievement, skillfully depicting images of humans, animals and birds. Such items may have been charms worn by shamans, or were representations of guardian spirit powers, or the beginnings of the crest art so well known for many of the historic groups.

Some of the finest surviving Marpole artworks are sculptures in stone, most commonly steatite. Particularly striking examples feature a seated human holding a shallow bowl. Frequently adorning the bowl or merging with some part of the human are snakes, lizards or frogs—presumably powerful shamanic images. Although they cannot be dated, the discovery of three such bowls during early excavations at the Marpole midden suggests that most belong to the Marpole period.

Archaeological evidence indicates that ranked societies, with chiefly classes consolidating their power through lavish displays of wealth, had emerged by Marpole times. Quantities of beads, dentalium shells, native copper and other wealth goods are found in the graves of some individuals. Some had artificially flattened foreheads produced by binding the head during infancy, which may have served to mark people of noble birth. Labrets and earspools also may have been indicators of high status. The abundance of wealth items and finely carved artworks suggests that skilled artisans were creating display pieces to enhance the prestige of their wealthy patrons, as was typical of historic Northwest Coast cultures.

While Marpole is the best known of the late Middle period cultures, similar developments were occurring elsewhere on the coast. In the north, around the lower Skeena River, the growing importance of warfare is indicated by clubs of stone and bone, often elaborately carved, as well as by indications in skeletal remains of head and arm injuries produced by such implements. One cache of weapons included remains of copper-wrapped wooden rod armour, a beautifully carved whalebone war-club, a club made from a killer whale jaw, a stone club and a large stone dagger. Warfare frequently marks the growth of more complex societies, as populations became larger and chiefs vied for power and prestige. Ambitious leaders plundered their neighbours for slaves and booty, including ceremonial regalia and associated ritual prerogatives. Graves of these warrior-chiefs contain weapons and such exotic wealth goods as copper bracelets and amber beads.

A glimpse into emerging Northwest Coast art and technology in wood comes from the waterlogged Lachane site on the lower Skeena, where remnants of bent-wood boxes, bowls, adze and chisel handles, canoe paddles and various styles of basketry have been preserved. A finely carved cedar handle depicts an unidentifiable animal in a fluid style clearly foreshadowing the famous historic art of the northern Northwest Coast cultures.

By the end of the Middle period the Northwest Coast cultural pattern was firmly in place. Where only eroding shell middens are visible today, villages of large wooden houses once stood. We can imagine these villages bustling with activity, the beaches in front lined with canoes and filled with the comings and goings of fishermen and travelers, and the welcoming of traders or guests for feasts. Elaborate ceremonies filled the winter months, allowing chiefs to display their wealth and proclaim the glory of their ancestral heritage.

In the **Late** period (*ca.* 1500 years ago to European contact), Northwest Coast cultures take essentially their historic form. For the first time it becomes possible, with some caution, to equate precontact remains with known ethnic groups. As an example, an excavation inside a traditional plank-covered Salish longhouse, still standing on the Musqueam Indian reserve in Vancouver until the 1960s, was able to trace Coast Salish culture back to at least A.D. 1200.

On the south coast considerable differences exist between Late period and earlier assemblages, leading to debate as to whether Marpole populations were replaced by invading Salish-speakers, or whether there was simply a shift in some aspects of technology and lifestyle. Most archaeologists favour the latter view. Gone are barbed harpoons and most other antler tools, as well as the chipped basalt points so common in Marpole deposits. Instead, sites contain numerous sharpened splinters of bone which served as barbs on a wide range of fishing implements, as well as ground-slate knives used for splitting and scoring fish for drying. Barbed harpoons were replaced with three-piece toggling harpoon heads, which held in place by turning inside the body of the salmon or seal. A major difference lies in the near-total disappearance of art and personal ornamentation. Gone are labrets, earspools, beads, pendants and the fine carvings in antler and stone. This lack, however, may mean only a shift to woodcarving and weaving as the major artistic outlets. These are poorly preserved archaeologically but were well developed by the historic Coast Salish.

On the west coast of Vancouver Island stone tools of all kinds are relatively rare and chipped stone is almost absent. Most tools found are of bone, with small bone points being particularly abundant. Most would once have been parts of composite fishing gear. The importance of fishing is also shown by the great quantities of fish bones, representing many different species. The abundant remains of seals, sea lions and whales of several species also show the extent of the maritime way of life. The late precontact cultures in this area are easily recognizable as the direct ancestors of the historic Nuu-chah-nulth people.

On the north coast, artistic traditions continued to develop. Stone sculptures include bowls and hafted mauls, often decorated with human or animal figures. Fine detailed sculptures in bone and antler show many of the

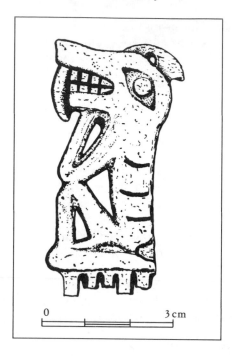

0   3 cm

This beautifully carved bone comb, depicting a wolf (or possibly a bear), dating to about A.D. 800, was excavated at a shell midden site near the mouth of the Skeena River. The exaggerated eye form, protruding tongue and depiction of the ribs ("x-ray vision") foreshadow historic northern Northwest Coast art.
CMC J19608-5

stylized features characteristic of the highly developed art of historic northern people.

Occasional wet site excavations give us a much broader understanding of Late period technology. Ozette, a Makah (the southern relatives of the Nuu-chah-nulth) village on the open coast of the Olympic Peninsula in Washington, provides the most spectacular example. Shortly before Europeans appeared, torrential rainfall loosened the hillside above the village, releasing a mudslide which rushed down the slope, crushing and burying at least four plank-covered houses. Although the force of the slide flattened dwellings and broke objects, the houses and their contents were sealed under mud, preserving the material culture of a society frozen in time—a North American Pompeii.

The Ozette site is unique in providing a nearly complete record of a Northwest Coast community prior to European arrival. It illustrates the variety of implements and the prevalence of artworks and ceremonial objects, almost entirely of wood and long vanished from other sites. The decorated bowls, boxes, seal or fish clubs, tool handles and other objects demonstrate that Northwest Coast art was highly developed prior to the arrival of Europeans and the fur trade. Its discovery stimulated the search for additional waterlogged deposits along the Northwest Coast. Although nothing as dramatic as Ozette has come to light in British Columbia, excavations at wet sites have yielded such normally perishable items as wooden

Many petroglyphs, such as this human figure pecked into the rock near Bella Coola, appear to have been inspired by shamanism. Photo by K. Fladmark

wedges, bent-wood fish hooks, basketry and cordage.

Warfare was prevalent in this Late period, becoming even more intense after the arrival of Europeans and increased competition over important trade routes. On the north coast, late precontact/early historic warrior-chiefs in armour defended their hilltop forts. All along the coast fortresses or defensive sites, frequently atop steep-sided headlands or islets, provided refuges to which people could flee during times of danger.

Mortuary practices also changed at this time. Rather than burying their dead in the middens, people began to place bodies in wooden boxes in trees, or in burial caves or small rock shelters, or in small plank-covered mortuary houses behind the villages. Remains of all of these can still be seen in remote regions of the coast, although surviving examples are probably historic.

The numerous pictographs and petroglyphs display a wide range of styles and, presumably, motivations for their creation. Some, particularly on the south coast, portray mythical creatures in a style unlike historic art. Many appear imbued with spiritual power, marking places where individuals recorded having had encounters with supernatural beings or where shamans communed with the spirit world. Others, particularly on the north coast, appear to be more secular displays of crest art in the historic style. The practice of carving or painting images on rocks may be ancient, but many examples are clearly recent. Images of European sailing ships, for example, are carved into the rock at a site on western Vancouver Island.

THE ETHNOGRAPHIC PERIOD

Villages of large plank-covered houses, monumental wooden sculptures, huge ocean-going dugout canoes and the potlatch ceremony at which chiefs gave away their wealth—these are the images for which ethnographic Northwest Coast cultures are famous. The basic pattern existed all along the coast, yet each group had its own distinct variations. Although all groups carved large sculptures in wood, the art of the Haida, for example, can be readily distinguished from that of the Kwagiulth or Salish. The coast is frequently divided into three sub-areas (northern, Wakashan and Coast Salish), but even within these sub-areas major cultural differences are evident.

Except for groups far inland along rivers, all Northwest Coast people shared the same basic economy. Trade and ritual exchange helped to balance local differences, as groups with abundant clams and sea urchins, for example, exchanged with others for seal meat or dried halibut. All along the coast, people relied heavily on the bounty of the sea, beaches and rivers. The three fundamental aspects of the Northwest Coast economy - fishing, sea mammal hunting and shellfish collecting - all relate to the sea. By comparison, food from the land played a more minor role in the economy, particularly for such outer-coast people as the Haida and Nuu-chah-nulth. Although the coast provided plentiful foodstuffs, making a living required hard work, skill and intimate knowledge of the local environment.

The fundamental resource was salmon—all five species of Pacific salmon, with annual spawning runs ranging from spring to late fall. Treatment varied: Sockeye, for example, was highly valued for its flavour and was primarily consumed fresh, while Chum (or Dog), which spawns late in the year and has a lower fat content, was ideally suited for preservation. Great quantities were dried or smoked, forming the staple food for winter months. Open-ocean groups had access to salmon year-round, taking them primarily on hook and line in salt water; however, the vast majority were taken during annual spawning runs, when people moved to fishing locations near the mouths of rivers or streams. Here the salmon could be harpooned, netted or taken in traps.

The vital role salmon played in the evolution of Northwest Coast cultures stems from several factors. First, salmon was a predictable resource. Native people could count on the salmon's appearance at the same locations at roughly the same time year after year and could schedule their annual round accordingly. Second, the salmon were abundant—native elders wistfully recounted the days when "you could walk across the rivers on their backs," and even the modern, greatly diminished runs are an impressive sight. Also, salmon are relatively easily taken—no great technology is required to harvest the spawning masses. A final and essential point is that salmon could be relatively easily preserved. Large stores of dried salmon meant that this could be a year-round staple rather than only a seasonal delicacy, allowing development of dense populations, complex social organization and elaborate material culture.

Although salmon were the essential resource, many other fish were extremely important in the Northwest Coast economy. The outer-coast Nuu-chah-nulth and Haida relied extensively on halibut. Men paddled to offshore halibut banks, often far out to sea, to go after the big fish. Specialized halibut hooks show great ingenuity and were often decorated with carving. Lingcod, flounder and rockfish, also taken on hook and line, offered welcome variety. Huge schools of herring could be taken during their spawning runs in nets or with an ingenious device termed a "herring rake"—a long pole studded with sharp bone teeth along the lower portion of one side. While a helper paddled the canoe, the fisherman swept the rake through the water, impaling small fish on the teeth and flipping them into the canoe on the follow-through. Early European observers record with astonishment how quickly those adept at this type of fishing could fill their canoes. Native people also sank evergreen boughs attached to floats into the spawning beds, later collecting the thick, sticky herring spawn to be consumed fresh as a delicacy or dried and stored for the winter months. In addition, the eulachon, a small oily smelt which spawns in the spring, could be netted in quantity, allowed to "ripen" for a short period, then cooked in large wooden vats to extract the oil. Eulachon oil was a highly prized condiment, greatly enhancing the flavour of dried salmon and other foods. It was served at feasts, given away at potlatches and traded far into the interior.

Also essential to the coastal diet were the readily available clams, mussels, abalone and other shellfish. In addition, sea urchins, sea cucumbers, octopus, crabs and seaweeds added variety. There is considerable truth to the old adage "When the tide is out, the table is set"; however, villages of several hundred people could quickly deplete nearby supplies. The task of gathering such food fell largely to the women, who required only a hard-pointed stick for digging and prying and an open-weave basket for carrying. The huge shell middens all along the coast are ample testimony to their industry.

As well as fishing and collecting intertidal foods, Northwest Coast people hunted both land and sea animals. It was the mammals of the sea, however, which were most prized in the diet and conferred the most prestige on the hunter. Seals, sea lions and porpoises were hunted by almost all groups, generally by harpooning from canoes. Agile hunters also clambered over rocky islets to club seals and sea lions. Only the Nuu-chah-nulth of western Vancouver Island took their frail craft out onto the open ocean in search of whales, an activity which served to enhance the prestige of the noble whaler as much as to provide food to the group.

A wide range of other animals was hunted, but their flesh was less valued than the oil-rich meat and blubber of sea mammals. Waterfowl were taken

Kwagiulth eulachon fishing at Knight Inlet, 1968. Above: *bringing in the catch;* Left: *skimming oil from the surface of the cooking tanks.* RBCM

by some groups, in nets or with multi-pronged spears. Of the land animals, deer, elk and bear were most important. These could be hunted with bows and arrows, or taken in traps such as snares and deadfalls. Among some inland groups the mountain goat had considerable importance, this diffi-cult-to-obtain prey providing a test of young hunters' abilities.

Although vegetal foods played a lesser role in the diet, a wide range of plants was gathered. In spring, green shoots of salmonberries and fireweed were relished as a welcome change from the dried foods of winter. Clover and fern roots, as well as edible bulbs and tubers, were dug. The inner bark of the hemlock tree was scraped and pressed into starchy cakes. When the berries ripened—salalberries, salmonberries, huckleberries and others—they were enjoyed fresh as well as being pressed into flat cakes and dried for win-ter use. Native recipes included mixing fresh berries with salmon eggs and with eulachon oil. In addition, soapberries were whipped into a frothy treat known as "Indian ice cream," eaten with specially carved wooden spoons. Ethnobotanical research has demonstrated considerable native knowledge of plant uses, for medicine, for ritual purposes and in technology, as well as for food.

As well as skill and hard work, the food quest required a certain rapport with the supernatural world. In mythic times humans and animals were essentially the same, and animals were believed to retain the ability to transform from one realm to another. The Salmon People, Killer Whale People, Wolf People and others were viewed as having their own houses, where they took off their animal cloaks and lived parallel lives to humans. Numerous myths, such as the widespread "woman-who-married-the-bear," discuss interrelationships between these realms and the transfer of animal powers to human beneficiaries. Because the Salmon People voluntarily left their underwater villages to offer their flesh to humans, it was essential that they be respected. All groups practiced some variant of the First Salmon rite, where the earliest fish of the season were ceremonially welcomed, being placed on new mats in the chief's house and sprinkled with white eagle down. After the flesh was consumed the bones had to be carefully returned to the water, so that the salmon could come again the following year. Minor rituals were also carried out to thank a bear or mountain goat for allowing itself to be killed by the hunter. Even the cedar tree was thanked in prayer when humans stripped off its cloak of bark to weave their own clothing.

Paramount to the technology of Northwest Coast cultures was the red cedar. Lightweight, strong and rot-resistant, the aromatic cedar wood could be easily shaped by woodworkers using tools of stone, bone and shell, later replaced by iron. The long, straight grain allowed large planks to be split from a cedar log, using wedges of antler or hardwood gently tapped with a stone hammer. The bark and roots provided raw material for weavers, who crafted beautiful basketry, matting and clothing. The slender, flexible branches or withes were split and twisted to make rope. Although other trees were used for specific purposes, none came close to rivaling the importance of red cedar.

Impressive cedar homes lined the beach wherever food and fresh water could be found. People moved from place to place during the year while gathering seasonal resources, often maintaining homes at both summer and winter villages, and perhaps less substantial shelters at various camps. As the storms of winter approached, people loaded their canoes with provisions and returned to the sheltered locations of their winter villages. Here they spent the dark, wet months, comfortable in their large multi-family houses. Although each region of the coast had its own architectural style, all followed a basic pattern. Massive cedar posts supported huge roof beams and a series of rafters, forming a framework which was covered with split-cedar planks. Decorative patterns of adze marks might embellish beams, and posts were occasionally carved in the form of crest animals. Roof planks were often channeled and overlapped, serving both to hold them in place and to control rain runoff. Planks were important possessions and could be

*Beautifully carved
Tsimshian chest with
beaver design.*
CMC 59642

transported to other village sites as people moved with the seasons.

Wood, particularly cedar, was the major medium for the great artistic achievements of coastal carvers. The so-called "totem poles" are the best-known examples of Northwest Coast art. In addition to the tall, free-standing poles in front of the houses, artists carved crests into frontal poles (against the front of the houses, incorporating the doorway) and on interior house posts. Although regional styles are clearly distinct and not all groups carved free-standing poles, all had some tradition of monumental artwork in wood. Most were heraldic in function, as important chiefs hired renowned artists to depict family crests for all to see. Wealthy patrons also commissioned spectacular masks, rattles and feast dishes to use in their winter ceremonials. Everyday items, such as bowls, spoons and storage boxes, were frequently embellished with finely carved designs. Even such roughly used objects as seal or fish clubs were frequently transformed into works of art.

A good example of the skill of Northwest Coast woodworkers is the bent-wood box. The four sides of these containers were formed from a single plank, cut partly through where the corners were to be and then steamed until the fibres could be bent at ninety-degree angles. The fourth corner was pegged or sewn with root, as was the bottom. A fitted lid completed the box. Most were so skillfully constructed that they were watertight and could be used as cooking boxes (adding hot rocks from the fire with tongs to keep the water boiling), water buckets or containers for other liquids. Others were used to store foods, such as dried salmon, halibut, shellfish, roots and cakes of berries. Still others, frequently beautifully decorated with incised and painted designs inlaid with decorative shells, were "boxes of treasures" in which high-ranking people stored their ceremonial regalia. These finely crafted containers served all the roles pottery played across most of North America. The absence of pottery in Northwest Coast cultures does not mean that people lacked suitable clay or the technological ingenuity to make pots—it simply demonstrates their mastery of the woodworkers' craft which met all their needs.

One of the great accomplishments of Northwest Coast woodworkers was the graceful, ocean-going dugout canoe. Construction of these vital craft

Above: *Beautifully crafted dugout canoes, such as these Kwagiulth examples, made the maritime Northwest Coast lifestyle possible.* E.S. Curtis/NAC C30189
Left: *Nuu-chah-nulth women wait for the canoe, with their digging sticks and open-weave baskets used for collecting shellfish.* E.S. Curtis/NAC C20845

was a skilled job, and some carvers became specialists. After the huge cedar log had been laboriously adzed to shape, the canoe was filled with water, which was heated by adding red-hot stones. Once the hot water and steam had softened the wood, the crucial task of spreading the sides to the desired shape could be accomplished. For large ocean-going canoes, separate prow and stern pieces were carved and carefully fitted and sewn to the hull. The exterior was singed with torches to harden the wood and remove any splinters, then polished with the sandpaper-like skin of the dogfish, so that the canoe would glide swiftly and silently through the water. Canoes ranged from small two-person fishing and sealing craft to vessels for trade or warfare capable of carrying forty or fifty people. They had to be treated with care; men cleared runways on the beach where they could draw up their canoes without damaging them and covered them with mats so they would not crack in the sun. Canoes made the Northwest Coast way of life possible. Almost all travel was by sea as people moved around their rugged homelands, or set out on lengthy voyages to attend feasts, to trade or to raid their enemies. Familiar from early childhood with the vagaries of waves, wind and weather, paddlers skillfully propelled their craft over great distances.

Whereas woodworking was primarily a male task, the female art was weaving. A variety of plant fibres, including cedar bark, split cedar and spruce root, and various grasses were used to produce elegant basketry in regionally distinct styles. Basketry containers served a variety of carrying and storage functions, some woven so closely that they were watertight and could be used for cooking.

Clothing was also woven from plant fibres, particularly cedar bark. For this purpose, the strips of bark were pounded until they became supple and soft, then were woven on a simple loom. Men wrapped cedar bark blankets around their bodies, while women wore skirts of shredded cedar-bark and blankets or cloaks. The blankets were usually fastened at the front with a wooden or bone pin. Wide-brimmed hats protected the wearer from the sun and rain. The tailored hide clothing worn across the rest of aboriginal Canada was useless in the drizzle and fog of the coastal rainforest; the soft and water-resistant bark provided much better protection from the elements. For colder weather people added robes of bear fur or sea otter pelts. Footwear was worn only by upriver groups—the hide moccasins of the interior were useless to coastal people who were constantly getting in and out of canoes.

All important locations, including house sites, salmon fishing stations, hunting territories, berry patches and major stands of cedar, were considered private property. Ownership was held by kinship groups sharing a name and a tradition of descent from a common ancestor. This corporate group held not only territory but also important privileges such as names, ritual dances, songs and the right to depict certain crests.

Northwest Coast people placed great emphasis on inherited rank and privileges. Chiefs and nobles held high-ranking names and controlled access to group-held territories and rights. Skillful management of the group's resources allowed chiefs to accumulate wealth, which could be publicly distributed at feasts and potlatches to enhance their status. Commoners, who lacked inherited claims to titles or ceremonial privileges, shared in the group's greater prestige and were essential to provide the labour necessary to accumulate food and wealth. Slaves, usually purchased or captured in war, made up a considerable portion of the population. Although they had to perform menial tasks, their lives were not greatly different from commoners. However, they were considered chattel and could be sold, given away at potlatches or killed by a high-ranking chief to demonstrate indifference to his great wealth.

Raiding and warfare were commonplace, even among people speaking the same language. Raids were frequently to revenge insults or injury, or to take slaves. Less common was full-scale warfare over territory. After a successful raid, warriors burned the houses and turned homeward, their canoes laden with booty, the severed heads of their vanquished foes, and women and children taken as slaves.

Marriages were contracted with individuals of equivalent rank in other kin groups. For high-ranking people this frequently meant marriage to someone from another village, often at a considerable distance. These marriages served as political alliances and involved transfers of wealth, including names and ceremonial prerogatives.

Central to the whole concept of status and rank was the potlatch. Any change in the status quo required a chief and his kin to invite others to witness their claim. A high-status marriage, the birth of an heir, the assumption of an inherited name, the completion of a new house or the raising of a carved pole were all such occasions. Chiefs might also potlatch to "erase a shame," when they had stumbled during a ceremonial performance or had been taken captive by enemies and ransomed by their people. No individual was recognized in a particular status, even if he was clearly the proper heir, until his name was "made good" by public validation at a potlatch.

A prominent feature of the potlatch was the distribution of property (the term "potlatch" actually comes from the word for "gift" in the Chinook jargon, a trade language widely used on the coast in historic times). The largest and most valuable gifts went to high-ranking visitors. Indeed, the potlatch served not only to validate the status of the giver but to reaffirm that of the guests. Great care had to be taken that the seating arrangements, order of distribution and size of gifts all reflected the status of the recipients. All present listened to speakers for the host group recount their history and their hereditary rights, and all had to be paid as witnesses. Late-nineteenth-century photographs show huge stacks of Hudson's Bay Company blankets, sacks of flour and other items ready for general distribution.

Anthropological descriptions of the potlatch all refer to late time periods, when massive social upheavals were affecting native life. During this time potlatches became more extravagant and more competitive, as great chiefs fought to outdo their rivals with wealth. Not only were enormous quantities of goods given away, but valuable items were destroyed as gestures of rivalry. Coppers (the shield-shaped copper objects which were the ultimate wealth items in the potlatch system) were broken, canoes were placed on the fire and slaves were killed. Chiefs poured boxes of valuable eulachon oil onto the fire in an attempt to force back high-ranking guests, who would thus be defeated by this show of wealth. The government banning of the potlatch was at least partly due to these historic excesses.

Few ethnographic topics have received greater attention than the potlatch. Anthropologists have argued over its interpretations and its functions

Nuu-chah-nulth men playing lehal, *the "bones game," 1975. The man in the foreground holds the "bones," while the drummers attempt to confuse their opponents.* Photo by author

in native societies. Certainly it played a pivotal role in social organization. In the absence of a writing system, the potlatch served to publicly recognize an individual's claim to a particular status or inherited right. It also served an economic role, redistributing food and goods. Far from impoverishing a potlatching chief, it was a system of "banking" or investment, as he would be a recipient at subsequent potlatches.

Potlatches were enlivened by performances of masked dancers. Supernatural forces were felt to dwell close to the villages and were most accessible during winter. Ceremonies kept people occupied and entertained during this time, when economic activities were greatly reduced. More theatre than dance, the performances re-enacted ancestral encounters with supernatural beings, when important rights were transferred to the human world. Skilled artists created dramatic masks and other regalia to enhance the image of supernatural presence.

More secular entertainments occurred year-round, whenever groups of people got together. Racing and feats of strength were common, but nothing was as passionately played as the gambling games. Particularly popular was lehal (the "bones game"), played with pairs of bone cylinders, one of each pair marked, which could be hidden in the hand. While one team guessed at the location of the unmarked bones, their opponents attempted to confuse them with drumming and singing. The game could be lengthy, with both participants and spectators betting heavily over each exchange of the bones.

Any successful endeavour—in hunting and fishing, in gambling, in warfare, in amassing wealth and potlatching—required supernatural aid. To gain such assistance people had to be ritually clean, requiring a period of "training." This involved fasting, sexual abstinence and frequent bathing, rubbing the body with hemlock boughs until the skin bled. Some acquired particular skill in controlling supernatural forces and became shamans, blessed with the ability to cure illnesses. In dramatic firelit performances shamans sang and drummed over their patients, sucking out the disease-causing object or embarking on a perilous psychic journey to restore the lost soul. The curing profession was open to both men and women, who were usually attracted to the field by heightened prestige and payment for successful cures. They were feared as well as respected, since they also had the power to inflict illness or death, and many were suspected of practicing witchcraft.

Exploits of supernatural beings and their encounters with human ancestors served as the basis for a rich oral tradition. The skies were filled with terrifying supernatural birds, such as the whale-hunting thunderbird; the woods contained giant human-like monsters; and numerous powerful beings, some capable of bestowing great wealth, dwelt beneath the waves. Prominent among the myths were those of the trickster/transformer, who put the world and all living things in their present form, a role played by Raven along most of the coast. It was Raven who brought light to the world, releasing the sun from a wooden chest where it had been kept by a mighty chief. Typical of transformer figures, Raven could be foolish, greedy or obscene as well as benevolent, and the stories of his adventures and mishaps made amusing telling. Although myths could be instructive, they were primarily enjoyed as entertainment, helping to while away long rainy evenings as people sat around the fires in their large wooden houses.

THE NORTHERN GROUPS

Speakers of three language isolates—Haida, Tlingit and Tsimshian—occupy the northern Northwest Coast. Although their unrelated languages clearly indicate separate origins, these three peoples shared a similar lifestyle, achieving the greatest elaboration of material culture and most sophisticated art style on the coast.

The Haida homeland was the cluster of islands, islets and sheltered waterways making up the Queen Charlotte Islands, known to the Haida as Haida Gwaii. Somewhat prior to European arrival some groups expanded across Dixon Strait to the north, establishing villages in southernmost Alaska. As a result, the international boundary now divides the Haida, although considerable social interaction still exists. The rugged lands of these island-dwellers ensured that their main orientation was to the sea. Their large dugout canoes took them out after salmon, halibut and sea mammals, and allowed trading expeditions or war parties to reach the mainland. The vast stands of red cedar on Haida Gwaii allowed the Haida to become master carvers and canoe-builders, their canoes being eagerly sought in trade. Newly carved canoes might be paddled across to the Tsimshian on the Nass River, towing an older craft in which they would return laden with eulachon oil received in exchange.

To the north were the Tlingit, along the myriad islands making up the archipelago of southeastern Alaska. The Tlingit were famed as seafaring traders, exchanging copper and mountain-goat wool blankets for such goods as slaves and shell ornaments. During the historic fur trade they also traveled far into the interior, taking European goods to the Athapaskans in exchange for furs in demand by the foreigners. Groups which owned strategic trade routes to the interior, along the valleys of the Chilkat, Taku and Stikine rivers, prospered in this trade. Some intermarried with Athapaskans and became the Inland Tlingit of extreme northwestern British Columbia and the adjacent Yukon. While they resembled the Athapaskans in many respects, their language, social organization and ceremonies remained Tlingit.

Several languages exist among the largest group, the Tsimshian of British Columbia's northern mainland. The four Nisga'a communities occupied the Nass River valley, plus adjacent saltwater territory. The seven winter villages (or "tribes") of the Gitksan (literally "People of the Skeena") lay along the Skeena River and its tributaries. Unlike other groups, the Gitksan relied solely on their rivers and mountains, and lacked any access to coastal resources. Although they were politically and culturally distinct, linguists consider the Gitksan and Nisga'a to speak two dialects of one Tsimshian language. A second language, Coast Tsimshian, was spoken by eleven tribes with villages on the lower Skeena and the islands near its mouth. In addition, three winter village groups pushed far to the south, taking over the outer islands formerly held by the northern Wakashans. Their language, the nearly-extinct Southern Tsimshian, is considered by most linguists to be a distinct dialect of Coast Tsimshian.

The territory of the Tsimshian peoples was rich and varied, with salmon in the rivers and the most important eulachon run on the Northwest Coast in the Nass. While most groups had access to the whole range of coastal resources, the Gitksan and Nisga'a were riverine people, devoting more time to the hunting of land mammals. Trade helped even out local shortages, and such important commodities as eulachon oil and mountain-goat wool were traded far afield.

The social organization of the northern groups distinguished them from other coastal peoples. The Haida and Tlingit divided themselves into two groups (termed "moieties" by anthropologists). Among the Haida these were the Eagles and Ravens, each subdivided into lineages named for their original villages. Tsimshian social organization was similar, except that there

*The Haida village of
Skidegate, 1878.* CMC 255

were four divisions (termed "phratries") rather than two. Each person had to seek a mate from outside their moiety or phratry; marriage within would have been incestuous. Descent was traced through the female line, each child taking the affiliation of the mother. A chief could not transmit his name and property to his own sons since they belonged to a different kin group; instead his sister's sons were his heirs. As high-status marriages were frequently alliances between groups, young men might have to set out for the villages of their maternal uncles to seek their inheritance.

The highly acclaimed northern art primarily depicted crest animals or images from myths. Display of such figures was a jealously guarded family prerogative. Much of the material culture of these northern people was embellished with such crests, from the finely carved miniature figures along the handles of gracefully bent horn spoons to massive wooden sculptures in front of houses. Among the Haida, men also frequently had their upper bodies tattooed with crest figures. Unique to the Haida was the practice of placing their high-status dead at the top of carved poles, hidden from view behind elegantly carved wooden boards displaying their main crest figures. The fluid lines and complex, stylized images of northern art, carefully wrapped in shallow carving around the poles and other objects without detracting from their basic shape, contrasts sharply with the bolder and more sculptural Wakashan forms to the south.

The northern groups also reached the greatest achievements in architecture on the coast. Carefully fitted cedar planks were placed vertically and relatively permanently to form the walls. Frontal poles, with the body or gaping mouth of the lowest figure forming an oval entranceway, were most common among the Haida. Interior house posts were often carved in the form of animals owned as crests by house occupants. Frequently there was an excavated central area in which people could sit around the fire. Important houses might have several levels, each covered with floorplanks

The abandoned Haida village of Ninstints, on the southern Queen Charlotte Islands, has been declared a World Heritage Site. Photo by author

Tsimshian chief in ceremonial regalia, including a Chilkat blanket of mountain goat wool. NAC C56768

and connected by stairs. The chief and his family slept in cubicles of planks, often painted with crest designs, at the rear of the house, while people of lesser rank slept along side walls and slaves had the least desirable locations near the door. Boxes and baskets stacked along the walls contained stored food supplies and personal gear. Houses of high rank, like people, had names and histories.

The northern people were noted warriors and slave-raiders, the Haida in particular being feared by groups far to the south. The sudden appearance of a Haida canoe, paddles flashing rhythmically as the craft bore down on its victims, could mean sudden death or enslavement for people as distant as the Fraser River Salish. Northern warriors wore wooden slat armour, large wooden helmets surmounted with frightening images and carved wooden visors to protect their faces. In a Gitksan legend, a warrior-chief named Nekt ventured forth from his hilltop fortress to do battle in his armour made from grizzly bear skin lined with slate tablets. Fortifications were constructed by ambitious chiefs at strategic locations to control access to major trade routes.

The lives of high-ranking northerners, as befitting people of vast wealth, were punctuated with major feasts and potlatches. Although various life crises required such ceremonies, the most important event was the mortuary potlatch. This ceremony served as both a memorial to the greatness of the deceased chief and validation of his successor's right to that position. It also allowed the host group to pay debts incurred during the lengthy period of mourning.

At such public occasions chiefs appeared richly attired in the distinctive northern ceremonial costume. The Chilkat blanket, a robe of mountain-goat wool finely woven with elaborate designs, was worn over the shoulders, often with leggings or a tunic of the same material. The ceremonial head-dress included a carved wooden frontlet surmounted with long sea lion whiskers, with numerous ermine skins hanging down the back. A hollow at the top of the headdress was filled with eagle down, a symbol of peace, which floated through the air and settled on spectators as high-ranking chiefs sedately danced.

Smallpox and other pressures of the historic period resulted in abandonment of many traditional villages. When Fort Simpson was established in 1834 most of the Coast Tsimshian moved near the post, leaving only large shell middens to mark where their ancestors had lived for millennia. Declining populations forced the Haida to coalesce at two villages, Massett and Skidegate. At the others, the great cedar houses collapsed and the finely carved poles gradually toppled over and were lost to decay. Only at Ninstints, a remote village at the southern end of Haida Gwaii, has an attempt been made to arrest this gradual destruction. Ninstints has been proclaimed a World Heritage Site by the United Nations, a fitting recognition of the genius and talents of the nineteenth-century artists who carved the still-standing poles.

THE WAKASHANS

The Wakashan language family has two main branches, Kwakiutl and Nootka (although some linguists prefer to call them simply Northern and Southern Wakashan). The term Wakashan comes from the observations of Captain James Cook, among the people he called "Nootka," in 1778:

the word *wakash* . . . was very frequently in their mouths. It seemed to express applause, approbation, and friendship. For when they appeared to be satisfied, or well pleased with any thing they saw, or any incident that happened, they would, with one voice, call out *wakash! wakash!*

(Cook 1784:337)

Although primarily used as a linguistic term, it also designates the central sub-area of the Northwest Coast. In this case it includes the Nuxalk, who are Salishan in language but possess most Wakashan cultural traits.

The groups in the Wakashan sub-area historically have been known by inappropriate or erroneous names, which are largely rejected by the people to whom they refer. Today all these groups have adopted names which better reflect their own concepts of their identity. As their languages had no words for such large social units, new terms have had to be created. "Nootka," for example, is an error dating to Cook's visit. It is still uncertain what the natives were actually saying to the famed navigator when he concluded that they called themselves Nootka. The people today refer to themselves as the Nuu-chah-nulth (roughly "all along the mountains"). Similarly, "Bella Coola" is an anglicized version of a Heiltsuk word for people who now prefer to be called Nuxalk, from their name for the Bella Coola valley. "Kwakiutl" is a poor rendering of a native word ("Kwagiulth" is closer), which in any case refers only to the people at Fort Rupert. For the southern groups, who speak a language known as Kwakwala, the term Kwakwaka'wakw ("those who speak Kwakwala") has been proposed, but is not yet in widespread use.

Three languages make up the northern branch of the Wakashans. The farthest north are the Haisla, who have been influenced by extensive contact with the Tsimshian. South of them are the Heiltsuk, a large group with their main centre at Bella Bella, on the central coast. Farther south are the many politically separate villages of the Kwakwaka'wakw or Kwagiulth on northern Vancouver Island and the adjacent mainland coastline.

The Nuu-chah-nulth, occupying the storm-lashed west coast of Vancouver Island and the tip of the Olympic Peninsula in Washington, are also divided into three languages. The northern and central Nuu-chah-nulth groups speak dialects of one language, while the Ditidaht of southern Vancouver Island and the Makah on the Olympic Peninsula speak separate but closely related languages. Their rugged environment made the Nuu-chah-nulth among the most maritime of all Northwest Coast peoples. Like the Haida, the Nuu-chah-nulth were famed canoe-builders, skillfully carving graceful ocean-going vessels from the huge cedar trees which grow on the outer coast. In such craft they set far out to sea to fish for halibut and hunt sea mammals.

The Nuxalk are a relatively small enclave of Salish-speakers on the central coast. Their territory included the valleys of the Bella Coola and Dean rivers, plus the long steep-sided inlets that cut through the mountains from the outer coast, giving them access to both inland and saltwater resources. Culturally they more closely resemble their Heiltsuk neighbours than their Salish kin to the south. Their artwork and ceremonial performances, while distinctively Nuxalk, follow the general Wakashan pattern.

The social organization of the Wakashans differed considerably from that of northern groups. Inheritance, including membership in the kin group, could come from either the mother's or father's side, although there was an emphasis on the male line. Members of each kin group (known as *namima* among the Kwagiulth) traced descent from a common ancestor. Such ancestors were often supernatural beings who became humans early in the history of the world. Kin groups owned fishing sites and other economic resources, as well as such important assets as names, dances, songs and crests, including the rights to depict their supernatural forebears or to re-enact myths in ceremonial performances. Rank came from the closeness of the relationship with these ancestors, based on primogeniture. The rank-conscious Kwagiulth counted rank not only within the *namima* but also ranked *namima* within the "tribe" (the winter village group), and even ranked the tribes. No political authority extended this widely; the highest chief of the first-ranking *namima* of the first-ranking tribe simply had the greatest prominence on all ceremonial occasions.

The striking appearance of these people was described by late-eighteenth-century explorers and fur traders. Cook commented that the natives of Nootka Sound "rub their bodies constantly over with a red paint of a clayey or coarse ochry substance mixed with oil" and frequently sprinkled mica on the paint to make it glitter. For festive occasions the hair was greased and sprinkled with bird down. Although facial hair was usually plucked by the young men, older men often allowed their beards to grow. The earlobes and the nasal septum were pierced for ornaments. Dentalium shells, a wealth item obtained by the Nuu-chah-nulth from deep offshore waters, were worn in the ears and as necklaces. Even the shape of the skull was altered by binding the foreheads of infants in the cradleboards. The Kwagiulth of northern Vancouver Island practiced the most extreme form, tightly bandaging the child's head to produce a narrow and elongated shape consistent with their ideals of beauty.

Wakashan houses differed considerably from northern styles. The planks which made up the walls were structurally separate from the large permanent framework of posts and beams. A family group might have several house frames at different seasonal villages, and the planks were intended to be easily dismantled and transported. When people moved, planks could be placed across two canoes, providing a convenient platform on which to stack household goods. Once at each location, the planks were tied horizontally between pairs of upright poles to form walls. Planks also covered the roof, being weighed down with poles and rocks against the high winds

Top: *The inside of a Nuu-chah-nulth house, 1778. This engraving, from a painting by Cook expedition artist John Webber, provides a wealth of information on native life at the beginning of European contact.* CMC J-2434
Centre: *The Kwagiulth village of Blunden Harbour, 1901.* RBCM
Bottom : *The Kwagiulth village of Alert Bay, 1917.* CMC 41968

of winter storms. Although they lacked the plank floors and recessed levels of high-status northern homes, there were benches for sitting and sleeping, and back-supports near the fires. Boxes and baskets of preserved foods and personal goods were stacked nearly to the roof, and large quantities of fish hung drying from the rafters. Cook complained of the "filth and confusion" and the "stinking of fish, train-oil [whale oil], and smoke," but to the natives such odours must have been only testimonials to the warmth of their fires, the reassuring winter's supply of food and their success in hunting such mighty quarry as the whale.

Of all Northwest Coast peoples, only the Nuu-chah-nulth actively ventured out to sea in pursuit of whales, particularly the California gray and the humpback. The whaling crew had to be well trained to silently propel their canoe alongside their prey, allowing their leader the privilege of thrusting his harpoon deep into the animal. Then the crew frantically back-paddled to escape the thrashing of the wounded beast's tail as it dove, taking with it a long line with large floats made from inflated sea lion skins. Struggling against the floats eventually exhausted the whale, which then could be dispatched with a killing lance. A successful hunt provided a large amount of meat and the highly prized blubber to be rendered into oil, and also enhanced the prestige of the whaling chief.

Success at whaling involved far more than rigorous training for the crew. The whaler had to be ritually pure, requiring long periods of fasting and sexual abstinence. Prolonged ritual bathing, the whaler diving and spouting like a whale, was followed by vigorous scrubbing of the body. Sometimes the whaler's wife shared in the ritual bathing, and while the whaler was on the hunt she remained motionless in her bed so that the whale would similarly be docile. Some whalers kept shrines in the woods, where they set up human skulls or corpses and carved wooden figures representing dead whalers around an image of the whale. The dead were believed to have power over whales and could aid the whaler on the hunt or cause dead whales to drift ashore near the village.

The Wakashans shared a distinctive and exuberant art style. Cook noted several large carved wooden figures in the Nuu-chah-nulth house he visited and commented that: "Nothing is without a kind of frieze-work or the figure of some animal upon it." Wakashan carving was much more sculptural than the applied northern forms, extending the basic shape with projecting wings, beaks, legs and other appendages. Thunderbirds soar on outspread wings, and the tsonoqua, a cannibal ogress, reaches with outstretched arms. When commercial paints became available, these were enthusiastically adopted, adding to the flamboyant nature of Wakashan art. Late-nineteenth-century photographs show villages with tall, deeply carved poles and elaborate paintings embellishing the fronts of some houses.

It was the Wakashans who held the largest potlatches and developed winter ceremonials to their greatest extent. The Kwagiulth forbade economic activities during a sacred winter period, so that all their energies could be turned to ceremonies. Secular ranking was replaced by the ranking of the dances. Elaborate costumes, masks that "transformed," theatrical tricks such as carved figures that "flew" through the darkened houses, all enhanced the illusion of supernatural presence.

The Wolf featured most prominently in the winter rituals of the Nuu-chah-nulth. The sound of whistles from the woods warned people that the Wolf spirits were nearby, ready to abduct their children. Suddenly, men dressed as wolves attacked the villagers and in the confusion made off with the children, of both sexes, who were to be initiated. When the children were finally returned they were "wild" and had to be "tamed" through ritual dances. Finally the initiates danced in their wolf costumes, demonstrating their return to human state but with new powers received from the Wolves. The flat-sided wooden headdresses worn by dancers as part of their wolf costumes are among the best known of Nuu-chah-nulth artworks.

Among the Kwagiulth, there were several distinct dance series, featuring many different supernatural beings. Dances were hereditary and ranked, with dancers often working their way through a number of lesser positions before being initiated into the most highly ranked dances, such as the *hamatsa* or "Cannibal Dancer." Believed living in the home of the fearsome "Cannibal at the North End of the World," the initiate was actually hidden in the woods for a long period of seclusion and instruction. When he returned he was possessed with cannibalistic frenzy, leaping through the smokehole from the roof onto the fire or rushing into the house to bite members of the audience. Such "victims" were forewarned and were later publicly paid for their role. A small concealed knife could draw a convincing display of blood, and the image could be enhanced by placing small blood-filled bladders in the mouth to be burst at appropriately dramatic moments. Relatives attempted to "tame" the *hamatsa* with their rattles and songs as he circled the fire. Then the "Cannibal Birds" made their appearance. Dancers, wearing long strips of cedar bark to cover their bodies, performed with the large elaborate masks representing "Cannibal Raven," "Crooked-Beak-of-Heaven" with its distinctive hooked beak, and *hokhokw* with its long straight beak which crushed men's skulls. These were among the most dramatic of all performances, as the dancers high-stepped around the fire, swaying the huge masks and loudly clacking their beaks. Finally the *hamatsa* returned, dressed in ceremonial finery, now "tamed" and restored to his human state.

Many dances relied on theatrical trickery for their effect on the audience. A good example is a woman's dance, the *tokwit*, which involved apparent death and resurrection. In one version, as the woman danced sedately around the fire, she was attacked by a man emerging from the shadows. Knocking her to the ground, the warrior hacked off her head with his whalebone "sword," holding the severed head, streaming with blood, up to

Top left: *The thunderbird sits atop* tsonoqua *on this fine example of a Kwagiulth totem pole, now standing at Alert Bay, by the master carver Willie Seaweed.* Photo by author
Top right: *Kwagiulth mask representing* tsonoqua, *the cannibal ogress.* RBCM
Left: *A Nuu-chah-nulth chief wears a distinctive thunderbird headdress.* NAC PA140976

Kwagiulth dancers pose in their elaborate costumes for the winter ceremonials.
E.S. Curtis/NAC C20857

the firelight. In actuality, the *tokwit* dancer had covered her head with her blanket, and the warrior had removed a carved wooden likeness, complete with the *tokwit's* own hair, that she had been concealing. Bursting the blood-filled bladders attached to the wooden head completed the effect. Attendants rushed in to remove the "body," yet later in the performance the *tokwit* re-emerged, unharmed, to dance again.

Many masterpieces of Wakashan artistry were created specifically for winter ceremonials. The magnificent masks, representing a wide range of supernatural beings, were deeply carved to enhance the effect of eerie shadows from the firelight. Early historic headdresses often have mica set into pitch in the eyes, to flash as they reflected the fire. Later examples use copper strips or bits of mirror to enhance this dramatic effect. Many masks, such as those of the Cannibal Birds, were mechanical, allowing the dancers to pull concealed strings to make the beaks open and close with a loud clacking sound. In other cases, the masks could "transform"; pulling the concealed strings caused the mask to burst open and reveal an inner being. Skilled artists who could produce new and dramatic effects were eagerly sought by chiefs who wished to amaze their guests. When we see these masks displayed in our well-lit museums we should remember that their context has been lost. Try to imagine them in use, in darkened houses lit only by the central fire, as skilled dancers conveyed the image of supernatural presences to their audience.

THE COAST SALISH

The southern coast of British Columbia and south far into Washington was the homeland of the Coast Salish. Excluding the northern enclave of Nuxalk at Bella Coola, six distinct Salishan languages were spoken on the British Columbia coast. In the north are the Comox people, bordering the Kwagiulth on both Vancouver Island and the mainland and borrowing from them many Wakashan cultural traits. South of the Comox on Vancouver Island were the Pentlatch, who largely succumbed to disease and native warfare in the nineteenth century. Below the Comox on the mainland are the Sechelt and the Squamish people. The largest Salishan language is Halkomelem, which includes such important groups as the Cowichan and Nanaimo on Vancouver Island and all the people along the lower Fraser River, collectively termed the Sto:lo from their name for the river. Finally, the Straits language is spoken on both sides of the Juan de Fuca Strait, with most groups in British Columbia near the modern-day city of Victoria.

Most of the Coast Salish had a typical Northwest Coast economy, based primarily on the sea. The Sto:lo, however, were riverine people, with most lacking any access to salt water. The river provided plentiful salmon, eulachon and other fish, and the men hunted waterfowl in the marshes and deer, bear and mountain-goat on the surrounding land. Particularly important was the sturgeon, which could be taken year-round in the Fraser and its larger sloughs and tributaries. The Sto:lo devised ingenious techniques to harpoon these large fish while they rested, fat and sluggish, in deep water during the winter, and used a variety of fishing techniques in summer when the sturgeon moved into the sloughs to spawn.

Social organization of the Coast Salish was not as rigid as that of groups to the north. No clear-cut class distinctions were evident. True "chiefs" appear not to have existed, the native term being better translated as "leader." Although people of high birth had a great advantage, the system was flexible enough to accommodate upward mobility for talented individuals of more humble origins. Leaders spoke only for their extended families or "households," as they tended to be the group occupying one house. Households were the largest effective political groups, even winter villages being essentially only clusters of households. The loose social organization allowed frequent shifting of households into different winter village groups. Slaves, purchased or obtained in war, were not numerous in Salish villages.

The winter village houses consisted of permanent frameworks of posts and beams, covered with split cedar planks, slung horizontally between uprights to form walls. Houses were of the "shed-roof" variety, with a single pitch on the roof sloping gently from front to back. The near-flat roofs provided convenient platforms for spectators at public events such as potlatches. A number of houses might be joined side by side under a common roof to create one long segmented structure. Simon Fraser observed such dwellings on his famed 1808 journey. One in the Fraser Valley he described as:

640 feet long . . . under one roof. The front is 18 feet high, and the covering is slanting. All the apartments, which are separated in portions, are square . . . on the outside, are carved a human figure large as life, and there are other figures in imitation of beasts and birds.

(Fraser 1960:103)

217

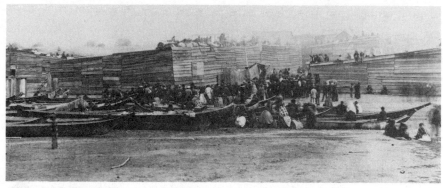

Potlatch in progress at a Salish village at Victoria, 1872. RBCM

Another, near the mouth of the Fraser, he described as a "fort . . . 1500 feet in length." Interior partitions of planks or mats provided privacy for family groups but could be removed to create a large open space for social or ceremonial occasions.

Winter dances of the Salish were very different from the masked performances of the Wakashans. They lacked theatrical illusions and elaborate costumes, instead emphasizing personal acquisition of spirit power. Young people ritually purified themselves by fasting and bathing before embarking on a quest for a guardian spirit. Those fortunate enough to obtain guardian spirit power received the ability to cure sickness, to foretell events or to be exceptionally successful at hunting or fishing. Guardian spirits also imparted details of songs and dances, through which humans could express their spirit power. During the winter months spirit power became stronger and overwhelmed the human recipients, who danced and sang as directed. Dancing and feasting were almost continual during these months, frequently involving reciprocal visiting with inhabitants of nearby villages.

The only masked dance among the Salish was the *sxwaixwe*, featuring a distinctive mask with protruding eyes and bird-like elements. This mask was unique to the Salish, and the right to dance wearing it was an important inherited privilege. Its use was not part of the winter spirit dances but enlivened such events as potlatches, weddings and the reception of visitors.

With the exception of the *sxwaixwe* mask, elaborate ceremonial art was lacking among the Salish. In addition, they did not embellish their household goods with crest designs. Only the Comox, in contact with the Kwagiulth, raised free-standing totem poles. More typical of Salish art are house posts carved in human or animal form and grave figures carved to represent deceased ancestors. Smaller artworks include carved rattles and engraved designs on spindle whorls and combs. Although fewer objects were decorated by the Salish, much of their work was of considerable artistic merit. Its personal and religious associations, however, meant that it was

Left: *A Coast Salish* sxwaixwe *dancer, wearing the distinctive dance mask.*
E.S. Curtis/PAC C20825 □ Right: *Carved wooden spindle whorls are among the finest of Coast Salish artworks.* CMC 72850

less likely to be sold to collectors and museums, and today it is less known to the general public than other variants of Northwest Coast art.

The art of weaving was well developed by the Salish. Beautiful coiled baskets of split cedar root were decorated with geometric designs in cherry bark and other materials, in the same style as those produced by the Interior Salish. Created in a variety of sizes and shapes, they served many carrying and storage functions. As well as the woven cedar-bark capes and blankets for everyday use, women also produced a "nobility blanket" of mountain-goat wool mixed with dog hair and other materials, which was woven on a loom. Such blankets ranged from elegantly simple, with only a decorated border breaking the plain appearance, to those covered with complex geometric designs. The recent revival of this art among several Fraser River bands has led many women to a great appreciation for the talents of their ancestors as the women attempt to duplicate past achievements.

HISTORIC IMPACT

Ships of the pale-skinned invaders finally reached the remote coast of what is today British Columbia in the 1770s. Alarmed by the Russian presence in the north, the Spanish attempted to strengthen their claims to western North America with coastal expeditions in 1774 and 1775. Fleeting contact was made with Haida and Nuu-chah-nulth groups during these voyages.

Far from being overawed by these strange new people in their floating houses, coastal natives paddled out to the ships, tossing feathers on the water or making other gestures of peace, and initiated trade. Eagerly sought was anything of metal, a wondrous substance that these wealthy newcomers seemed to possess in abundance.

It was not until 1778, when Captain James Cook arrived at Nootka Sound during his third voyage of exploration, that intensive contact began. Cook spent almost a month among the Nuu-chah-nulth, and his journal provides the earliest major account of Northwest Coast native life. Much of the interaction between the two races centred on trade. In exchange for metal implements, the British obtained handicrafts and furs. Cook's initial speculation that a profitable fur trade could be established was confirmed when the ships reached China and it was discovered that the thick, soft pelts of the sea otter obtained from the Nuu-chah-nulth could be sold at high prices. This was a discovery of momentous consequence for Northwest Coast peoples, turning Nootka Sound into a scene of international commerce within only a few years.

By the mid-1780s the rush for fur trade wealth had begun. Initially British, French, Spanish and American vessels vied for pelts collected by the natives, but the trade soon dwindled to the British (called "King George men" by the Indians) and the Americans (known as "Boston men" from their main home port). Ships set out laden with goods for the native trade; initially iron tools were the major trade items, but as the market became glutted traders shifted to other commodities which might catch the natives' fancy. After driving the best deal possible, traders set sail for China with their valuable cargoes of sea otter pelts. This trade continued into the second decade of the nineteenth century, until relentless pursuit of the sea otter finally resulted in its extinction along the British Columbia coast.

While ship captains stood to make great profits, it is also true that some fortunate and astute native leaders were able to establish themselves as intermediaries in the trade, greatly increasing their own wealth and power. European traders and aboriginal leaders interacted as equals, each controlling access to goods desired by the other. Many European journals grudgingly acknowledge the trading skills of native chiefs.

In fact, this early maritime trade bolstered the traditional native economy. Newly wealthy chiefs invested their profits in traditional ways, holding impressive ceremonies and distributing quantities of goods at potlatches. With iron carving tools and new wealth, great works of art could be commissioned on a scale previously unknown. The "forest of totem poles" which greeted later arrivals to the northern villages was possible only as a result of this trade. Not all of the effects of this early period of contact were positive, however; outbreaks of epidemic diseases carried by European traders took a dreadful toll in many native villages. Although the traders were only interested in making a profit and had no desire to usurp the land or convert the heathens, individuals who held such goals were not far behind.

The next major period of contact was the land-based fur trade. Explorers in the employ of the great fur trade companies had forged routes from the interior to the coast, and permanent trading posts sprang up in their wake. The earliest coastal Hudson's Bay Company post was Fort Langley, built among the Fraser River Salish in 1827. Fort Simpson on the northern coast became the centre for nine Tsimshian tribes clustered in a single village around it after 1834. Similarly, Fort Rupert, constructed on northern Vancouver Island in 1849, became the permanent home of four formerly separate Kwagiulth tribes. Also, the burgeoning town which grew up around Fort Victoria after 1843 attracted large numbers of natives from all along the coast.

This period of permanent fur trade posts had much greater impact on native life than the fleeting contacts of earlier maritime traders. Wherever forts were established, native communities grew up around them, often abandoning much of their former economic cycle. Many traditional skills were lost, as laboriously produced native items were replaced by readily available European goods, such as the Hudson's Bay Company blanket. Firearms from traders made intertribal warfare more deadly, and alcohol brought social problems and demoralization to many groups.

In some cases, such as the Tsimshian at Fort Simpson and the Kwagiulth at Fort Rupert, the merger of separate tribal units into a single large village created conflicts. How could tribal chiefs, each jealous of his power and prestige, work out their relative ranking in the new social group? The solution was through rivalry potlatching, as chiefs competed for status through competitive gestures and the destruction of goods. These aggressive performances and the "whiskey feasts" held around the posts alarmed the growing white communities and eventually led to legal prohibition of the potlatch.

The most serious of the many problems besetting native communities at this time was infectious disease. Aboriginal people lacked immunity to such European-introduced contagions as measles and smallpox, and periodic epidemics had begun as early as the 1780s. Increased contact with Europeans in this more settled period led to more widespread and deadly epidemics. Particularly devastating was the smallpox epidemic which began in Fort Victoria in 1862. As the disease took its toll on the large groups of natives around the fort, alarmed white authorities put the camps to the torch and forced the natives out. Many died during their canoe journey home, but others spread the disease wherever they went. Soon the epidemic raged along the entire coast and far into the interior. It is estimated that about 20,000 people, roughly one third of British Columbia's native population at the time, succumbed to this catastrophe. As their population dwindled, survivors abandoned many villages, often coalescing around European trading posts or missions. These weakened and demoralized groups were often will ing to surrender their surviving traditions for promises of assistance and salvation offered by missionaries.

Unlike the traders who preceded them, the missionaries arrived with the intention of radically transforming native lifestyles. They were convinced that the only hope aboriginal people had for salvation, or even survival, lay in their total assimilation to European beliefs and habits. Filled with the moral virtue of their age, they attributed the misery of the native camps not to the ravages of European diseases but to an inferior lifestyle that had to be changed as rapidly as possible. In their evangelical zeal, they saw themselves as bringing the light of the Gospel to a "dark and revolting picture of human depravity," enveloped in a "dark mantle of degrading superstition" (William Duncan, cited in Fisher 1977:128).

The famous missionary William Duncan provides the clearest example of this association between religious conversion and cultural assimilation. Duncan arrived at Fort Simpson in 1857, sent by the Anglican Church Missionary Society as a result of disturbing reports concerning native conditions around the post. Energetic and hard-working, Duncan soon mastered the Tsimshian language and began preaching. After establishing a sizable following, Duncan decided to move his converts from the debauched atmosphere of Fort Simpson to establish a model Christian community nearby. Metlakatla, one of the old Tsimshian village sites, was chosen as a suitable location and Duncan moved his flock there in 1862, narrowly missing the smallpox epidemic which ravaged Fort Simpson. Under Duncan's strong-willed direction, the community soon grew and prospered. Rows of identical two-story houses, complete with such Victorian flourishes as picket fences, were constructed of lumber from the community's sawmill. The schoolhouse and an elaborate church, capable of seating 800 people, dominated village life. As well as the sawmill, a trading post, cannery, blacksmith shop and other industries made the village economically self-sufficient. Residents had to abide by a list of rules established by Duncan, forbidding most of their traditional practices and stressing the values of their new Europeanized Christian lifestyle. As missionary, teacher and magistrate, Duncan held all authority.

Duncan's social experiment at Metlakatla flourished for several decades. His stubbornness and inflexibility, however, alienated both government and church authorities. Dissension became inevitable when the church sent a bishop, holding considerably different views on appropriate ritual for Indians, to Metlakatla as Duncan's superior. In 1887, after a successful appeal to the American government, Duncan led his followers out of British Columbia to a location in southern Alaska. With characteristic zeal, Duncan re-created his Christian industrial village at New Metlakatla, while the original settlement lapsed into a small remote fishing community.

The first steps in Indian administration came after the declaration of Vancouver Island as a crown colony in 1849. Increasing numbers of

Duncan's model community of Metlakatla, 1881. PABC HP55793

colonists clamouring for property pressured the government to free the land by providing reserves for Indian use. Between 1850 and 1854, Governor James Douglas negotiated fourteen treaties with individual tribes on Vancouver Island, particularly those in the vicinity of Fort Victoria. By the terms of these treaties the land became "the entire property of the white people forever" in exchange for small payments of compensation and the establishment of reserves. Despite expanding white settlement, Douglas was unable to obtain additional funds to continue his policy of treaty-making and these remain the only treaties ever signed with natives of the British Columbian coast.

Continued pressure of white settlement meant that reserve allocation had to continue, both on Vancouver Island and in the new colony of British Columbia after 1858. Douglas's policy was simply to assign lands the natives requested, based on their traditional use. As a result, a patchwork pattern of reserves evolved, with each band holding a number of traditional villages and campsites. These plots were much smaller than those later established under federal policies. Even these small holdings were opposed by Douglas's successors, who felt that too much good agricultural land had been given out. The many small, scattered reserves throughout British Columbia today reflect this historic practice.

British Columbia's entry into confederation in 1871 shifted responsibility for B.C. natives to the federal government. The west coast tribes were far from the new administrative centre of Ottawa, and knowledge of their particular situation was limited. What's more, the new Indian Act was seen by government agents and missionaries as a weapon in their battle against native practices such as the potlatch, which they felt were hindering efforts at conversion. Accordingly, they lobbied the federal government to enact legislation which would ban such performances. Their efforts were successful, and in 1884 the potlatch became illegal under the Indian Act.

Native groups reacted strongly to such a fundamental assault on their customs. Some protested vigorously; others potlatched in secret, evading the agents by holding ceremonies at fishing camps rather than the winter villages. Initially, prosecution attempts were unsuccessful owing to the vague wording of the law; however, by the early 1920s there were several highly publicized trials and convictions. Legal prohibitions against the potlatch remained in effect until the Indian Act was rewritten in 1951.

By the early decades of the twentieth century, native economies had shifted to new activities with natives as employees of white enterprises. Some Nuu-chah-nulth and Kwagiulth men signed aboard sealing schooners as fur seal hunters, setting out on voyages that took them as far afield as Japan or Hawaii. This industry collapsed in 1911 when an international treaty halted commercial sealing. Others found work in the logging industry or in the commercial fishery. Fish canneries employed large numbers of native women, whose families left their villages each summer to camp nearby. The closure of canneries all along the B.C. coast in the mid-twentieth century meant the loss of a major source of income for many native families.

One of the main causes of native discontent was the loss of most traditional lands. Particularly those groups in more isolated areas could not understand how the government could force them onto small reserves when they had never sold or ceded the rest of their territory. As early as the 1880s the Nisga'a were protesting the loss of their lands and demanding compensation. In 1913 they formed the Nisga'a Land Committee and sent a petition, the first clearly defined native land claim in the province, to Ottawa. In 1916 they joined other native groups to form the Allied Tribes of British Columbia, which continued to press for a settlement. In 1927 a government committee established to examine this issue denied the aboriginal claim to the land and declared that the question was closed. An amendment to the Indian Act, making it illegal to raise funds for the purpose of pressing any aboriginal claim, indicated the government's resolve to end the debate. Despite such declarations of finality, land claims remain a contentious issue between Northwest Coast First Nations and the governments of Canada and B.C.

FIRST NATIONS OF THE NORTHWEST COAST TODAY

After decades of neglect and suppression, a cultural resurgence is now taking place. Northwest Coast art has been recognized as one of the world's great artistic achievements, sparking renewed demand for the works of coastal carvers. In a flurry of artistic production, new artists have contributed to what has been termed the "Northwest Coast renaissance." Not all of their work is produced to meet the near-insatiable demand of non-native collectors. New totem poles proudly stand with the few remaining ancient examples in native villages, and young dancers once again are performing in beautifully carved masks and headdresses at native ceremonies. Potlatches are no longer illegal, and many modern events are marked by feasting and public distribution of gifts. Some First Nations have established cultural programs and museum displays to interpret their heritage, and many on-reserve schools are teaching native languages. The Nisga'a operate their own school district, supplementing the standard provincial curriculum with courses in Nisga'a language and culture.

Events in the recent history of the Kwagiulth provide a good example of these changes. Potlatching had continued throughout the period of illegality. In 1922, after a large potlatch, the agent at Alert Bay prosecuted those involved, striking an infamous bargain in which those who surrendered their masks, rattles and other potlatch regalia could buy their freedom from jail. Some of these items were sold to an American collector, while the rest were divided between what are today the Canadian Museum of Civilization and the Royal Ontario Museum. In recent decades, when potlatching no longer needed to be conducted in secret, a large dance house was constructed on the reserve and native pressure began to mount for return of their lost treasures. Finally, the Canadian government agreed to return the goods, provided that they be put on public display. By 1980 museums had been constructed in the villages of Alert Bay and Cape Mudge, with the newly returned artifacts forming the basis of the collections. These museums serve not just as static displays of objects, but as dynamic community cultural centres, enhancing Kwagiulth language and traditions.

Northwest Coast native artists have achieved a prominent place within Canadian art. Living master artists such as Bill Reid provide a link with the anonymous great artists of the past. Reid draws heavily upon his Haida heritage for inspiration, yet he has stamped his own strong personal style on his work. Other prominent contributors include the Haida artist Robert Davidson and Joe David, a Nuu-chah-nulth. Both are thoughtful and innovative artists who have mastered their regional styles and are intent on taking the art in new directions. Many younger artists, from virtually all coastal First Nations, are now gaining recognition. New media for their artistic expression, such as gold and silver, silkscreening and even cast bronze, are added to the more traditional carvings in wood. While strongly rooted in tradition, contemporary Northwest Coast art is not simply a reflection of nineteenth-century achievements but continues to expand and evolve.

Fishing continues to be the economic mainstay for many Northwest Coast people, the fleet of fishing boats being a prominent feature of such native villages as Massett, Bella Bella and Alert Bay. More recently, logging has played an important role in the native economy, and a number of First Nations have formed logging cooperatives. Some have developed industries

Left: *The design of the modern museum and cultural centre at Alert Bay was based on an old-style plank house, with its painted depiction of the thunderbird over a whale.* Photo by author □ Right: *A fine example of contemporary northern art, this portrait mask is the work of Haida carver Freda Diesing.* Photo by author

or recreational enterprises on their lands, or leased them for such purposes. In general, however, the small, scattered and isolated nature of the reserves has frustrated native attempts at economic development. The lack of employment opportunities forces many people to leave the reserves for the cities. Nearly half of B.C. natives now live off-reserve.

Land claims continue to be of central concern to coastal First Nations, involving legal battles with both levels of government. Although such provincial organizations as the Native Brotherhood of British Columbia and the Union of B.C. Indian Chiefs were once major voices, action has shifted to the local level. Individual bands or tribal councils are fighting for compensation for lands lost from their traditional territories, which were never sold or surrendered.

The Nisga'a Tribal Council took their case through each level of the Canadian legal system, finally receiving an inconclusive verdict in 1973. In their ruling, three Supreme Court judges upheld the Nisga'a claim, three rejected it, and the seventh ruled against the Nisga'a on procedural grounds without commenting on the question of aboriginal rights. While it was a technical defeat for the Nisga'a, this case indicated that considerable legal support existed for the native position and forced re-evaluation of federal policy. The Nisga'a continue to press for recognition of their rights to self-determination in their traditional territory.

More recently, in the longest and most costly aboriginal court case so far, the Gitksan-Wet'suwet'en Tribal Council, representing seven bands in the Upper Skeena area, took its claim covering a large area of northwestern British Columbia to the B.C. Supreme Court. In a 1991 decision the court ruled against the Gitksan-Wet'suwet'en, greatly angering many aboriginal

leaders by dismissing the testimony of the elders, who had carefully presented their oral histories to the court, as well as anthropologists giving evidence on their behalf. An appeal court decision in 1993 somewhat softened
the blow by ruling that aboriginal rights had not been extinguished, as
claimed in the original judgment, but still denied the Gitksan-Wet'suwet'en
title to their traditional territories.

At the same time, other groups, such as the Council of the Haida Nation
and the Nuu-chah-nulth Tribal Council, were pressing for resolution of
their own claims. A major obstacle has been the reluctance of the British
Columbia government to become involved in such issues, maintaining that
these are entirely federal concerns. Recently, however, the province has
reversed its long-standing position. An agreement between the governments
of Canada and British Columbia and the First Nations of the province in
1992 created the B.C. Treaty Commission. The Commission is designed to
facilitate treaty negotiations in an attempt to resolve these lengthy disputes
over aboriginal title.

Both the Haida and Nuu-chah-nulth have led highly publicized demonstrations protesting logging in their traditional territory. They have declared
certain islands "tribal parks," under native jurisdiction as part of their aboriginal claim. Coastal groups also maintain that resources of the sea and
rivers are included in their claims, sparking a number of disputes over fishing rights. After a series of protests, the Haida were successful in stopping
logging and exerting Haida control over the southern portion of Haida
Gwaii, the South Moresby area. These lands, now known as Gwaii Haanas,
are jointly managed by the Haida Nation (as a Haida Heritage Site) and the
government of Canada (as a National Park Reserve), pending resolution of
aboriginal claims issues.

The First Nations of the west coast have been active in such national
issues as the constitutional debate and recent attempts to establish aboriginal self-government through a constitutional amendment. However, the
Sechelt, a Coast Salish people on the mainland coast, have negotiated a separate route to self-government. Federal legislation transfers ownership of
reserve lands to the band and gives them the right to establish their own
constitution and local government. The Sechelt are free to develop their
lands as they wish, unencumbered by the restrictions of the Indian Act.

It was the grandparents of today's elders who paddled their canoes along
the rugged coastline, seeking the resources of this bountiful environment.
These were the people who suffered through the years of population
decline, loss of their land and suppression of their culture. In only a few
generations their world was transformed into one of dependence and white
government control. Today, the situation is again changing, as Northwest
Coast First Nations are intent on restoring and preserving their cultural traditions, transferring their heritage to a new generation and fighting to
ensure that they have the resources to shape their own future.

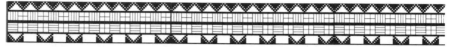

CHAPTER 9 *The Western Subarctic*

The northern boreal forest and forest-tundra transition of the Western Subarctic stretches from interior Alaska to Hudson Bay. In the north it is bounded by the tree line, though some Subarctic natives made seasonal forays after caribou out onto the barrenlands. In the south it grades into the Plains and Plateau. Lakes, rivers and muskeg cover much of its surface. Winters are long and piercingly cold, with deep accumulations of snow, but the forest provides shelter. Summers are short and pleasantly hot, but are plagued by swarms of biting insects. From a southern urban perspective it seems a harsh and demanding environment, yet it was home to many groups of nomadic hunters and fishers, whose modern descendants are determined to maintain traditional ties to the land.

Physiographically diverse, the Western Subarctic can be divided into three broad regions. In the east is the rocky Canadian Shield, extending from the Eastern Subarctic across northern Manitoba and Saskatchewan and much of the Northwest Territories. The western Northwest Territories, along with northern Alberta and northeastern British Columbia, are in the Mackenzie Lowlands, sloping gradually to the Mackenzie River delta. In the west is the Cordillera, the array of mountains ranges and valleys that characterizes the Yukon and central British Columbia. In this region many of the rivers flow to the Pacific, providing native groups with access to bountiful salmon runs and bringing them into contact with coastal cultures.

For the big game hunters of the Western Subarctic, caribou and moose were essential resources. Bison herds were also available to some of the more southerly groups, and in the Cordillera mountain goats and sheep were

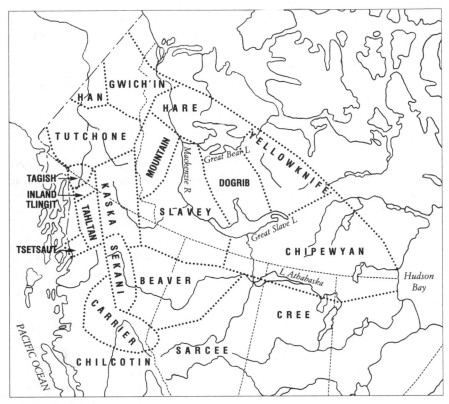

Ethnographic groups in the Western Subarctic.

hunted. Smaller mammals, especially the snowshoe hare, played an important role in the diet. Great numbers of migratory waterfowl could be taken for brief periods each year, and the lakes and rivers provided whitefish, lake trout, pike, grayling and other fish.

Throughout this vast region roamed the Athapaskans, or Dene as many now prefer to be called. More than twenty Athapaskan languages, including those in Alaska, have been defined for the Subarctic. All are closely related, indicating relatively recent differentiation. Classification is somewhat arbitrary since they tend to grade into one another through a series of intermediate dialects. Communication between neighbouring groups was usually possible.

Athapaskan migrations and their fame as "cultural borrowers" have attracted considerable anthropological interest. From their northern homeland the Athapaskans spread far to the south in a series of separate movements. The Sarcee on the Plains and the Nicola and Chilcotin in the Plateau appear to be relatively recent examples. The Navajo and Apache of the American Southwest, as well as the cluster of Athapaskan languages on the Pacific coast around the Oregon-California border, provide evidence of more extensive migrations. Wherever they spread, the Athapaskans adopted whole new patterns of cultural traits from other groups. Even in their northern homeland such borrowing is evident, since the Cordilleran groups absorbed many aspects of Northwest Coast cultures. Such diffusion, along with adaptation to differing local environments, accounts for the considerable cultural diversity among Subarctic Athapaskans. However, no matter how far they traveled or how intensive the cultural borrowing, they tenaciously maintained their Athapaskan language.

Two non-Athapaskan aboriginal languages occur in the Western Subarctic. Tlingit is spoken in extreme northwestern British Columbia and the southern Yukon, reflecting inland movement of the coastal Tlingit in their quest for furs during the historic fur trade. Intermarriage and widespread use of Tlingit as a ceremonial language have resulted in its spread at the expense of Athapaskan languages in the southern Yukon. Far more widespread and populous are the Cree, with communities throughout northern Manitoba, Saskatchewan and Alberta, often mixed with such Athapaskan groups as the Chipewyan and Beaver. Their culture differs little from the Cree of the Eastern Subarctic, described in Chapter 5.

The question of Cree antiquity in the Western Subarctic has recently been reappraised. The Cree frequently have been portrayed as historic arrivals, dramatically expanding their territory at the expense of the Athapaskans during the eighteenth century. In this view, the Cree had an economic and military advantage over their neighbours stemming from their involvement in the fur trade around Hudson Bay and their early acquisition of firearms. Recent research, however, indicates that the Cree have a more lengthy heritage in parts of the Western Subarctic. Several archaeological studies have suggested continuity from late precontact times to the historic Cree, and variants of precontact Selkirk pottery, usually associated with the Cree, have been found in northern Manitoba and Saskatchewan. Although some Cree-speakers, along with other aboriginal groups, were moving west during the historic fur trade, the dramatic surge from Hudson Bay to the Rockies presented by some earlier writers seems to have been exaggerated.

BEFORE WRITTEN RECORDS

This vast land of northern forests is one of the least-known archaeological areas in Canada and presents major challenges to interpretation. Small groups of hunters wandering across the landscape left few traces. Even these meagre remains have been reduced to simple stone tools by the acidic soils which destroy all but the most recent organic objects. Sites tend to be small and shallow, largely hidden by forest cover, and disturbed or mixed by frost action. Although the pace of archaeological research has recently accelerated, the emerging picture is still far from clear.

Early occupants were the Paleo-Indians, whose distinctive projectile points are relatively widespread. The earliest styles occur in the west, where fluted points similar to those described in Chapter 2 have been found. Most are undated surface discoveries. Only at Charlie Lake Cave in northeastern British Columbia, where Paleo-Indians hunted a large form of bison 10,500 years ago, has a fluted point been found in a radiocarbon-dated context. Later Paleo-Indian remains, marked by large unfluted spearpoints, are known as Plano or, in the north, Northern Cordilleran. Most archaeological finds are undated, but at the Canyon site in the southern Yukon, on a bluff today topped by historic Tutchone gravehouses, a small group of early bison hunters left behind several large stone spearpoints and the remains of a hearth which could be dated to 7200 years ago.

To the east, the huge Laurentide ice sheet blocked human entry until about 8000 years ago. The Plano hunters were the first people to move into this area, leaving behind the large lancelate spearpoints known on the Plains as Agate Basin. These distinctive objects are found at sites far out onto the barrenlands. The Plano people are assumed to have been big game hunters, attracted to the north by the large herds of caribou.

At the same time as Paleo-Indians were hunting across this region, a different population was entering from the west. These were people with a Eurasian technology, crossing into North America shortly before the final disappearance of Beringia. Their presence is marked by the distinctive small tools commonly termed microblades—thin, parallel-sided stone flakes with razor-sharp edges, set as the cutting or slicing edges into grooved bone or antler spearpoints or other tools. Stone knives, spearpoints, scrapers and other implements were also part of their tool-kits. After arrival in Alaska at least 10,700 years ago, microblade technology eventually spread to the Yukon, northern interior British Columbia and into the western Northwest Territories. In these regions microblades are considerably later and may represent gradual adoption of this technology by local peoples. Much later sites of the Northern Archaic tradition, marked by notched stone projectile points, are often found with microblades, suggesting the mixture of people and ideas throughout a large area.

The microblade technology did not spread east past the Mackenzie River valley. In eastern regions late Plano hunters seem to have developed into the more diversified archaic cultures. The Shield Archaic, in the rocky Shield country around Hudson Bay, emerged about 6000 years ago. This widespread culture, with its artifact inventory of notched stone spearpoints, knives and scrapers, extends from the Eastern Subarctic to the eastern portions of the Western Subarctic. Many researchers associate it with the culture history of the Algonkians.

Between about 3500 and 3000 years ago a new group from the north pushed into the lands east of the Mackenzie River. These were an Arctic people, leaving behind the small stone tools which mark the Paleo-Eskimo variant known as Pre-Dorset. Their expansion is associated with colder climatic conditions which pushed the tree line far to the south. Following the caribou herds, the Pre-Dorset hunters moved south as far as what is today northern Saskatchewan and Manitoba. Their occupation of these lands was short-lived, lasting only a few centuries. Traces of their ancient camps consist only of a scatter of stone tools around the fire-cracked rocks that once were hearths use to heat their shelters.

When people we can identify as Athapaskans first appeared is a much-debated question. Some have associated the Athapaskans with the early appearance and spread of microblades, giving them an ancient heritage in the Western Subarctic. Others have traced Athapaskan migrations through later styles of projectile points. Such attempts face the problem of defining linguistic and social units through the distribution of stone tools. Why would we expect the modern distribution of razor blades or pocket knives, for example, to identify any one specific culture? In addition, the Athapaskans were culturally diverse, occupying a wide range of environments, and can be expected to have left a varied pattern of remains. Nevertheless, the late precontact emergence of specific Athapaskan cultures has been charted in several regions.

In the east, the Taltheilei tradition spans the last 2500 years in the historic homeland of the Chipewyan, Yellowknife and Dogrib Athapaskans. Best known around Great Slave Lake and Lake Athabasca, it extends across much of the eastern Northwest Territories and northern Manitoba, Saskatchewan and parts of Alberta. Sites appear far out on the barrenlands, suggesting that these people, like their historic counterparts, ranged between the forests and tundra following the migrating caribou herds. The Migod site in the Northwest Territories, for example, was sequentially occupied by Agate Basin, Shield Archaic, Pre-Dorset and Taltheilei peoples, all hunting the caribou herds out on the barrenlands. Fishing was also a vital part of the economy, as suggested by the location of many sites ("Taltheilei" refers to water). Stone stemmed and lancelate spearpoints, changing in form over time, as well as knives, endscrapers and stone-slab or boulder-flake hide scrapers (generally known by the Athapaskan term *chi-thos*) are the characteristic tools. Small notched points which presumably tipped arrows appear late in the sequence. Implements of native copper are also relatively common from that time. Finally, beads and other European goods mark the transition to such historic Athapaskans as the Chipewyan.

About 1250 years ago (A.D. 700) a cataclysmic event greatly affected the people of the southern Yukon. A massive volcanic eruption in the St. Elias Range, at the southern end of the present Yukon-Alaska border, blasted immense quantities of volcanic ash into the air. Winds swept the ash about a thousand kilometres to the east, blanketing the southern Yukon with a thick layer of grit. Today visible along river banks and road cuts, the horizontal white band in the otherwise brown soil is known as White River ash. Its arrival must have terrified the local people, darkening the sky, fouling the water and covering the land. Areas most affected must have been rendered temporarily uninhabitable.

Such conditions would have forced many groups to set out in search of unaffected lands, dispersing to the north and south of the ashfall area. As people moved into already occupied regions local hostilities likely resulted. Many groups might have been forced to continue their wanderings for considerable distances. Alaskan archaeologist William Workman has pointed out the correspondence in time of this environmental disaster and linguistic estimates of Athapaskan divergence. He suggests that the ashfall served as a "triggering mechanism," stimulating the southward migrations which eventually resulted in the Navajo and Apache of the American Southwest. As such movements would be very difficult to demonstrate archaeologically, this remains a speculative, although attractive, hypothesis.

As plant and animal life gradually returned to normal in the ashfall area, humans reoccupied the land. In the layers overlying the White River ash archaeologists find tools of the late precontact Aishihik culture. These include stone spear and arrow points, knives, *chi-thos* and wedges for splitting wood. Also found are distinctive arrowpoints, awls and other tools of copper, nuggets of which occur locally and could be heated and hammered to shape. Such tools persist into the early historic period and can be related to the Tutchone people who occupy the area today.

In the northern Yukon, the deeply stratified Klo-kut site, occupied from approximately A.D. 950 into the historic period, reveals development to the historic Gwich'in. Precontact stone tools include such distinctive Athapaskan items as tapered-stem projectile points (known as Kavik points) and *chi-thos*. Unusually good preservation led to the recovery of such bone tools as barbed points, fish hook components and a carved fish effigy lure, as well as trays and other items of birchbark. A stable economy of caribou hunting and fishing is indicated, extending into the historic period.

At the southeastern edge of the Western Subarctic, in northern Manitoba and Saskatchewan south of the Taltheilei sites, the archaeological sequence resembles the Eastern Subarctic (see Chapter 5). The introduction of pottery transforms Shield Archaic lifeways into the Laurel culture of the Initial Woodland period. In the Terminal Woodland, after about A.D. 1000, archaeological remains consist of the distinctive fabric-impressed Selkirk pottery, small side-notched arrowpoints, and other stone tools. Selkirk sites take us into the historic period and are generally associated with Algonkian people such as the Cree.

Closely paralleling the distribution of Selkirk pottery is that of red ochre pictographs. Paintings on prominent rock outcrops along major waterways are common across much of northern Manitoba and adjacent

Human figure pictograph in northern Saskatchewan. Upraised arms on humans are a common feature of Canadian Shield rock art. Photo by Tim Jones

Saskatchewan. Humans, game animals and such mythological beings as thunderbirds are common depictions. The subject matter, as well as occasional small offerings left near the paintings, suggest that they served a religious function. They closely resemble the numerous pictographs of northern Ontario, and all appear to be the work of Algonkian artists, in this area presumably the Cree.

THE ATHAPASKANS (DENE)

The broad term "Athapaskan" (or "Athabascan") is simply a linguistic label, indicating a common origin for all the related languages from interior Alaska to western Hudson Bay. Its origins, however, come not from the people to whom it refers but from the Cree. The native inhabitants of the Mackenzie basin refer to themselves as Dene ("people"). Similar, although varying, terms are used by Athapaskan groups in other areas. The term "Dene Nation" has today become the preferred collective self-designation in the Northwest Territories.

The fluid Athapaskan social groups cannot be equated with political "tribes." Small, highly mobile bands tended to resemble their neighbours in speech and lifestyle. Any division into named units is somewhat arbitrary and often reflects administrative or anthropological convenience rather than aboriginal reality. Most group names reflect linguistic differences, yet not all are separate languages. The now-extinct Yellowknife, for example, were once a distinct ethnic entity, yet spoke a dialect of Chipewyan. Similarly, some modern linguists class Slavey, Hare and Mountain as all speaking dialects of the same language. Even separate languages, such as Beaver and Sekani, grade into one another through a series of dialects. Modern group names frequently derive from terms applied by European traders or the Cree. As the explorer David Thompson described for the Chipewyan, "the country is occupied by a people who call themselves 'Dinnie', by the Hudson Bay Traders 'Northern Indians', and by their southern neighbours 'Cheepawyans'." This Cree term means "pointed skins," referring either to their manner of preparing beaver pelts or to the pointed tails on their shirts.

All northern Athapaskans lived by hunting and fishing, with the gathering of plant foods playing only a minor role. During the historic fur trade many shifted their emphasis to hunting and trapping furbearing animals. Athapaskan lifeways were flexible, with each group closely adapted to the territory it inhabited. A major environmental and cultural division occurred between the Cordillera on the west, where most rivers drain to the Pacific, and the Shield and Mackenzie Lowlands to the east, where the rivers flow north to the Arctic or into Hudson Bay.

ATHAPASKANS OF THE SHIELD AND MACKENZIE LOWLANDS

Few environments in aboriginal North America presented such challenges to human survival. The seasons are characterized by long severe winters and short warm summers, separated only by brief intervals. It was the winters, with intense cold, deep snow and limited daylight, that posed the greatest threats. Starvation and death by exposure were constant dangers. The pleasant months of summer were marred by dense swarms of mosquitoes and blackflies, requiring that the body be kept covered at all times. David Thompson, on western Hudson Bay in 1784, commented: "Summer such as it is, comes at once, and with it myriads of tormenting Musketocs; the air is thick with them, there is no cessation day nor night of suffering from them . . . and [we] were thankful for the cold weather that put an end to our sufferings" (Thompson 1962:17).

Although the land provided huge herds of barren-ground caribou in the northern transitional forest and tundra, woodland caribou and moose in the full boreal forest and numerous fish in the lakes and rivers, these were not always predictable resources. Failure to find animals or poor luck in fishing could mean disaster for the entire group.

In the east are the Chipewyan, the most numerous and widespread of the northern Athapaskans. These were an "edge-of-the-forest" people, occupying the northern transitional forest east of Hudson Bay and far out onto the tundra or barrenlands. The barren-ground caribou were essential to the Chipewyan, who based their economy on following the herds in their seasonal movements. Winter was spent in the forests, where both humans and caribou could find shelter. When the animals began their migrations out onto the barrenlands in spring, the Chipewyan hunters ambushed them

Chipewyan caribou hunting camp on the barrenlands near Fort Churchill, ca. 1880.
CMC 74880

along their major routes. During the summer humans and the herds ranged far out onto the barrenlands. In the fall, the caribou could again be taken in large numbers along their migration routes south. Their flesh was cut into thin strips, dried in the sun and pounded into pemmican for winter provisions.

One productive method of taking caribou was in large empoundments, built near a caribou migration path. A stout enclosure of brushy trees was constructed to contain the animals. Samuel Hearne, who traveled with the Chipewyan in the late eighteenth century, claimed to have seen some "that were not less than a mile round." Inside was a maze of fences, with snares placed in every opening. Long lines of brush fences, claimed by Hearne to be sometimes "not less than two or three miles," funneled the animals to the pound's narrow entranceway. Once the caribou had been driven inside, this entrance was blocked with brush. Women and children raced around the fence to prevent animals from escaping, while men speared those entangled in the snares and shot with arrows those which still ran loose. When such techniques were successful, so many caribou could be taken that people could remain in one place for much of the winter.

Out on the barrenlands during the summer the caribou could be hunted with bows and arrows or speared from canoes as they crossed rivers or lakes. Small, light bark canoes were carried from the woods for this purpose. Hearne also described use of lines of sticks to direct the caribou to a narrow pass, where concealed hunters waited.

Caribou were essential for more than food. The Chipewyan relied on caribou hides for clothing and lodge covers, and cut them into strips for snares, fish nets, snowshoe lacings and many other purposes. Antlers and bones provided raw materials for many of their tools, and sinew was used in sewing clothing. A complete suit of winter clothing, according to Hearne, required eight to eleven hides, obtained in August and September when they were thick and unmarred by warble fly holes. Hearne states that many animals were killed for their hides at this time, with only the choicest portions of meat taken.

While the caribou were the staff of life to the Chipewyan, much as bison were to the Plains tribes, other animals played a role in the diet. Musk-oxen were occasionally hunted while out on the barrenlands, Arctic hares were frequently shot or snared and waterfowl were seasonally abundant. Fishing was second only to caribou hunting in importance, with large quantities being taken in nets or with bone hooks. In 1785 David Thompson commented that: "When the land is scarce of Deer [caribou] . . . they take to the Lakes to angle Trout or Pike at which they are very expert."

Although the Chipewyan did not participate in the historic fur trade as enthusiastically as the Cree, some changes in their culture and distribution did occur. The northern transitional forests provided the caribou which sustained them but contained few of the furbearing animals in demand by European traders. Some bands responded to the traders' urgings and pushed into the boreal forests to the south and west, reaching as far as northeastern Alberta. Those who remained in their former territory became known as the "Caribou-Eater" Chipewyan, the most conservative members of the group.

To the west were the Yellowknife, who spoke a dialect of the Chipewyan language. Their name comes from their copper tools, manufactured from deposits found in their territory along the Coppermine River. Although linguistically and culturally Chipewyan, they are mentioned in the historical literature as a separate entity and were apparently considered as such by Hearne's Chipewyan guides, who plundered them, taking young women, furs, and bows and arrows. The Yellowknife, in turn, harassed the Dogrib and other neighbouring groups. In the nineteenth century many perished through disease and retaliatory attacks by the Dogrib. Finally, they disappeared as a distinct group, the survivors and their lands being absorbed by the Dogrib and Chipewyan.

The Dogrib occupy the land between Great Bear and Great Slave lakes. Their culture was similar to the Chipewyan, though they did not venture as far out onto the barrenlands. Caribou were the essential resource, with moose, hare and fish being of secondary importance.

The Hare, between Great Bear Lake and the Mackenzie River, speak a language closely related to Dogrib and differ little from them. They lived by hunting and fishing, pursuing the barren-ground caribou out onto the tundra in summer. Big game was relatively scarce in their territory, resulting in reliance on fish and hares throughout much of the year. Their dependence on hares for food and clothing sufficiently distinguished them from their neighbours to give them their name but resulted in a precarious existence. Since hares go through a population cycle every seven to ten years, the people suffered periodic food shortages, frequently resulting in starvation.

Closely related to the Hare are the Bearlake and Mountain Indians. The Bearlake or Sahtu Dene, today recognized as a distinct group, are an historic fusion of Hare, Dogrib and Slavey people whose ancestors settled around the fur trade posts near Great Bear Lake. The Mountain Indians are the aboriginal inhabitants of the Mackenzie Mountains, where they hunted moose, woodland caribou and mountain goat. Difficulty in killing large game during the winter, along with a scarcity of small game and lack of large lakes for ice fishing, made winter survival difficult. Historic records of starvation are common.

A closely related language is Slavey (or Slave, as they are more commonly known in the southern portions of their distribution). Their territory covers a large area of the Northwest Territories west of Great Bear and Great Slave lakes, plus northeastern British Columbia and northwestern Alberta. Unlike more northerly Athapaskans, the Slavey were fully a people of the forest, hunting moose and woodland caribou. These are not herd animals like the barren-ground caribou and had to be hunted individually with bows and arrows or speared when crossing water. Both large and small game were also taken in snares. In addition, fishing played a major role. The numerous small bands speaking dialects of the Slavey language did not constitute any cultural or political unit, but they have in recent times developed something of a common identity by use of the term "Slavey" to distinguish themselves from other Athapaskans when speaking English.

To the south, the Beaver Indians occupy a large area along the Peace River of northern British Columbia and Alberta. The Beaver once dwelt farther to the east but, according to Alexander Mackenzie, were pushed westward by gun-bearing Cree in the late eighteenth century. The Peace River apparently takes its name from the truce negotiated between these two peoples. The Beaver lifestyle was based almost entirely on big-game hunting. Herds of bison came into the open lands along the Peace and were driven into pounds in a technique similar to that used by the Plains tribes. Moose were available throughout Beaver territory, and woodland caribou could be hunted in some areas. The abundant beaver were sought for both their meat and fur. Fishing was not an important activity, being considered beneath the dignity of a hunter, and was resorted to only when the search for game failed.

Throughout the Shield and Mackenzie Lowlands, Athapaskan societies were small, simple and highly mobile. The basic unit was the family, composed of a man and his wife or wives, their children and perhaps an aged parent or two. Polygyny occurred in most groups, but only exceptional men could provide for several wives and defend them from other men; Matonabbee, the powerful Chipewyan chief described by Hearne, had seven wives. Several families, bound by ties of kinship and marriage, lived and traveled together throughout much of the year. When fishing was good or more men were needed for communal caribou hunting, much larger groups might gather. Hearne encountered a Chipewyan summer camp of seventy tents, which he estimated "did not contain less than 600 persons."

Leadership was based on ability, with the best hunter or most experienced warrior taking charge for the duration of that activity. The Chipewyan and Dogrib, with their communal caribou hunts, placed greater emphasis on leadership than did groups such as the Slavey, in which hunting was an individual activity. Such leadership roles were temporary, and all adults felt free to come to their own decisions or join another social group. Flexibility and respect for individual autonomy are at the core of Athapaskan culture.

Although the Athapaskans were not known as ferocious warriors, hostilities were common. Raids between Athapaskan groups were usually motivated by desires for revenge or to steal women. Long-standing enmities existed with the Cree to the south and the Inuit in the north. Hearne recounted the savage slaughter of a small Inuit camp by his Chipewyan guides as they traveled to the mouth of the Coppermine River in 1771.

The requirement for mobility meant that housing was simple and lightweight. Throughout the area the most common year-round dwelling was the conical tipi covered with caribou or moose hide, banked with snow in winter. Some groups made more substantial winter structures of poles chinked with moss. In summer, simple lean-tos were all that was required.

For most groups summer travel was primarily by water, in canoes covered with spruce bark or birchbark. In a few areas moose hides were used to cover the canoe frame. Lacking good navigable rivers, the Chipewyan traveled out onto the barrenlands on foot but carried small lightweight canoes. In winter, snowshoes were essential. Goods were carried on toboggans, which were hauled by the women. Dog sleds were unknown until the fur trade period.

Clothing was generally made of tanned caribou or moose hides, with some groups also making use of hare skins. Clothing was similar for men and women, generally consisting of a long pullover shirt or dress, leggings with attached moccasins, and breechcloth. Mittens, a cap and a robe were added in winter. Some northern groups attached hoods onto their winter coats, but this is thought to be a late Inuit influence. Fringes and designs in moose hair or porcupine quills were added for decoration. People also enhanced their appearance by tattooing parallel lines on their cheeks or chin and occasionally perforating their nasal septum for insertion of a quill or other ornament.

The late-eighteenth-century explorers—Hearne, Thompson and

Mackenzie—noted a lack of obvious religious practices or ceremonies. These early observers, however, did not delve into the spiritual beliefs held by their native guides and acquaintances. Later anthropological studies revealed complex religious thought, centring on the relationship between hunters and the animals on which they depended. Among the Beaver, children were sent into the bush on vision quests, to seek supernatural power from the animals. Such experiences were not to be revealed but to be reflected upon and nurtured as private knowledge. As an adult, the person who "knew a little something" controlled power. Hunters slept near their "medicine bundles," containing images or charms relating to supernatural aid received as children. In their dreams they encountered animals and gained assistance and knowledge from their spirit power.

Few restrictions applied to a young man entering puberty, but young women were secluded. They were placed in a small hut, often at some distance from the main camp, where they were attended and instructed by female relatives. They would eat only dried meat and had to take liquids through a bone drinking tube; a scratching stick had to be used to avoid touching the body. Throughout most of their lives women were subjected to periodic restrictions, since menstruating women were believed to be offensive to the animal spirits and thus threatened the hunting success and survival of the entire group. They were prohibited from walking on hunting trails or on ice where men fished or hunted beavers, and could never touch or step over the personal gear of the hunter. Among the Beaver, menstruating women could not even walk behind the lodges for fear of severing the sacred link between the hunter or his medicine bundle and the animals in the bush.

The eighteenth-century accounts paint a dismal picture of the lives of women in these societies. They were required to do all the heavy work of hauling loads, could be beaten or killed by their husbands, or exchanged after wrestling contests or gambling. In times of shortage, they were the first to starve. Among the Chipewyan, Hearne stated that "they are inured to carry and haul heavy loads from their childhood, and do all manner of drudgery." Similarly, among the Beaver, Mackenzie referred to the "abject state of slavery and submission" of the women, who "alone perform that labour which is allotted to beasts of burthen in other countries." Thompson referred to the high rate of female infanticide among the Chipewyan and noted that it was considered "an act of kindness." However, such harsh treatment of women seems foreign to later studies of Athapaskan cultures, and it is difficult to assess the reliability of these early observations.

Old age was a difficult time in societies which had to keep on the move after game. Individuals who could no longer keep up with the group were left behind. When a person died, the Chipewyan might simply leave the body on the ground surface; other groups interred their dead or raised them on scaffolds. Some personal possessions of the deceased were burned or left

Left: *Slavey shaman at Fort Rae, 1913.* CMC 26080 □ Right: *Gwich'in hunters in the 1840s.* CMC 73453

behind and the camp was abandoned.

Uncertainties of everyday life could be dealt with through supernatural means. Dreams provided guidance in making decisions. Shamans could call upon their spirit powers to locate game or to overcome their enemies. Illness was treated by blowing on the afflicted part of the body, or by sucking out a small object believed to have caused the disease. As well as such individual practices, occasional group ceremonies fostered social cohesion. Such gatherings featured feasting, singing, drumming, dancing and gambling.

THE CORDILLERAN ATHAPASKANS

The majestic mountains and plateaus of the Subarctic Cordillera extend from northern Yukon to central British Columbia. Vast stretches of boreal forest cover the rugged landscape, but there are also large areas of meadows, floodplains and muskeg, as well as alpine tundra at higher elevations. Climate varies from among the harshest in the Subarctic in the northern territory of the Gwich'in to more benign among the Carrier in the south. Latitude is not the only consideration; local climatic conditions vary widely according to altitude and proximity to the coast. In the south the Subarctic grades into the open country of the Plateau, and the Chilcotin have been placed in that culture area.

The rivers which flow to the Pacific provided salmon runs to all but the easternmost Cordilleran peoples. This assured food supply allowed a greater

241

population density and more settled way of life than among the eastern Athapaskans. Other resources, however, played at least as large a role in the economy of most groups. Caribou were essential, particularly to such northerners as the Gwich'in. Mountain sheep and goats, moose, bear and smaller game were also hunted and taken in snares. Freshwater fish were important to many groups, and plant foods were more abundant and played a larger role in the diet than among the eastern Athapaskans. Local resources could also be exchanged for exotic foodstuffs, such as eulachon oil, in trade with their coastal neighbours. Numerous influences from the Northwest Coast permeated the lives of the Cordilleran Athapaskans, distinguishing them from their kin to the east.

In the north, bordering on the Inuit, are the Gwich'in (formerly known as the Kutchin; eastern groups around the lower Mackenzie River are also known by the French term "Loucheux"). The Alaska-Yukon boundary today bisects their traditional lands. Salmon ascended the Yukon River system far into Gwich'in territory, although the Mackenzie River groups in the east relied on Arctic char and whitefish instead. Traps were the most productive means of taking fish, and summer camps were established to construct and operate them. Moose, smaller animals and waterfowl were also important. Caribou were paramount to the Gwich'in, providing the greatest amount of food, as well as hides for shelter and clothing. Although they could be pursued by individual hunters, the major technique was the communal surround. Long lines of posts directed caribou to roughly circular enclosures, in which they were snared and then speared or shot with arrows.

South of the Gwich'in are the Han, a distinct though little-known society. Their territory is on the Yukon River drainage, straddling the Yukon-Alaska border. Fish, particularly salmon, were paramount in their diet, though hunting animals also played a major role.

The Tutchone occupy the southern Yukon. Some bands depended heavily on annual salmon runs, while others were primarily hunters. Native copper was found in Tutchone territory and was extensively used for making tools. With the advent of the historic fur trade, the Tutchone were drawn into a trading relationship with the Chilkat Tlingit, who tended to dominate their inland partners. Ties of trade and intermarriage resulted in extensive Tlingit influences in Tutchone culture. Society was divided into two moieties, Wolf and Crow (the latter equivalent to the Tlingit Raven), each of which might have several clans in the Tlingit style. Marriage partners had to be of the opposite moiety, and all children took the affiliation of their mother.

The spread of Tlingit dominance into the Cordillera is most clearly seen in northwestern British Columbia and the adjacent southern Yukon—the territory of the Inland Tlingit and Tagish peoples. Extensive trade and intermarriage with the Tlingit in the nineteenth century resulted in the adoption of Tlingit language and social organization by the local

Sekani man setting trap for lynx, 1914.
RBCM

Athapaskans. They held potlatches, divided their society into Wolf and Crow, and used crests to denote their kin groups. The Tagish language went into gradual decline and is virtually extinct today.

Also in northwestern British Columbia, along the Stikine River drainage, are the Tahltan. The Stikine provided dependable salmon runs and a major trade route to the Stikine Tlingit on the west. The Tahltan were able to establish themselves as intermediaries in trade between coastal groups and Athapaskans farther inland. Intensive social relations with the Tlingit, including intermarriage and reciprocal potlatching, resulted in the adoption of many elements of Tlingit culture. Matrilineal moieties (Wolf and Raven) were divided into clans in the Tlingit fashion.

One group of Athapaskans, the Tsetsaut, penetrated the mountains and reached the Pacific at the end of several long inlets on the British Columbia-Alaska border. Their economy was based more heavily on inland game hunting than on fishing, apparently lacking a full coastal adaptation. They were harassed and raided by adjacent groups, particularly the Tahltan, with the survivors finally being absorbed by the Nisga'a. By the early twentieth century they were extinct.

In the eastern Cordillera of northern British Columbia and southern Yukon are the Kaska and Sekani. The Sekani are virtually indistinguishable from the Beaver and appear to have diverged from them only recently. To the north they are mixed with the Kaska, whose speech is closely related to Tahltan. Both lived by hunting moose, woodland caribou and mountain sheep, with fishing being of lesser importance. Since their rivers are in the Mackenzie drainage they lacked direct access to salmon but could take trout and whitefish. Although further removed from the Northwest Coast than most Cordilleran Athapaskans, some coastal influences were felt. The Kaska divided their society into Wolf and Crow, with descent traced through the female line. Several western Sekani bands briefly adopted the matrilineal clans of the Gitksan and western Carrier. Both held modest potlatches. Their cultures seem transitional between the Cordillera and the Mackenzie Lowlands.

Left: *Totem pole at the western Carrier village of Moricetown.* Photo by author
Right: *Carrier woman scraping moose-hide with a stone-bladed scraper, 1922.* CMC 56902

Occupying a large area of central British Columbia are the many groups known collectively as the Carrier. They differ somewhat in culture and language, with those in the northwest, who today prefer to be known as the Wet'suwet'en, speaking a dialect sufficiently distinct that some linguists classify it as a separate language. The upper reaches of both the Fraser and Skeena river drainages extend through Carrier territory, providing teeming masses of spawning salmon. Salmon were the staple for most Carrier groups, resulting in a relatively settled lifestyle and the highest population density in the Western Subarctic. The period of the salmon runs was one of abundance, when many plant foods were available and hunting was most productive. In the lean months of late winter, however, supplies of dried foods often ran low, forcing some groups to seek the hospitality of the Gitksan or Nuxalk to the west.

The basic Carrier social group was the extended family, usually consisting of several brothers, their wives and children, and married sons' wives and children. Each social group held rights to a hunting territory and fishing sites. This typically simple Athapaskan organization began to be elaborated in the early historic period, as extensive trade and intermarriage with coastal peoples brought in the potlatch and ranking systems. In the north the Wet'suwet'en, bordering on the Gitksan of the upper Skeena, adopted clan organization with descent traced through the mother. Southern groups, in contact with the Nuxalk in the Bella Coola valley, lacked such clans and traced descent through either the male or female line. In both cases, crests, generally depicting animals, were painted or carved in

Northwest Coast style to denote particular kin groups. Those closest to the Gitksan adopted much of their ceremonial system. Totem poles were raised to display crest privileges, the intricate Chilkat blankets of mountain goat wool were worn by nobles on important occasions, and high-ranking women slit the lower lip to wear a labret as a badge of status.

The Carrier situation was typical of most Cordilleran groups. Under the influence of the Tlingit, Gitksan and Nuxalk the simpler Athapaskan societies became organized into descent groups, traced matrilineally from the Gwich'in to the northern Carrier. "Big men" or "chiefs" began to emerge as the rank system spread inland, new wealth obtained in trading being transferred into status through potlatching. While these "chiefs" had great prestige and were accorded respect, they lacked real political authority; the basic individual autonomy of the Athapaskans was retained.

Although modest events compared to the extravagances of the Northwest Coast, some vestiges of the potlatch spread to all Cordilleran groups. Each event of importance—the naming of a child, the assumption of a family crest, a marriage or funeral—demanded a feast and distribution of goods. Newly wealthy families could purchase high-ranking titles or crests, or acquire them through sponsoring the funeral potlatch of a former owner. Frequent potlatches, with distributions of wealth, were required to maintain high status.

Trade relations between coast and interior were of long standing. In exchange for furs and prepared hides, the Athapaskans received wealth goods, such as dentalium shells and woven blankets of mountain-goat wool, and exotic foods, such as eulachon oil, dried clams and seaweed. The "grease trails," so-called for the numerous boxes of eulachon oil carried far into the interior, were major arteries of trade and travel, along which natives guided such European explorers as Alexander Mackenzie.

The arrival of Europeans, with their shining array of metal tools and other goods eagerly sought by natives, intensified this relationship. Coastal groups denied the Athapaskans direct access to the newcomers, while trading them European goods for the furs required in the coastal trade. In turn, the Athapaskans with closest ties to the coast became intermediaries in trade with those further inland. The coastal peoples, while continuing to regard interior groups with disdain, now found them to be important sources of wealth. Coastal chiefs made trading excursions far into the interior and sought to consolidate their influence through marriages, offering young women of high rank to Athapaskan leaders. Such kin ties brought many Cordilleran Athapaskans, particularly the Tagish, Tahltan and Carrier, into the Northwest Coast sphere of influence, resulting in rapid adoption of many elements of their social organization.

The requirement of mobility meant that housing was kept simple. The northern Cordilleran peoples—the Gwich'in, Han and Tutchone—made portable dome-shaped winter houses, with moose or caribou hides covering a framework of bent and tied poles. The Han, like many of the Alaskan Athapaskans, also built rectangular pit-houses, heavily banked with turf to withstand the cold. In the south, the Carrier made winter homes of split poles covered in spruce bark. The Sekani in the east lived in conical lodges covered with bark or hide. All of the western groups, from the Gwich'in to the Carrier, constructed rectangular bark-covered structures at summer fish camps, used as living quarters as well as for smoking and drying fish. The Carrier borrowed two additional house types—the plank house used for potlatches from the Northwest Coast and, in the south, the semi-subterranean pit-house characteristic of the Plateau.

The rugged lands and turbulent rivers of the Cordillera meant that most travel was on foot. Only in the north was water travel practical for any distance. Most groups lacked birchbark and constructed their canoes of the heavier spruce bark. Many made small dugout canoes, but these were not steamed and spread like coastal dugouts. Rafts and other temporary craft were constructed to transport people and goods short distances. In winter, travel was on snowshoes, dragging loads on toboggans, though the Carrier deny that they used either until the historic period.

In clothing and appearance, the Cordilleran people differed little from other northern Athapaskans. Robert Campbell, traveling among the Gwich'in and Han in 1851, left a good description of their apparel.

> Their dress which when new is pretty & picturesque, is made of the skin of the moose or the reindeer, principally the latter. The skirt [shirt] or coat is finished in a point, both before & behind, & reaches down to the knees, being frequently ornamented with coloured beads, porcupine quills or long hair. The coat has a hole large enough to admit the head, but does not open in front, & is provided with a hood which can be used, when wanted, as a head-dress. The trowsers or leg covering, & shoes are made of the same material, & the garment made with the hair inside for warmth.
>
> (Osgood 1971:91)

Dentalium shells obtained in trade with the coast were also in frequent use as decorations on clothing and in the hair, as necklaces, and as ornaments worn in perforations through the ears and nasal septum. Tattooing, particularly on the cheeks and chin, was common. The Carrier also had a unique ceremonial costume, featuring an elaborate wig and a breast-plate of dentalium.

In contrast to other Athapaskans, the Cordilleran groups generally cremated their dead. The Carrier derive their name from the custom of requiring a widow to carry on her back a bag containing the charred bones of her husband. This was done throughout the mourning period of a year or more, supposedly discouraging early remarriage. At the end of the mourning period, the remains were placed in a box on top of a post carved with the crest of the deceased.

In many other traits the people of the Cordillera shared the basic Athapaskan lifeways. Shamans interceded with the supernatural world, removing some of the uncertainty of daily life. Religious concepts centred on respect for animals and the quest by the hunter to obtain at least one spirit helper. Girls underwent a period of seclusion at puberty, and menstruating women had to be isolated and subjected to taboos for fear of offending the spirits of game animals and fish. Oral traditions told by the elders described how the world came into being and stressed the relationship between humans and animals. While some of the stories clearly owe their origin to the Raven myths of the coast, others reflect pan-Subarctic themes. Under the veneer of Northwest Coast influences, the simpler egalitarian Athapaskan culture was intact.

HISTORIC CHANGES

The Chipewyan were the first of the Canadian Athapaskans to come into contact with Europeans. York Factory, established on southwestern Hudson Bay in 1682, was dominated by trade with the Cree. Shortly thereafter, the Chipewyan were drawn into the trade. The Cree used their newly acquired firearms to plunder the Chipewyan, who suffered severe losses in warfare. The English traders eventually became aware of these "Northern Indians," as they were called, through slaves held by the Cree. In an effort to bring them into direct trade, the Hudson's Bay Company organized an expedition to Chipewyan lands and negotiated a peace with the Cree during the winter of 1715-1716. This was followed in 1717 by the construction of Fort Churchill, at the mouth of the Churchill River, specifically for the Chipewyan trade.

The Chipewyan, however, failed to wholeheartedly embrace the fur trade lifestyle, as the Cree had done. The caribou herds provided for all their needs, and furbearers were scarce in the northern transitional forests. As Samuel Hearne noted: "The real wants of these people are few, and easily supplied; a hatchet, an ice-chisel, a file, and a knife, are all that is required to enable them, with a little industry, to procure a comfortable livelihood." He observed that those who went to the fort with furs risked starvation on the long trip across the barrenlands and were not better off than those who remained behind with the caribou. Nevertheless, some of the Chipewyan joined their fortunes to those of the fort, controlling trade with groups further west. It was partially to break this trade monopoly that Hearne made his famous journey in 1770-1771, traveling from Churchill to the Arctic coast at the mouth of the Coppermine River in an attempt to bring the "Far Indians" into the post to trade.

The threat to both the Hudson's Bay Company and Chipewyan dominance in the fur trade came with the movement of "free traders," shortly to form the Montreal-based North West Company, into the interior. This began in 1778, when Peter Pond established a post near Lake Athabasca. In 1786 a post, later known as Fort Resolution, was built on the southern shore of Great Slave Lake. In 1788 Fort Chipewyan was constructed on Lake Athabasca. Many of the Chipewyan had pushed south into this region for its more abundant furbearers and preferred to go to the new post rather than undertake the arduous journey to Churchill. The Hudson's Bay Company was forced to abandon its long-standing policy of requiring natives to bring their furs to the coastal forts and began to establish numerous posts inland. A period of intense rivalry ensued, continuing until the merger of the two companies in 1821.

It was as an agent of the North West Company that Alexander Mackenzie explored to the north and west, reaching the mouth of the mighty river that now bears his name in 1789. Setting out from Fort Chipewyan, he traversed the lands of the Slavey, Hare and eastern Gwich'in. Following this journey, the North West Company established several posts in the lower Mackenzie valley, beginning with Fort Good Hope in 1805. The Gwich'in became intermediaries in trade with the Inuit, denying the latter access to the posts. They also were able to obtain Russian goods through the Alaskan Athapaskans.

In a second ambitious expedition in 1793, Mackenzie set out to find a route to the Pacific. His travels took him through Beaver, Sekani and Carrier territory, finally reaching salt water at Bella Coola. Although Mackenzie was the first European in the Carrier homeland, he found people who were already accustomed to European goods through trade with the Nuxalk. He saw iron and brass tools in their possession and noted one man carrying "a lance that very much resembled a serjeant's halberd." His party fell in with a Carrier group heading to the coast to trade, taking skins of beaver, otter, marten, bear and lynx, as well as dressed moose hides obtained from the "Rocky-Mountain Indians" (Sekani). Again, trading posts soon followed exploration. A post existed among the Beaver of the upper Peace River by at least 1798. Farther west, Fort McLeod was constructed among the Sekani in 1805 and Fort St. James and Fort Fraser among the Carrier in 1806.

Modern scholars have disagreed sharply in their assessment of the impact the early years of trade had on the Athapaskans. June Helm and other Subarctic ethnographers have championed a model stressing continuity. In this view, the Athapaskans remained essentially in their homelands, making only minor territorial adjustments in attempts to secure greater access to furbearing animals or European goods. The new trade items made life easier and were eagerly sought as status goods but were essentially grafted onto the pre-existing culture without drastically altering it. This stable fur trade era is seen as persisting without major disruptions until the extension of federal administration in the Canadian north after 1945.

An alternative point of view, held primarily by ethnohistorians such as Shepard Krech III, is that massive cultural changes and population dislocations occurred. Warfare with the Cree resulted in major losses in population and land for the Chipewyan, Slavey and Beaver. Such northern peoples as the Dogrib and Hare once lived farther south but were forced into the relatively impoverished northern transitional forest, resulting in their precarious existence and later dependency on the trading posts for survival. In this view, the common practice among the Mackenzie Lowlands Athapaskans of tracing kinship bilaterally (through either the mother or the father) was not an ancient trait but a late adaptation to provide greater flexibility in times of decreasing populations.

Certainly one of the major disruptions brought by Europeans was epidemic outbreaks of disease. How early such scourges as smallpox wrought their destruction, or how dreadful the toll, cannot be known. By 1781, we have historic records of a devastating smallpox epidemic among the Chipewyan and Cree near Hudson Bay. Hearne estimated that nine-tenths of the Chipewyan around Churchill perished. Influenza, measles, whooping cough and scarlet fever also caused huge losses. Starvation often followed outbreaks of disease, as the survivors were too weakened to provide for themselves. Krech's study of the Gwich'in refers to the "almost constant sickness, disease and mortality" of the nineteenth century and estimates that the population was reduced by approximately 80 percent.

Aboriginal people also suffered through the widespread use of liquor as an inducement to trade. As early as 1785, David Thompson lamented the liberal dispensation of "brandy" to the natives of western Hudson Bay, commenting that: "No matter what service the Indian performs . . . strong grog is given to him, and sometimes for two or three days Men and Women are all drunk, and become the most degraded of human beings" (Thompson 1962:36). The use of alcohol in trade was particularly prevalent during the years of intense rivalry between the two great fur trade companies, after which it was discouraged.

As trading posts continued to be established throughout Athapaskan lands in the nineteenth century, natives became increasingly dependent on items of Euro-Canadian manufacture. Metal tools and European clothing rapidly replaced their aboriginal counterparts. Firearms and ammunition were among the most important trade goods. Hunting became more of an individual activity, no longer requiring the communal effort to construct corrals or drive the herds to where hunters waited. Steel traps came into use but did not replace native snares and deadfalls. Commercial twine fishnets supplanted laboriously produced native examples. The greater quantity of fish and meat obtained could be used to feed dogs, allowing development of dog-teams trained to pull sleds or toboggans. To obtain these necessities the Athapaskans spent the winters trapping, bringing to the posts furs valued in the international market.

A state of mutual dependence developed, with the posts existing only for the furs brought in by native trappers and natives altering much of their traditional lifestyle to obtain furs to exchange for goods. The fur trade companies, however, were driven by market considerations rather than a sense of reciprocal obligation. After the merger of 1821, many posts were closed as a cost-saving measure, despite the effect this had on local bands. A group of outraged Beaver massacred five company employees at a post on the Peace River scheduled for closure. In retaliation, the company closed all posts in the area, subjecting the Beaver to considerable hardship.

Throughout the rest of the nineteenth century most Athapaskans continued to be tied to the fur trade. In isolated northern communities, this way of life persisted well into the twentieth century. It was this complex of rifles, dog teams, trap lines and a market economy that became the "traditional" Athapaskan culture described by native informants to anthropologists.

The latter half of the nineteenth century also saw the arrival of missionaries, predominantly Roman Catholic. Missions were established, generally at the trading posts; however, the priests had to travel extensively to bush camps and isolated communities to keep contact with their converts. Unlike the traders, the missionaries attempted to transform native cultures, bringing them into greater conformity with Euro-Canadian practices. They introduced schools, serving to acculturate as much as educate native children. While most education was in English, an Anglican missionary among the Gwich'in devised a writing system for their language. By the end of the century, all but the most isolated Athapaskans were at least nominally Christian.

The increased movement of Euro-Canadian males into the Western Subarctic led to the growth of a mixed population, now generally known as Métis. In the Mackenzie district, two distinct groups emerged. One was the so-called "Red River Métis," descended from French-Canadian workers in the fur trade and their Indian, usually Cree, wives. They moved into the area as the fur trade spread to the northwest, later being joined by refugees from the Plains after the final defeat of the "Métis Nation" in 1885. The second group emerged in the north from the union of Scottish and English Hudson's Bay Company employees with Athapaskan women. The Métis served as post employees, interpreters and canoemen. They were not a distinct population but served as cultural intermediaries between natives and Euro-Canadians.

Massive cultural disruption occurred among the Cordilleran Athapaskans with the discovery of gold in their lands. The Cariboo gold rush, which climaxed in 1862, brought a mass of gold-seekers into Carrier territory. In the 1870s lesser gold strikes occurred to the north, in the lands of the Sekani, Kaska and Tahltan. Finally, the 1898 Klondike gold rush in the Yukon profoundly affected the Tagish, Tutchone and Gwich'in and almost destroyed the Han, the native occupants around what became

Dene gambling at Arctic Red River, N.W.T., ca. 1930. NAC 102486

Dawson City. In a matter of months Dawson's population swelled to an estimated 40,000, making it the largest Canadian city west of Winnipeg. The few hundred Han were simply swamped by the newcomers. Although Dawson was an ephemeral settlement, it boasted such amenities as saloons, dance halls and brothels. These novel attractions, plus opportunities for wage labour, drew many Athapaskans to Dawson. Some became prospectors or packers, while others worked cutting cordwood or as deckhands on the steamers. Unlike their essential role in the fur trade, however, the Athapaskans remained on the margins of the new economy. When the gold rush waned, they found themselves largely abandoned.

Increased movement of non-Indians into the north led to the Canadian government's negotiation of treaties, similar to those signed across the prairie provinces in the years following confederation. Treaty No. 8, signed in 1899, covers northeastern British Columbia, northern Alberta, northwestern Saskatchewan and north as far as Great Slave Lake. Increased development in the north and the discovery of oil in the Mackenzie valley led to the signing of Treaty No. 11 in 1921—the last of the historic federal treaties with Canadian natives. It covers the lands from Great Slave Lake to the Arctic Ocean, including the entire Mackenzie valley. No treaties were ever signed in the Yukon or with the Cordilleran peoples of British Columbia. Native leaders saw the treaties essentially as pacts of friendship and assistance, rather than as deeds of sale. However, the terms of the treaties specified removal of aboriginal title to the land in exchange for small annual payments, reserves and guarantees of continued hunting, fishing and trapping rights. Some promises have yet to be fulfilled, such as the establishment of reserves for all treaty groups in the Northwest Territories, while other rights were continually eroded prior to their protection in the 1982 constitution.

The "frontier," based on the rate of Euro-Canadian settlement, gradually moved to the north and west. Homesteaders took suitable farming and ranching lands in central British Columbia and along the Peace River of northern British Columbia and Alberta. Further north, the transportation corridors opened up by the gold rush continued to attract new settlers. Mining camps and permanent towns sprang up throughout much of the Western Subarctic. As new roads were built, the pace of non-Indian settlement increased. Construction of the Alaska Highway during World War II opened up the formerly remote lands of the Slavey, Kaska and Tutchone to a steady stream of Euro-Canadian arrivals. By the end of the war some Athapaskans, particularly in the south, had long since been displaced from most of their land and had become minorities, while in the north many remote and isolated groups were still living a life centred on the trading posts.

THE MODERN DENE

The postwar years saw an accelerated pace of Euro-Canadian expansion into Athapaskan lands. Mining, logging and other extractive industries brought in a stream of transient workers from the south. Aboriginal people increasingly became minorities in their homelands. As the population grew, new government services were provided, improving living conditions for the Dene but increasing their dependency.

Particularly important were new government programs in health, education, housing and welfare. Medical facilities were established to combat high rates of tuberculosis and infant mortality. Schools were constructed in many native communities, while elsewhere children were sent to residential schools in central locations. Such schools separated children from their parents and their culture, educating them in a language their parents could not understand and instilling foreign values. Only recently has this trend been reversed, with education serving to enhance Dene languages and culture, as well as providing skills essential for the modern world. Financial assistance also became available, in the form of family allowances, welfare and old age pensions. All of these programs have tended to encourage sedentary life in towns.

Dene communities in northern Canada today rely on some combination of trapping, government assistance and wage labour. While most jobs in the mining and lumber industries are taken by transient southern whites, an increasing number of Dene are finding employment. Guiding big-game hunters, fighting forest fires and clearing brush for roads also provide seasonal income. Commercial fisheries exist in a few places, such as around

Great Slave Lake, and cattle ranches have been established among the Beaver. Declining fur prices have led to a reduction in the number of people trapping, but this is still an important economic activity throughout the north. Subsistence hunting and fishing continue to put food on the table in most Dene households and provide important reaffirmation of native identity.

Modern Dene villages frequently include a store, school and church. The trading posts have become stores, offering a variety of southern goods for cash sale, though they often buy furs as well. Older homes are log cabins, which are gradually being replaced with wood-frame housing built under government subsidy. These permanent facilities discourage mobility, although men might leave the villages for short periods to tend their traplines or hunt, and whole families might depart to fish-camps during the summer.

Northern communities are becoming increasingly less isolated with modern advances in transportation. Snowmobiles and manufactured boats with outboard motors have almost totally replaced earlier methods of travel. New roads are being cut into Athapaskan lands as part of mining and oil exploration. Increasing use is being made of small chartered planes. Hunters and trappers can now quickly travel from their villages to distant locations to find game.

Modern studies of the Dene stress the maintenance of traditional individualism. Ideal personality traits include self-reliance and respect for the autonomy of others. In her study of one Slavey settlement, June Helm (1961:87) discussed this behavioural norm:

> . . . minding one's own business is a cardinal principle in Slavey life. Precepts, aid, or warnings are seldom volunteered to others. Even one's own children . . . are allowed, to a great extent, to govern their own lives.

The Dene of the Northwest Territories have become very active politically in recent decades. The Indian Brotherhood of the Northwest Territories was formed in 1970, later changing its name to the Dene Nation. While dedicated to enhancing education, health and communication among the Dene, it also has had their claim to the land as a primary focus. To advance their claim, it has been necessary to refute the government interpretation of Treaties 8 and 11. The Dene position is that they surrendered neither their sovereignty nor their rights to their lands in these treaties.

In 1973, the Dene filed a legal caveat to halt all further development on their traditional lands. A series of hearings in native communities was conducted by Justice William Morrow of the Supreme Court of the Northwest Territories. After listening to native testimony, particularly from individuals who had actually attended the signing of Treaty 11, he concluded that the treaties had been misrepresented or inadequately explained. His ruling favoured the Dene, stating that they should be permitted to advance a claim for title to the land and that "notwithstanding the language of the two treaties . . . there is sufficient doubt on the facts that aboriginal title was extinguished." This judgment was subsequently overturned on technical grounds, but it forced recognition by the federal government that the Dene had a strong negotiating position. The government failure to establish reserves promised by treaty also strengthens the Dene argument.

In 1975 the Dene and Métis of the Northwest Territories issued the Dene Declaration. It states, in part:

> We the Dene of the N.W.T. insist on the right to be regarded by ourselves and the world as a nation. Our struggle is for the recognition of the Dene Nation by the government and people of Canada and the peoples and governments of the world. What we seek then is independence and self-determination within the country of Canada.
>
> (Dene Nation 1984:28)

Shortly after, the Dene and Métis began their lengthy negotiations with the federal government over land claims and aboriginal rights.

Meanwhile, oil and gas development threatened Dene lands. Particularly worrisome were plans for a pipeline down the Mackenzie valley. Strong opposition by aboriginal peoples and environmentalists led to a federal inquiry headed by Justice Thomas Berger. Beginning in 1975, Berger traveled to each Dene and Inuit community on the Mackenzie to hold hearings. The southern media were captivated by this soft-spoken judge and the quiet conviction of native northerners who expressed opposition to the pipeline. Primary concerns were the impact on game and furbearing animals, and the failure of the government to settle land claims prior to construction. In his 1977 report, Berger recommended that any such project be postponed to allow time to settle native claims. In his words (1977:200):

> If we build the pipeline, it will seem strange, years from now, that we refused to do justice to the native people merely to continue to provide ourselves with a range of consumer goods and comforts . . . the pipeline, if it were built now, would do enormous damage to the social fabric in the North, would bring only limited economic benefits, and would stand in the way of a just settlement of native claims . . . It would leave a legacy of bitterness.

The heavy publicity given Berger's recommendations, plus uncertain economic conditions, led to shelving plans for the pipeline.

More recently, one Treaty 8 band won a major victory involving gas and oil revenues. The Slavey around Fort Nelson, in northeastern British Columbia, had been promised reserves when they signed the treaty. Continuing in their migratory lifestyle, they did not settle and take reserve lands until much later. When the province transferred title to the lands to the federal government in 1961, it withheld all subsurface rights. Since other reserves established under this treaty received mineral rights, the Fort

Nelson Slavey took their case to court. Their 1980 victory gave them $15 million in retroactive royalties and a 50:50 split with the province on future profits.

In the Yukon, where no historic treaties were signed, land claims have been a paramount concern. The Council for Yukon Indians has vigorously pressed its case in negotiations with the federal government. Concern over surrender of aboriginal title to their lands led individual Yukon First Nations to reject a 1984 agreement-in-principle. Finally, in 1993 an Umbrella Final Agreement was signed between the Government of Canada, the Government of the Yukon and the Council for Yukon Indians. The Yukon First Nations agreed to "cede, release and surrender" their aboriginal claims to non-settlement land in return for title to over 40,000 square kilometres and financial compensation which will total over $240 million. The interests of Yukon First Nations will also be protected through membership on various boards and committees dealing with wildlife management, resource development and heritage preservation. Specific issues are dealt with in separate agreements with individual Yukon First Nations. The Umbrella Agreement also commits the federal government to negotiate self-government with each Yukon First Nation which so requests.

In the Northwest Territories, a final agreement remains elusive. The Dene Nation and the Métis Association of the Northwest Territories have jointly negotiated with the federal government. Although a final agreement was signed in 1990, it was rejected at an assembly of the Dene and Métis organizations later that year. Concern over the agreement's extinguishment of aboriginal rights and title to the land were at the heart of the rejection.

Not all Dene groups, however, supported that assembly's position. The Gwich'in of the Mackenzie delta withdrew from the broader Dene-Métis claim to negotiate on their own. The Gwich'in Comprehensive Land Claim Agreement was finalized in 1992. Its terms follow the model of the proposed Dene-Métis agreement, providing title to lands (over 20,000 square kilometres, only a portion of which includes rights to subsurface minerals), financial compensation ($75 million), royalties on resources removed from Gwich'in land and membership on regulatory boards dealing with land and resources. It also calls for separate negotiations on the issue of self-government. The neighboring Sahtu Dene and Métis of Great Bear Lake also withdrew from the broader claim, striking a similar agreement in 1993. This agreement also provides financial compensation, title to lands, resource royalties and a commitment from the federal government to negotiate self-government.

In British Columbia, where the Cordilleran Athapaskans lack historic treaties, land claims negotiations are proceeding through separate tribal councils. The Wet'suwet'en are fighting their legal battle in cooperation with the neighbouring Gitksan. Their lengthy but unsuccessful court case is discussed in Chapter 8. Other Athapaskan groups in British Columbia with claims accepted for negotiation by the federal government include the Kaska-Dena Council, the Association of United Tahltans, the Carrier-Sekani Tribal Council and the Nazko-Kluskus (Carrier) Bands.

Farther east, Treaty No. 8 encompasses the lands of the Dene and western Woods Cree. In northern Alberta the Lubicon Cree have been involved in a lengthy and bitter land claims dispute. This isolated group was apparently missed during treaty signing and did not apply for lands until much later. A reserve proposed in 1940 was never surveyed due to disputes about the number of band members and consequent reserve size. In subsequent decades oil exploration resulted in roads opening up what had been a remote area and the destruction of much of the game upon which the Lubicon depended. Under their young chief, Bernard Ominayak, the Lubicon organized court challenges, roadblocks and highly publicized protests at the 1988 Winter Olympics in Calgary, along with the boycott of a major exhibition of aboriginal art at Calgary's Glenbow Museum. Negotiations were complicated by the Lubicon position that they held aboriginal title to the land and were entitled to compensation for the destruction of their hunting and trapping way of life, as opposed to government insistence that this was simply a specific treaty entitlement claim. After the bitter collapse of a near-agreement, a number of Cree in the area, with government encouragement, formed separate bands and negotiated reserve lands and financial compensation, leaving the remaining Lubicon in a difficult and unresolved position.

Today there are over 50,000 Canadian Athapaskans. The most populous groups are the Chipewyan, Carrier and Slavey, with registered members totaling about 14,000, 10,000, and 6500, respectively. With the exception of Han and Tagish, which face extinction, their languages are relatively healthy. This is particularly the case in the Northwest Territories, where many villages are unilingual in Chipewyan, Dogrib, Slavey or Gwich'in. It is less true in British Columbia and Alberta, where the Beaver, Sekani and Kaska languages are considered endangered, with only a few hundred speakers; Carrier, however, is in a stronger position (the 1991 census indicates that about 2600 people speak the Carrier language). Modern programs to teach native languages in the schools help to ensure survival.

The later history of the Dene was one of progressive loss of control over their own lives. In recent decades, however, the Dene have managed to reverse this trend. Unlike natives in southern Canada, who have lost most of their lands and traditional economy, the Dene have the opportunity to retain much of their heritage. Indeed, many see it as not just a question of survival but an opportunity to flourish—following a Dene lifestyle with the advantages of modern technology and without the traditional fears of winter starvation or the sudden appearance of enemy warriors.

CHAPTER 10 *The Arctic*

Dwelling on the fringe of the habitable world, the Inuit have long fascinated more southerly Canadians. Despite our self-identity as a northern nation, most Canadians inhabit a narrow strip along the south of the country, visualizing the Arctic as a vast frozen wasteland, caught in the grip of near-continual winter. The Inuit, in their ancient occupation of the Arctic, have become symbols of our northern aspirations, exciting admiration for their ingenious adaptation to a harsh environment.

The tree line defines the Arctic's southern limit. Only a short distance from the Arctic coastline in the west, it drops sharply to the southeast, taking in the eastern Northwest Territories and a small portion of northern Manitoba. To the east of Hudson Bay, northern Quebec and much of the Labrador coast are included. The area is one of treeless tundra, presenting a forbidding vista of glaciated mountains, boulders and gravel, with sparse vegetation. Small patches of stunted trees such as willow occur in sheltered areas, but even such limited growth is rare on the islands of the High Arctic. Physiographically, the land varies from the rugged mountains and deeply cut fiords of the eastern High Arctic islands, to the rocky rolling terrain of the interior barrenlands, to the flat plain of the Mackenzie delta.

Throughout the lengthy winters the Arctic fulfills its image of a windswept, snow-covered, harsh and barren land. Temperatures drop to extremes, capable of freezing exposed flesh in minutes. For nine months or more each year the seas and lakes are frozen solid. Darkness reigns uninterrupted for weeks in midwinter, with only a brief twilight at midday. Despite the presence of snow and ice everywhere, the land is a desert, with very little precipitation.

The brief summer restores life and colour to the landscape.

257

Temperatures, while not hot by southern standards, are pleasant, though freezing conditions and snow flurries can occur at almost any time. The days are long and generally sunny, with a period near midsummer when the sun never sets. Colourful plants spring to life across the tundra. The permafrost prevents meltwater from seeping away, turning the land surface into innumerable bogs and ponds. Such conditions are ideal for mosquitoes and blackflies, which plague humans and animals during this otherwise pleasant season.

The inhabitants of this region are the Inuit, who are a distinct aboriginal people in Canada. They belong to a linguistic stock termed Eskimo-Aleut, named for its two major branches. The Aleuts, on the Aleutian Islands of Alaska, are the most divergent. The larger branch, Eskimo, has a major division near Bering Strait. On one side, the Yupik comprise people with at least five separate languages in eastern Siberia and central and southern Alaska. On the other, the Inuit extend from northern Alaska to Greenland, including all of Arctic Canada. In Canada, the word "Inuit" (meaning "people"; the singular is "Inuk") has now almost totally replaced "Eskimo" (generally, although probably erroneously, believed to be derived from a derogatory Algonkian term meaning "eaters of raw meat"). Throughout their vast distribution, the Inuit speak a single language (Inuktitut), although a number of dialects are known. In their physical features, all Eskimos and Aleuts are classified with eastern Siberian native peoples in a category known as "Arctic Mongoloids."

Throughout the Arctic the Inuit and their predecessors survived on whatever resources were available. Their economy was based on some combination of hunting land and sea mammals and fishing, with gathering playing a very limited role. Caribou and seals were the essential resources, providing a steady, if somewhat monotonous, diet. The hunters' quests were not always successful, and starvation was an ever-present threat. Resources in Arctic Canada were more limited than to either the west or east, supporting a lower population density than Alaska or Greenland.

ARCTIC CULTURES PRIOR TO EUROPEAN ARRIVAL

The Arctic poses major challenges to southern researchers trying to decipher its ancient heritage. Field seasons are necessarily short, access to many areas is difficult, and the frozen ground only gradually yields its secrets to the archaeologists' patient scraping. Despite the difficulties, the rewards of Arctic archaeology are great. With little or no vegetation or soil to obscure or bury sites, and little disturbance from nature or humans, most remains sit on the surface as they were originally abandoned. The continuously frozen ground has acted as a deep-freeze, preserving intact materials which are rarely recovered from archaeological sites elsewhere. In addition to objects of bone, antler and ivory, at some locations even such perishable materials as wood and hide have emerged after centuries in the frozen soil, allowing a more complete understanding of the rich material culture of these ancient Arctic-dwellers.

In the southern Arctic, people of Eskimoan stock were not the first inhabitants. Stone tools, including Plano spearpoints of the Agate Basin form, show that late Paleo-Indian hunters pursued the caribou herds far out onto the barrenlands of Keewatin. It is likely that they retreated to the shelter of the forests in winter, as did the historic Chipewyan. The rest of the Canadian Arctic, however, far removed from the tree line, sat empty until the arrival of people already adapted to sea mammal hunting and the harsh climate. Termed "Paleo-Eskimos," these people appeared somewhat over 4000 years ago. Although not directly ancestral to the historic Inuit, they brought an "Eskimo" way of life.

Initial arrivals came from the west, spreading rapidly from Alaska to Greenland. They brought with them the distinctive assemblage of tiny chipped-stone tools known to archaeologists as the Arctic Small Tool tradition. Their sites are littered with finely crafted miniature implements of stone, such as razor-blade-like microblades, a variety of small scrapers and tiny sharp tools used as tips or side-blades on arrows or harpoons. The first wave seems to have taken them into the High Arctic by about 2000 B.C. Termed **Independence I**, their meagre remains consist of small, briefly occupied campsites. The people apparently kept on the move, primarily hunting musk-oxen and small game, as well as taking seals. Life must have been harsh for these Arctic pioneers, who apparently lacked the dog sled, blubber lamps and the technology required to build snowhouses (igloos). Huddled in their tents against the cold and dark of an Arctic winter, these early Paleo-Eskimos must have struggled on the edge of survival. Yet they spread into the northern reaches of the High Arctic islands, a land not occupied by Inuit in historic times. Their hold on the High Arctic was tenuous, and they disappeared after only a few centuries.

Further to the south another Paleo-Eskimo variant, the **Pre-Dorset**, made a more lasting adaptation. They spread throughout the Low Arctic, including the interior barrenlands, east as far as northern Labrador. This was a richer environment, with a greater abundance of caribou and sea mammals, resulting in larger and more numerous sites than in the far north. Only later did their travels take them into the islands of the High Arctic, typically settling near polynyas (bodies of water which remain open much of the year), where seals and birds were abundant. Their dwellings appear to have been tents, indicated by circular clearings, often surrounded by a ring of boulders which once held down the tent edges. It is possible that winter homes were igloos out on the sea ice, where seals could be hunted, but these would disappear without a trace. Occasional discoveries of

Paleo-Eskimo (Independence I variant) artifacts from Devon Island. Clockwise from upper left: *two antler harpoon heads, bone needle, two stone points, endscraper, concave sidescraper, knife, endblade, three microblades.* Courtesy R. McGhee, CMC

soapstone lamps for burning blubber may indicate their use, since other fires could not be lit in the close confines of an igloo. Miniature stone tools of the Arctic Small Tool tradition were used for cutting meat, shaping wooden and ivory objects, scraping hides and myriad other tasks. Small bone needles were essential in preparing warm clothing. Bows and arrows were used for hunting land mammals and harpoons for sea mammals. The harpoon heads, almost as important to Arctic archaeologists for classifying cultures as stone projectile points are on the Plains, are of the socketed "toggling" type—that is, they "toggle" or turn to hold fast inside the body of the seal, walrus or small whale, the most important prey throughout most of Pre-Dorset distribution.

A period of cooler climate characterizes the late Pre-Dorset period. Environmental stress appears to have led to a lower population on the Arctic islands, through local extinctions or southward migrations. Other groups followed the retreating tree line far to the south, eventually reaching what is today northern Manitoba and Saskatchewan. In the interior barrenlands these Pre-Dorset became highly specialized caribou hunters. However, dependence upon any one resource is perilous in the Arctic, with extinction the eventual fate. After about 800 B.C. the Pre-Dorset disappeared from the barrenlands, which reverted to sporadic use by Indian groups from the south. Not until the arrival of the historic Caribou Inuit would the barrenlands return to Eskimoan peoples.

Unlike the preceding or subsequent stage, the **Dorset** culture (ca. 800 B.C. to A.D. 1000) appears in place in the Canadian Arctic, emerging gradually out of Pre-Dorset. Sites are larger and more numerous, with a greater number and variety of artifacts. Many objects, such as stone tools and harpoon heads, resemble their Pre-Dorset antecedents but have gone through changes in style. The small chipped-stone burins used by the Pre-Dorset to

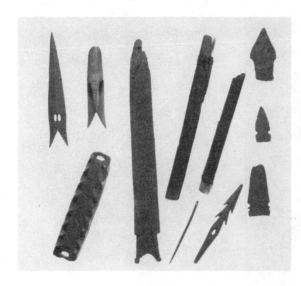

Dorset artifacts.
Clockwise from upper left: *two harpoon heads, lance head, microblade mounted in wooden handle, burin-like tool in wooden handle, two chipped stone points, ground slate blade, dart head, needle, ice-creeper.*
Courtesy R. McGhee, CMC

carve bone and ivory were replaced by burin-like tools which were ground to shape. Similarly, ground-stone knives and other tools became common, replacing earlier chipped-stone varieties. Large bone knives were possibly used to cut snow blocks for constructing igloos. Rectangular lamps of soapstone, used to burn oil from sea mammal blubber, were used to light and heat their homes. Other new inventions included ivory sled shoes (pegged over the sled runners to protect them on rough ice or gravel) and "ice-creepers" (notched strips of bone or ivory tied under the boots to prevent slipping on the ice). Such traits suggest that the practice of hunting seals on the sea ice was fully developed. In the midst of this technological ingenuity, there are some surprising absences. Gone are the drill and the bow and arrow, both of which existed in Pre-Dorset times.

People of the Dorset culture eventually spread throughout the Arctic, including the northernmost islands. Only in the interior barrenlands and the western region around the Mackenzie delta did Dorset culture not spread to where Pre-Dorset people had lived. In the east, the Dorset continued their travels far beyond the Pre-Dorset distribution, eventually colonizing the entire coast of Labrador and the island of Newfoundland. Their occupation of Newfoundland, which lasted for over a millennium, represents the most southerly extension of any Eskimoan people.

Like all Arctic inhabitants, the Dorset followed the seasons to wrest a living from their harsh environment. In spring and summer, seals and walrus were harpooned from the ice edge and perhaps from kayaks in open water. Caribou were hunted in the summer, as were musk-oxen and birds, and Arctic char were speared at favoured fishing locations. In winter, it appears that many bands built snowhouses out on the sea ice, where they hunted

261

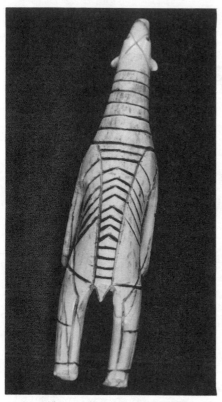

Above: *Dorset life-sized wooden mask from Bylot Island, possibly used by a shaman. Traces of red paint still survive. Wooden pins along the side may have been used to fasten the mask to clothing.* CMC K75-493

Dorset ivory carving of a polar bear (16 cm long). Typical of such figures, it shows skeletal elements and joints. A slit on the throat contains a sliver of ivory. It may represent the spirit helper of a shaman. Photo by Diane Lyons

seals at their breathing holes. Their way of life was not greatly dissimilar to that of the historic Central Inuit.

Housing also varied with the seasons, as it did for later groups. Summer dwellings were tents, probably of sealskin. Winter homes were more substantial, being dug slightly into the ground and having walls built up of sod and rocks. Floors were paved with flat stone slabs, and small sleeping platforms flanked the central working area. Dorset people probably also built igloos while sealing on the ice, but these leave no archaeological trace and can only be inferred by the presence of bone snow-knives and soapstone lamps. Near the end of the Dorset time span, they also constructed long, rectangular boulder enclosures, known as "longhouses," which have been claimed by several writers to be Norse ruins. Lacking evidence that they were ever roofed over or served as residences, these enigmatic structures may have had some unknown social or ceremonial function.

Also occurring in the late Dorset period was the climax of a remarkable art form. Tiny sculptures, some miniature masterpieces, were carved in bone, antler and ivory. Small carvings in soapstone also occur, particularly in northern Labrador. Where wood has been preserved, it also appears as an important medium for the carvers' skill. Images of humans, animals and birds provide insight into the Dorset world. Wooden and soapstone carvings of people give details of clothing, indicating that Dorset parkas had a high collar rather than a hood. Clusters of human faces peer out from segments of caribou antler. Polar bears predominate among the many animals depicted, which is hardly surprising considering that they are the major predators of the Arctic, capable of stalking humans for food. Despite the danger, the Dorset apparently hunted the bears, at least occasionally, and their images in the art may be related to the hunt. Some depictions seem simply playful, as in several small soapstone figures of seated bears and small ivory sculptures depicting people at play or adults with children on their shoulders.

Much of the art gives the overwhelming impression of supernatural matters and shamanic activity. Masks range from full-size wooden examples, possibly worn by shamans, to small bone and soapstone maskettes. Many of the polar bears appear as if they were flying through the air and are covered with designs indicating skeletal elements and joints. This may represent butchering of the animal, but it may also reflect shamanic vision. Powerful shamans among the historic Inuit were supposed to be able to divest themselves of flesh and blood, flying through the air as skeletons. The power of the polar bear, along with its man-like qualities, would make it an ideal spirit helper. Carvings range from detailed naturalism to highly abstracted forms, and from complete figures to only parts of an animal's body, such as a head or hoof. Several man-animal carvings suggest the link between the shaman and his spirit helper. Some of the bears have slits in the throat, into which have been placed red ochre and slivers of wood or ivory, suggesting a hunting ritual. More sinister is the occurrence of similar slivers in the chests of human figures, a practice suspiciously resembling witchcraft rituals in many cultures.

How were the Dorset related to other "Eskimo" people? Skeletal remains are rare in the Arctic, but burials from Newfoundland indicate that they were Arctic Mongoloids, distinct from Indian populations of the area. Yet they were not directly related to the historic occupants of the Arctic, and we cannot use the term "Inuit" for them. In their legends the Inuit refer to an earlier race, people whom they called the Tunit. These were strong and peaceful people, who were great seal hunters. It is likely that these legends reflect ancient traditions from when the ancestors of the Inuit met their predecessors in the Canadian Arctic, the Dorset.

Around A.D. 1000 the Dorset were challenged by new conditions and new arrivals. A warming trend in the Arctic possibly disrupted the distribution of animals on which they depended and allowed the spread of alien peoples into their lands. To the east, the Norse established colonies in Greenland and possibly made occasional forays to Baffin Island or Labrador, bringing Arctic natives into their first contact with Europeans. Far more significant, however, was the flood of new arrivals from the west. These people were the Thule, the direct ancestors of the modern Inuit, who rapidly expanded across the Arctic to Greenland and northern Labrador.

Extinctions are a common theme in the Arctic archaeological record and we cannot be certain that the Dorset survived to meet these new arrivals. If the Dorset and Thule did briefly coexist, what fate befell the Dorset? Inuit legends describe a period of peaceful coexistence with the Tunit, before the two groups quarreled and the Tunit were driven away. The elaborate technology of the Thule must have given them a competitive edge over the more conservative Dorset, who were either killed, displaced or absorbed. Only a few tantalizing hints of cultural contact and borrowing exist in the archaeological record. Although the Dorset were gone from the central Arctic by about A.D. 1000, they appear to have hung on for a few more centuries around the eastern shores of Hudson Bay and in northern Quebec. Some authorities even point to the now-extinct Sadlermiut of Southampton Island, with their distinct dialect and an emphasis on chipped-stone tools, as the last vestige of the Dorset, surviving into the early twentieth century.

The **Thule** (*ca.* A.D. 1000 to 1600) brought a dynamic Alaskan culture into the Canadian Arctic. Their arrival coincided with a general warming trend which would have reduced the amount of sea ice, thereby opening up a larger area for bowhead whales and other large sea mammals. Climatic changes could only allow the spread, not be the cause, which may have had more to do with population pressure in Alaska or the invention of a more efficient whaling technology. Thule whale hunters, traveling in skin boats and dog sleds, moved rapidly eastward, bringing with them a rich and varied material culture. Almost certainly speaking Inuktitut, these were the direct ancestors of the Arctic's historic inhabitants.

Many new items of technology for sea mammal hunting were introduced by the Thule. They had both the *kayak* (a small, single-person hunting boat, completely enclosed except for an opening at the top to admit the hunter) and the *umiak* (a larger, open, hide-covered boat, used for transporting goods and people and for hunting whales). New forms of large harpoon heads were used with floats, allowing the hunting of sea mammals, including large whales, on the open water. Winter hunting of seals on the ice is shown by a number of specialized tools. Long bone probes were used to detect the shape of the seals' breathing holes, small stools provided comfort for the sealer in his long wait, plugs prevented loss of blood from the seal's wound, and snow goggles reduced the glare off the ice to prevent snow-blindness in the winter. Travel over the ice was made easier by the dog sled, which seems to have been a Thule introduction. While the Dorset possessed small sleds, there is no evidence that they employed dogs to pull them. Thule sites yield various toggles and buckles used in harnessing the dogs, as well as physical remains of the dogs themselves.

Numerous other ingenious innovations were brought from their Alaskan homeland. *Ulus*, the semicircular "women's knives," with ground-slate blades and wooden or bone handles, were the major tools for cutting meat or preparing hides. Fine bone needles were kept in decorated bone needle-cases, and small bone thimbles were kept on anchor-shaped thimble holders. The bow-drill, where the drill shaft was rapidly turned by looping the bowstring around it and moving the bow back and forth, was widely used to work bone and ivory. For land hunting, the bow and arrow was reintroduced and small weights of antler and bone were used in bolas to capture low-flying ducks and geese.

The Thule also brought the Alaskan practice of manufacturing pottery lamps and other vessels. Pottery is common at Thule sites in the western Arctic and occurs at early levels in sites farther east. Thule pottery is thick, poorly fired, coarse and crumbly, thoroughly earning its unflattering designation by Arctic archaeologists as "Thule crudware." Difficulty in obtaining clay and the wood needed to fire it led to the abandonment of pottery-making throughout most of the Canadian Arctic. Instead, the Thule carved much more durable lamps and cooking pots of soapstone, a trait perhaps learned from their Dorset predecessors.

The art of the Thule people is much less dramatic than that of the Dorset. Frequently adorning functional objects, its purpose appears decorative, lacking the supernatural power suggested by Dorset art. Incised designs on bone and ivory surfaces depict tents, hunters with bows and arrows, and whalers in umiaks. Decorative patterns of circles and dots, produced with the bow drill, appear on a variety of objects. Small sculptures include humans (usually female) in wood, bone and ivory, and flat-bottomed ivory figures of swimming birds, often with a woman's head and torso. The latter were likely tossed in a game but may have had a mythological basis, representing the Inuit belief in an association between women and the sea animals.

The Thule built substantial winter houses, which must have offered much greater comfort than the Dorset enjoyed. They brought the basic style from Alaska but in the wood-scarce Canadian Arctic had to substitute whale ribs and jaws for driftwood logs as construction materials. The entrance tunnel sloped downwards, trapping cold air below the level of the house. Inside, the floor was paved with flat stones, which were also used to construct a sleeping platform, elevated to take advantage of the warmer air, with storage space below. Baleen (the tough, fibrous material from the mouths of bowhead whales) was placed on the platform to form a springy mattress, which was covered with caribou hides. Walls were of stone, with rafters of whalebone supporting the roof, which was formed of hides covered with a thick layer of turf. Heated and lit with oil-burning lamps, these

Top: *A Thule winter house, after removal of the collapsed roof. A raised sleeping area is in the foreground, while a sunken entrance tunnel can be seen at the rear of the house.* Courtesy R. McGhee, CMC

Bottom left: *Thule artifacts.* Top row: *whaling harpoon head, two sealing harpoon heads, arrowhead, fish-spear prong; middle row: ulu with native copper blade, adze head, knife with iron blade, bird-spear sideprong; third row: dog harness buckle, thimble holder, needle case, comb, snowknife; bottom: snow goggles.* Courtesy R. McGhee, CMC

Bottom right: *Copper Inuit man using a bow drill.* NAC PA117148

Inuksuit ("like men" cairns) channel caribou to where the hunters wait. NAC PA129873

must have provided warm and secure refuge against the Arctic winter. Ruins of such structures, today visible as small circular mounds of rock, whalebone and baleen, are found across the Arctic, including the northernmost islands. Evidence that they also built snowhouses, although probably only as temporary camps, comes from such specialized tools as snow-probes (for judging the snow's depth and consistency) and snow-knives (for cutting blocks suitable for building). In summer, the Thule were much more mobile, camping in hide-covered tents.

Whaling played a major role in Thule life. As the large bowhead whales moved into their summer feeding grounds along the gulfs and straits of the Arctic islands, swimming slowly and near the surface, they could be hunted with large harpoons by men in umiaks. Even if a successful hunt was a relatively rare event, it would have provided several tonnes of meat and blubber, meeting the food requirements of a Thule village for many months. Nowhere, however, were the Thule exclusively dependent upon whales. Some moved into areas where whaling would not have been feasible, relying instead on seals and walrus. Caribou, musk-oxen and waterfowl, as well as fish, were also important sources of food.

The readily available boulders of the Arctic landscape were used by the Thule for a variety of constructions. Circles of rocks mark where tents stood, and jumbles of rock and whalebone identify the winter villages. Boulder cairns were piled over their dead and over caches of meat. Piled boulders supported umiaks and kayaks, keeping them off the ground and away from dogs. Stone dams or weirs were built at favoured fishing locations, to intercept the annual runs of Arctic char. *Inuksuit* (*inukshuk* is singular), rocks piled to resemble humans, were used to funnel caribou to where the hunters waited, and some perhaps also served as landmarks on flat and featureless snow-covered terrain. As great "movers-of-boulders," the Thule altered the landscape, leaving numerous traces of their presence for modern archaeologists.

In the east the Thule were in contact with the Norse, who had established colonies in Greenland. Although the Norse sagas tell only of hostility with the natives (whom they termed *skraelings*, or "savages"), archaeological discoveries of smelted iron, bronze and copper at a number of Canadian Thule sites suggest that trade also occurred. Particularly dramatic was the discovery on Ellesmere Island of fragments of chain mail, the typical armour of medieval Europe, along with woolen cloth, iron boat rivets and sections of wooden barrels dating to the mid-thirteenth century. Such objects may have found their way there through trade with Greenlandic Thule; however, the discovery of part of a folding bronze balance, of the type used by Norse traders for weighing small objects, suggests that the Norse might have traveled to Ellesmere. It is probable that they were occasional visitors to Baffin Island, and a small wooden figure excavated from a thirteenth-century Thule house there appears to show a European, dressed in the long robes of his time, with a cross on his chest. Was this little figure carved by a Thule after an encounter with strangers of another race? Trade could have been profitable on both sides, with the Thule anxious to acquire metal for their tools and the Norse seeking wealth in the form of polar bear skins, walrus hides and ivory.

Iron-bladed tools appear to have become an important part of Inuit technology by the thirteenth century. Despite the common image of being remote until very recently, the Inuit of the central Arctic were using iron tools hundreds of years before direct contact with Europeans. Analysis indicates that they had access to both meteoric iron from Greenland and smelted iron of Norse origins. Indeed, Arctic archaeologist Robert McGhee has suggested that we should consider the Thule an "Iron Age" people and that demand for this important material may have been one of the motivations behind the Thule migration into the eastern Arctic.

At the end of the Thule period they again came into brief contact with outsiders. The European "Age of Discovery" brought ships into eastern Arctic waters in search of the fabled Northwest Passage, beginning with Martin Frobisher in 1576. One of his officers provided a description of natives they encountered, stating "they be like to Tartars, with long blacke haire, broad faces, and flatte noses, and tawnie in colour, wearing Seale skinnes . . . The women are marked in the faces with blewe streakes downe the cheekes, and round about the eies." An artist who accompanied the expedition in the following year left paintings which show people essentially identical to the nineteenth-century Inuit.

The Inuit cultures described by later explorers, however, seem less complex than the Thule. Their technology appears simpler and the way of life less secure. Cooler conditions after about A.D. 1200 caused the Thule to adapt increasingly to local resources, removing some of the uniformity which characterized early Thule culture. The climate continued to cool until reaching the "Little Ice Age," lasting from about A.D. 1600 to 1850. Worsening climate greatly affected the distribution of animals and the people who were dependent upon them. Increased sea ice blocked the large whales from their former feeding grounds, resulting in collapse of the Thule whale hunt. Cultures became specialized on locally available foods, usually some combination of seal, caribou and fish, and became increasingly different from each other. In the central Arctic such basic Thule traits as the umiak and the permanent winter house were abandoned, the people retaining only such temporary shelters as the skin tent and domed snowhouse. On the northern islands of the High Arctic, worsened conditions meant starvation or migration for the local inhabitants, leaving the land unoccupied. Some families may have joined relatives around the open water and bird cliffs of northwestern Greenland. There an isolated remnant population known as the Polar Eskimo survived, believing themselves to be the only people in the world until nineteenth-century contact with Europeans. While the historic Inuit are clearly the inheritors of a rich Thule tradition, not all of this legacy survived the colder climate.

TRADITIONAL INUIT CULTURE

Although eastern groups had been in fleeting contact with Europeans for many centuries, sustained Euro-Canadian presence was late in the Canadian Arctic. The more isolated Central Inuit had few contacts until late in the nineteenth century, maintaining their traditional hunting and fishing lifestyle, with the addition of some imported material items, into the twentieth century. These were the people studied by Diamond Jenness as part of the Canadian Arctic Expedition (1913-1918) and by the Danish team of Knud Rasmussen, Therkel Mathiassen and Kaj Birket-Smith as part of the Fifth Thule Expedition (1921-1924). Unlike anthropologists in more southerly parts of Canada, who had to reconstruct earlier ways of life from the memories of informants, these researchers were able to observe functioning traditional societies, living with them and recording their activities. This large body of information on the Central Inuit, who are among the best known of Canadian natives, tends to overshadow the regional diversity exhibited by Inuit elsewhere in the Canadian Arctic.

For all but a few inland-dwelling groups, the sea provided the most important resources. The small ringed seal, which lives under the sea ice in winter, could be taken throughout the Arctic, as could the larger but less numerous bearded seal. The Greenland or harp seal, which requires open water, was only available to the eastern Inuit. Seals provided food for humans and dogs, oil to heat homes and cook food, and hides which could be made into boots, summer clothing, tents, harpoon lines and dog harnesses. The walrus, which also requires open water, could be hunted by groups from Igloolik and Baffin Island to Labrador. The walrus provided meat and blubber, ivory from their tusks and tough hides which could be used for various purposes, including covering boats. While large whales were hunted in the east and west, most Canadian Inuit pursued smaller species, the narwhal and beluga.

The harpoon was essential for hunting sea mammals, and a variety of ingenious forms was developed for different species and different hunting techniques. The prey were commonly pursued in open water by hunters in kayaks or, in some places, umiaks. They could also be taken along the edge of the ice, or where seals hauled themselves out of the water to bask in the sun. The most ingenious technique was that developed by the Central Inuit to hunt seals at their breathing holes in the winter ice. After his dogs had sniffed out the breathing hole under the snow, the hunter used a long probe to determine its shape, so that he would know where to thrust the harpoon. A small piece of down might be carefully set over the hole, so that its movement would indicate the arrival of the seal. Perhaps sheltering himself from the winter wind with a low wall of snow-blocks, and with his harpoon at the ready, the hunter patiently settled himself for what might be a long wait. If the seal finally returned to the hole and the harpoon thrust hit its target, the hunter enlarged the hole to draw out his kill, plugged the wound to preserve the blood, and dragged the seal to his sled.

On land, caribou was by far the most important prey. As well as meat, the caribou provided hides for warm winter clothing, sinew for thread and antler as an important raw material for tools. Caribou could be hunted with the bow and arrow or speared from kayaks as they swam across lakes or rivers. One common technique, used earlier by the Thule, was to drive the caribou between converging lines of *inuksuit*, which directed the caribou to where archers were concealed in shallow pits or to a water crossing where the hunters waited by their kayaks.

Other land mammals played a lesser role. Musk-oxen were easy to hunt, owing to their habit of standing in a defensive circle when attacked. This worked well against wolves, but not against hunters with bows and arrows. Even polar bears, despite being fearsome predators, were hunted for their meat and hides. Various birds, from waterfowl to ptarmigan, were also taken by hunters.

Fishing was the other major part of the economy for most Inuit groups. Fish could be speared from the ice edge or a rock over the water. Occasionally men fished from their kayaks. In winter, people laboriously chipped holes through the thick ice to jig for fish with hook and line. Many of the central groups moved inland in late summer to intercept the runs of Arctic char at their stone weirs. After repairing the damage to the rock walls caused by the winter ice, the people awaited the arrival of the fish, which were channeled into a central enclosed basin. When enough fish had arrived, men and women waded into the frigid water with their leister spears. These consisted of wooden shafts, at the end of which were two flexible prongs of antler or horn with sharp bone barbs to slip over and grasp the fish while a sharp central point impaled it. Staying in the water as long

Central Inuit spearing fish at a stone weir, ca. 1915. CMC 37080

as their numbed limbs would allow, people quickly speared large numbers of fish with this ingenious implement, stringing them on a long line which could then be hauled to shore. Some of the catch was eaten fresh, while the rest was dried and cached under rocks for later use.

The Inuit lived almost totally on the flesh of animals and fish, differing from most non-agricultural societies by relying little on gathered foods. Wherever birds nested, eggs could be collected to provide a welcome change of diet. Except in more southerly regions, such as Labrador, plant foods were very limited, being restricted to a few berries. Some plant food was obtained indirectly, as after a caribou kill the warm, partially digested contents of the animal's stomach were eagerly consumed.

Although meat alone cannot provide proper nutrition, the Inuit diet was healthy because it consisted of nearly every part of the animals killed. Sea mammals were valued for their thick layer of blubber as much as their meat. *Muktuk*, the skin with attached blubber of the beluga and other whales, was highly prized. Caribou bones were broken to extract the marrow. Brains, heart and other organs were eaten. After the kill of a seal, hunters gathered for a snack of raw liver. Fish and animal eyeballs were eaten as tasty morsels during the task of butchering, and seal intestines were braided and dried, to be stored as a delicacy.

Most of the food was eaten raw, particularly in the central area, where fuel for cooking was scarce. However, even there some meat was cooked in soapstone pots over small fires of moss or willow twigs, or over the blubber lamp. It was frequently boiled, with blubber and blood added to make a thick broth. The typical method of eating was to bite into a strip of meat, then cut it off near the lips with a knife. In winter, caribou meat was eaten frozen by chipping off and chewing small pieces. Although the Arctic provided a natural deep-freeze, allowing storage of food for a considerable period of time, some putrefaction did occur. This, however, only enhanced the taste, and some traditional recipes required it. For example, one delicacy called for a whole sealskin, complete with the blubber layer, to be stuffed with small sea birds and left under rocks until the contents had turned to the consistency of cheese.

Sharing of food was essential for small groups of people living together harmoniously. By sharing in all hunters' successes, they could adjust for the vagaries of individual luck and reduce jealous hostility. Sharing reached its most formal level among the central groups at their winter sealing camps. Each hunter was bound to the others by precise rules in a pattern of sharing partnerships. When a man killed a seal it was taken to his igloo, where his wife butchered it, giving different portions to the wives of the other hunters in accordance with their specific relationship. The hunter kept little for himself but would share in the future successes of all his partners.

The successful food quest also required strict observance of taboos. Most pervasive throughout the Arctic was the belief that the products of land and sea must not be mixed. Seal and caribou meat could never be cooked together, for fear of supernatural retribution bringing storms, starvation or sickness. For the same reason, all sewing of caribou skins for winter clothing had to be completed before the people moved to their sealing camps on the sea ice. In addition, as among most hunting people, menstruating women had to obey numerous restrictions to avoid offending the animals.

There were times, however, when the hunters' skills and strict observation of taboos failed, and the community faced starvation. This threat meant that population size had to be kept low. Infanticide was relatively frequent, particularly for females, most families preferring to raise boys who would become hunters. Elderly people who could no longer keep up with the group had to be abandoned. The elderly and the very young were usually the first to perish when food ran out in late winter, and starvation of whole villages was not unknown. Under such extremes of distress it is not surprising that people occasionally resorted to cannibalism in order to survive, yet this act was regarded with abhorrence.

Dogs were important to the Inuit, but their drain on food supplies meant that only a few were kept. They were invaluable in hunting, sniffing out the seals' breathing holes under the snow and holding musk-oxen and polar bears at bay. In summer they were used as pack animals and in winter they pulled sleds.

The snow and frozen seas of winter made travel by dog sled over long distances possible. The sled (*komatik*) consisted of crossbars lashed with sealskin thongs to the runners, making it very flexible. Runners were covered with mud or moss and water, freezing into a hard, slick coating which allowed the sled to glide easily over the snow. Where wood was available it was used in sled construction, but elsewhere Inuit ingenuity found substitutes. Caribou bones or antlers could be used for crossbars, and runners could be made of rolled-up and frozen musk-ox skins or even of frozen fish wrapped in sealskin. In summer, the Central Inuit moved inland by walking, a difficult task on the marshy tundra, packing their goods on their backs and on dogs. Only the Mackenzie Delta Inuit and the eastern groups traveled by water to any extent, transporting their goods in umiaks.

Caribou hides, taken in fall when they were in best condition, were essential for winter clothing. Caribou hair is hollow, trapping air as insulation. Winter apparel consisted of two layers of coats, trousers, stockings and boots, the outer with the hair on the outside and the inner with the hair next to the body. Summer clothing was a single layer and in many areas was of sealskin. Sealskin boots were also essential for these wetter months. Women's clothing was often more elaborate than men's, with baggy trousers, large hoods and extra space at the back where babies were carried against the mother's skin. Strips of white hide from the underside of the caribou provided decoration. Although the basic design was the same, regional differences did exist.

The women's skill in preparing warm winter clothing was as essential to the group's survival as the men's ability to bring in food. Women spent much of their time making and mending clothing, particularly boots, which wore out quickly. Boots also became stiff and hard after use and had to be thoroughly chewed to restore them to their former soft and supple condition.

Another task performed by the women was care of the soapstone lamp (*kudlik*), used to heat and light the home, cook food, melt water and dry clothing. Seal blubber stored in bags gradually produced oil which could be burned, but fresh blubber had to be pounded. The moss wick also required constant tending.

Although personal adornment was limited, it was customary for women to tattoo their faces. Straight lines radiated from the nose and mouth across the forehead, cheeks and chin. The operation was performed by older women, who drew a needle threaded with soot-darkened sinew under the skin. Some women also had their hands and arms tattooed.

Marriage occurred at an early age, with girls in particular often being betrothed at birth. As survival would be difficult without a spouse, virtually all adults married, males as soon as they developed the necessary hunting skills and girls at puberty. The practice of female infanticide, however, meant a marked shortage of women among such Central Inuit as the Netsilik. Despite this, polygyny was relatively common, although only the most skilled hunters could support several wives and almost never were there more than two. Polyandry was less common, but occasionally women had several husbands, particularly in areas where there was a marked imbalance in numbers between the sexes. This imbalance also led to such prac-

Left: *Tattooed lines in traditional fashion adorn the face of this Copper Inuit woman,*
1949-50. Richard Harrington/NAC PA145007
Right: *Central Inuit drummer, ca. 1915.* CMC 50918

tices as spouse exchange and "sexual hospitality." Men might lend or
exchange wives on a short-term basis or as part of a longer semi-ritualized
bond of friendship and mutual aid. In the latter case the men usually were
song-fellows during drum dance festivals and wife-exchange was part of a
broader pattern of sharing.

Social groups varied with the seasons. Several families, generally related
through the males (brothers or father and sons), remained together
throughout most of the year. When food was abundant or more people
were needed, larger social groups formed. The winter sealing camps of the
Central Inuit required many hunters to watch the breathing holes, resulting
in communities of about 100 people. Similarly, the caribou hunt among
the Caribou Inuit and whaling among the Labrador and Mackenzie Delta
Inuit brought together large numbers. Leadership was informal, with the
opinion of the most experienced and respected elder carrying greatest
weight.

Competition over women and the jealousies engendered by living in
close quarters throughout the long winters occasionally led to hostility.
Without any strong positions of leadership, methods of social control were
limited. One technique of conflict resolution was the song duel, where two
opponents publicly ridiculed each other's behaviour through carefully composed songs. Each was expected to accept this rebuke with good grace.

Another way of dealing with unacceptable behaviour was for the band simply to move, leaving the offender behind. Anger sometimes led to murder, which early historic accounts indicate was not uncommon. The murderer and his family might flee to avoid retribution from the victim's kin, or a blood feud between the two families might ensue, resulting in additional deaths. In rare cases, the group might feel sufficiently threatened by the actions of an individual that a collective decision for his execution would be reached.

Sporadic conflict between Inuit and their Indian neighbours occurred, although avoidance was the more common practice. The Mackenzie Delta Inuit came into contact with the Gwich'in and Hare, the Caribou Inuit held overlapping territory with that of the Chipewyan, and the Inuit of northern Quebec and Labrador frequently encountered the Cree and Innu. Suspicion and hostility were deep-seated, with traditions of violence and murder being common. However, trade and occasional intermarriage also occurred.

Some control over an uncertain world came from the *angakok* (shaman). Both men and women could obtain spirit power, enabling them to communicate with the supernatural realm. In public performances the *angakok* went into a trance, speaking in the voice of a spirit helper. Their powers enabled them to cure the sick, prophesy the future, and summon supernatural aid when the animals could not be found or storms kept the hunters trapped in their homes.

Inuit myths and legends helped explain the spirit world. Supernatural beings, often malevolent, were everywhere, howling in the winter storms or lurking under the surface of the water. One widespread myth is the story of the sea goddess, who is known by many names among the various Inuit groups but is commonly called Sedna. The myth is lengthy, with many versions, involving a young woman who married a dog and a bird (a petrel or fulmar), who appeared in human form. When her father came in his skin boat to rescue her from the rocky island where her bird husband had taken her, a great storm came up and threatened to capsize the boat. To lighten the load the young woman was tossed overboard. When she tried to climb back in, the father cut off the joints of her fingers, which fell into the sea and became seals. Still she clung to the side of the boat, so her father cut off the rest of her fingers, which became walruses. Still failing to dislodge her, the heartless father cut off her hands, which became whales. The young woman sank to the bottom of the sea, where she lives today as the mother and protector of all sea mammals. She demands respect and strict observance of taboos or she will withhold her bounty and the people will starve.

An important ceremony was held in the fall, prior to winter sealing, to appease the wrath of Sedna for any taboo violations. The *angakok* went into a trance, during which he visited Sedna in her underwater home to discover the cause of her displeasure. Wearing strange clothing and a leather mask, the *angakok* also performed a trick where he appeared to be harpooned like a seal but recovered from the ordeal without harm. A tug-of-war was held between those born in summer and those born in winter, the belief being that if the winter side won there would be enough food that season. Then the *angakok* paired off the men and women for a brief spouse exchange, which was thought to be pleasing to the sea goddess.

Various types of recreation, generally performed in specially constructed buildings, brought together members of the community to enjoy each other's company, particularly during the relatively inactive winter period. Festivals were held, at which people played drums, danced and sang. In some communities women performed "throat singing," making resonant sounds from deep in the throat. One of the more popular of the many games was cup and pin, in which the player held a bone pin attached with sinew to a bone drilled with holes, which he swung into the air and attempted to skewer with the pin. A favourite pastime of the women was "cat's cradle," or string figures, in which players showed great ingenuity in creating a variety of patterns from a length of sinew stretched between the hands. The Inuit were also great story tellers, captivating their audience with tales that ranged from recent adventures to ancient legends. As the winter storms raged outside their homes, the Inuit passed the long dark days with games, songs and stories.

THE MACKENZIE DELTA INUIT

The Inuit of the western Canadian Arctic, around the Mackenzie delta and the Yukon coast, differed from other Canadian Inuit, most closely resembling their kin in northern Alaska. Their territory was rich in sea mammals and fish, allowing the largest villages and densest population in Arctic Canada. Estimates of the mid-nineteenth-century population range from 2000 to 4000 people. They were divided into five sub-groups, each with its own territory, known collectively as the Chiglit.

Large bowhead whales came into the Beaufort Sea and were hunted from umiaks by people living along the coast. In the Mackenzie delta the major prey was the beluga, which came into the shallow waters in large numbers to feed during summer. The estuary provided a natural trap, as men in kayaks could form a line across the river and drive the beluga upstream onto the shoals, where they could easily be killed. Several hundred of these small whales could be taken in a single drive, providing plenty of meat and blubber for winter use. Fishing, sealing and caribou-hunting were also part of their economy.

During the summer beluga hunt, the delta people clustered at their village of Kittigazuit. With a population of up to 1000 people, it was the largest Inuit community in Canada. Houses were large, permanent, semi-subterranean structures, built of driftwood logs covered with earth for insulation. Long sunken entrance tunnels, acting as cold traps, led to trap doors into the house level. Several families occupied each house. The proximity to the forest and the numerous drift logs in the river meant that wood was at hand for construction and fuel. Snowhouses were built only as temporary shelters, such as when jigging for fish out on the ice during late winter.

Many traits link the Mackenzie Delta Inuit with those in northern Alaska. Their house styles, plus the presence of separate "men's houses" in the villages, were essentially Alaskan. Pottery was used for lamps and cooking pots, though these were less important than farther east as there was an abundance of wood for open fires. Wood was also used for trays, ladles and many other objects. Men wore labrets of polished stone or ivory through perforations on each side of the mouth. Village "headmen," hereditary chiefs with the office passing through the male line, emerged through late Alaskan influence.

The Chiglit, as the original inhabitants of the Mackenzie delta area, were nearly exterminated by epidemics in the late nineteenth and early twentieth centuries. As their population decreased they were supplanted by Alaskan Inuit moving eastward, first attracted by trade with American whalers on the coast and later by the rich trapping potential of the delta. The few remaining Chiglit have been largely assimilated by those with a more recent Alaskan heritage. The inhabitants of the western Canadian Arctic today consider themselves separate from other Canadian Inuit and prefer to be known as Inuvialuit (literally, "real people").

THE CENTRAL INUIT (COPPER, NETSILIK, IGLULIK, BAFFINLAND)

The "Eskimo" stereotype, with its image of fur-clad, igloo-dwelling seal hunters, comes from the Central Inuit. These groups occupy much of the Canadian Arctic, from Victoria Island and the Coppermine River on the west to Baffin Island in the east. The Caribou Inuit are often included in this category but differ in their inland orientation and near-total reliance on caribou. The Central and Caribou Inuit all stem from a Thule base, but increasing regional specialization during the Little Ice Age resulted in greater loss of their Thule heritage than among other Canadian Inuit.

In the west, the Netsilik ("people of the seal") and the Copper Inuit (named for the native copper found in their area) lived an annual rhythm of summer and winter, land and sea. The shallow coastal waters froze each winter into an unbroken expanse of ice joining the islands and peninsulas, which meant that larger sea mammals, such as whales and walrus, were absent. Instead these people depended almost entirely during the winter on hunting seals at their breathing holes in the ice. In summer they moved inland to hunt caribou and to fish. Musk-oxen and polar bears were also hunted but were relatively minor in the diet. The umiak was unknown, and the kayak was used only for hunting caribou on inland lakes and rivers.

The groups farther east lived in an environment more richly stocked with sea mammals. The Iglulik, on Melville Peninsula and northern Baffin

Iglulik hunter pulling in two captured seals, 1952-53. The small umiak at right is for retrieving seals shot from the floe edge. Richard Harrington/NAC PA129874

Sealskin tent on Baffin Island, 1924. CMC 68941

Copper Inuit igloos, ca. 1915. Harpoons and other gear are stuck in the walls and sleds are raised on snow blocks to protect their rawhide lashings from the dogs. CMC 37018

Inside a Central Inuit igloo, 1903. The women are sitting on a platform covered with furs. At left is the cooking area, with pots suspended over an oil-burning lamp. CMC 2883

Island, and the Baffinland Inuit, who occupied the rest of the island, were near large areas of water that remained open during the winter and supported such sea mammals as bearded seal, walrus, beluga and narwhal. Even the large Greenland whale, as the bowhead is known in the east, was occasionally taken. In winter, hunters harpooned sea mammals from the floe edge, as well as seals at their breathing holes. In summer, some remained on the coast, hunting sea mammals from kayaks, while others went inland to hunt caribou.

The Central Inuit, with their migratory lifestyle, built no permanent structures. In winter, they lived in the domed snowhouse or igloo, a dwelling which could be quickly constructed from material that was available everywhere. Long entrance passageways provided cold-storage and acted as traps for colder air. Raised sleeping platforms of snow were covered with musk-oxen or polar bear skins and caribou-hide sleeping robes. A block of clear ice acted as a window. Some groups lined the interior walls with skins suspended from the roof, trapping a layer of colder air against the walls, which allowed heating the room to a higher temperature without melting the snow blocks. Two or three houses might be built close together, sharing an entrance passageway. For festivals a large dance house might be constructed, incorporating several houses, whose interior walls were then removed. Soapstone lamps burning blubber supplied heat and light. In spring, when igloos began to drip, structures with walls and entranceway of snow and roof of caribou hide were briefly occupied. Such dwellings were also built in autumn, when the snow had not yet reached sufficient firmness to construct an igloo. In summer, people carried only light tents of caribou hide or sealskin on their migrations inland.

Raw materials were scarce in this central region. The Copper Inuit were most fortunate, with good sources of native copper and soapstone and somewhat more abundant driftwood. Elsewhere, people relied on trade or on their ingenuity in finding available substitutes. They developed an elaborate technology, meeting all their material needs, with only a few tools of wood, copper and stone, relying mainly on ice and snow, bone and antler, and hide and fur.

One other group, the now-extinct Sadlermiut (or Sallirmiut) of Southampton Island in Hudson Bay, should be included among the Central Inuit. They were apparently distinct, speaking a separate dialect and manufacturing tools of chipped stone rather than the more common ground stone. They were maritime hunters, with walrus and polar bear being particularly important. Some writers have claimed Dorset ancestry for the Sadlermiut; however, most of their technology indicates the same Thule heritage as their neighbours. An epidemic disease introduced by a whaling ship led to their destruction in the winter of 1902-1903.

THE CARIBOU INUIT

The barren interior west of Hudson Bay was home to the Caribou Inuit, fascinating anthropologists who have long puzzled over their origins. After members of the Fifth Thule Expedition provided the first extensive description of their culture in the 1920s, Kaj Birket-Smith proposed his model of interior origins for the Inuit. The Caribou Inuit, with their simple way of life and impoverished material culture, were seen as "Proto-Eskimos," the last vestiges of a way of life that existed prior to most Inuit becoming coastally adapted sea mammal hunters.

Later research shattered the notion of inland origins for the Inuit and indicated that Caribou Inuit culture, far from being a survival of an ancient primitive stage, was recent, emerging only in the historic period. When Samuel Hearne traveled through the barrenlands with his Chipewyan companions in the 1770s, the only occupants were other Athapaskans. Over a century later, when the Tyrell brothers crossed the southern barrens in the 1890s, they met only Inuit. The Chipewyan hold on the barrenlands had been broken by disastrous epidemics which depleted their numbers and by construction of trading posts inland, making unnecessary the long trek across the barrens to Hudson Bay. The Inuit, descendants of the Thule people who had settled along the coast of Hudson Bay, began to spread inland sometime in the late eighteenth or early nineteenth century. This was largely a result of European presence on the coast, as firearms made hunting caribou more efficient and the fur trade provided the incentive for inland trapping. The simplicity of their way of life and meagreness of their aboriginal material culture in the ethnographic descriptions stemmed not from being an early primitive stage but from cultural disintegration and more than a century of dependence on Euro-Canadian technology.

The Caribou Inuit became highly specialized to an interior way of life, with near-total reliance on the caribou herds. Their hunting techniques were identical to those of other Inuit, including stalking with bows and arrows, spearing from kayaks at water crossings and the use of *inuksuit* to direct the caribou to convenient ambush spots. Great quantities had to be taken during the autumn migrations, so that warm clothing could be made from their hides and much of the meat could be cached. In winter, when most of the caribou had retreated south to the forest, people relied on their stores of caribou meat, supplemented with fishing through the ice and hunting musk-oxen. Such a specialized economy could provide only a precarious existence. Failure of the caribou to appear in sufficient numbers would mean winter starvation.

In most aspects of their culture the Caribou Inuit resembled other Central Inuit. Their technology was simpler, however, for most of their Thule heritage had been abandoned as useless in the barrenlands. They lacked blubber for their lamps, which were often merely flat stones with natural depressions. Occasionally caribou fat was burned, providing light but little heat. In winter, people lived largely in darkness in igloos, which were unheated except for the body warmth of the occupants. Inside temperatures were bearable but not comfortable and were insufficient to dry clothing. The only method they had to accomplish this was to take their wet apparel into their beds, sleeping with it next to their skin. Any cooking had to be done over a small fire built in a separate alcove off the entrance tunnel. As a result, most food was eaten frozen and raw. Even the eastern bands, with access to seals and beluga along the coast of Hudson Bay, preferred to follow the herds of caribou inland.

Periodic shortages and starvation continued into the twentieth century as hunting with rifles took a heavy toll on caribou and musk-oxen numbers. In the few years just prior to 1920 scarcity of caribou meant starvation for hundreds, greatly reducing the Caribou Inuit population. The people described in the ethnographies, known primarily through the writings of Birket-Smith and Rasmussen, should really be seen as the weakened survivors of these disastrous years. Epidemic diseases and periodic famines continued into the mid-twentieth century, leading the Caribou Inuit to the verge of extinction. Their plight was brought to public attention by Farley Mowat in his popular books *The People of the Deer* (1952) and *The Desperate People* (1959). Mowat's stinging charges of administrative incompetence added to a growing awareness of the appalling conditions under which Inuit across the Arctic were living. The government response was to encourage Inuit groups to move into permanent settlements where services could be provided. With the exception of Baker Lake, the Caribou Inuit settlements are on the coast, leaving their former homeland, the barrens, largely abandoned.

THE INUIT OF NORTHERN QUEBEC AND LABRADOR
The Thule were late to spread east of Hudson Bay, arriving in the Ungava region of northern Quebec about A.D. 1350 and along the coast of Labrador by about 1450. This area seems to have been spared the worst effects of the Little Ice Age, and much of the Thule heritage was maintained well into historic times.

The waters of this eastern region are richly stocked with sea mammals. Walrus, ringed seal, bearded seal, harp seal, narwhal, beluga and even the large Greenland or bowhead whale were pursued by Inuit hunters. In summer, they were harpooned from kayaks, or umiaks in the case of the large whales, and in winter from the ice edge. In most areas, seals were also hunted at their breathing holes in the ice. Whaling required ritual preparation, involving observation of taboos, magical treatment of implements and shamanic consultation with spirit helpers for information in planning the hunt. Such rituals strongly resemble those performed by Inuit whalers in Alaska, suggesting the former presence of a widespread Thule whale cult that was lost in the central area.

Inuit hunter with kayak and two freshly killed belugas. The harpoon line with inflated float is still attached to the whale in the foreground. Photograph taken at Little Whale River, northern Quebec, in 1865. NAC C8160

Caribou hunting in the interior was practiced by almost all groups, particularly in the fall when hides were needed for winter clothing. A few small bands in northern Quebec remained inland for much or all of the year, drawing almost all of their needs from the caribou herds in the same fashion as the Caribou Inuit. Other bands lived year-round on the islands of eastern Hudson Bay, subsisting on sea mammals, polar bears and birds. Lacking sufficient caribou skins for clothing, they developed local alternatives, such as eider-duck skin parkas and polar bear pants and winter boots.

Fishing was also important, both in the sea and inland, where Arctic char were taken during their annual runs. Birds and bird eggs were a major source of food in some areas. Although only minor aspects of the diet, berries and other plant foods were more plentiful along the Labrador coast than elsewhere in the Arctic. In addition, the tidewaters of northern Quebec yielded mussels and sea urchins, providing a minor food source which could become important in times of famine.

While the igloo was the standard winter home of the Quebec Inuit, it was used only as a temporary shelter in Labrador. Labrador Inuit lived for up to six months of the year in large, permanent, semi-subterranean structures, similar to those of the Thule period. The walls were of sod or stone, with a sod-covered roof supported on rafters of whale bones or timber. A long covered entrance passage led to the house, and a skylight of translucent seal intestine was set into the roof over the entrance. In Quebec, stone and turf houses with hide roofs were used in the transitional periods, when the igloos began to drip in the spring and when the autumn snow was too soft to build igloos. As elsewhere in the Arctic, skin tents were the summer dwellings.

Although much of the Thule heritage had survived the colder climate, it could not long withstand the onslaught of European contact. Explorers, whalers, traders and missionaries wrought dramatic changes on their culture. Although the eastern groups were the first to feel the impact, a wave of change was about to engulf the entire Canadian Arctic.

INUIT AND OUTSIDERS

Contact between Inuit and Europeans goes back to the Norse settlement of Greenland, taking the form of both battles (according to Norse sagas and Inuit legends) and trade (as revealed by archaeology). This pattern was to continue for centuries. The Inuit eagerly sought the iron tools and other goods of the foreign invaders, yet through mutual misunderstanding and suspicion the encounters often ended in bloodshed. Fishers and whalers of several European nations were in the rich waters off the Labrador coast by at least the early sixteenth century and undoubtedly came into contact with natives, but they have left few written records. The search for the fabled Northwest Passage to the riches of the Orient provided the next major incentive for European exploration, beginning with the first of Martin Frobisher's three voyages in 1576. Sailing into what is now Frobisher Bay on Baffin Island, he encountered "men in small boates made of leather" who kidnapped five of his men. Frobisher captured three natives to take back to England, where they succumbed to illness. Hostility marked nearly every meeting, and Frobisher himself received an Inuit arrow in the buttocks. Trading vessels followed those of exploration, particularly after the establishment of the Hudson's Bay Company in 1670. However, most trade from Hudson Bay was with the Indians of the fur-rich forest, giving these people the advantage of firearms long before the Inuit.

The earliest continuous contact was in Labrador, where Moravian missionaries, familiar with the Inuit language from Greenland, helped the English governor of Newfoundland negotiate peace with the Inuit in 1765. Shortly after, the Moravians began establishing missions along the Labrador coast, beginning with Nain in 1771. As well as a church, each mission contained a trading post to supply the goods upon which the Inuit had become dependent. The Inuit settled in permanent wooden houses at these self-contained communities. Although many elements of their culture were lost under Moravian influence, they enjoyed a lengthy period of near-isolation from other outside influences.

Only in the nineteenth century did European explorers break the barriers of ice and cold to reach the Central Inuit. Early contacts were fleeting, peaceful, and made no changes in Inuit culture except the introduction of a few items of European manufacture. The romantic search for the Northwest Passage still lured adventurers, who wintered with their ships in the Arctic ice so that their search could continue over several years. Beginning in 1821 William Parry and George Lyon explored western Hudson Bay and Melville Peninsula, spending two winters in the territory of the Iglulik. They were peacefully received by the natives, who entertained them with dancing in their snowhouse village. Descriptions from these contacts provide the most important ethnographic data until the comprehensive study of the Fifth Thule Expedition a century later. Sir John Franklin also surveyed parts of the Arctic coast but is best known for the tragic expedition of 1846. Attempting to thread his way through an ice-choked passage in the central Arctic, his ships were trapped and the entire crew of 129 men perished. In the following years many ships searched unsuccessfully for survivors, in the process exploring much new coastline and bringing most Inuit groups into contact with Europeans.

The nineteenth century also brought commercial whalers into the Canadian Arctic. At first the whalers pursued their prey along Davis Strait and Baffin Bay, off the coast of Baffin Island, but by 1860 much of the hunt took place in northern Hudson Bay, where the whalers typically wintered over. This brought them into close contact with the Inuit, who clustered around the whaling bases and were employed as crew on the whaleboats and as hunters to provide the ships with fresh meat. In return they received such typical trade goods as firearms, iron tools, metal pots and kettles, woolen clothing, beads and tobacco. Even such items as kerosene lamps and canvas tents became common among the Inuit, and whaleboats largely replaced the umiak. Although the whalers hastened the erosion of traditional Inuit culture in the eastern Arctic, their impact here was far less damaging than in the west. There American whalers, after depleting Alaskan stocks, moved into Canadian waters by 1890. Herschel Island, off the Yukon coast, became their wintering base, attracting both Alaskan and Mackenzie Delta Inuit. There the whalers liberally dispensed alcohol, debauched the women and brought destruction through diseases. The whaling period came to a rapid end after 1910, when diminished whale populations and the collapse of the market for baleen made it no longer profitable.

Immediately following were the fur traders, who stepped into the gap in the Inuit economy left by the whalers. In the nineteenth century, permanent fur trade posts among the Inuit were few. Some took their furs far to the east, to the Moravian missions in Labrador or, after 1830, to Fort Chimo on Ungava Bay, while others made the long trek south to Fort Churchill. In the west, the fur trade began with the construction of Fort McPherson in the upper Mackenzie delta in 1840. However, it was not until the early decades of the twentieth century, with a steady rise in fur prices, that the Hudson's Bay Company built many posts across the north. In order to satisfy their need for imported goods, the Inuit had to supply the traders with furs. Those of white fox were most valued, along with muskrat in the Mackenzie delta region. Firearms and steel traps became essential as the Inuit based their economy on the fox, trapping inland in winter rather than hunting on the coast as formerly. Booming fur prices in the 1920s meant relative wealth for many, but a market collapse in the 1930s put an end to this period of affluence.

With the growth in the fur trade came a spread of the missionaries, both Roman Catholic and Anglican. Often establishing their missions alongside the posts, the missionaries brought about major cultural changes. Traditional practices such as polygamy, spouse exchange and shamanism were attacked, but missionaries also introduced education and medical assistance.

The whaling era in particular had taken a toll on Inuit populations. Smallpox, measles and influenza epidemics devastated many groups. Syphilis and other venereal diseases became rampant among those near the whaling bases. Alcohol, particularly in the western Arctic, led to murders and demoralization. Famine frequently followed outbreaks of disease, as there were too few able-bodied hunters to provide food. Extinction was the fate of the Sadlermiut, and the Chiglit of the Mackenzie delta also nearly succumbed. Neither the curing techniques of the shamans nor the medical knowledge of the newcomers could halt the drastic decline in numbers across the Arctic.

The Canadian government was late in making its presence felt in the north, requiring a threat to its sovereignty in the High Arctic before taking action. For several decades the major government representatives in the Arctic were members of the North West Mounted Police (later the Royal Canadian Mounted Police). In 1903 a police post was established at Fullerton Harbour, a wintering station for whalers in Hudson Bay. In the same year, two police posts were created in the western Arctic, at the whaling station of Herschel Island and at the fur trade post of Fort McPherson. Although they were not there to administer the Inuit, the police brought new concepts of law and justice and forcefully suppressed such practices as infanticide and the blood feud. Aside from the police presence, the government provided no services, leaving the missionaries to do the best they could in providing rudimentary education and health care.

Major changes and new economic opportunities came with World War II as Canadian and American military personnel moved into strategic Arctic locations. Construction of roads, airfields, hangars, barracks and other facilities created an employment boom for the Inuit. In the following Cold War era of the 1950s, construction of the DEW (Distant Early Warning) line of radar installations, stretching from Alaska to Baffin Island, brought another surge of job opportunities, as did the building of Inuvik, the administrative centre of the western Arctic. Newly focused attention on the north exposed the government's neglect of the native occupants and forced increased government involvement in their welfare.

THE MODERN INUIT

By the 1950s the Canadian government took a more active role in Inuit administration. Services formerly provided by missionaries, fur traders or police were transferred to government administrators, who came to be a permanent feature of northern communities. Tuberculosis was rampant and many Inuit were uprooted from their families and culture for lengthy hospital treatment in southern Canada. Continued high rates of infant mortality and other health problems led to establishment of nursing stations and health programs in the north. Schools were built at many Inuit settlements. Family allowances, welfare and old age pensions were extended to the Inuit on the same basis as to other Canadians.

In order to administer their Inuit charges, the federal government encouraged them to settle in permanent communities and lead a more sedentary lifestyle. Many Inuit abandoned their hunting camps for the lure of government-subsidized housing, education for their children, health care and other services. The church and the trading post were also features of the settlements, although the latter was shortly to be challenged by Inuit-run cooperative stores. Several administrative centres, such as Inuvik in the west and Iqaluit in the east, have become large towns, with shopping malls, hotels, hospitals, regular air service and other amenities of southern Canadian life.

A caste-like social system quickly developed between the Inuit and the *Qallunaat*, the White, generally temporary, residents of the north. As government administrators, teachers, missionaries, shopkeepers or police, these non-natives held the positions of authority. Status differences were clearly evident in the communities, often with the *Qallunaat* occupying a separate part of the town. Failing to understand the nature of the new institutions, and not speaking the language in which they were conducted, the Inuit found themselves excluded from the realm of decision-making. Only in recent years have the Inuit begun to reclaim control of their lives.

While the benefits of life in the settlements are evident, there was also a price to pay. The hard work and self-sufficiency of the camps was replaced with unemployment and idleness for many. Readily available alcohol led to social and health problems and brought many Inuit into conflict with the law. Depression and anxiety encouraged alcohol abuse and led to high levels of violence and suicide. Food purchased from the stores became increasingly important, despite being expensive and nutritionally inferior to a traditional diet. Values and beliefs that have survived for millennia are being

Inuit family at hunting camp near Pond Inlet, Baffin Island, 1975. Photo by Jeff Hunston

eroded by a constant barrage of stimuli from the south, through television, radio and the frequent turnover of *Qallunaat* in their midst. The transplanted suburban life of southern Canada in a few decades proved more destructive to Inuit culture than the previous centuries of contact.

Inuit from many smaller settlements were relocated to larger centres for administrative convenience and economy. Some Inuit were induced to settle in remote areas, presumably for good access to seals and other game. Such schemes, however, were also designed to bolster Canadian sovereignty over the northern islands. In the mid-1950s Inuit families from northern Quebec and from Baffin Island were relocated to the High Arctic, unoccupied since Thule times. They established the small communities of Resolute, on southern Cornwallis Island, and Grise Fjord, on southern Ellesmere. The Inuit of Grise Fjord became Canada's most northerly permanent residents. These moves were not without government coercion, however, and some Inuit are now demanding an apology and compensation for suffering. Testimony to the Royal Commission on Aboriginal Peoples in 1993 referred to the "cruel and inhumane" policy of forced relocations and charged that the Inuit were used as "human flagpoles" to ensure Canada's sovereignty in the High Arctic.

The introduction of new technology links the Inuit of the settlements with mainstream modern life. Boats with outboard motors have replaced kayaks. Snowmobiles have largely replaced dog sleds, though they are noisy, require expensive fuel and frequent repairs, and, unlike dogs, cannot be eaten in emergencies. Three-wheeled all-terrain vehicles are also common. Air travel links the scattered Arctic communities and provides access to cities in the south. Satellite communication systems bring southern television programs to northern homes. Modern and traditional elements of Inuit life are merged, as Inuit children in their prefabricated homes watch television beside mothers cutting seal meat with *ulus*.

Since most Arctic communities lack any real economic base, unemployment levels are high. Many of the few available jobs are part-time or seasonal. Government assistance payments are required by most families. Trapping cannot provide a living but can supplement other sources of income. Hunting continues to put meat on the table for most families, though the high cost of fuel and ammunition is an inhibiting factor. Hunting and trapping expeditions help reaffirm traditional values and maintain ancestral ties to the land.

Various government programs have been introduced to provide an economic base. Earlier in this century attempts to establish reindeer husbandry in Labrador and in the western Arctic met with failure. More successful was the introduction of Inuit-run cooperatives during the 1960s. Originally these produced northern goods for sale, later expanding to provide stores and other services in the north. Along with governments, cooperatives have become the major employers of northern natives.

Most successful of the federal programs was the introduction of a commercial art form. Although small carvings were being made for sale in historic times, modern Inuit art had its beginning just prior to 1950, when the Canadian artist James Houston visited several communities in northern Quebec. Impressed with some small sculptures he collected, he encouraged the Inuit to produce more work, particularly in soapstone, as a much-needed source of new income. Backed by the federal government and the Hudson's Bay Company, Houston's experiment in marketing Inuit art achieved rapid success. The newly produced sculptures were in great demand in the south, and soon carvers were active in many northern communities.

Inuit soapstone sculptures have a raw power and vitality that make them attractive to southern art collectors. Market demands largely determine their form, however, and they differ considerably from what had previously been considered "Eskimo art." Earlier sculpture was primarily in ivory, with soapstone being used only for lamps and cooking pots. Such carvings also tended to be small, portable and often functional, rather than the current large, heavy stone sculptures destined for art galleries and mantelpieces. The subjects of the modern art commonly depict Arctic animals or hunting and domestic scenes, although spirit beings from the legends also occur. Several carvers have acquired national prominence for the quality of their work, and carving continues to provide a source of income for many northern residents.

The success of soapstone carving quickly led to experiments in other media, such as printmaking. Most important is the stone-block print, where the design is carved onto a slab of soapstone, which is inked and the paper pressed onto it. Stenciled prints and copper-plate engravings are also produced. Printmaking was first introduced by James Houston to Cape Dorset on Baffin Island, and that community has remained the dominant

Top left: *Kenojuak with two of her prints, Cape Dorset, 1980.* Judith Eglington/NAC PA140297
Top right: *Two Inuit artists working on a stone block print at the art centre in Cape Dorset, 1961.* B. Korda/NAC PA145607
Bottom: *A fine example of modern Inuit soapstone carving.* CMC J8609

print centre. From Cape Dorset have come such renowned artists as Kenojuak, Kananginak and Pitscolak. Kenojuak's flamboyant depictions of fantasy birds are among the most famous Inuit works of art.

Until recently, many Inuit were able to supplement their income through the sale of sealskins. Outrage against the bloody clubbing of infant ("whitecoat") harp and hooded seals along Canada's east coast led to a European boycott of all seal products in 1982. This destroyed the market for skins of the adult ringed seal traditionally taken by the Inuit, causing considerable hardship in areas with few other sources of income.

On the political level, the Inuit Tapirisat of Canada (ITC) was formed in 1971. Its mandate is to promote Inuit culture and identity, and to present a common front on political, economic and environmental issues concerning the Inuit. Its role is national, with regional affiliates to handle local concerns. There were originally six such regional organizations, from Labrador to the Mackenzie delta, but the Inuvialuit of the western Arctic later withdrew from the ITC. A major item of business has been negotiations on land claims for all traditional Inuit territory. Three final agreements, covering all Inuit lands in Arctic Canada except for Labrador, have now been reached.

The James Bay and Northern Quebec Agreement, signed in 1975, was the first native land claims settlement in Canada. In return for surrendering their aboriginal title to the land so that the Quebec government could proceed with hydroelectric development, the Cree and Inuit of northern Quebec received a cash settlement (the Inuit share was about $90 million), ownership of certain lands (nearly 9000 square kilometres for the Inuit), and exclusive hunting, fishing and trapping rights over a much larger area. The Makivik Corporation was founded to administer the Inuit share of the compensation money, part of which was used to establish regional businesses. Air Inuit now links the scattered communities in northern Quebec, and various cultural programs and publications in Inuktitut have been financed with this money. The Kativik School Board is responsible for education in the Inuit villages, ensuring that one of the languages of instruction is Inuktitut. Unlike the Cree, the Quebec Inuit chose a municipal government model, where each village has control over local matters. Local self-government, however, remains in Inuit control only as long as they maintain a population majority.

Not all Quebec Inuit communities accepted the agreement, however. In addition, many Inuit feel that neither the federal nor the provincial governments have fully honoured the provisions of the agreement. Dissatisfaction also exists with what many see as Quebec's excessive interference with local self-government. Steps are now underway to implement a regional government which would have its own assembly and constitution, recognizing the Inuit as a distinct society and Inuktitut as an official language. The Quebec Inuit are also split over the province's plans to proceed with Great Whale, the next phase of the James Bay hydroelectric project. Like the Cree, many Inuit oppose any further development in their lands, although the Makivik Corporation negotiated compensation for environmental damage before the Quebec government shelved this controversial project in 1994.

In the western Arctic the six communities of the Inuvialuit signed an agreement in 1984, surrendering their aboriginal title in exchange for $45 million in compensation and title to about 91,000 square kilometres of land. Some of the land includes subsurface rights, an important consideration in the potentially oil-rich area of the Beaufort Sea. Inuvialuit corporations own the land and initiate business ventures and investments with the money. The agreement also provides hunting and fishing rights, measures to protect Arctic wildlife and Inuvialuit membership on various management boards.

For the rest of the Northwest Territories, the Inuit are represented by the Tungavik Federation of Nunavut (TFN). In lengthy negotiations the TFN pressed forward on two related fronts: settlement of their land claim and a political accord to create an Inuit homeland to be known as Nunavut ("Our Land" in Inuktitut). After an agreement-in-principle was reached in Igloolik in 1990, the land claim settlement was ratified and signed in 1993. The Inuit of the Nunavut Settlement Area agreed to "cede, release and surrender" all aboriginal claims to the land in exchange for title to about 350,000 square kilometres, with mineral rights included on just over 10 percent. On all other lands the Inuit will have joint control with the federal government over land-use planning, wildlife management and environmental issues. They will keep the right to hunt, fish and trap throughout Nunavut. The settlement also provides about $1.15 billion in financial compensation and resource royalty sharing. The Nunavut Trust will administer the fund, using the interest to support Inuit businesses and education, and to provide an income-support program for Inuit hunters. An Inuit Heritage Trust will administer all archaeological resources of the Nunavut area, including controlling the issue of permits to researchers. The Government of Canada also committed itself to the establishment of the separate territory of Nunavut, with its own legislative assembly.

To create Nunavut, the present Northwest Territories has to be divided. For the Inuit communities in the north, the territorial government in Yellowknife is not just distant but also culturally alien. A 1982 government plebiscite on division was narrowly passed, with the eastern Arctic solidly in favour and the western regions generally against. A subsequent contentious issue was the establishment of a boundary which would separate Nunavut from the lands of the Dene, Métis and the majority of non-aboriginals, provisionally to be called Denendeh. The initial proposal called for a boundary along the tree line, from the Mackenzie delta to the N.W.T.-Manitoba border near Hudson Bay. The Inuvialuit, however, opted not to join Nunavut. Problems also developed over Dene claims to hunting territories out on the barrenlands. After considerable debate an essentially east-west division was approved by a narrow margin in a 1992 referendum.

The creation of Nunavut, presently targeted for 1999, will be the first major change to the map of Canada since Newfoundland joined confederation in 1949. Stretching from the Manitoba border to the northern tip of Ellesmere Island, Nunavut will be the largest of Canada's provinces and territories. Iqaluit is the probable capital, although government operations will have to be highly decentralized in a vast land of scattered settlements lacking any road links. Inuktitut will be the language of government in a legislative assembly dominated by Inuit. As the Inuit comprise about 80 percent of the population, Inuit self-government is assured. Barring political or economic crises in Canada, Nunavut seems destined to become a reality in the near future.

At the international level, a "Pan-Inuit" movement has emerged, allowing Inuit of different countries to compare experiences and strengthen their common identity. The first Inuit Circumpolar Conference was held at Barrow, Alaska in 1977, bringing together Inuit from Alaska, Canada and Greenland. Although several thousand Inuit live in Siberia, Russian Inuit have only been able to participate since 1989. The Conference officially adopted the term "Inuit" for all people formerly known as "Eskimo," despite major linguistic differences among them. Attainment of "home rule" by Greenlandic Inuit (Greenland is a self-governing province of Denmark) encouraged Canadian Inuit to seek greater political control. Similarly, the settlement of native land claims in Alaska in 1971 stimulated Canadian Inuit in their negotiations. For the first time in their long history, the Inuit are addressing their problems as a united people.

The Inuit population in Canada has grown rapidly over the past few decades. The estimated 33,000 Inuit today number more than triple their 1950 population. Inuktitut is the language of the Arctic settlements and is being taught to children in the schools. Two written forms of Inuktitut, one based on syllabics and the other using the Roman alphabet, were introduced by the missionaries and are still in widespread use. Dictionaries are being developed, coining new words for objects and concepts that did not exist in the traditional language. Newspapers and radio programs in Inuktitut reach many Inuit homes, and a television network, the Inuit Broadcasting Corporation, produces programs in both Inuktitut and English. Place names are being changed from English or French to Inuktitut, a process underway in the Northwest Territories and largely completed in Quebec.

Within only a generation the Inuit have been catapulted into the modern world. Many people now resident in Arctic towns lived as nomadic hunters only a few decades ago, and some families still prefer to live off the land. Most of the amenities of southern life are now available, but they require considerable changes in Inuit lifestyle. Southern demands for the north's energy supplies continue to threaten Inuit lands. Their land claims settlements and the eventual creation of Nunavut, however, will ensure that the Inuit remain in control of their own destinies.

CHAPTER 11 *The Métis*

The Métis (from a French word meaning "mixed") emerged during the fur trade, the offspring of European men and native women. Although the term can be applied to anyone of mixed racial heritage ("half-breed," "half-caste," "country-born" and *bois brûlé* are other terms used historically), it came primarily to refer to those who forged a common identity on the Plains of western Canada in the nineteenth century. There they proclaimed the "New Nation," identifying themselves as a people distinct from both their First Nations and European progenitors.

Historically the term "Métis" referred particularly to those part-native people who were French-speaking and Catholic, while "half-breed" more commonly was applied to English-speaking and Protestant individuals. The latter term, with its derogatory connotations, has almost disappeared, with Métis assuming more general use. Today it is applied to a diverse population, not all of whom can trace any ties to the nineteenth century New Nation on the Plains.

The process of racial mixture which eventually led to the Métis began with earliest contact. The all-male crews of the fishing, trading or exploring vessels sought casual relations with native women, who were receptive to the newcomers owing to the valuable trade goods they brought. French fishermen from the Brittany coast left many descendants among the Mi'kmaq and Maliseet. Such children were raised as Indians, with no separate social group developing.

In New France, racial mixture was initially encouraged in order to bol-

293

ster the population and strengthen French claims to the land. Samuel de Champlain told his native allies: "Our young men will marry your daughters, and we shall be one people." Many Acadian communities grew through extensive admixture with local natives. Frequently the process worked in reverse, as young men opted for a freer life among the Indians. A French official complained in 1685 that: "Those people with whom we mingle do not become French, our people become Indian" (Peterson 1978:47). In either case, the children were raised as Indian or European, and no distinct Métis identity emerged.

The fur trade lured many French *coureurs de bois* westward, where they established stable unions with native women, particularly Cree and Ojibwa. Marriages were *à la façon du pays* ("in the custom of the country"), lacking any formal ceremony. Kinship ties from such marriages forged alliances that facilitated trade. Native wives were invaluable, serving as interpreters in trade and performing such skilled domestic tasks as making moccasins and snowshoes, drying meat and dressing furs. As male children frequently followed their fathers into the fur trade, the voyageurs became increasingly of mixed heritage.

A somewhat different process was occurring to the north, around Hudson Bay. There the English and Scottish employees of the Hudson's Bay Company remained in their coastal forts, surrounded by the Cree who provided furs and provisions. Initially, the Company's policy was to discourage any mixing of the races. Indians were barred from the forts except during trading, and employees were to refrain from visiting the native camps. Some officers imposed a near-military abstinence on their men, while others themselves took "country" wives. Later, as the Company was forced inland by competition with the North West Company, the policies were relaxed and such unions became commonplace. Unlike the French *coureurs de bois* and voyageurs, who often spent their lives among their native kin, Hudson's Bay Company men in the early period usually returned to Britain, and most of their progeny were absorbed into native groups. Only a few high-ranking officers sent their sons to be educated in England or Scotland. Other country-born sons of officers found employment at the posts, as traders, interpreters or labourers.

By the mid-eighteenth century, a large "mixed-blood" population had congregated around the Great Lakes. The French *coureurs de bois* were the first to settle with their native families, later followed by the Scottish employees of the North West Company. Substantial communities of log cabins emerged at such strategic locations as Sault Ste. Marie. Some inhabitants were farmers, while others worked as voyageurs and clerks in the fur trade. As the population grew, marriages within the mixed-blood group became common. The Great Lakes Métis were beginning to become a distinct society, merging the separate elements of their heritage into a shared identity. However, depleted fur stocks and increased settlement from the east early in the nineteenth century stopped the process. Many Métis drift-ed westward to the Plains, where the birth of a distinctive Métis culture finally occurred.

THE RED RIVER MÉTIS

The "classic" Métis culture emerged early in the nineteenth century on the Plains, particularly near the confluence of the Red and Assiniboine rivers (today in the heart of Winnipeg). There they established themselves as buf-falo hunters and provisioners for the North West Company, serving as an essential link in the long trade chain from Montreal to the far-off fur posts of the Athabasca region. Geographic and social isolation, as well as a shared lifestyle, promoted a group identity, but it was the years of bitter confronta-tion between the two great fur trade companies that forged the concept of a New Nation in the Canadian West.

The Métis lifestyle and freedom in the eastern Plains were threatened when the Hudson's Bay Company, which controlled the vast area of Rupert's Land, granted Lord Selkirk land along the Red River for an agri-cultural colony. The first Scottish settlers arrived in 1812. The North West Company, incensed that the new colony lay directly on its main trade route from Montreal, fueled the sparks of nationalism that were developing among the Métis. The Métis were warned that the new arrivals would usurp their land and put an end to their livelihood. Leaders of the new colony seemed to confirm these fears when they prohibited the running of buffalo on horseback and forbade the sale of pemmican to the North West Company, striking at the very heart of Métis culture in order to bolster the economy of the settlement.

In response to this threat the Métis organized under Cuthbert Grant, the Montreal-educated son of a Scottish Nor'wester and a native woman, as the "Captain General of all half-breeds." The inevitable clash, known as the Battle of Seven Oaks, left the colony's governor and 20 settlers dead, while the Métis lost one man. Although they were unsuccessful in permanently driving out the colonists, the Métis had firmly established their rights in the area. Symbols such as a flag and the commemorative songs of the Métis bard Pierre Falçon bolstered Métis nationalism. Several years after Seven Oaks, Cuthbert Grant founded the Métis settlement of Grantown to the west of the Red River colony, providing a protective buffer for the colony against marauding Dakota war parties.

The years of intense rivalry came to an end with the merger of the two great fur trade companies in 1821. With the reduction in the number of posts that followed, former employees were encouraged to settle with their native wives and country-born offspring along the Red River. Many of the more nomadic Métis also drifted into the settlement. The Métis tended to have large families and their numbers grew dramatically, soon making them the majority of the population. Most marriages were within the mixed-blood group, strengthening their common ties, although Métis women were also in demand among the white settlers. No new outside attempt at colonization disrupted the Métis, and the New Nation flourished in virtual isolation for half a century.

Despite their newly gained political consciousness as a single people, there were strong divisions within the Red River settlement. The French Métis, who formed the largest part of the population, were devout Roman Catholics, while the English Métis were Anglicans and those of Scottish descent were Presbyterians. Many of the English-speaking half-breeds maintained small farms, while the French Métis tended to live a more nomadic lifestyle. Social and racial distinctions led to tension and strife. Many ties of intermarriage, however, helped to bind members of the community, as did common participation in such activities as the communal bison hunt. Many spoke both European languages, plus Cree or Ojibwa from their mother's side. In time a distinct composite language, known as Michif, emerged, based primarily on Cree and French.

Crucial to their economy and central to their group self-identity was the buffalo hunt. As well as providing food, this was a commercial endeavour, during which meat was made into pemmican and traded to the Hudson's Bay Company. The Métis met at Pembina, on the Red River just south of the American border, traveling in their distinctive two-wheeled Red River carts pulled by horses or oxen. The carts, which were essential for transporting equipment and hauling meat, were made entirely of wood bound with rawhide. The axles could not be greased, since the dirt that then collected soon cut through the wood. As a result, the Métis cart brigades filled the prairie air with the hideous creaking of wood rubbing on wood, producing such disturbing noise that some Indians blamed them for driving away the bison. The hunts quickly grew to major proportions; in 1840 over 1600 people and 1200 carts met at Pembina. Cart trails rutted the prairies as hunting parties set out after the herds.

Strict rules attended the hunt, resembling those imposed by the Plains Indian military societies. Punishment could be meted out to anyone who threatened the general hunt by disturbing the herds. Officers were chosen and strict discipline imposed, both to ensure success on the hunt and as a precaution against raids by hostile Dakota.

The favoured hunting technique was "running the buffalo." Mounted on swift "buffalo horses," the Métis raced into the stampeding herd. Riding at full gallop alongside his selected target, the Métis hunter poured gunpowder into the barrel of his gun, spat in a lead ball from a supply carried in his mouth, pounded it down by abruptly striking the butt on his saddle, and lowered the barrel to fire. Quickly dropping a glove or some other personal object to mark his kill, the hunter raced on to select another animal and

"Half-breeds Running Buffalo," by the Canadian artist Paul Kane, captures the excitement and the dangers of the Métis bison hunt. Kane participated in this hunt near Fort Garry in 1846. ROM

repeat the process. An experienced hunter on a good horse could kill as many as ten or twelve animals on a run.

The excitement of the hunt was enhanced by its obvious dangers. Men might be gored, thrown from their horses and trampled, or accidentally shot in the dust, noise and confusion. As one nineteenth-century observer, zoologist William Hornaday, described the events:

> It often happened that the hunter found himself surrounded by the flying herd, and in a cloud of dust, so that neither man nor horse could see the ground before them. Under such circumstances fatal accidents to both men and horses were numerous. It was not an uncommon thing for half-breeds to shoot each other in the excitement of the chase; and, while now and then a wounded bull suddenly turned upon his pursuer and overthrew him, the greatest number of casualties were from falls.
>
> (Verbicky-Todd 1984:145)

As the dust of the hunt settled, men sought the animals they had killed and immediately began the task of skinning and butchering. The bulk of the labour, however, fell to the women. They cut the meat into strips, dried it in the sun and over fires, pounded it into coarse powder, mixed it with melted fat and berries, and stored it in hide bags. Creaking brigades of Red River carts hauled back huge loads of pemmican, destined as provisions to the distant posts of the fur trade.

Métis traders, 1872-75.
NAC C4164

As the buffalo hunts spread far out onto the Plains, the Métis came into bitter conflict with the Dakota. Not only were they depleting the bison herds in Dakota hunting grounds, but the Métis were closely associated by blood and marriage with the Cree and Ojibwa, the traditional enemies of the Dakota. The military discipline and large group size were Métis adaptations to the ever-present threat of Dakota attacks. Numerous skirmishes led to a decisive battle in 1851. Although greatly outnumbered, the Métis placed their carts in a defensive circle and dug shallow rifle pits, from which sharpshooters with their buffalo guns directed a withering fire against attackers. After suffering terrible losses, the Dakota withdrew, leaving the Métis in undisputed control of the eastern Plains.

Bison herds soon dwindled under the sustained onslaught of the hunters. By the 1850s, the Métis were having to move farther and farther afield in search of game. With such distances to travel, many families began to "winter over" on the Plains, at such wooded oases as Moose Mountain, Wood Mountain and the Cypress Hills. Known as *hivernants* ("winterers"), these hunters reduced their reliance on manufactured goods and lived a lifestyle similar to that of the Plains Indians. A member of the Palliser expedition, visiting a *hivernant* camp near Fort Edmonton in 1858, described them as:

> a motley troop with loaded horses and dogs, travelling in a style hardly different from Indians. There were about 200 men, women, and children in the band, with forty tents, which were merely Indian wigwams of buffalo skins sewn together and stretched over poles . . . They wore clothes of European manufacture, but even those of the men who could speak French preferred to speak Cree.
>
> (Spry 1963:109-110)

More permanent *hivernant* settlements of log cabins soon began to spring up across the Plains.

The distinct identity the Métis had established was expressed in a variety of clothing styles, mixing elements of European and Indian heritage. Men commonly wore the capote (a long hooded coat), with a brightly coloured sash or belt, trousers and moccasins. Women wore European dresses, with a dark shawl or blanket covering the head and shoulders, and moccasins. Alexander Ross, a prominent member of the Red River colony, described one individual:

> we met a stout, well-made, good-looking man, dressed in a common blue capote, red belt, and corduroy trousers; he spoke French, and was a Canadian. That, said I, pointing to his dress, is the universal costume of both Canadians and half-breeds.
>
> (Ross 1856:190)

The red sash, a tradition adopted from the French voyageurs, is particularly important as an emblem of Métis identity. In addition, Métis women were skilled at beadwork, producing elaborate floral designs as decorations on moccasins, pouches and other items. So distinctive a trait was this that the Dakota knew them as "the flower beadwork people."

Social gatherings and festivities also drew on the various aspects of their heritage to strengthen Métis identity. Houses were cleared of furniture to make room for dancing. The fiddle, a legacy of their French and Scottish background, became their beloved musical instrument. Fiddlers provided the vigorous dance music which was essential for any major gathering. Dances of the Plains Indians, French jigs and Scottish reels were combined to produce such distinctive steps as the famous "Red River jig." Men, in particular, prided themselves on their energy, often dancing until they wore through their moccasins.

Such boisterous gatherings seem to have been typical of the Métis. In this regard, they clearly considered themselves to be different from either parent race. Métis writer Maria Campbell commented:

> There was never much love lost between Indians and Halfbreeds. They were completely different from us—quiet when we were noisy, dignified even at dances and get-togethers. Indians were very passive . . . whereas Halfbreeds were quick-tempered—quick to fight, but quick to forgive and forget.
>
> (Campbell 1973:26)

After a half-century of control over the eastern Plains, the Métis found their way of life threatened in the 1860s. The fur trade which had given them birth was in decline, and steamships had appeared on the Red River to replace the creaking Red River carts. The bison were rapidly disappearing from the Plains, forcing many either to abandon the hunt or move west in search of the last herds. Crop failures resulted in hardship in the colony. Even more serious to the Métis way of life was the threat from the east, as the Métis communities stood in the way of Sir John A. Macdonald's dream of a Canada that stretched from sea to sea.

By 1869 the Hudson's Bay Company had been pressured into turning over the vast Rupert's Land to the new Canadian government. Even before final transfer of the title, a stream of settlers from Ontario began claiming lands along the Red River. Surveyors began to lay out square lots in the Ontario township system across the long and narrow Métis riverlots. The Métis, who held no legal title to the lands they occupied, were understandably alarmed. The government did nothing to ease their fears or hostility, conducting the transfer as a simple real estate transaction with little concern for the area's occupants.

Through these events the young Louis Riel emerged as leader of the Métis. He was Montreal-educated, had a basic familiarity with the law and could unite the various factions through his fluent command of French, English and Cree. The French Métis took the initiative in resistance, while the Anglophone half-breeds either reluctantly supported them or remained neutral. Other factions in the community welcomed the arrival of Protestant settlers from the east. Backed by a force of armed men experienced in buffalo hunts and skirmishes with the Dakota, Riel seized Fort Garry, the centre of the Red River settlement, and proclaimed a provisional government. Representatives were elected to draft the conditions under which they would enter confederation. Their demands included rights to their own elected legislature, representation in the parliament of Canada, and official status for both the French and English languages.

Riel, however, made a major political blunder. Thomas Scott was one of the recent arrivals from Ontario who sought to overthrow the provisional government and bring the area quickly into confederation. A Protestant Orangeman from Ulster, Scott was violently anti-Catholic and thoroughly disdainful of the Métis. As a result of his attempts to incite an uprising, Scott was captured by angry Métis, court-martialled and shot. Riel's failure to stop the execution earned him the bitter enmity of Ontario, forcing his exile and contributing eventually to his own execution.

The demands of Riel's provisional government led directly to the Manitoba Act of 1870. The new province of Manitoba was created (although, at a mere 100 square miles, it was only a small portion of the modern province), while the rest of the former Hudson's Bay Company lands in the north and west became the Northwest Territories, governed directly from Ottawa. Several provisions of the Act dealt with Métis concerns over lands. The federal government maintained control of the land but the Métis were to be assured title to their riverlot holdings and an additional 1.4 million acres were to be made available to Métis families. These provisions were amended several times, however, and the entire process was characterized by lengthy delays and mismanagement. Scrip certificates for land largely ended up in the possession of speculators. This flawed process, plus pressures from the new flood of arrivals into Manitoba, meant that few Métis received any long-term benefit.

Negotiations preceding Manitoba's entry into confederation called for general amnesty for those involved in the "resistance." Despite this, Riel and other leaders were forced into exile south of the border when British and Canadian troops arrived. Riel was not forgotten by the Métis, who still see him as the Father of Manitoba, and he was elected three times to Parliament in Ottawa, although he was unable to take his seat.

Although in many ways the Métis had been victorious, it was a brief victory. Protestant farmers from Ontario soon owned most of the land. The Métis, who were the dominant population along the Red River in 1870, were soon reduced to a small minority. The new arrivals were openly contemptuous of the Métis and hostile to anyone who had taken part in the "rebellion." Several Métis who had been prominent in the provisional government were killed and others were beaten. Many Anglo-Protestant half-breeds were able to continue on their farms north of Fort Garry, gradually blending in with the new settlers. Those who were French-speaking and Catholic bore the brunt of discrimination. Such social pressures encouraged many to move west, following the migrations begun by the *hivernants* decades earlier. Substantial Métis log-cabin communities appeared in what are today Saskatchewan and Alberta, where the Métis attempted to continue their lifestyle as hunters, freighters and farmers. In less than a decade and a half, however, they were again overrun.

THE NORTH-WEST REBELLION OF 1885

The disappearance of the bison herds caused great unrest in the Canadian West. The Cree and Assiniboine were starving on their reserves. Métis communities relied increasingly on farming, forcing an end to their nomadic lifestyle. Few owned title to their land, and they felt threatened by the increasing tide of settlers brought in by railroad and steamships. As along the Red River, the government sent surveyors to divide the land into square lots, disrupting the traditional Métis practice of narrow lots extending back from the rivers. Fearing that they were to be dispossessed once again, the Métis petitioned for recognition of their land rights. Although they were not totally ignored, the government response was far too slow to allay their fears, and there was no firm commitment that their requests would be granted.

The focus of their discontent was around the fork of the Saskatchewan River, where a number of Métis communities had emerged. One of the most prominent leaders was Gabriel Dumont, a former sharpshooter and buffalo hunter who had turned to homesteading and operating the ferry and a small store near Batoche. More at home with his horse and rifle than

Gabriel Dumont, the famed Métis buffalo hunter and military leader of the 1885 Rebellion, after his flight from Batoche. Glenbow Archives, Calgary

in dealing with government, Dumont knew that the Métis required a more educated and articulate voice. At a meeting attended by white settlers and anglophone half-breeds as well as Métis, it was decided that Louis Riel, who had defended their interests so vigorously at Red River, was again needed. Dumont and three others set out to find Riel and bring him back to the service of the Métis people.

The Riel they located in Montana was considerably different from the man who had been the focus of the resistance at Red River. Forced into exile and pursued by bounty hunters, he suffered a nervous breakdown and had been placed in mental asylums in Quebec. He had become obsessed with the idea that he had a divine mission to fulfill, to create a new French-Catholic state in the North-West. The invitation to return to the Métis people was seen as part of this ordained mission.

A politician and religious zealot rather than a soldier, Riel at first busied himself with preparing petitions, outlining Métis grievances to the government. Many of the Métis, however, were anxious for more direct action. Finally, Riel and his men seized the parish church at Batoche and proclaimed a provisional government, much as he had done at Red River in 1869. A slate of officers was elected, although most power was held by Riel and by Gabriel Dumont, who became "head of the army."

The Saskatchewan River in 1885, however, was quite different from the Red River in 1869. The North-West was now firmly under the control of Canada, which had an army in the east as well as the North West Mounted Police in the west. The west's isolation, which meant it took several months for British troops to reach Red River in 1870, was coming to an end with construction of the transcontinental railway. Despite gaps in the rail link with the east, troops could be quickly moved to the scene of the uprising. From proclamation of the provisional government to the fall of Batoche, the North-West Rebellion lasted scarcely two months.

The first skirmish took place near Duck Lake, where the North West Mounted Police arrived to assert the authority of the Dominion of Canada. Dumont's Métis, with a few Indians from nearby reserves, controlled the surrounding woods. Twelve police soon lay dead upon the ground and the rest were forced to flee. The Métis would have pursued them and inflicted greater casualties but were forbidden by Riel. This defeat caused the police to abandon Fort Carlton and move to the larger settlement of Prince Albert.

News of the Métis victory at Duck Lake spread quickly among the Indian camps. Messengers from Riel urged them to join in common cause with their Métis kin. Disillusioned with the treaties, chafing under the restraints of life on their reserves and starving due to a misguided government restraint policy, many Indians were eager to join the rebellion. Several hundred Cree besieged the fort at Battleford, looting and burning surrounding homes and stores. There they were joined by Assiniboines who had left their reserve after killing their farm instructor and a settler. Further to the northwest, the Cree warriors of Big Bear's band killed the Indian agent, two priests and six others at Frog Lake and forced the abandonment of Fort Pitt, which they pillaged and burned.

It was the shock of the deaths at Frog Lake that forced the government to act decisively. While the Métis had not caused a great deal of government concern, the spectre of a general Indian uprising across the west certainly did. Troops were hastily dispatched, dividing into a three-pronged assault on the insurgents. One column headed after Big Bear's Cree, while another proceeded to relieve Battleford, and the main force, under General Middleton, moved against the Métis capital of Batoche.

Dumont's tactics of guerrilla warfare were opposed by Riel, who still hoped to negotiate peacefully with the government. The advance of the army, however, required action and Dumont hastened to meet the troops before they could reach Batoche. At the Battle of Fish Creek, Métis sharpshooters, though greatly outnumbered, temporarily halted the army's advance. Meanwhile, a second army column moved against the Cree on Poundmaker's reserve but was counter-attacked at Cut Knife Hill and forced to retreat. Poundmaker and his warriors headed towards Batoche but were too late to join the fight.

The final outcome of the Battle of Batoche could never have been in doubt. A few hundred Métis with smooth-bore muzzle-loaders were no match for nearly a thousand soldiers with rifles, cannons and the rapid-fire Gatling gun. Métis supplies of ammunition were low, and by the end of the conflict many were reduced to firing nails and pebbles. Nevertheless, deeply dug into rifle pits and trenches, the Métis held off the military onslaught

Top: *Big Bear (seated at left, with youngest son Horse Child) and Poundmaker (seated at right) in custody at Regina after the Rebellion.* NAC C1872 □ Bottom: *Métis prisoners at Court House in Regina, August 1885.* O.B. Buell/NAC PA118760

for four days. Finally, the rifle pits were overrun, and the Métis defenders fled to the woods.

As fugitives, Riel and Dumont acted in characteristically different fashion. Riel agreed to surrender, to "fulfill God's will" and to continue to plead the cause of the Métis to the government of Canada. Dumont, the man of action, reacted to Middleton's demand for his surrender with the terse response: "I have still ninety cartridges to use on his men." He soon fled to the United States, where, for a brief period, this colourful frontiersman entertained audiences with his shooting and riding skills in Buffalo Bill Cody's Wild West Show. Later, he quietly returned to his homeland and lived out his life around Batoche. Poundmaker surrendered shortly after Riel, but Big Bear eluded the troops for several months. Many Indians and Métis fled to Montana, where their descendants today are the Cree of Rocky Boy reservation.

The trials which followed sent a number of Métis and Indians to prison. Big Bear and Poundmaker each received a three-year sentence. Their spirits and health broken by imprisonment, both men died shortly after their release. Eight Cree and Assiniboine were hanged at Battleford for the murders at Frog Lake and elsewhere. Most attention, however, was focused on the trial of Louis Riel.

A central issue in the trial was Riel's mental stability. A plea of insanity would almost certainly have saved him from the gallows. Riel, however, strongly believing in his divine mission, refused to weaken his impassioned speeches by allowing a claim of insanity. Despite a recommendation for mercy from the jury which convicted him, Riel was sentenced to hang.

This verdict embroiled much of the country in controversy. English Canada, having never forgiven Riel for the death of Thomas Scott fifteen years earlier, saw him as a traitor and demanded his execution. French Canada saw him as the defender of its language and religion in the west and demanded a pardon. Appeals to commute the death sentence came from around the world. The infuriated Macdonald declared: "He shall hang though every dog in Quebec bark in his favour." Disapproval was so strong in Quebec that Macdonald's Conservative party went into a century of political decline there. In Regina, on 16 November 1885, the Métis dreams of a New Nation in the Canadian West died on the gallows with Louis Riel.

THE LAST CENTURY

The Métis defeat marked the end of the "Old West." Hunters, trappers and traders had to give way to new arrivals, eager to fence and plow the land for their farms. Once again, the Métis were dispersed. Some sought the open spaces of Montana, while others retreated northward into the boreal forest, reaching as far as the Mackenzie River, where they could continue to live by hunting and trapping. Those who remained were left on the fringes of the new economic order.

Métis self-identity had been shattered by the events following the battle at Batoche. They had become "non-people," refused recognition of separate status by government policy. As Macdonald stated: "If they are Indians, they go with the tribe; if they are half-breeds they are whites." Some chose to emphasize the "French" and "Catholic" aspects of their heritage, while others, particularly in the north, merged with Indian groups and later took treaty. Not until the Constitution Act of 1982 would the Métis again achieve widespread recognition as a distinct people.

Acknowledgment that the Métis held some aboriginal rights can be seen in the practice of issuing "half-breed scrip," a certificate for a certain number of acres of Dominion land or cash value redeemable in purchase of such lands (commonly $240 or 240 acres). When Indian treaties were signed, individuals of mixed heritage were offered the option of scrip rather than treaty, providing an immediate financial inducement to surrender their native status. Few obtained any long-term benefit, as poverty forced most to sell the certificates to speculators who followed the scrip commissions. The Métis were dealt with very differently than their Indian kin, with their rights extinguished individually rather than collectively and in a fashion which worked to deny them a land base and other benefits of treaty. Many Métis today insist that their aboriginal rights cannot have been extinguished by such an inadequate process.

Well into the twentieth century, many Métis lived in deplorable economic conditions, shut out from mainstream Canadian life yet excluded from the reserves and federal programs for Indians. Where hunting and trapping were no longer possible, people earned a bare existence through cutting wood and other odd jobs. Métis shanty-towns grew up on the outskirts of villages and alongside reserves; other Métis built cabins on Crown land such as road allowances. The Depression pushed many Métis even further into poverty and despair.

By the 1930s political action finally brought the desperate situation of the Métis to government attention. This was particularly true in northern Alberta, where many Métis squatters on Crown land were threatened by a transfer to provincial jurisdiction. The Métis Association (today the Métis Nation) of Alberta was formed to bring attention to their situation. Leaders such as Malcolm Norris and Jim Brady forcefully articulated Métis grievances and helped revive Métis nationalism. As a result, the Alberta government formed the Ewing Commission to investigate, leading to passage of the Métis Betterment Act in 1938. Twelve Métis colonies, similar in nature to Indian reserves, were established in north-central Alberta. Although four were later rescinded, the remaining eight Métis settlements are home to about 6000 Métis today. The western settlements are largely agricultural, while ranching has been more important in those to the east. Until recently this was the only communal Métis land base in the country (in Saskatchewan, a Métis farm originally run by the Catholic church has now been transferred to a Métis corporation and the Métis of the Northwest Territories are negotiating a land base through land claims settlements).

Differences in perception, however, set the stage for continuing conflict. The commissioners and government agents viewed the settlements as "colonies," run by the government to assist destitute Métis to become successful farmers. The Métis aspirations, articulated by such leaders as Norris and Brady, were for a self-governing Métis land base. The Métis resented what they saw as excessive government control, and their lack of land security was reinforced in 1960 when the Alberta government terminated one of the occupied settlements in spite of Métis objections. Another major source of friction, which developed into a prolonged legal battle, was a dispute over control of subsurface rights to oil and gas resources.

This continuing conflict led the Conservative government of Peter Lougheed to establish a committee, chaired by former lieutenant-governor Grant MacEwan, to review the Métis Betterment Act. The committee's 1984 report called for a greater degree of self-government and transfer of land ownership to the settlements. These recommendations, plus a desire to end the lengthy court proceedings over oil and gas revenues, led to a 1989 agreement. In exchange for dropping their legal suit the Métis communities are to receive $310 million over seventeen years. Legislation was enacted in 1990 to allow for limited self-government, full title to the lands that make up the settlements and an amendment to the Alberta Act to constitutionally entrench the legal title.

Métis political activity has intensified in the last few decades. Most provinces now have Métis associations, often including non-status Indians. The Gabriel Dumont Institute in Regina, which promotes research on Métis history and provides a variety of educational services, has helped heighten Métis self-awareness. The term "Métis" is becoming much more widely applied than its historic usage, often including anyone of partial Indian heritage who is not legally classified as an Indian. This is a far cry from its specific use for the nineteenth-century French-Cree Métis of the Plains, and many of their descendants resent the wider application of the term. However, the much larger numbers have given the Métis greater political clout. Métis political organizations primarily are seeking improved social and economic conditions, a land base and the redress of historical grievances.

As "aboriginal peoples of Canada" specified in the Constitution, the Métis are entitled to share in land claims settlements reached with First Nations. Accordingly, government negotiations over land claims in the Yukon and Northwest Territories have included both Dene and Métis. In addition, the Métis have claims which stem from their own unique history. In 1986 the Manitoba Métis Federation launched legal action against the governments of Manitoba and Canada over lands reserved for the Métis in the Manitoba Act of 1870. They maintain that amendments to the Manitoba Act, which served to deprive many Métis of their land entitlements, were unconstitutional. They also claim that the government mismanaged the grant program and did not fulfill the conditions agreed upon when Manitoba entered confederation. As descendants of the Métis at Red River in 1870, the Manitoba Métis argue that they are entitled to compensation in money and land. A 1990 Supreme Court of Canada decision cleared the way for the Métis to proceed with their legal action. The stakes are considerable as large areas of modern-day Winnipeg and the surrounding communities sit on lands of the former Red River settlement, much of which the Métis maintain was set aside for them under the terms of the Manitoba Act.

From the "forgotten people" of a few decades ago, the Métis have again emerged in public consciousness. The events at Fort Garry and Batoche, so crucial to the history of western Canada, have inspired renewed interest. Batoche is now a National Historic Park, and statues of Louis Riel have been raised outside the provincial legislative buildings in both Regina and Winnipeg. Riel's execution remains a subject of debate, and demands have been presented for a retroactive pardon. The charismatic Métis leader continues to symbolize the tensions in Canadian society, between East and West, French and English, native and non-native.

CHAPTER 12 *Native Canadians:*
Major Contemporary Issues

At Canada's birth, the British North America Act (now known as the Constitution Act, 1867) assigned the federal government responsibility for "Indians, and Lands reserved for Indians." Treated as wards of the federal government, Indians were placed under separate legislation (the Indian Act, 1876), which put them in a different legal category from all other Canadians. Later, as Canada's attention finally turned to its vast northern regions, the Inuit were also recognized as falling directly under federal jurisdiction. Two other categories, the Métis and "non-status Indians," consist of individuals who consider themselves to be aboriginal Canadians but lack formal recognition as such by the federal government. Consequently, they have been denied special rights and receive most services from the provinces in the same manner as other Canadians. Not until the Constitution Act, 1982, did the Métis gain official recognition as one of the three "aboriginal peoples of Canada." Unlike the other two groups, however, the Métis population and their relationship with "non-status Indians" remain undefined.

INDIANS: THE STATUS ISSUE
"Status" (or "registered") Indians are those who fall under the provisions of the Indian Act and are recognized by the federal government through the Department of Indian Affairs and Northern Development, which maintains an Indian Register. For the vast majority of Indians, the right to be registered comes from membership in a band, the political-administrative unit recognized by the federal government. Status Indians have rights to use of reserve lands held by their band, access to federal funding for various

programs (such as housing and education) and the limited benefits of the Indian Act.

The terms "status Indian" and "treaty Indian" are not synonymous. Even in such treaty areas as Ontario and the prairie provinces there are groups of legally recognized Indians (such as the Iroquois and Dakota) that lack federal treaties as a result of their historic arrival in Canada. In other areas (Quebec, the Yukon, most of British Columbia), no treaties were ever signed. While "status" can exist without treaty, "non-status" Indians do not receive treaty benefits, even in treaty areas.

From its inception, the Indian Act has been divisive, applying to some Indians while excluding others. Until 1985 it contained the concept of "enfranchisement," whereby individuals or even entire bands, simply by majority vote, could surrender their status as Indians and become Canadian citizens. Since all Canadian natives are citizens today, there has been little incentive for such voluntary enfranchisement in recent decades. Earlier, however, individuals had to give up their status in order to vote, own property or purchase liquor. When a man surrendered his status, his entire family was enfranchised.

The blatant sexual discrimination in the Act was its most infamous feature. Indian women who married non-Indian males, along with their dependent children, were stripped of their status. Even on marriage to an aboriginal person, unless the male was legally registered as an Indian his wife was "deemed not to be an Indian within the meaning of this Act." The wives of Indian men, on the other hand, automatically became Indians under the Act regardless of racial origin. "Indian" is thus a legal category, with only a partial correspondence to biological reality. Despite the archaic nineteenth-century assumptions about women taking the identity of their husbands, this discriminatory section of the Indian Act remained in place until 1985, surviving several court challenges.

In 1973 the Supreme Court of Canada ruled against Jeannette Lavell, an Ojibwa from Manitoulin Island who had lost her status as a result of marriage. Basing her case on the Bill of Rights, Lavell had been successful in a lower court. The Supreme Court, however, ruled that the Indian Act took precedence. Later, the Human Rights Act specifically excluded the Indian Act from its jurisdiction. Blocked from further court challenge, Sandra Lovelace, a Maliseet from the Tobique reserve in New Brunswick, took a similar case to the United Nations. There, in 1981, Canada was found to be in violation of an international covenant on human rights. Although this was an embarrassment to Canada, it could not force any changes.

It was not until April 1985 that the Act was finally rewritten to remove sexual discrimination, as required by the Charter of Rights and Freedoms in the Constitution. Bill C-31, which revised the Indian Act, repealed all sections dealing with enfranchisement. No longer is it possible to gain or lose status through marriage. Anyone who lost status, whether voluntarily, through marriage, or from being a dependent child when his or her mother was enfranchised, can reclaim Indian status. In addition, the children of such people also are eligible to apply for status. In future, those with two Indian parents will be able to transmit Indian status to their offspring, while those with one Indian parent will be considered Indian but will not be able to transmit status to their children without marrying another Indian. Not all reinstated Indians, however, will be eligible to join bands. Thus the Act creates a new division within the status Indian population, between those who have band membership and those who do not, with the latter having no rights to reserve lands or resources.

The status Indian population, already with a growth rate well above the national average, was swelled as a result of these changes. By late 1994, more than 92,500 people had obtained status as Indians through the provisions of Bill C-31, and this number continues to grow. Approximately 16 percent of all status Indians in Canada are now Bill C-31 registrants. This surge of newly registered Indians has placed considerable pressure on Indian bands across Canada, straining existing lands and resources, and not all bands have been receptive to extending their membership. The numbers of "non-status Indians" and, to a lesser extent, Métis have been reduced as many individuals have taken advantage of their eligibility for Indian status. Despite Bill C-31, however, there will still be some people who consider themselves of Indian heritage who will not be eligible for registration.

At the end of October 1994, the status Indian population in Canada was 570,197. This is a young and rapidly growing population, whose number has doubled in the past twenty years. Over half are under twenty-five years of age, compared to 35 percent for Canada as a whole. Status Indians comprise, however, only 1.9 percent of the total national population. The largest number of Indians, about 130,000, is in Ontario, followed by British Columbia, Saskatchewan and Manitoba. Overall, Indians form less than 1 percent of the total population in eastern and central Canada. Only in Saskatchewan and Manitoba is the Indian population more than 5 percent of the provincial total. In the north, status Indians make up about 20 percent of the total population of the two territories. Only in the Northwest Territories do aboriginal peoples collectively form the majority.

The national political organization representing status Indians is the Assembly of First Nations (formerly the National Indian Brotherhood). The Assembly has been the major Indian voice to the federal government, strongly advocating the entrenchment of aboriginal rights and self-government in Canada's Constitution. The First Nations it represents are the bands, which divide traditional cultural and linguistic groups. While there are approximately fifty-three aboriginal languages in Canada, there are 605 Indian bands. The Mi'kmaq, for example, are divided into twenty-eight bands spread across the easternmost five provinces. The Assembly has been weakened by the division between treaty and non-treaty groups and by the different aspirations of its members. Disagreements over strategy have caused some bands to withdraw. Partly as a result of this instability, most government negotiations with Indian groups have been at the local, rather than the national, level.

Non-status Indians are represented nationally by the Congress of Aboriginal Peoples (formerly the Native Council of Canada), which also represents status Indians living off reserves. Their position is that Canada's responsibility to Indians, as stated in the Constitution Acts of 1867 and 1982, should refer to all people of aboriginal descent, not just those recognized by the provisions of the Indian Act. Since non-status Indians are not considered by government to be Indians, no accurate estimates of their numbers exist. In the 1981 federal census only 75,110 people, an unrealistically low number, identified themselves as "non-status Indians." Although this category disappeared in the 1991 census, nearly 800,000 people identified their ethnic origins as at least partially "North American Indian." Not all would consider themselves to be aboriginal people, and many would have status as Indians, but this large population figure suggests that there is a considerable number of people with Indian heritage who do not have legal recognition.

MÉTIS

Confusion exists over the term "Métis." In western and northern Canada it generally refers to the distinct Métis society which emerged in the nineteenth century, with its beginnings along the Red River. Elsewhere, it is often used to designate anyone of mixed Indian-European heritage. In this broader sense no clear distinction can be made between Métis and non-status Indians, and provincial organizations representing both have emerged across the country. In the 1991 census 75,150 people identified themselves as "Métis," and an additional 137,500 claimed partial Métis origins.

Although the former Native Council of Canada was a strong voice for Métis nationalism, it suffered from tensions between western Métis and eastern non-status Indians. As a result, the Métis of Manitoba, Saskatchewan and Alberta broke away to establish the Métis National Council in 1983. Similar divisions occurred at the provincial level; the Association of Métis and Non-Status Indians of Saskatchewan, for example, split into two separate organizations in 1988.

The Métis gained a great victory with their inclusion as "aboriginal peoples" in the Constitution. Denied a separate identity and ignored for a century after the fall of Batoche, the Métis were finally accorded official recognition. However, it is unclear who should be considered "Métis" and what rights have been gained.

These uncertainties were addressed as part of the constitutional negotiations in 1992. An agreement, the Métis Nation Accord, was struck between the Métis National Council, along with provincial and territorial Métis groups, and the federal and corresponding provincial governments. This agreement defined a Métis as an aboriginal person who self-identifies as Métis and is a descendant of those Métis who were entitled to land grants or scrip under the provisions of the Manitoba Act of 1870 or the Dominion Lands Act. It called for federal responsibility for Métis, as for other aboriginal peoples, and for enumeration of Métis populations. It also committed the federal and provincial governments to negotiate with the Métis regarding self-government and a land base. The rejection of the 1992 Charlottetown Accord by the Canadian public, however, makes implementation of this agreement uncertain.

INUIT

In the 1991 census 30,085 people identified themselves as Inuit, with an additional 19,165 claiming partial Inuit origins. Like Indians, the Inuit are administered federally, although the governments of Quebec and Newfoundland provide services to Inuit communities within their jurisdictions. A dispute between Quebec and the federal government led the Supreme Court of Canada to determine in 1939 that the Inuit were included when the British North America Act made "Indians" a federal responsibility. However, they are specifically excluded from the Indian Act, do not have reserves and are administered somewhat differently from Indians.

Their national organization is the Inuit Tapirisat of Canada, which has been active in pressing for settlement of land claims and in the constitutional debate over aboriginal rights. Unlike other Canadian natives, the Inuit form a relatively homogeneous group and have remained the majority population throughout most of their traditional lands. Modern land claims settlements from the western Arctic to northern Quebec have given the Inuit a certain level of self-government and economic security. The proposed split of the Northwest Territories would create the self-governing Inuit homeland of Nunavut in the eastern Arctic, which could eventually achieve status similar to that of a province. The Inuit Tapirisat has also been concerned with forging stronger circumpolar ties with the Inuit of Greenland and Alaska.

THE INDIAN ACT

Assimilation and paternalism have been the foundations of Canadian Indian policy. From the beginning, the goal was to protect Indians while attempting to "civilize" them and prepare them to enter mainstream society. Native populations were declining throughout the late nineteenth and early twentieth centuries, and the government plan was to encourage the gradual disappearance of Indians as Indians. The twin pillars of Indian policy conflicted, however, since the paternalistic protection of the Indian Act served to isolate Indians from the rest of the society they were expected to join. It also created the deep division among Canadian Indians between those recognized under the Indian Act and all others.

The administration of Indians as colonized people was implemented with the passage of the first Indian Act in 1876. The assimilation goal is evident in the peculiar provision for enfranchisement. It was clear that the category of "Indian" was to be a legal rather than a racial one, and that anyone considered "ready" would be removed from status. This included women who married non-Indian men, and, after later amendments, anyone who obtained a university degree or entered a profession. Government officials (Indian agents) had the right to determine who was an Indian, could decide on the best uses for reserve lands and had other sweeping powers. For decades prairie Indians could not even leave their reserves without a pass from the agent. Amendments to the Act banned the potlatch on the Northwest Coast and the Sun Dance of the Plains, striking at the heart of native cultures to promote assimilation. A 1927 amendment even prohibited the raising of money to pursue land claims. The Indian Act served to suppress Indian cultures and keep Indians locked in a state of dependency, with little control over their own affairs.

Major revisions were made to the Indian Act in 1951. While much of the 1876 legislation remained intact, some government powers were curtailed. The ban on Indian ceremonies was dropped, as was that on raising money for political purposes, and Indians were allowed to consume liquor in public places. Except for the repeal of the enfranchisement provisions in 1985 and an amendment allowing bands to tax businesses on reserves in 1988, the present Act is largely as it was rewritten in 1951.

In 1960, federal voting rights were extended unconditionally to Canadian Indians. For the first time it was possible to be both a Canadian citizen and an Indian. The concept of multiculturalism had finally prevailed over the earlier requirement of assimilation for rights as a citizen. John Diefenbaker, the prime minister at the time, was jokingly hailed by native leaders as "the Lincoln of the North."

The spirit of social change in the 1960s and the liberal ideology of the Trudeau government required further action. The Indian Act and reserve system had become stigmatized as "Canada's apartheid policy." Accordingly, the government proposed a radical restructuring of its relationship with First Nations. In 1969 it presented a proposal, the White Paper on Indian Policy, to end paternalism and discrimination. Essentially, the White Paper called for an end to any special status for Indians. The Indian Act was to be repealed, the bureaucracy of Indian administration dismantled and all federal responsibilities for Indians ended.

Reaction of First Nations across Canada was immediate and vehemently negative. The policy was viewed as an abrogation of treaty and aboriginal rights, a betrayal of the historic relationship with the Crown. Harold

Cardinal, a Cree political leader from Alberta, described the policy in his scathing book *The Unjust Society* as "cultural genocide" and "a thinly disguised programme of extermination through assimilation." So violently opposed were native leaders that the government was forced to withdraw the proposal. It has left a legacy of distrust and suspicion.

Many provisions of the Indian Act still reflect the paternalism of 1876. Clauses included to protect Indians from unscrupulous whites may today inhibit bands from economic development. A good example is the protection of Indian property on reserves. Since First Nations do not own title to their reserve lands, and since all personal property of an Indian or band on a reserve is not subject to mortgage or legal seizure, bands have had great difficulties in financing on-reserve developments.

Other provisions of the Act, such as those on taxation, work to the benefit of First Nations today. Indian or band property on a reserve cannot be taxed, nor can income earned on a reserve. A 1983 Supreme Court decision confirmed that Indians who live and work on their reserve are exempt from income tax. Income from employment off the reserve, however, is taxed at the same rate as for all other Canadians.

Although the provisions of the Indian Act still regulate the lives of Canadian Indians, the tendency has been away from the paternalism of the past and towards the transfer of responsibility to First Nations. Indian agents have long been withdrawn from the reserves, and the decisions are being made by band councils. More than half of the bands control their own finances. Several have achieved self-government and are no longer bound by the Indian Act. The concept of Indian self-government has been endorsed by the federal government, and the days of the Indian Act, at least in its present form, seem numbered.

INDIAN RESERVES

Indian reserves ("reservation" is the American term) are lands set aside, according to the Indian Act, for the "use and benefit" of specific bands. Title to the land, however, is held by the Crown, making the reserves pockets of federal jurisdiction within the provinces. Under the terms of the Indian Act, a band cannot sell or otherwise dispose of reserve lands without surrendering them to the Crown. Proposals for Indian self-government involve transferring ownership of the land to the bands, and this already has been achieved in several places.

The earliest reserves were established in New France by the Catholic Church. Later, reserves were set aside through treaties and grants by the governments of Upper and Lower Canada, the Maritime colonies and British Columbia. After confederation, most reserves were established through treaties, extending from Ontario to the Rocky Mountains. In other areas, such as Quebec and most of British Columbia, reserves were allocated without treaties. The process remains incomplete, as few reserves have been established in the Yukon and Northwest Territories, even where promised by federal treaties. Most band members in the territories live in "settlements," generally on Crown land. Some more southerly bands also lack reserves; the Innu settlements in Labrador do not have federal reserve status and the Lubicon Cree in Alberta have led an unresolved and highly publicized battle over their reserve entitlement.

Of Canada's 2364 reserves, over 1600 are in British Columbia. This reflects a different history of reserve allocation, rather than any huge native land base. In British Columbia the bands received each of their small seasonal village locations as reserves, on a per capita base far below that in use for the federal treaties across the rest of western Canada. As a result, each band holds a number of reserves, which tend to be small, scattered and in many cases economically useless today.

Many reserves are inaccessible by road and can be reached only by trails, watercraft or airplanes. Of reserve residents in Canada, over 60 percent live in rural or remote areas. Federal statistics for 1992 indicate that 41.8 percent of people who live on reserves are in rural areas, 18.3 percent are in "special access zones" (lacking any year-round road access into their community) and 1.8 percent are "remote" (more than 350 kilometres from the nearest service centre with road access).

Reserves have tended to isolate status Indians from the rest of Canadian society. Unemployment and poor living conditions on reserves have led many Indians to chose off-reserve life. For those who remain, the reserves continue to offer a physical and spiritual refuge, a place where aboriginal values and beliefs are not endangered by pressures of the outside world.

TREATIES AND TREATY GRIEVANCES

> Let no one forget it . . . we are a people with special rights guaranteed to us by promises and treaties. We do not beg for these rights, nor do we thank you . . . because we paid for them . . . and God help us the price we paid was exorbitant. (Chief Dan George, Squamish Nation, in Waubageshig's *The Only Good Indian*)

The historic treaties signed between Canada and the First Nations continue to be of great legal and symbolic significance. Perceptions of their nature and importance, however, vary considerably. Native people whose ancestors signed treaties tend to view these documents as recognition of their sovereign status and affirmation of their aboriginal rights. The treaties provide for a continuing relationship between Canada and the First Nations. Governments and non-aboriginals, however, tend to see the treaties as historic agreements which extinguished aboriginal rights to the land and estab-

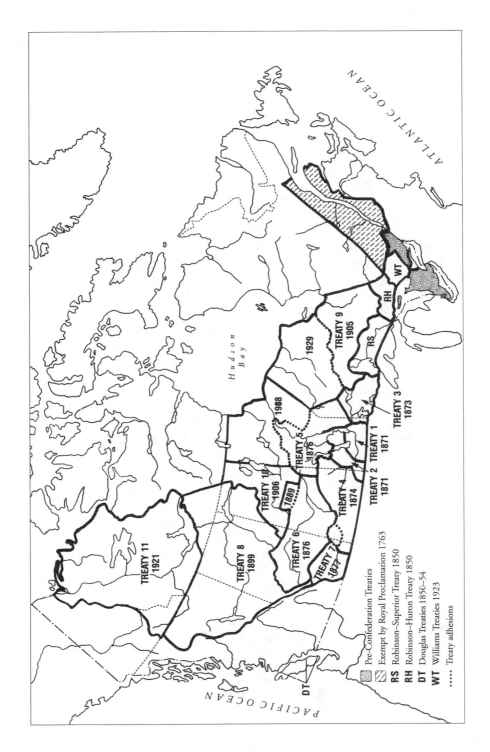

Treaty areas in Canada

lished federal control over the lives of native people.

The earliest treaties were between the British government and aboriginal peoples of what is today Atlantic Canada. These were the "peace and friendship treaties," signed during the late seventeenth to late eighteenth centuries. The British sought agreements to forge political alliances with Indian groups and gain their assistance in wars with the French. These early treaties do not include purchase or surrender of the land, nor do they promise reserves or annuities.

After defeat of the French and with increased European settlement, the focus of the treaties shifted from "peace and friendship" to land surrenders. Between about 1780 and 1850 small land conveyance treaties were negotiated with the Indians of what was to become southern Ontario. These treaties varied greatly but often involved small, one-time payments; for example, the "Chippewas and Mississaugas" (Ojibwa groups) surrendered their lands in a 1781 treaty for 300 suits of clothing. Only occasionally were reserves granted or hunting and fishing rights guaranteed. Some were imprecise, such as the so-called "Gunshot Treaty" of 1787, which covered lands along the shores of Lake Ontario as far inland as a gunshot could be heard on a clear day.

In 1850 Commissioner W.B. Robinson was dispatched to Sault Ste. Marie to negotiate treaties with the Indians of the upper Great Lakes. Known as the Robinson-Superior and Robinson-Huron treaties, they involved the surrender of large areas of land in exchange for reserves, lump-sum cash payments, annual payments to each member of the band and promises of hunting and fishing rights over unoccupied Crown lands. These large-scale treaties set the stage for the later federal treaties, which were similar in form.

On the Pacific coast, the colony of Vancouver Island also began to purchase native title to the land to make way for European settlement. James Douglas, as chief factor of the Hudson's Bay Company and governor of the colony, negotiated agreements with individual bands, extinguishing native title to the lands around Victoria, Nanaimo and Fort Rupert between 1850 and 1854. In return for surrendering their land, which became "the Entire property of the White people for ever," the Indians were confirmed in possession of their village sites and fields, assured that they would be "at liberty to hunt over the unoccupied lands, and to carry on fisheries as formerly," and given small payments. The amounts were trifling, the entire Victoria area being obtained for 371 blankets. Shortage of funds kept Douglas from conducting further agreements, and most of British Columbia remains non-treaty.

After confederation, the new Dominion of Canada began to look to the west. Construction of a railroad to the west coast and agricultural settlement on the prairies made it advisable for the government to seek to extinguish any aboriginal claims to the land. The "numbered treaties" began with Treaty No. 1, affecting the Ojibwa and Cree of southern Manitoba, in 1871. By the time Treaty No. 7 was signed with the Blackfoot, Sarcee and Stoney of southern Alberta only six years later, the lands from western Lake Superior to the Rockies had been covered. Except for a northward addition to Treaty No. 6, treaty-making came to a halt for twenty-two years, until gold and oil discoveries in the north brought about a new spate of negotiations. Between Treaty No. 8 in 1899 and Treaty No. 11 in 1921, native title was extinguished in northern Ontario, the rest of the prairie provinces, northeastern British Columbia and the western half of the Northwest Territories. Finally, the Williams treaties of 1923, which extinguished native title to the last unsurrendered lands in southern Ontario, brought treaty-making in Canada to a close.

While there were minor differences, all federal treaties were similar. First Nations agreed to "cede, release, surrender, and yield up" their rights to the land in exchange for reserves, small cash payments, ammunition and fishing twine, uniforms and medals for the chiefs, annual payments to each band member and promises of continued hunting and fishing rights. For decades annual "treaty days" featured a government official flanked by uniformed Mounties dispensing payments. Members of treaty bands still receive an annual payment, amounting to only $5 per person under most treaties.

Native people received very little for their surrender of nearly half of Canada's land surface. What is more, it appears that there were great differences between what they were told they were signing and the actual written words of the treaties. Gifts such as flags and medals enhanced the illusion that these were pacts of friendship and mutual assistance between nations, while the written provisions more closely resembled deeds of sale. First Nations today want the treaties interpreted in the broadest possible way, reflecting the spirit in which they were signed. They maintain that their treaty rights include the recognition of aboriginal self-governments.

A number of specific claims have developed over unfulfilled treaty promises. Not all the reserve lands promised in treaties were ever allocated. In Saskatchewan, for example, thirty-seven bands claim additional treaty land entitlements. A 1992 framework agreement between the federal and provincial governments and the Federation of Saskatchewan Indian Nations provides $500 million over twelve years for the purchase of up to 1.7 million acres of additional reserve lands. Other bands are looking at treaty provisions that were never fulfilled; for example, in 1984 the Blackfoot (now the Siksika Nation) received $1,675,000 in financial compensation for cattle promised over a century earlier under Treaty No. 7. Others seek wider interpretation of treaty promises, arguing that a contentious clause unique to Treaty No. 6, calling for a medicine chest to be kept at the agent's house, should be interpreted as full free medical care, a viewpoint not upheld in the courts.

A more widespread grievance is the abrogation of treaty-promised hunting and fishing rights. Various commissioners remarked that without assurances of such rights the Indians could never have been persuaded to sign the treaties. Some treaty hunting rights still exist. In a court case (*R. v. White and Bob*) two Nanaimo Indians were acquitted of hunting deer out of season due to hunting rights promised in their band's 1854 treaty. Similar decisions have been made in the prairie provinces. However, these rights have clearly been eroded by subsequent federal legislation. In a Supreme Court decision, a Northwest Territories treaty Indian was convicted under the Migratory Birds Convention Act for shooting a duck, though the court also chastised the federal government for breaching its treaty obligations. Similarly, fishing rights promised by the Douglas treaties on the west coast have been removed by federal fisheries legislation. The entrenchment of treaty rights in the constitution should halt further erosion but will not restore rights lost prior to 1982.

LAND CLAIMS

Massive rejection of proposed Indian policy in 1969 and the partial success of the Nisga'a in a 1973 Supreme Court decision forced the federal government, despite a long-standing hostility to claims based on aboriginal rights, to rethink its position. Shortly after the Nisga'a decision the government announced that it was prepared to negotiate settlements in areas where aboriginal title had never been extinguished by treaty. The Office of Native Claims was opened in Ottawa in 1974 to receive proposals for negotiation. Native claims are of two types: comprehensive (based on aboriginal title) and specific (based on lawful obligations).

COMPREHENSIVE CLAIMS

Comprehensive claims exist for those areas where aboriginal title has never been extinguished through treaty or other legal process. Aboriginal title derives from native ownership of the land prior to European colonization. While most commonly thought of as rights to the land and resources, many First Nations are demanding that aboriginal rights be considered in a broader perspective, including offshore fisheries, respect for traditional cultural practices and the right to self-determination.

The cornerstone of the legal argument is the Royal Proclamation of 1763. In a section dealing with aboriginal peoples, this decree by George III refers to "any Lands whatever, which, not having been ceded to or purchased by Us . . . are reserved to the said Indians." Thus, it has been argued, treaties are legally mandatory to extinguish aboriginal title, and any land not ceded by treaty is still native land. It is uncertain, however, how widely the Proclamation applies. For example, as the lands of British Columbia were unknown to the British sovereign at that time, the province has argued

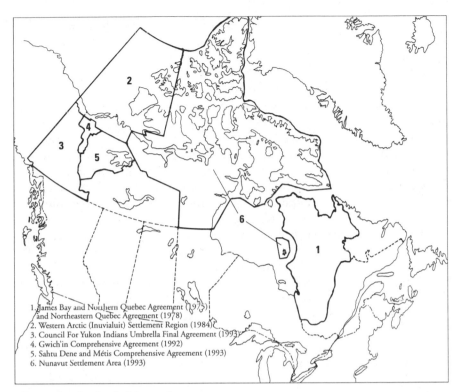

1. James Bay and Northern Quebec Agreement (1975) and Northeastern Quebec Agreement (1978)
2. Western Arctic (Inuvialuit) Settlement Region (1984)
3. Council For Yukon Indians Umbrella Final Agreement (1993)
4. Gwich'in Comprehensive Agreement (1992)
5. Sahtu Dene and Métis Comprehensive Agreement (1993)
6. Nunavut Settlement Area (1993)

Comprehensive land claim settlement areas

against its application. Nevertheless, the colonial and dominion practice of signing treaties with First Nations across much of Canada clearly indicates some recognition of aboriginal rights to the land.

It was the Nisga'a of northern British Columbia who most vigorously kept native land claims alive. The 1973 outcome of an appeal to the Supreme Court of Canada, however, left the essential issue unresolved (see Chapter 8). Although resulting in a technical defeat for the Nisga'a, the strength of their case led the federal government to reappraise its policy on native claims. It also marked a shift away from the courts and into the political sphere, with negotiations handled through the Office of Native Claims.

Modern land claims agreements have now been reached with aboriginal groups across most of northern Canada. The first was the James Bay Agreement of 1975, involving the Cree and Inuit of northern Quebec (see Chapters 5 and 10). This agreement was extended in 1978 to northeastern Quebec to include one group of Innu (the Naskapi of Schefferville). The Western Arctic (Inuvialuit) Agreement in 1984 and the huge Nunavut Land Claims Agreement of 1993 (see Chapter 10) completed settlements for all Inuit traditional lands except in Labrador. In the Yukon, a 1993

Umbrella Final Agreement with the Council for Yukon Indians provided a general settlement for all Yukon First Nations and a framework on which agreements with individual Yukon Indian Nations are based. In the Northwest Territories, prolonged negotiations with the Dene Nation and the Métis Association have collapsed. Instead, separate agreements were struck with the Gwich'in of the lower Mackenzie River in 1992 and with the Sahtu Dene and Métis around Great Bear Lake in 1993 (see Chapter 9). Other comprehensive claims are in active negotiation.

Although comprehensive claims agreements vary considerably, there are many common features. All extinguish native claim to the land in exchange for monetary compensation, ownership of certain lands and provisions for continued hunting and trapping rights. Some of the lands include subsurface mineral rights, an important point in Canada's resource-rich north. Membership on decision-making boards ensures the protection of aboriginal interests concerning such areas as wildlife management, resource development and heritage preservation. Control of social programs, such as education and health, is a feature of some agreements, as is a commitment from the federal government to negotiate self-government. Once completed, land claims agreements are constitutionally protected, having the same status as treaties.

The modern settlements resemble the historic treaties in the requirement for extinguishment of aboriginal title. They specify that aboriginal groups "cede, release and surrender" any aboriginal claim. This has been a sore point for some native groups, who reject the surrender of their aboriginal rights as a "sell-out," no matter what the financial compensation. The James Bay Agreement was denounced by some as "another beads and blankets deal—just more beads and more blankets." The government requirement for extinguishment, among other factors, caused the collapse of an agreement with the Dene and Métis of the Northwest Territories.

The 1985 report of the federal task force on comprehensive claims (*Living Treaties: Lasting Agreements,* commonly known as the Coolican Report) calls for flexible agreements that recognize and affirm aboriginal rights. Aboriginal self-governments can be negotiated as part of the comprehensive claims process. It also recommends that settlements apply to all aboriginal peoples who continue to use and occupy traditional lands, not just those who are at present recognized as Indians or Inuit by the federal government.

The Métis are involved in a number of comprehensive claims. Provisions in the Manitoba Act and the Dominion Lands Act acknowledge that the Métis had some aboriginal claim to the land, as do several of the numbered treaties. The inclusion of the Métis as aboriginal peoples in the Constitution suggests that they are entitled to share in any agreements based on aboriginal rights. Yet who should be considered a Métis for such purposes, and what about non-status Indians? Only in the north does the situation seem relatively clear, and negotiations in both the Yukon and the Northwest Territories include the Métis.

Frustration with lengthy delays in the negotiation process has driven some groups to seek resolution of their claims through the courts. The British Columbia Supreme Court, after lengthy proceedings, dealt aboriginal land claims a serious blow when it ruled against the Gitksan and Wet'suwet'en in 1991. The presiding judge ruled that the Royal Proclamation did not apply to British Columbia, that aboriginal interest in the land did not include ownership and that aboriginal rights had been extinguished by actions of the Crown. This judgment, which contradicts earlier decisions of other courts, was widely criticized for its ethnocentric comments and its dismissal of oral testimony by native elders and anthropologists. Another blow, also in 1991, was the rejection by the Supreme Court of Canada of the Teme-Augama Anishnabai claim in the Lake Temagami area of northern Ontario. Both groups protested against the continued despoliation of their traditional lands by logging companies while their cases slowly proceeded through the courts. Both organized highly publicized blockades of logging roads to protect aboriginal lands. Ultimately, the courts may be inappropriate vehicles in such cases, which are essentially political matters.

Comprehensive claims remain to be settled for considerable areas of Canada. Negotiations continue with Dene and Métis groups in the Northwest Territories, the Labrador Inuit Association, the Innu Nation in Labrador and the Conseil Attikamek-Montagnais in Quebec. In British Columbia, such groups as the Nisga'a Tribal Council, Gitksan-Wet'suwet'en Tribal Council, Council of the Haida Nation, Nuu-Chah-Nulth Tribal Council, Heiltsuk Nation and Nuxalk Nation have had their claims accepted for negotiation. Successful completion of negotiations across much of Canada's north and the establishment of the British Columbia Treaty Commission involving the provincial government may set the stage for additional agreements in the near future. When announcing the creation of the Royal Commission on Aboriginal Peoples in 1991, the federal government also declared an intention to "fast-track" native land claims, setting the target date for completion as A.D. 2000.

SPECIFIC CLAIMS

Specific claims stem from the government's obligations in law to aboriginal people. They generally involve claims for fulfillment of treaty provisions or relate to the management of Indian lands and assets under the Indian Act.

A good example of specific claims is the "cut-off lands" issue in British Columbia. Reserve allocations had caused tension between the federal and provincial governments, with the province attempting to restrict the size of reserves. A federal-provincial commission was established in 1912 to make final decisions on all reserve lands. Their 1916 report confirmed the existing reserves in most cases, but it also added some new reserve land while cutting off other land, generally because of its agricultural value, from twenty-two bands. This was a unilateral action by the commission, removing lands earlier assigned through negotiations. Settlements of this historic grievance began in 1984, when the Penticton band received some of the land they lost in 1916, plus $14 million for lands that could not be returned.

Other claims involve allegations of mismanagement. For example, it is alleged that in 1901 several hundred Assiniboine were forced off two reserves in Saskatchewan and settled among the Cree of the White Bear reserve so government officials could make a real estate profit. A settlement of $19 million was announced for this grievance. In another example, the Ojibwa of the Kettle Point reserve near Sarnia accepted $2.4 million in 1980 as compensation for reserve land surrendered for a military camp at below-market prices. Similarly, the Supreme Court of Canada in 1985 awarded the Musqueam band in Vancouver $10 million in compensation for government mismanagement in leasing reserve lands at unrealistically low rates.

ECONOMIC CONDITIONS

> Without a great improvement in our economic development, self-government is a meaningless phrase. (Chief Gabriel Gopher, North Battleford District Chiefs, to the Task Force on Indian Economic Development, 1985)

On-reserve economic development is hindered by the isolated nature of most reserves, their generally small size and their limited resources. Not all, however, are isolated; First Nations such as Squamish in Vancouver and Kahnawake in Montreal hold extremely valuable real estate.

The poor economy of most reserves is reflected in the state of their housing. A 1985 evaluation of reserve housing indicated that conditions in general remain poor (particularly in Saskatchewan, Manitoba and Ontario, as well as all rural and remote areas). Almost half of the housing failed to meet basic physical standards, and more than one-third was seriously overcrowded or lacked basic amenities such as running water. Federal statistics for 1993 show that most reserve housing had running water and sewage disposal, yet over half of dwellings required replacement or extensive renovation. Inadequate and overcrowded housing subjects the occupants to greater risk of disease and fire, and inhibits the children's academic performance in school.

Health problems also reflect poor economic conditions. Despite progress in recent decades, native life expectancy is still below the national average. The infant mortality rate is dropping, but is still well above national levels. Deaths by violence and accidents, often related to alcohol abuse, occur at about three times the national average. Suicide rates are extremely high for native teenagers and young adults. Although the near-epidemic levels of tuberculosis once found among Indians and Inuit have greatly declined, chronic diseases such as tuberculosis and diabetes remain serious problems in aboriginal communities. Improvements in native health and lowered infant mortality have contributed to rapidly growing native populations, putting increased economic pressures on available lands and resources.

The great concern for many First Nations is to initiate developments that will provide employment for their members. Native businesses have sprung up on reserves across the country. Some fortunate bands with oil and gas revenues or valuable real estate have been particularly successful. For isolated reserves with few resources, federal assistance may be the only source of income.

Native economic development boasts many successes. In Alberta, the Samson Cree Nation owns and operates a federally chartered trust company, Peace Hills Trust, with several branches. Similarly, the oil-rich Sawridge band has a chain of hotels, including ones at Slave Lake and Jasper, as well as other business enterprises. In British Columbia, the Kwagiulth at Cape Mudge have constructed a luxury lodge based on traditional longhouse design. Tourism provides employment for many native people across the country, who run motels, campgrounds and museums; act as guides for hunting, fishing or sightseeing expeditions; and operate shops which sell native arts and handicrafts. Several aboriginal communities, such as the Cree at The Pas in Manitoba, have opened shopping malls on their reserves. Band-owned cooperatives run logging, fishing and other operations. Where land claims settlements have provided an adequate economic base, as among the Cree and Inuit of northern Quebec and the western Arctic, native development corporations manage a wide range of commercial enterprises and real estate investments. Aboriginal entrepreneurs have become major participants in the economy of many parts of Canada.

Leasing of reserve lands provides income for many First Nations. On-reserve industries also provide opportunities for native employment. The Kamloops band of British Columbia and the Chippewas of Rama First Nation of southern Ontario, among others, have created industrial parks on their reserves, yielding both income from the lease and ongoing employment for band members.

As reserve communities seek new sources of income and employment, gambling has become a very tempting option. On-reserve casinos and high-stakes bingo parlours, operating tax-free and outside of provincial laws, generate considerable profits from the primarily non-aboriginal clientele. Although gambling is generally under control of the provincial governments, various First Nations maintain that provincial jurisdiction does not extend to their reserves. The militant Mohawk communities in Quebec were the first to encourage large-scale gambling, but other groups soon seized the opportunity as well. Roseau River in Manitoba and White Bear in Saskatchewan are two of a number of bands that opened casinos on their reserves. Both were subjected to RCMP raids to shut down the gambling, but the jurisdictional issue remains unresolved. Meanwhile, various First Nations across the country are considering the possibility of developing their own on-reserve gambling facilities.

Economic opportunities are far fewer for Métis and non-status Indians. Only on the few Métis settlements in Alberta do the Métis have a land base, where they are involved in farming, ranching and logging. Although federal statistics are lacking, poverty and high unemployment rates characterize many Métis communities.

In general, many reserves lack adequate housing and a viable economic base. Increasing numbers place greater pressure on available resources. High rates of unemployment are common, particularly for the more isolated reserves. Under such conditions an increasing number of Indians choose to leave their home communities and attempt to find a new life in the city.

URBANIZATION

Over 40 percent of status Indians in Canada normally reside off-reserve, a figure nearly double that of two decades ago. Bill C-31 has contributed to this growth, as it allowed the registration of large numbers of people who had never lived in reserve communities. The figures are highest for Ontario, Saskatchewan and British Columbia, where almost half of registered Indians do not live on reserves. Most off-reserve migration has been to urban centres. Métis, non-status Indians and, to a much lesser extent, Inuit are also arriving in the cities in unprecedented numbers.

The motives for urbanization vary; however, the search for employment and better economic conditions is consistently most important. One survey of urban Indians in British Columbia listed the four main reasons for leaving their reserves as: greater employment opportunities, general preference for life off the reserve, lack of housing on reserve and desire to attend school or gain greater educational opportunities for their children.

The native influx has created social problems. Although some urban natives pursue successful careers and adjust well to city life, for others, lacking education or specialized job training, the search for employment is in vain. The "good life" visualized when they left their reserves remains elusive, and their poverty restricts their opportunities. They remain at the economic margins of urban life, ghettoized in run-down low-rent areas of the city and dependent upon government assistance. Alcohol abuse is a problem for many, often leading to clashes with the law. Several Canadian cities have instituted native liaison programs, in which aboriginal people are hired to mediate between police and other urban natives.

Although the federal government provides few services directly to Indians living off reserves, some programs are available. Most cities with substantial native populations also have native-run educational or cultural centres. Services provided include cultural awareness programs, job and housing referrals, drug and alcohol therapy, legal counseling and recreational activities.

In only a few decades aboriginal people have gone from the "invisible minority," largely tucked away out of sight on isolated reserves, to a highly visible population with a large urban component. This is particularly evident in western Canada. Of all major Canadian cities, Regina appears to have the highest native proportion, estimated at 15 to 20 percent of the total population. Larger centres such as Toronto and Vancouver have substantial native populations, representing a wide range of backgrounds and income levels.

ABORIGINAL PEOPLE AND THE CRIMINAL JUSTICE SYSTEM

Without understanding there cannot be justice. Without equality there can be no justice . . . Aboriginal people want a judicial system that recognizes the native way of life, our own values and beliefs, and not the white man's way of life. (Elijah Harper, speaking to the Manitoba Aboriginal Justice Inquiry)

The justice system thrives in this country, and the commodity that provides the fuel is Indian people. (Chief Louis Stevenson, Peguis band, to the Manitoba Aboriginal Justice Inquiry)

Aboriginal people are over-represented at every stage of the Canadian criminal justice system. They are incarcerated in provincial, territorial and federal institutions at rates greatly above their proportion of the general population. Aboriginal inmates are particularly over-represented in the prairie provinces and in the north. Particularly alarming are the statistics for aboriginal women, who are many times more likely than non-aboriginal women to serve jail sentences. In general, the dismal picture provided by these facts suggests that the criminal justice system has been inadequate to meet the needs of aboriginal Canadians.

The reasons behind native over-representation in the criminal justice system are complex and have been the subject of numerous studies. Poverty plays a role for many, as defaults on court-ordered fines are a major cause of jail sentences. Alcohol and drug abuse have led many natives afoul of the law. A variety of destructive behaviours, including criminal offenses, family violence and suicide, stem from the disempowerment and loss of self-esteem that are the heritage of colonialism. Many aboriginal people view the courts as a foreign system imposed upon them, perpetuating that colo-

327

nialism. This perception is reinforced by the lack of aboriginal people employed throughout the justice system and by the general failure of the courts to acknowledge and respect cultural differences.

Several legal inquiries have recently examined how the justice system has failed aboriginal people. In Nova Scotia, a Royal Commission examined the case of Donald Marshall, Jr., a young Mi'kmaq man who spent eleven years in prison after being wrongly convicted of murder. In its 1989 report, the Commission found that the criminal justice system had failed Donald Marshall at every point and the fact that he was an aboriginal person had contributed to the miscarriage of justice. In Alberta, the Task Force on the Criminal Justice System and Its Impact on the Indian and Métis People released its report in 1991. Similarly, twin task forces on Indian Justice and Métis Justice in Saskatchewan reported in early 1992. Particularly far-reaching in its recommendations was the Aboriginal Justice Inquiry in Manitoba. This three-year inquiry was stimulated by the deaths of two aboriginal people, one whose murder had been improperly investigated by police and one who had been shot by police in an alleged case of mistaken identity. Unlike the other reports, which called for more aboriginal police and other justice system employees and for more cross-cultural awareness in the courtroom, the Manitoba report of 1991 concluded that such incremental improvements would be insufficient. Instead, it stated that the justice system had failed the aboriginal people of Manitoba on such a massive scale that the establishment of a separate aboriginal justice system was the only appropriate response.

Aboriginal police forces are being established by First Nations across the country. The federal government's Indian Policing Policy provides for two options: a special contingent of First Nations officers within an existing police force or a First Nations police service organized on a band, tribal or regional basis. Independent aboriginal police forces include the Dakota-Ojibwa Police Service in Manitoba, the Louis Bull Police Service in Alberta, and the Stl'Atl'Imx Tribal Police Service at Lillooet in British Columbia. Canada's only aboriginal justice academy for training native police officers is the First Nations Tribal Justice Institute in Mission, British Columbia.

Cultural differences are also evident in aboriginal approaches to sentencing offenders. The emphasis is on healing and restoration of harmony to the community, rather than on punishment and institutionalization of the offender. Sentencing circles are being used in some First Nations communities, bringing together the offender, the victim, their families, elders and other community members in face-to-face discussion. The elders play a vital role in guidance and spiritual support. Sentencing circles have also been adopted by Métis communities in northern Saskatchewan, as a result of recommendations in the Métis Justice Task Force. In addition, tribal courts with on-reserve jurisdiction are operated by a few First Nations, such as the Kahnawake and Akwesasne Mohawk.

In prisons, the use of traditional healing practices is becoming more widespread. Sweat lodges, ceremonies and spiritual guidance from native elders can provide a renewed sense of identity and the strength to change life patterns. A few First Nations run their own corrections facilities. The Blood Tribe in Alberta, for example, through an agreement with the provincial government, operates the Kainai Corrections Centre for inmates in the final months of their sentences. Blood elders conduct spiritual ceremonies and counsel inmates in preparation for their return to the community.

Many First Nations, as recognized by the inquiry in Manitoba, view their own justice systems as part of their inherent right to self-government. As self-government negotiations proceed, additional aboriginal police forces and other elements of the justice system will emerge. These will provide services which are culturally responsive to the needs of the community, rather than continuing to impose external dictates upon them.

EDUCATION

Education plays a key role in native plans for the future, serving to enhance traditional languages and cultures as well as to provide the skills and knowledge essential for future economic success. Many see control of their own education systems as an essential battle in the fight for aboriginal self-government.

After confederation, federal responsibility for Indian education was largely met through the establishment of residential schools run by religious orders. In the colonialist spirit of Indian administration at the time, the schools were vehicles for assimilation, where students were forced to adopt the ways of the dominant society. Children were severely punished for speaking their own languages or practicing native customs. Contact with their families was discouraged. Much of their school time was spent in religious indoctrination and in vocational training, with a corresponding neglect of academic subjects. School routines were highly regimented, with strappings and beatings to enforce discipline. Ojibwa author Basil Johnston, recalling his childhood experiences at the residential school in Spanish (near Sudbury), Ontario, writes that the very name of the town "inspired dread . . . It was a word synonymous with residential school, penitentiary, reformatory, exile, dungeon, whippings, kicks, slaps, all rolled into one." Native students tended to react to this alien, harsh and inadequate system by leaving it as soon as possible. The failure of the residential schools to provide adequate education was finally acknowledged by the gradual closing down of the system. By the 1960s most Indian students were attending integrated provincial schools, although the last residential schools were not closed until the late 1980s.

The residential schools have left a bitter legacy. The loss of language

329

which afflicts many native communities is at least partially attributable to residential school policies. Students were alienated from their own cultures, contributing to the loss of identity experienced by so many aboriginal people. The removal of children from their parents led to a loss of parenting skills in subsequent generations. Accounts of physical and sexual abuse, apparently rampant at some institutions, have begun to emerge. As the abused often later becomes the abuser, these residential school experiences have contributed to the social problems facing many aboriginal communities. Alcohol abuse, suicide and family violence were linked to childhood experiences in the residential schools by participants in the health and social issues hearings of the Royal Commission on Aboriginal Peoples in 1993.

By the 1950s federal policy favoured integration into the provincial school system. Wherever Indian or Inuit children could attend the regular public schools, the federal government entered into a financial agreement with the provincial school boards. Attendance at such schools ensured native students the same quality of education as was offered to other children in the province. This policy also promoted assimilation, however, as the education program was geared to the white middle-class norm, with little or no recognition of aboriginal cultures.

A more recent policy shift finally enabled aboriginal people to assert control over the education of their children. Particularly important was a 1972 proposal of the National Indian Brotherhood, the predecessor of the Assembly of First Nations, entitled "Indian Control of Indian Education," which was adopted as federal policy in the following year. It called for increased local community control of education, more native teachers, the development of curricula relevant to aboriginal peoples today and increased instruction in native languages and culture. On-reserve federally funded schools run by individual First Nations have increased dramatically, from 53 in 1975/76 to 353 in 1992/93. More than three-quarters of Canada's Indian bands now administer all or part of their education programs. Band-run schools teach the provincial curriculum but add culturally relevant subjects such as native language instruction. Some First Nations have taken this well beyond simply offering courses in their language; the Nisga'a of British Columbia operate a school program stressing a bilingual and bicultural approach while the Kahnawake Survival School offers an immersion program in the Mohawk language. By the 1992/93 school year, 49 percent of on-reserve Indian children in Canada were attending band-operated schools, as opposed to 46 percent in the provincial schools and 5 percent in federal schools.

The policy of aboriginal control over education has had considerable success. The number of on-reserve Indian students remaining in school until grade 12 has increased dramatically, from about 3 percent in 1960/61 to over 60 percent in 1992/93. Native teachers and administrators are becoming increasingly numerous. Three aboriginal groups, the Nisga'a of

British Columbia and the Cree and Inuit of northern Quebec, operate their own school boards. In addition, a 1990 agreement with the Assembly of Manitoba Chiefs allows First Nations in that province to administer their own education system on reserves. Many urban centres with large native populations have established alternative schools for native children. The large gap in educational attainment that once existed between natives and non-natives is closing.

At the post-secondary level, rapidly increasing numbers of native students are attending universities, colleges and institutes. In 1992/93 nearly 22,000 status Indians attended post-secondary institutions, a figure nearly double that of only seven years earlier. Native participation rates in higher education are not greatly below the Canadian average, which is also increasing. Status Indians and Inuit are eligible for federal funding to cover tuition and living costs, although a spending "cap" was imposed by the federal government in 1989. This limit, which sparked demonstrations by native students across the country, means that not all qualified candidates are able to attend. Critics of this policy point to the high levels of unemployment among aboriginal people and note that education is a better investment than welfare.

Many universities have established Native Studies programs, and separate native post-secondary institutions have emerged. The Saskatchewan Indian Federated College, administratively separate from but academically linked with the University of Regina, is jointly funded by the provincial and federal governments. Also in Regina is the Gabriel Dumont Institute, an aboriginal college and cultural centre active in Métis heritage. Although not directly funded by Indian Affairs since it does not primarily serve status Indians, it does receive some federal funding for specific programs. Federally funded institutions in Alberta include Blue Quills Native Education Centre (affiliated with Athabasca University) in the north and Old Sun College (affiliated with Mount Royal College and the University of Calgary) on the Siksika Nation reserve. Similarly, the Secwepemc Cultural Education Society in British Columbia offers university degrees at the Kamloops reserve through an agreement with Simon Fraser University. Young, articulate, university-educated leaders have emerged in many native communities.

ABORIGINAL SELF-GOVERNMENT AND THE CONSTITUTION

The principle is simple. Only Indian people can design systems for Indians. Anything other than that is assimilation. (Carrier-Sekani Tribal Council, to the Special Committee on Indian Self-Government, 1983)

Canada's Constitution, enacted with great fanfare on 17 April 1982, along with the negotiations which led up to it and the subsequent First Ministers conferences, greatly increased awareness of aboriginal rights and grievances. Many native leaders saw it as the vehicle to achieve their aspirations for a new role within Canada. Their battle was long and frustrating, and the benefits they have won fall far short of what they still hope to achieve.

In its original drafts the Constitution contained no specific references to aboriginal rights. Native demands for recognition of their unique place in Canadian society were accompanied by vigorous lobbying efforts. The most publicized was the "Constitutional Express," a train which left Vancouver in November 1980 and picked up more than a thousand people before arriving in Ottawa for demonstrations on Parliament Hill. In England, bemused British onlookers and foreign tourists were treated to the spectacle of Canadian Indians pounding drums outside the Houses of Parliament in London to protest repatriation of the constitution without recognition of aboriginal rights.

Native protests were rewarded when the federal government added a statement guaranteeing aboriginal rights to the proposed constitution. This brief mention, however, fell far short of satisfying native aspirations, and the protests continued. What natives received instead was a betrayal. When the federal government finally sat down at the bargaining table with the provinces, at a meeting which excluded natives, the section on aboriginal rights was dropped to placate provincial concerns. Native outrage and adverse publicity, however, forced reinstatement of the clause.

The brief but important statement on aboriginal rights is contained in Section 35 of the Constitution Act. It states: "The existing aboriginal and treaty rights of the aboriginal peoples of Canada are hereby recognized and affirmed." The word "existing," added due to objections raised by the premier of Alberta, creates a certain ambiguity. While treaty rights are relatively straightforward, few aboriginal rights could be conclusively demonstrated as "existing" in 1982. Native leaders strongly opposed this addition as an attempt to limit their rights. However, it could also be interpreted in a broader framework as constitutionally entrenching all rights, including an inherent right to self-government, never directly surrendered through treaty.

Two other sections touch upon native affairs. Section 25 ensures that aboriginal rights are not adversely affected by the Charter of Rights and Freedoms, specifically protecting any aboriginal rights recognized by the Royal Proclamation of 1763 or acquired through land claims settlements. Section 37 called for the federal and provincial governments to meet within one year, including on their agenda "constitutional matters that directly affect the aboriginal peoples of Canada" and inviting native leaders to participate. This was a recognition that the Constitution remained incomplete on aboriginal issues, that aboriginal and treaty rights had been entrenched but not yet defined.

The required First Ministers Conference was held in March of 1983. This marked the first time that native leaders fully participated in constitu tional debate. Yet the conference accomplished relatively little. Section 35 was amended to specify that "treaty rights" include rights obtained through land claims agreements and that aboriginal and treaty rights are guaranteed equally to men and women. Provisions were made for subsequent meetings, carrying through to 1987. No progress was made on the definition of aboriginal and treaty rights, nor on the broader native concerns for self-government.

A major breakthrough came with the 1983 release of *Indian Self-Government in Canada*, the report of the Special Committee on Indian Self-Government (usually referred to as the Penner Report, after its chairman). This all-party committee made several far-reaching recommendations. Particularly important was the call for the federal government to establish a new relationship with Indian First Nations, that an essential element of this relationship be recognition of Indian self-government, and that the right to self-government be entrenched in the Constitution. The Committee, dismissing the Indian Act as "antiquated" and "completely unacceptable as a blueprint for the future," recommended the phasing out of Indian Affairs programs. Federal grants and settlement of native land claims would be necessary to provide the required economic base. First Nations governments would have control over all Indian lands and resources and would have jurisdiction over many matters affecting their members. They would become a distinct third order of government within Canada.

The First Nations visualized by the Committee, whose mandate was restricted to status Indians, was clearly the bands or voluntary associations of bands (as in existing Tribal Councils). The Inuit could achieve self-government on a similar basis. Since they lack any collective land base for economic development, however, it is difficult to see how this model of self-government could be applied to Métis and non-status Indians, as well as those status Indians who live off-reserve.

Armed with the Penner Report, the federal government attempted to constitutionally entrench native self-government at the following First Ministers Conferences. Prime Minister Pierre Trudeau stated at the 1984 conference: "we are not here to consider whether there should be institutions of self-government, but how these institutions should be brought into being"; similarly, Inuit representative Zebedee Nungak declared that their goal was "to do some constructive damage to the status quo." Such optimism proved to be unwarranted. At the following meetings, in 1985 and 1987, the government of Prime Minister Brian Mulroney attempted to make the proposal acceptable to the provincial premiers. In the end, however, the talks collapsed in rancour and squabbling between the federal government, the provinces and leaders of the four major national native organizations. The federal proposal for recognition of an aboriginal right to self-government, without full definition of terms and costs, was unacceptable to the governments of British Columbia, Alberta, Saskatchewan and

Newfoundland. Constitutional reform on aboriginal issues appeared to be at an impasse.

Shortly after the failure of the final conference, Mulroney and the provincial premiers signed the Meech Lake Accord, recognizing Quebec as a "distinct society" in the constitution. Aboriginal leaders, while not hostile to Quebec's aspirations, were outraged that they had been denied similar status by the same provincial leaders. The rhetoric of "two founding nations" was highly offensive to First Nations people. They also distrusted the shift to greater provincial powers, which was another feature of the Accord. Ultimately, this agreement met defeat at the hands of an aboriginal politician, Elijah Harper, an Ojibwa-Cree from northern Manitoba and NDP member of the Manitoba legislature. By June 1990 the three years required for the provinces to approve the Accord had dwindled to a few days and procedural regulations required unanimous consent to bring it to a vote in the Manitoba legislature. Harper, in consultation with the Manitoba chiefs led by Phil Fontaine and Assembly of First Nations' leader Ovide Mercredi, also from Manitoba, defied personal and political threats in order to block the deal. Holding an eagle feather for spiritual strength, Harper's quiet repeated "no" effectively killed the Accord. Aboriginal people had demonstrated that they are a political force that cannot be ignored and that they will not be left out of constitutional reform.

Despite the failure of Meech Lake, constitutional issues continued to dominate the national agenda. Lengthy negotiations finally culminated in August 1992 with the Charlottetown Accord. The Canadian voter was to be asked to approve a constitutional package that dealt with such wide-sweeping issues as Quebec's status in Canada, Senate reform and aboriginal rights. A major feature of the proposals for aboriginal peoples was the recognition of the inherent right to self-government. Aboriginal governments would become one of three constitutionally recognized orders of government in Canada. Aboriginal people would also be guaranteed representation in the Senate. The federal government committed itself to consultation with First Nations in a treaty review process, interpreting the treaties in a broad and liberal manner. A separate agreement with the Métis, the Métis Nation Accord, would finally define and enumerate the Métis and place them with other aboriginal peoples under federal jurisdiction. Self-government negotiations would include the transfer of Crown lands to Métis corporations to provide a land base.

The Charlottetown Accord dealt with too many diverse and complex issues in one "take it or leave it" package to be acceptable to the Canadian public. Despite some impressive gains, it was also not supported by large numbers of aboriginal people. Ovide Mercredi, National Chief of the Assembly of First Nations, was instrumental in drafting the Accord and had campaigned tirelessly for its acceptance, yet could not deliver a solid backing of First Nations. Yvon Dumont, head of the Métis National Council,

Elijah Harper, the only aboriginal member of the Manitoba legislature, holds an eagle feather for spiritual strength as he quietly denies the unanimous consent required to pass the Meech Lake Accord, 1990. Wayne Glowacki/ Winnipeg Free Press.

championed the Accord as a major victory for Métis people, yet the Métis also were far from unanimous in their support. The Mohawk opposed the Accord because it did not recognize their sovereignty. The Native Women's Association of Canada, after failing to win a seat at the negotiating table, opposed the Accord as a continuation of male-dominated aboriginal politics. Mercredi's insistence on the protection of collective rights, which would allow First Nations to opt out of the Charter of Rights and Freedoms, was felt by many aboriginal women to violate their individual constitutional rights. Other First Nations felt that the process had been too rushed and that they were not yet ready to implement aboriginal governments. On 26 October 1992 the Charlottetown Accord was rejected in a national referendum. Voter turnout everywhere was low, including on reserves, where some First Nations refused to allow polling stations. The rejection by on-reserve voters was even greater than the national rate, and reached particular heights in Mercredi's home province of Manitoba.

Although the process of constitutional reform has faltered, constitutional change may not be necessary to accommodate aboriginal rights to self-government. Many people believe that Section 35 of the present constitution, guaranteeing the existing aboriginal and treaty rights of aboriginal peoples, includes an inherent right of self-government. First Nations and Métis organizations have urged the federal government to implement relevant sections of the Charlottetown Accord and Métis Nation Accord without constitutional amendment. The political will, however, is no longer present.

Aboriginal self-government can also be achieved through bilateral agreements between First Nations and the federal government. The Cree and Naskapi of northern Quebec have essentially achieved self-government through the terms of their land claims settlements, later set out in federal legislation as the Cree-Naskapi (of Quebec) Act in 1984. Other groups, such as the Yukon First Nations, the Gwich'in of the Northwest Territories and the Nisga'a of British Columbia, are in the process of negotiating self-government as part of land claims. The first to negotiate self-government as a separate issue was the Sechelt band of coastal British Columbia. Through the terms of the Sechelt Indian Band Self-Government Act (1986), the Sechelt received title to their reserve lands, the right to draft their own constitution and laws, and are no longer bound by the Indian Act. According to federal figures for mid-1993, one additional proposal was in final stages of drafting and fourteen others, representing forty-four bands, had reached the framework agreement stage. These include groups as diverse as the Kahnawake Mohawk outside Montreal, the Grassy Narrows Ojibwa near Kenora, the Cree and Dene bands of the Meadow Lake Tribal Council in northern Saskatchewan, the Siksika Nation in Alberta, and the Gitksan-Wet'suwet'en and Cape Mudge Kwagiulth in British Columbia.

Not all First Nations see the Sechelt agreement as a model to follow. Some native groups wish to remain under the Indian Act, seeking only greater control over their own affairs. Others have a concept of aboriginal rights which goes far beyond the essentially municipal model achieved by the Sechelt. The form of self-government desired might be very different for the Inuit, the Mohawk or the Haida, and self-government has to be seen as an evolving process, with no one definition.

Problems in providing an economic base plague most self-government plans. Many First Nations also reject the idea that their self-government jurisdiction would extend only to their reserve lands, and tie their self-government aspirations to settlement of land claims over their traditional territories. To quote one aboriginal view: "Self-government for Indian nations or self-government for Indian reserves? That's the question that comes first." (Leonard Andrew, band chief of Mount Currie, B.C., *Vancouver Sun*, 7 March 1984).

NATIVE CANADIANS FACE THE TWENTY-FIRST CENTURY

Who would have thought in 1969, when the federal government attempted to abolish special status for Indians, that less than a decade later natives would be negotiating land claims over large areas of Canada, and less than two decades later aboriginal leaders would be sitting with provincial premiers and the prime minister in televised debates over native self-government? Aboriginal issues, in the form of both negotiated settlements and violent confrontations, have been in the forefront of Canadian politics for the last several decades. Paternalistic attitudes of the past have shifted to recognition of aboriginal peoples' rights to shape their own future. Despite great progress, however, major social and economic problems still trouble many aboriginal communities.

In an attempt to clarify native issues and seek new directions, the federal government announced in 1991 the creation of the Royal Commission on Aboriginal Peoples. The Commission, which held its first hearings in 1992, is co-chaired by Georges Erasmus, a Dene and the former head of the Assembly of First Nations, and Quebec Appeal Court Justice René Dussault. Five additional Commissioners provide a balance of males and females, Anglophones and Francophones, and Indian, Inuit, Métis and Euro-Canadian ethnicity. The Commission's mandate is very broad, including social and economic issues, education, health, aboriginal justice, comprehensive and specific claims, treaties, the Indian Act and the constitution. It will also look specifically at the constitutional and legal position of Métis and off-reserve Indians, as well as the special difficulties of northern natives. The Commission has already released reports from National Round Tables on several specific topics, but final recommendations have not been completed as of this writing.

Responsibility for administering their own affairs is being transferred gradually to First Nations. Many participate in an Alternate Funding program with the Department of Indian Affairs and Northern Development, whereby they manage their own federal program funds. As of 1993, 139 such agreements, representing 244 bands, had been struck. Self-administration, however, is a far cry from self-determination, which involves the ability to plan and implement their own programs to meet their needs. In 1994, Indian Affairs Minister Ron Irwin announced his intention to gradually dismantle the federal bureaucracy and allow aboriginal peoples, beginning with those in Manitoba, to run their own affairs. This is a goal which many aboriginal leaders hope to achieve in the next few decades.

In many areas natives are also taking charge of resolving their social problems. Some communities have instituted "healing circles," allowing people to confront publicly such social problems as family violence and child abuse. A few have established more permanent "healing lodges," such as Poundmaker's Lodge, a native-run treatment centre on the outskirts of Edmonton. Alcohol has been the bane of many native communities, but determined action by some groups has put an end to abuse. One example is the Shuswap of Alkali Lake, British Columbia. After decades of apathy and child neglect caused by heavy drinking, a movement to sobriety led by the chief and his wife gradually attracted converts. Bootleggers were charged under the Indian Act, and government assistance cheques were replaced with vouchers for food and clothing so the money could not be spent on liquor. Eventually almost the entire band stopped drinking. People began to improve their economic lot, building new houses and organizing cooperatives for logging and agriculture. Attention turned to reviving their lan-

In June 1993 the Native Council of Canada (now the Congress of Aboriginal Peoples) organized a caravan across Canada to the "Gathering of Aboriginal Peoples" on Parliament Hill. The Gathering protested cut-backs in federal funding for housing, education and other programs, and the lack of government attention to off-reserve and non-status natives. The United Aboriginal Youth Council delegation, with National Youth Representative Melanie Jackson in front, is shown here. Photo by L. Weissmann, with approval by United Aboriginal Youth Council.

guage and culture through their school program. Other bands seek to emulate their success; a 1985 conference on social issues at Alkali Lake attracted more than a thousand people, and a native-made film on their story has been distributed to many reserves across the country.

In the Canadian north, the emphasis is on maintaining a traditional way of life. Hunting, fishing and trapping still provide a viable economic base, and native leaders seek to ensure that this continues. The preservation of native ties to the land and its traditional resources is an essential feature of modern land claims agreements. Native leaders see this not simply as protecting an economic resource but as the fundamental basis of their culture. In a similar vein, natives on both the east and west coasts have claimed that harvesting the rich runs of salmon and other fish is a fundamental part of their culture and an unextinguished aboriginal right.

Aboriginal people have become increasingly involved in Canadian politics. Native politicians now represent their people in Parliament and in provincial and territorial legislatures. James Gladstone, a Blood, became Canada's first native senator in 1958. At present, three aboriginal people sit in the Senate: Charlie Watt, an Inuk from northern Quebec; Len Marchand, an Okanagan Indian from British Columbia; and Walter Twinn, chief of the Sawridge band in Alberta. Ralph Steinhauer, a Stoney, became lieutenant-governor of Alberta in 1974, the first native to hold such an office. In 1993, Yvon Dumont, a descendant of the Red River Métis and former head of both the Manitoba Métis Federation and the Métis National Council, became lieutenant-governor of Manitoba.

Native people are making contributions to nearly every aspect of Canadian life. In the arts, there are native painters, sculptors, actors, singers, authors, poets and film-makers. The three major native art traditions (Northwest Coast, Woodlands and Inuit) are thoroughly part of Canadian identity, producing artists of international stature. Other native artists are using Western art styles as vehicles for social commentary on native experiences. Douglas Cardinal, an Alberta Métis, is the architect who designed the majestic new Canadian Museum of Civilization in Hull. Buffy Sainte-Marie, a Cree singer and songwriter from Saskatchewan, has achieved widespread success in the entertainment industry. Kashtin, an Innu rock band, has brought an aboriginal voice into contemporary Canadian music. Other natives have distinguished themselves in sports; for example, Alwyn Morris, a Mohawk canoeist from Kahnawake, won a gold medal for Canada in the 1984 Olympics. Many young natives now entering university have their sights set on the professions, and their contributions will increasingly enrich Canadian life.

Canada's historic policy of assimilation of aboriginal peoples, as seen in the residential schools, the Indian Act and an administrative bureaucracy which removed all decision-making powers from the people affected, was a dismal failure. Despite all obstacles, aboriginal people have resisted loss of their distinct identities. The colonialism of the past has taken its toll, however, and aboriginal people are now attempting to heal their damaged societies and restore their languages and cultures. Taking control is a vital step in decolonization, and many aboriginal groups are now asserting their rights to self-determination.

Despite the debacle of constitutional reforms, Canada can forge a new relationship with aboriginal peoples. This could come largely through implementation of the agreements reached with First Nations and Métis as part of the failed 1992 constitutional talks. Self-government as enshrined in these agreements is an inherent or already existing right, not one granted by government. Separate mechanisms would also have to be developed to meet the self-government aspirations of urban Indians and Métis. The diversity within aboriginal groups would have to be recognized and respected, requiring flexibility in any agreements. With public acceptance and political will a suitable relationship can yet be reached with aboriginal peoples in Canada, so that they can chart their own paths to the future.

SOURCES

Chapter One *Introduction: Canada's First Nations*

The classic ethnographic study of Canadian First Nations, although now badly out of date, is that of Jenness (1977, originally published in 1932). Miller (1989) and Dickason (1992) provide historical overviews. Brizinski (1993) has developed an introductory text for Native Studies. Articles on native groups across Canada appear in books of readings edited by Morrison and Wilson (1986), Fisher and Coates (1988) and Cox (1988). A popular account of precontact life as seen through archaeology is given in McGhee (1989).

Swayze (1960) reviews the lives of three prominent Canadian anthropologists: Diamond Jenness, Marius Barbeau and W.J. Wintemberg. Dyck and Waldram (1993) examine the role of the anthropologist in public policy involving aboriginal peoples.

Brizinski, Peggy 1993. *Knots in a String: An Introduction to Native Studies in Canada* (2nd ed). University Extension Press, University of Saskatchewan, Saskatoon.

Campbell, Lyle and Marianne Mithun (eds.) 1979. *The Languages of Native America: Historical and Comparative Assessment*. University of Texas Press, Austin.

Cox, Bruce A. (ed.) 1988. *Native People, Native Lands: Canadian Indians, Inuit and Métis*. Carleton University Press, Ottawa.

Dewdney, Selwyn and Franklin Arbuckle 1975. *They Shared to Survive: The Native Peoples of Canada*. Macmillan, Toronto.

Dickason, Olive P. 1992. *Canada's First Nations: A History of Founding Peoples from Earliest Times*. McClelland & Stewart, Toronto.

Dyck, Noel and James B. Waldram (eds.) 1993. *Anthropology, Public Policy and Native Peoples in Canada*. McGill-Queen's University Press, Montreal and Kingston.

Fisher, Robin and Kenneth Coates (eds.) 1988. *Out of the Background: Readings on Canadian Native History*. Copp Clark Pitman, Toronto.

Foster, Michael K. 1982. Canada's first languages. *Language and Society* 7:7-16.

Glenbow Foundation 1987. *The Spirit Sings: Artistic Traditions of Canada's First Peoples*. McClelland & Stewart and Glenbow Foundation, Toronto and Calgary.

Jenness, Diamond 1977. *The Indians of Canada* (7th ed.). University of Toronto Press, Toronto.

Kehoe, Alice B. 1981. *North American Indians: A Comprehensive Account*. Prentice-Hall, Englewood Cliffs, NJ.

Leechman, Douglas 1957. *Native Tribes of Canada*. Gage, Toronto.

McGhee, Robert 1989. *Ancient Canada*. Canadian Museum of Civilization, Ottawa.

Miller, J.R. 1989. *Skyscrapers Hide the Heavens: A History of Indian-White Relations in Canada*. University of Toronto Press.

Morrison, R. Bruce and C. Roderick Wilson (eds.) 1986. *Native Peoples: The Canadian Experience.* McClelland & Stewart, Toronto.
Price, John 1979. *Indians of Canada: Cultural Dynamics.* Prentice-Hall, Scarborough, ON.
Rohner, Ronald P. (ed.) 1969. *The Ethnography of Franz Boas.* University of Chicago Press, Chicago.
Swayze, Nansi 1960. *The Man Hunters: Famous Canadian Anthropologists.* Clarke, Irwin, Toronto.

Chapter Two *The Earliest Arrivals*

Edited volumes of papers on the initial arrival in North America are those of Bryan (1978) and Shutler (1983). Fagan (1987) provides a full-length popular account of the peopling of the Americas, while Meltzer (1993) presents a recent scholarly review. Also recommended is the article by Fladmark (1979) assessing possible migration routes into North America.

Adovasio, J. M. and R. C. Carlisle 1984. An Indian hunters' camp for 20,000 years. *Scientific American* 250(5):130-136.
Adovasio, J. M., J. D. Gunn, J. Donahue and R. Stuckenrath 1978. Meadowcroft Rockshelter, 1977: An overview. *American Antiquity* 43(4):632-651.
Bonnichsen, Robson and K. L. Turnmire (eds.) 1991. *Clovis: Origins and Adaptations.* Center for the Study of the First Americans, Oregon State University, Corvallis, OR.
Bryan, Alan L. (ed.) 1978. *Early Man in America from a Circum-Pacific Perspective.* Occasional Paper no. 1 of the Department of Anthropology, University of Alberta, Edmonton.
Buchner, A.P. 1981. *Sinnock: A Paleolithic Camp and Kill Site in Manitoba.* Papers in Manitoba Archaeology, Historic Resources Branch, Department of Cultural Affairs and Historical Resources, Winnipeg.
Carlisle, R. C. (ed.) 1988. *Americans Before Columbus: Ice–Age Origins.* University of Pittsburgh Ethnology Monographs 12.
Cinq-Mars, J. 1979. Bluefish Cave I: A late Pleistocene eastern Beringian cave deposit in the northern Yukon. *Canadian Journal of Archaeology* 3:1-32.
Fagan, Brian M. 1987. *The Great Journey: The Peopling of Ancient America.* Thames and Hudson, London.
Fladmark, Knut R. 1979. Routes: Alternate migration corridors for early man in North America. *American Antiquity* 44(1):55-69.
Fladmark, Knut R. 1981. Paleo-Indian artifacts from the Peace River district. In *Fragments of the Past: British Columbia Archaeology in the 1970s* [Special Issue, *BC Studies* 48], ed. K. R. Fladmark, pp. 124–135.
Fladmark, Knut R., Jonathan C. Driver, and Diana Alexander 1988. The Paleoindian component at Charlie Lake Cave (HbRf 39), British Columbia. *American Antiquity* 53(2):371-384.
Forbis, Richard G. 1968. Fletcher: A Paleo-Indian site in Alberta. *American Antiquity* 33(1):1-10.
Fox, W.A. 1975. The PaleoIndian Lakehead Complex. In *Archaeological Research Report no. 6*, pp. 28–49. Historical Planning and Research Branch, Ontario Ministry of Culture and Recreation, Toronto.
Fox, W.A. 1980. The Lakehead Complex: new insights. In *Collected Archaeological Papers*, ed. D. S. Melvin, pp. 117–151. Archaeological Research Report no. 13, Historical Planning and Research Branch, Ontario Ministry of Culture and Recreation, Toronto.
Gramly, Richard M. 1982. *The Vail Site: A Paleo-Indian Encampment in Maine.* Bulletin of the Buffalo Society of Natural Sciences, Buffalo, NY.
Greenberg, Joseph H. 1987. *Language in the Americas.* Stanford University Press, Stanford, CA.
Greenberg, Joseph H. and Merritt Ruhlen 1992. Linguistic origin of Native Americans. *Scientific American* (Nov.): 94-99.
Greenberg, Joseph H., Christy G. Turner II and Stephen L. Zegura 1986. The settlement of the Americas: A comparison of the linguistic, dental, and genetic evidence. *Current Anthropology* 27:477-497.
Gryba, Eugene M. 1983. *Sibbald Creek: 11,000 Years of Human Use of the Alberta Foothills.* Archaeological Survey of Alberta Occasional Paper no. 22, Edmonton.
Gryba, Eugene M. 1985. Evidence of the fluted point tradition in Alberta. In *Contributions to Plains Prehistory*, ed. D. Burley, pp. 22–38. Archaeological Survey of Alberta Occasional Paper no. 26, Edmonton.
Haynes, C. Vance, Jr. 1964. Fluted projectile points: Their age and dispersion. *Science* 145:1408-1413.

Haynes, C. Vance, Jr. 1966. Elephant hunting in North America. *Scientific American* 214(6):104-1

Haynes, C. Vance, Jr. 1969. The earliest Americans. *Science* 166:709-715.

Hoffecker, J. F., W. R. Powers and T. Goebel 1993. The colonization of Beringia and the peopling of the New World. *Science* 259:46-53.

Hopkins, David M. (ed.) 1967. *The Bering Land Bridge.* Stanford University Press. Stanford, CA.

Hopkins, David M., John V. Matthews Jr., Charles E. Schweger and Steven B. Young (eds.) 1982. *Paleoecology of Beringia.* Academic Press, New York.

Julig, P.J. 1984. Cummins Paleo-Indian site and its paleoenvironment, Thunder Bay, Canada. *Archaeology of Eastern North America* 12:192-209.

Kehoe, Thomas F. 1966. The distribution and implications of fluted points in Saskatchewan. *American Antiquity* 31(4):530-539.

MacDonald, George F. 1968. *Debert: A Paleo-Indian Site in Central Nova Scotia.* Anthropological Paper no. 16, National Museums of Canada, Ottawa.

McGhee, Robert 1989. Who owns prehistory? The Bering Land Bridge Dilemma. *Canadian Journal of Archaeology* 13:13-20

Martin, Paul S. 1973. The discovery of America. *Science* 179:969-974.

Martin, P. S. and H. E. Wright, Jr. (eds.) 1967. *Pleistocene Extinctions: The Search for a Cause.* Yale University Press, New Haven, CT.

Meltzer, David R. 1993. Pleistocene peopling of the Americas. *Evolutionary Anthropology* 1(5):157-169.

Morlan, Richard E. 1977. Fluted point makers and the extinction of the arctic-steppe biome in eastern Beringia. *Canadian Journal of Archaeology* 1:95-108.

Morlan, Richard E. 1980. *Taphonomy and Archaeology in the Upper Pleistocene of the Northern Yukon Territory: A Glimpse of the Peopling of the New World.* National Museum of Man Mercury Series, Archaeological Survey of Canada Paper no. 94, Ottawa.

Nelson, D. E., R. E. Morlan, J. S. Vogel, J. R. Southon and C. R. Harington 1986. New dates on northern Yukon artifacts: Holocene, not Upper Pleistocene. *Science* 232:749-751.

Pettipas, Leo 1985. Recent developments in Paleo-Indian archaeology in Manitoba. In *Contributions to Plains Prehistory,* ed. D. Burley, pp. 39–63. Archaeological Survey of Alberta Occasional Paper no. 26, Edmonton.

Roberts, Arthur 1984. Paleo Indian on the north shore of Lake Ontario. *Archaeology of Eastern North America* 12:248-265.

Roberts, Arthur 1985. *Preceramic Occupations along the North Shore of Lake Ontario.* National Museum of Man Mercury Series, Archaeological Survey of Canada Paper no. 132, Ottawa.

Rutter, N. W. and C.E. Schweger (eds.) 1980. *The Ice-Free Corridor and Peopling of the New World* [Special Issue, *Canadian Journal of Anthropology* 1(1)].

Shutler, Richard, Jr. (ed.) 1983. *Early Man in the New World.* Sage Publications, Beverly Hills and London.

Stork, P. L. 1979. *A Report on the Banting and Hussey Sites: Two Paleo-Indian Campsites in Simcoe County, Southern Ontario.* National Museum of Man Mercury Series, Archaeological Survey of Canada Paper no. 93, Ottawa.

Stork, Peter L. 1982. Paleo-Indian settlement patterns associated with the strandline of Glacial Lake Algonquin in southcentral Ontario. *Canadian Journal of Archaeology* 6:1-31.

Stork, Peter 1984. Glacial Lake Algonquin and early Paleo-Indian settlement patterns in southcentral Ontario. *Archaeology of Eastern North America* 12:286-298.

Szathmary, Emöke J. E. 1993. Genetics of aboriginal North Americans. *Evolutionary Anthropology* 1:202-220.

Szathmary, Emöke J.E. 1993. MtDNA and the peopling of the Americas. *American Journal of Human Genetics* 53:793-799.

Chapter Three *The Atlantic Provinces*

Atlantic Canada prior to contact is discussed in two books by Tuck: *Newfoundland and Labrador Prehistory* (1976) and *Maritime Provinces Prehistory* (1984).

Most of our information on traditional Mi'kmaq life comes from the seventeenth-century accounts. Particularly important are those of Biard in *The Jesuit Relations* (Thwaites 1896-1901), Lescarbot (1907-14; originally published 1609), Denys (1908; originally published 1672) and LeClercq (1910; originally published 1691). The major published ethnography is by Wallis and Wallis (1955), who combine the ethnohistoric information with ethnographic data gathered in 1911. For the Beothuk, the classic source is Howley (1915), which compiles all early documentation on this group. Summary articles on the Beothuk, Mi'kmaq and Maliseet in the *Handbook of North American Indians*, vol. 15, *Northeast* (Trigger 1978) are also useful.

Bailey, Alfred G. 1969. *The Conflict of European and Eastern Algonkian Cultures, 1504-1700* (2nd ed.). University of Toronto Press, Toronto.

Bartels, Dennis 1991. Newfoundland Micmac claims to land and "status." *Native Studies Review* 7(2):43-51.

Bock, Philip K. 1966. *The Micmac Indians of Restigouche: History and Contemporary Description*. National Museum of Canada Bulletin no. 213, Ottawa.

Carignan, Paul 1975. *The Beaches: A Multi-Component Habitation Site in Bonavista Bay*. National Museum of Man Mercury Series, Archaeological Survey of Canada Paper no. 39, Ottawa.

Carignan, Paul 1977. *Beothuck Archaeology in Bonavista Bay*. National Museum of Man Mercury Series, Archaeological Survey of Canada Paper no. 69, Ottawa.

Davis, Stephen 1978. *Teacher's Cove: A Prehistoric Site on Passamaquoddy Bay*. New Brunswick Archaeology Series 1, no. 1, Fredericton.

Davis, Stephen 1991. *Micmac*. Four East Publications, Tantallon, NS.

Denys, Nicolas 1908. *The Description and Natural History of the Coasts of North America (Acadia)*. Champlain Society, Toronto.

Dickason, Olive P. 1976. *Louisbourg and the Indians: A Study in Imperial Race Relations, 1713-1760*. History and Archaeology 6, Parks Canada, Ottawa.

Fitzhugh, Willaim W. 1972. *Environmental Archaeology and Cultural Systems in Hamilton Inlet, Labrador*. Smithsonian Contributions to Anthropology no. 16, Smithsonian Institution Press, Washington, DC

Fitzhugh, William W. 1975. A Maritime Archaic sequence from Hamilton Inlet, Labrador. *Arctic Anthropology* 12(2): 117-138.

Fitzhugh, William W. 1978. Maritime Archaic cultures of the central and northern Labrador coast. *Arctic Anthropology* 15(2): 61-95.

Fitzhugh, Williaim W. 1978. Winter Cove 4 and the Point Revenge occupation of the central Labrador coast. *Arctic Anthropology* 15(2): 146-174.

Gonzalez, Ellice B. 1981. *Changing Economic Roles for Micmac Men and Women: An Ethnohistoric Analysis*. National Museum of Man Mercury Series, Canadian Ethnology Service Paper no. 72, Ottawa.

Gould, G. P. and A. J. Semple (eds.) 1980. *Our Land: The Maritimes*. Saint Annes Point Press, Fredericton.

Howley, James P. 1915. *The Beothucks or Red Indians: The Aboriginal Inhabitants of Newfoundland*. Coles, Toronto (1974 reprint).

Jackson, Doug 1993. *"On the Country": The Micmac of Newfoundland*. Harry Cuff Publications, St. John's.

LeClercq, Father Chretien 1910. *New Relation of Gaspesia, With the Customs and Religion of the Gaspesian Indians*. Champlain Society, Toronto.

Lescarbot, Marc 1907-1914. *The History of New France* (3 vols.). Champlain Society, Toronto.

McGee, H. F. (ed.) 1974. *The Native Peoples of Atlantic Canada: A Reader in Regional Ethnic Relations*. Carleton Library no. 72, McClelland & Stewart, Toronto.

McGhee, Robert 1984. Contact between native North Americans and the medieval Norse: A review of the evidence. *American Antiquity* 49:4-26.

McGhee, Robert and James A. Tuck 1975. *An Archaic Sequence from the Strait of Belle Isle, Labrador*. National Museum of Man Mercury Series, Archaeological Survey of Canada Paper no. 34, Ottawa.

Marshall, Ingeborg C. L. 1985. *Beothuk Bark Canoes: An Analysis and Comparative Study*. National Museum of Man Mercury Series, Canadian Ethnology Service Paper no. 102, Ottawa.

Martijn, Charles A. (ed.) 1986. *Les Micmacs et la mer*. Recherches Amérindiennes au Québec, Montreal.

Miller, Virginia P. 1976. Aboriginal Micmac population: A review of the evidence. *Ethnohistory* 23(2):117-127.

Miller, Virginia P. 1986. The Micmac: a maritime Woodland group. In *Native Peoples: the Canadian Experience*, ed. R.B. Morrison and C.R. Wilson, pp. 324-352. McClelland & Stewart, Toronto.

Pastore, Ralph T. 1992. *Shanawdithit's People: The Archaeology of the Beothuks*. Atlantic Archaeology Ltd., St. John's.

Rowe, Frederick W. 1977. *Extinction: The Beothuks of Newfoundland*. McGraw-Hill Ryerson, Toronto.

Sanger, David 1973. *Cow Point: An Archaic Cemetery in New Brunswick.* National Museum of Man Mercury Series, Archaeological Survey of Canada Paper no. 12, Ottawa.

Speck, Frank G. 1915. The Eastern Algonkian Wabanaki Confederacy. *American Anthropologist* 17:492-508.

Speck, Frank G. 1922. *Beothuk and Micmac.* Indian Notes and Monographs, Museum of the American Indian, Heye Foundation, New York.

Such, Peter 1978. *Vanished Peoples: The Archaic, Dorset and Beothuk People of Newfoundland.* NC Press, Toronto.

Thwaites, Reuben G. (ed.) 1896-1901. *The Jesuit Relations and Allied Documents* (73 vols.). Barrows Brothers, Cleveland.

Trigger, Bruce (ed.) 1978. *Handbook of North American Indians,* vol. 15, *Northeast.* Smithsonian Institution, Washington.

Tuck, James A. 1970. An Archaic Indian cemetery in Newfoundland. *Scientific American* 222(6):112-121.

Tuck, James A. 1975 The northeastern Maritime continuum: 8000 years of cultural development in the far northeast. *Arctic Anthropology* 12(2): 139-147.

Tuck, James A. 1975 *Prehistory of Saglek Bay, Labrador: Archaic and Paleo-Eskimo Occupations.* National Museum of Man Mercury Series, Archaeological Survey of Canada Paper no. 32, Ottawa.

Tuck, James A. 1976. *Newfoundland and Labrador Prehistory.* National Museum of Man, Ottawa.

Tuck, James A. 1976. *Ancient People of Port au Choix.* Institute of Social and Economic Research, Memorial University of Newfoundland, St. John's.

Tuck, James A. 1976. An Archaic Indian burial mound in Labrador. *Scientific American* 235(5):122-129.

Tuck, James A. 1984. *Maritime Provinces Prehistory.* National Museum of Man, Ottawa.

Turnbull, C. J. 1976. The Augustine site: A mound from the Maritimes. *Archaeology of Eastern North America* 4:50-62.

Upton, L. F. S. 1979. *Micmacs and Colonists.* University of British Columbia Press, Vancouver.

Wallis, W. D. and R. S. Wallis 1955. *The Micmac Indians of Eastern Canada.* University of Minnesota Press, Minneapolis.

Wallis, W.D. and Ruth S. Wallis 1957. *The Malecite Indians of New Brunswick.* National Museum of Canada Bulletin no. 148, Anthropological Series no. 40, Ottawa.

Whitehead, Ruth Holmes 1980. *Elitekey: Micmac Material Culture from 1600 AD to the Present.* The Nova Scotia Museum, Halifax.

Whitehead, Ruth Holmes 1982. *Micmac Quillwork.* The Nova Scotia Museum, Halifax.

Whitehead, Ruth Holmes 1991. *The Old Man Told Us: Excerpts from Micmac History 1500-1950.* Nimbus Publishing, Halifax.

Wien, F. 1986. *Rebuilding the Economic Base of Indian Communities: The Micmac in Nova Scotia.* The Institute for Research on Public Policy, Montreal.

Chapter Four *The Iroquoians of the Eastern Woodlands*

An extremely useful source, providing summary articles on all the Iroquoian groups, is the *Handbook of North American Indians,* vol. 15, *Northeast* (Trigger 1978).

A good overview of the precontact period is given in two popular books by J. V. Wright: *Ontario Prehistory* (1972) and *Quebec Prehistory* (1979).

The major primary sources for the seventeenth-century Iroquoians are *The Jesuit Relations* (Thwaites 1896-1901), Champlain (Biggar 1922-36) and Sagard (1939). Particularly important studies of Huron life are those by Trigger (1976, 1990), Tooker (1964) and Heidenreich (1971). A major ethnographic source for the Neutral is G.K. Wright (1963).

General accounts of the Mohawk confrontations of 1990 are given in York and Pindera (1991), Hornung (1991) and Johansen (1993).

Bechard, H. 1976. *The Original Caughnawaga Indians.* International, Montreal.

Biggar, H. P. (ed.) 1924. *The Voyages of Jacques Cartier.* Publications of the Public Archives of Canada no. 11, Ottawa.

Biggar, H.P. (ed.) 1922-1936. *The Works of Samuel de Champlain* (6 vols.). Champlain Society, Toronto.

Chapdelaine, Claude 1989. *Le Site Mandeville à Tracy: variabilité culturelle des Iroquoiens du Saint-Laurent.* Recherches Amérindiennes au Québec, Montreal.

Clermont, N. C. Chapdelaine and G. Barré 1983. *Le site Iroquoien de Lanoraie: témoignage d'une maison-longue*. Recherches Amérindiennes au Québec, Montreal.

Dodd, Christine 1984. *Ontario Iroquois Tradition Longhouses*. National Museum of Man Mercury Series, Archaeological Survey of Canada Paper no. 124, Ottawa.

Druke, Mary A. 1986. Iroquois and Iroquoian in Canada. In *Native Peoples: The Canadian Experience*, ed. R. B. Morrison and C. R. Wilson, pp. 302-324. McClelland & Stewart, Toronto.

Ellis, Chris J. and Neal Ferris (eds.) 1990. *The Archaeology of Southern Ontario to* A.D. *1650*. Ontario Archaeological Society, London.

Fenton, William N. 1971. The Iroquois in history. In *North American Indians in Historical Perspective*, ed. E. B. Leacock and N. O. Lurie, pp. 129-168. Random House, New York.

Finlayson, William D. 1977. *The Saugeen Culture: A Middle Woodland Manifestation in Southwestern Ontario* (2 vols.). National Museum of Man Mercury Series, Archaeological Survey of Canada Paper no. 61, Ottawa.

Finlayson, William D. 1985. *The 1975 and 1978 Rescue Excavations at the Draper Site: Introduction and Settlement Patterns*. National Museum of Man Mercury Series, Archaeological Survey of Canada Paper no. 130, Ottawa.

Foley, Denis P. 1977. Six Nations traditionalist social structure. *Man in the Northeast* 13:107-112.

Frisch, Jack A. 1976. Some ethnological and ethnohistorical notes on the Iroquois in Alberta. *Man in the Northeast* 12:51-64.

Heidenreich, Conrad 1971. *Huronia: A History and Geography of the Huron Indians 1600-1615*. McClelland & Stewart, Toronto.

Hoover, Michael L. and The Kanien'kehaka Raotitiohkwa Cultural Centre 1992. The revival of the Mohawk language in Kahnawake. *Canadian Journal of Native Studies* 12(2):269-287.

Hornung, Rick 1991. *One Nation Under the Gun: Inside the Mohawk Civil War*. Stoddart, Toronto.

Hughes, Ken (Chair) 1991. *The Summer of 1990: Fifth Report of the Standing Committee on Aboriginal Affairs*. House of Commons, Canada.

Hunt, George T. 1940. *The Wars of the Iroquois*. University of Wisconsin Press, Madison.

Jamieson, James B. 1983. An examination of prisoner-sacrifice and cannibalism at the St. Lawrence Iroquoian Roebuck site. *Canadian Journal of Archaeology* 7(2):159-175.

Jamieson, Susan M. 1981. Economics and Ontario Iroquoian social organization. *Canadian Journal of Archaeology* 5:19-30.

Johansen, Bruce E. 1993. *Life and Death in Mohawk Country*. North American Press, Golden, CO.

Johnston, Charles M. (ed.) 1964. *The Valley of the Six Nations*. Champlain Society, University of Toronto Press, Toronto.

Johnston, Richard B. 1968. *The Archaeology of the Serpent Mounds Site*. Occasional Paper no. 10, Art and Archaeology, Royal Ontario Museum, University of Toronto.

Johnston, Richard B. 1979. Notes on ossuary burial among the Ontario Iroquois. *Canadian Journal of Archaeology* 3:91-104.

Kenyon, Walter A. 1968. *The Miller Site*. Occasional Paper no. 14, Art and Archaeology, Royal Ontario Museum, University of Toronto.

Kenyon, Walter A. 1982. *The Grimsby Site: A Historic Neutral Cemetery*. Royal Ontario Museum, Toronto.

Kidd, Kenneth E. 1953. The excavation and historical identification of a Huron ossuary. *American Antiquity* 18(4):359-379.

Kurath, Gertrude P. 1968. *Dance and Song Rituals of Six Nations Reserve, Ontario*. Bulletin 220, National Museums of Canada, Ottawa.

Lennox, Paul A. 1981. *The Hamilton Site: A Late Historic Neutral Town*. National Museum of Man Mercury Series, Archaeological Survey of Canada Paper no. 103, Ottawa.

Miller, J. R. 1992. The Oka controversy and the federal land-claims process. In *Aboriginal Land Claims in Canada: A Regional Perspective*, ed. K. Coates, pp. 215-241. Copp Clark Pitman, Toronto.

Mitchell, Grand Chief Michael 1989. Akwesasne: An unbroken assertion of sovereignty. In *Drum Beat: Anger and Renewal in Indian Country*, ed. Boyce Richardson, pp. 105-136. Assembly of First Nations/Summerhill Press, Toronto.

Morgan, Lewis H. 1962. *League of the Iroquois*. Citadel Press, NJ.

Noble, William C. 1975. Canadian prehistory: The lower Great Lakes-St. Lawrence region. *Canadian Archaeological Association Bulletin* 7:96-121.

Noble, William C. 1978. The Neutral Indians. In *Essays in Northeastern Anthropology in Memory of Mariam E. White*, ed. W. E. Engelbrecht and D. K. Grayson, pp. 152-164. Occasional Publications in Northeastern Anthropology no. 5, Department of Anthropology, Franklin Pierce College, Rindge, NH.

Noble, William C. 1979. Ontario Iroquois effigy pipes. *Canadian Journal of Archaeology* 3:69-90.

Noble, William C. 1984. Historic Neutral Iroquois settlement patterns. *Canadian Journal of Archaeology* 8(1):3-27.

Noble, William C. 1985. Tsouharissen's chiefdom: An early historic 17th century Neutral Iroquoian ranked society. *Canadian Journal of Archaeology* 9(2):131-146.

Noon, John A. 1949. *Law and Government of the Grand River Iroquois.* Viking Fund Publications in Anthropology no. 12, New York.

Pendergast, James F. and Bruce G. Trigger 1972. *Cartier's Hochelaga and the Dawson Site.* McGill-Queen's University Press, Montreal and London.

Richter, Daniel K. 1992. *The Ordeal of the Longhouse: The Peoples of the Iroquois League in the Era of European Colonization.* University of North Carolina Press, Chapel Hill.

Sagard, Father Gabriel 1939. *The Long Journey to the Country of the Hurons* (ed. G. M. Wrong). Champlain Society, Toronto.

Schlesier, Karl H. 1976. Epidemics and Indian middlemen: Rethinking the Wars of the Iroquois. *Ethnohistory* 23(2): 129-145.

Schoolcraft, Henry R. 1846. *Notes on the Iroquois.* Bartlett & Welford, New York. (Kraus Reprint 1975).

Shimony, Annemarie A. 1961. *Conservatism among the Iroquois at the Six Nations Reserve.* Yale University Publications in Anthropology no. 65, New Haven, CT.

Stothers, David M. 1977. *The Princess Point Complex.* National Museum of Man Mercury Series, Archaeological Survey of Canada Paper no. 58, Ottawa.

Thwaites, Rueben G. (ed.) 1896-1901. *The Jesuit Relations and Allied Documents* (73 vols.). Barrows Brothers, Cleveland.

Tooker, Elisabeth 1964. *An Ethnography of the Huron Indians, 1615-1649.* Bureau of American Ethnology Bulletin 190, Smithsonian Institution, Washington, DC.

Trigger, Bruce G. 1976. *The Children of Aataentsic: A History of the Huron People to 1660* (2 vols.). McGill-Queen's University Press, Montreal and London.

Trigger, Bruce G. (ed.) 1978. *Handbook of North American Indians*, vol. 15, *Northeast.* Smithsonian Institution, Washington, DC.

Trigger, Bruce G. 1985. *Natives and Newcomers: Canada's "Heroic Age" Reconsidered.* McGill-Queens University Press, Montreal and London.

Trigger, Bruce G. 1990. *The Huron: Farmers of the North* (2nd ed.). Holt, Rinehart and Winston.

Vincent Tehariolina, M. 1984. *La Nation Huronne: son histoire, sa culture, son esprit.* Éditions du Pélican, Québec.

Wallace, Anthony F. C. 1969. *The Death and Rebirth of the Seneca.* Random House, New York.

Warrick, Gary A. 1984. *Reconstructing Ontario Iroquoian Village Organization.* National Museum of Man Mercury Series, Archaeological Survey of Canada Paper no. 124, Ottawa.

Weaver, Sally M. 1972. *Medicine and Politics among the Grand River Iroquois.* National Museums of Canada, Publications in Ethnology no. 4, Ottawa.

Wright, Gordon K. 1963. *The Neutral Indians: A Source Book.* Occasional Papers of the New York State Archaeological Association no. 4, Rochester, NY.

Wright, J. V. 1966. *The Ontario Iroquois Tradition.* National Museum of Canada Bulletin 210, Ottawa.

Wright, J. V. 1972. *Ontario Prehistory.* National Museum of Man, Ottawa.

Wright, J. V. 1974. *The Nodwell Site.* National Museum of Man Mercury Series, Archaeological Survey of Canada Paper no. 22, Ottawa.

Wright, J. V. 1979. *Quebec Prehistory.* National Museum of Man, Ottawa.

Wright, J. V. and J. E. Anderson 1963. *The Donaldson Site.* National Museum Bulletin 184, Ottawa.

Wright, J. V. and J.E. Anderson 1969. *The Bennet Site.* National Museum Bulletin 229, Ottawa.

Wright, Milton J. 1981. *The Walker Site.* National Museum of Man Mercury Series, Archaeological Survey of Canada Paper no. 103, Ottawa.

York, Geoffrey and Loreen Pindera 1991. *People of the Pines: The Warriors and the Legacy of Oka.* Little, Brown, Toronto.

Chapter Five *The Algonkians of the Eastern Woodlands and Subarctic*

Particularly important ethnographic sources are the works of Densmore (1929) and Landes (1937, 1938, 1968) on the Ojibwa. Speck's (1935) study of the Naskapi, dealing primarily with religious beliefs, is an ethnographic classic. Field studies from more recent periods include Roger's descriptions of the Round Lake Ojibwa (1962, 1983) and the Mistassini Cree (1963, 1967, 1972, 1973), Dunning's

(1959) of the Pekangekum Ojibwa and Hallowell's (1992) of the Berens River Ojibwa. Shkilnyk's (1985) disturbing book documents recent social disintegration on the Grassy Narrows reserve near Kenora. Bishop (1974) and Ray (1974) provide excellent historical analyses.

In addition, particularly useful are the relevant summary articles in two volumes of the *Handbook of North American Indians*, vol. 6, *Subarctic* (Helm 1981) and vol. 15, *Northeast* (Trigger 1978).

Ashini, Daniel 1989. David confronts Goliath: The Innu of Ungava versus the NATO Alliance. In *Drum Beat: Anger and Renewal in Indian Country*, ed. B. Richardson, pp. 45-70. Assembly of First Nations and Summerhill Press, Toronto.

Bishop, Charles A. 1970. The emergence of hunting territories among the northern Ojibwa. *Ethnology* 9:1-15.

Bishop, Charles A. 1974. *The Northern Ojibwa and the Fur Trade*. Holt, Rinehart and Winston, Toronto.

Bishop, Charles A. 1982. The Indian inhabitants of Northern Ontario at the time of contact: Socio-territorial considerations. In *Approaches to Algonquian Archaeology*, ed. M. G. Hanna and B. Kooyman, pp. 253-273. Department of Archaeology, University of Calgary.

Bishop, Charles A. and M. Estellie Smith 1975. Early historic populations in northwestern Ontario: Archaeological and ethnohistoric interpretations. *American Antiquity* 40:54-63.

Brightman, Robert A. 1993. *Grateful Prey: Rock Cree Human-Animal Relationships*. University of California Press, Berkeley and Los Angeles.

Brown, Jennifer S. H. 1986. Northern Algonquians from Lake Superior and Hudson Bay to Manitoba in the historical period. In *Native Peoples: The Canadian Experience*, ed. R. B. Morrison and C. R. Wilson, pp. 208-236. McClelland & Stewart, Toronto.

Cooper, John M. 1936. *Notes on the Ethnology of the Otchipwe of the Lake of the Woods and Rainy Lake*. The Catholic University of America, Washington, DC.

Danziger, Edmund J., Jr. 1978. *The Chippewas of Lake Superior*. University of OklahomaPress, Norman.

Dawson, K. C. A. 1976. *Algonkians of Lake Nipigon: An Archaeological Survey*. National Museum of Man Mercury Series, Archaeological Survey of Canada Paper no. 48, Ottawa.

Dawson, K. C. A. 1977. An application of the direct historic approach to the Algonkians of northern Ontario. *Canadian Journal of Archaeology* 1:151-181.

Dawson, K. C. A. 1982. The Northern Ojibwa of Ontario. In *Approaches to Algonquian Archaeology*, ed. M.G. Hanna and B. Kooyman, pp. 81-96. Department of Archaeology, University of Calgary.

Dawson, K. C. A. 1983. Prehistory of the interior forest of northern Ontario. In *Boreal Forest Adaptations: The Northern Algonkians*, ed. A.T. Steegman, Jr., pp. 55-84. Plenum Press, New York and London.

Densmore, Frances 1929. *Chippewa Customs*. Smithsonian Institution, Bureau of American Ethnology, Bulletin 86, Washington, DC.

Dewdney, Selwyn 1975. *The Sacred Scrolls of the Southern Ojibway*. University of Toronto Press, Toronto.

Dewdney, Selwyn 1978. Birth of a Cree-Ojibway style of contemporary art. In *One Century Later*, ed. I. A. L. Getty and D. B. Smith, pp. 117-125. University of British Columbia Press, Vancouver.

Dewdney, Selwyn and Kenneth E. Kidd 1967. *Indian Rock Paintings of the Great Lakes* (2nd ed.). University of Toronto Press, Toronto.

Dunning, R. W. 1959. *Social and Economic Change among the Northern Ojibwa*. University of Toronto Press, Toronto.

Feit, Harvey A. 1986. Hunting and the quest for power: The James Bay Cree. In *Native Peoples: The Canadian Experience*, ed. R. B. Morrison and C. R. Wilson, pp. 171-207. McClelland & Stewart, Toronto.

Francis, Daniel and Toby Morantz 1983. *Partners in Furs: a History of the Fur Trade in Eastern James Bay 1600-1870*. McGill-Queen's University Press, Kingston and Montreal.

Grim, John A. 1983. *The Shaman: Patterns of Religious Healing Among the Ojibway Indians*. University of Oklahoma Press, Norman.

Hallowell, A. Irving 1955. *Culture and Experience*. University of Pennsylvania Press, Philadelphia.

Hallowell, A. Irving 1992. *The Ojibwa of Berens River, Manitoba: Ethnography into History* (ed. Jennifer S.H. Brown). Holt, Rinehart and Winston, New York.

Helm, June (ed.) 1981. *Handbook of the North American Indians*, vol. 6, *Subarctic*. Smithsonian Institution, Washington, DC.

Henriksen, Georg 1982. *Hunters in the Barrens: The Naskapi on the Edge of the White Man's World*. Institute of Social and Economic Research, Memorial University of Newfoundland, St. John's.

Hessel, Peter 1993. *The Algonkin Nation: The Algonkins of the Ottawa Valley.* Kichesippi Books, Arnprior, ON.

Hickerson, Harold 1960. The Feast of the Dead among the seventeenth century Algonkians of the Upper Great Lakes. *American Anthropologist* 62:81-107.

Hickerson, Harold 1970. *The Chippewa and Their Neighbors: A Study in Ethnohistory.* Holt, Rinehart and Winston, New York.

Hind, Henry Y. 1863. *Explorations in the Interior of the Labrador Peninsula: The Country of the Montagnais and Nasquapee Indians.* Krause Reprint, New York (1973).

Hoffman, W. J. 1891. The Mide'wiwin or Grand Medicine Society. In *Seventh Annual Report of the Bureau of Ethnology,* 1885-86, pp. 143-300. Smithsonian Institution, Washington, DC.

Honigmann, John J. 1956. The Attawapiskat Swampy Cree: An Ethnographic Reconstruction. *Anthropological Papers of the University of Alaska* 5(1):23-82.

Jenness, Diamond 1935. *The Ojibwa Indians of Parry Island, Their Social and Religious Life.* Bulletin no. 78, Anthropological Series no. 17, National Museum of Canada, Ottawa.

Johnson, Basil 1976. *Ojibway Heritage.* McClelland & Stewart, Toronto.

Johnson, Basil 1982. *Ojibway Ceremonies.* McClelland & Stewart, Toronto.

Kenyon, Walter A. 1970. The Armstrong Mound on Rainy River, Ontario. *Canadian Historic Sites, Occasional Papers in Archaeology and History* 3:66-84.

Kenyon, Walter A. 1986. *Mounds of Sacred Earth: Burial Mounds of Ontario.* Royal Ontario Museum, Toronto.

Knight, Rolf 1968. *Ecological Factors in Changing Economy and Social Organization among the Rupert House Cree.* Anthropology Papers no. 15, National Museum of Canada, Ottawa.

Landes, Ruth 1937. The Ojibwa of Canada. In *Cooperation and Competition Among Primitive Peoples,* ed. M. Mead, pp. 87-127. McGraw-Hill, New York.

Landes, Ruth 1937. *Ojibwa Sociology.* Columbia University Contributions to Anthropology. (AMS Press reprint 1969)

Landes, Ruth 1938. *The Ojibwa Woman.* Columbia University Contributions to Anthropology. (W. W. Norton reprint 1971).

Landes, Ruth 1968. *Ojibwa Religion and the Midewiwin.* University of Wisconsin Press, Madison.

Leacock, Eleanor 1954. *The Montagnais "Hunting Territory" and the Fur Trade.* American Anthropological Association Memoir no. 78.

Leacock, Eleanor 1986. The Montagnais-Naskapi of the Labrador Peninsula. In *Native Peoples: The Canadian Experience.* ed. R. B. Morrison and C. R. Wilson, pp. 140-171. McClelland & Stewart, Toronto.

MacGregor, Roy 1989. *Chief: The Fearless Vision of Billy Diamond.* Penguin Books, Markham, ON.

McLuhan, Elizabeth and Tom Hill 1984. *Norval Morrisseau and the Emergence of the Image Makers.* Art Gallery of Ontario and Methuen Publications, Toronto.

Martin, Calvin 1978. *Keepers of the Game: Indian-Animal Relationships and the Fur Trade.* University of California Press, Berkeley.

Martijn, Charles A. and Edward S. Rogers 1969. *Mistassini-Albanel: Contributions to the Prehistory of Quebec.* Centre D'Etudes Nordiques 25, Université Laval, Quebec.

Mason, Leonard 1967. *The Swampy Cree: a Study in Acculturation.* Anthropology Papers no. 13, National Museum of Canada, Ottawa.

Morantz, Toby 1983. *An Ethnohistoric Study of Eastern James Bay Cree Social Organization, 1700-1850.* National Museum of Man Mercury Series, Canadian Ethnology Service Paper no. 88, Ottawa.

Morrisseau, Norval 1965. *Legends of My People, The Great Ojibway.* Ryerson Press, Toronto.

Noble, William C. 1982. Algonquian archaeology in northeastern Ontario. In *Approaches to Algonquian Archaeology,* ed. M. G. Hanna and B. Kooyman, pp. 35-55. Department of Archaeology, University of Calgary.

Preston, Richard J. 1975. *Cree Narrative: Expressing the Personal Meanings of Events.* National Museum of Man Mercury Series, Canadian Ethnology Service Paper no. 30, Ottawa.

Ray, Arthur J. 1974. *Indians in the Fur Trade.* University of Toronto Press, Toronto.

Reid, C. S. "Paddy" and Grace Rajnovich 1991. Laurel: A re-evaluation of the spatial, social and temporal paradigms. *Canadian Journal of Archaeology* 15:193-234.

Richardson, Boyce 1991. *Strangers Devour the Land.* Douglas & McIntyre, Vancouver.

Rogers, Edward S. 1962. *The Round Lake Ojibwa.* Royal Ontario Museum, Toronto.

Rogers, Edward S. 1963. Changing settlement patterns of the Cree-Ojibwa of northern Ontario. *Southwestern Journal of Anthropology* 19:64-88.

Rogers, Edward S. 1963. *The Hunting Group - Hunting Territory Complex among the Mistassini Indians.* National Museum of Canada Bulletin no. 195, Ottawa.

Rogers, Edward S. 1967. *The Material Culture of the Mistassini.* National Museum of Canada Bulletin no. 218, Ottawa.

Rogers, Edward S. 1972. The Mistassini Cree. In *Hunters and Gatherers Today,* ed. M. G. Bicchieri, pp. 90-137. Holt, Rinehart and Winston, New York.

Rogers, Edward S. 1973. *The Quest for Food and Furs: The Mistassini Cree, 1953-1954.* National Museum of Man, Publications in Ethnology no. 5, Ottawa.

Rogers, Edward S. 1983. Cultural adaptations: The Northern Ojibwa of the boreal forest 1670-1980. In *Boreal Forest Adaptations: The Northern Algonkians,* edited by A. T. Steegmann, Jr., pp. 85-141. Plenum Press, New York and London.

Salisbury, Richard F. 1986. *A Homeland For the Cree: Regional Development in James Bay 1971-1981.* McGill-Queen's University Press, Kingston and Montreal.

Schmalz, Peter S. 1991. *The Ojibwa of Southern Ontario.* University of Toronto Press, Toronto.

Shkilnyk, Anastasia M. 1985. *A Poison Stronger Than Love: The Destruction of an Ojibwa Community.* Yale University Press, New Haven, CT.

Sinclair, Lister and Jack Pollock 1979. *The Art of Norval Morrisseau.* Methuen, Toronto.

Southcott, Mary E. 1984. *The Sound of the Drum: the Sacred Art of the Anishnabec.* Boston Mills Press, Erin, ON.

Speck, Frank G. 1915. The family hunting band as the basis of Algonkian social organization. *American Anthropologist* 17:289-305.

Speck, Frank G. 1935. *Naskapi: The Savage Hunters of the Labrador Peninsula.* University of Oklahoma Press, Norman.

Tanner, Adrian 1979. *Bringing Home Animals: Religious Ideology and Mode of Production of the Mistassini Cree Hunters.* Institute of Social and Economic Research, Memorial University of Newfoundland, St. John's.

Teicher, Morton I. 1960. *Windigo Psychosis: A Study of a Relationship between Belief and Behavior among the Indians of Northeastern Canada.* American Ethnological Society, distributed by the University of Washington Press, Seattle.

Thompson, David 1916. ed. Tyrrell, J.B., *David Thompson's Narrative of His Explorations in Western America, 1784-1812.* Champlain Society, Toronto.

Thwaites, Rueben G. (ed.) 1896-1901. *The Jesuit Relations and Allied Documents* (73 vols.). Barrows Brothers, Cleveland.

Trigger, Bruce G. (ed.) 1978. *Handbook of North American Indians,* vol. 15, *Northeast.* Smithsonian Institution, Washington, DC.

Turner, Lucien M. 1894. *Ethnology of the Ungava District, Hudson Bay Territory.* Eleventh Report of the Bureau of Ethnology, Smithsonian Institution, Washington, DC.

Vastokas, Joan M. and Romas K. Vastokas 1973. *Sacred Art of the Algonkians.* Mansard Press, Peterborough, ON.

Vecsey, C. 1983. *Traditional Ojibwa Religion and its Historical Changes.* American Philosophical Society, Philadelphia.

Wadden, Marie 1991. *Nitassinan: The Innu Struggle to Reclaim Their Homeland.* Douglas & McIntyre, Vancouver.

Warren, William W. 1984. *History of the Ojibway People.* Minnesota Historical Society Press, St. Paul (originally published 1885).

Wright, J. V. 1965. A regional examination of Ojibwa culture history. *Anthropologica* n.s. 7(2):189-227.

Wright, J.V. 1967. *The Laurel Tradition and the Middle Woodland Period.* National Museum of Canada, Bulletin no. 217, Ottawa.

Wright, J.V. 1971. Cree culture history in the southern Indian Lake region. *Contributions to Anthropology 7: Archaeology and Physical Anthropology:*1-31. National Museum of Man, Bulletin 232, Ottawa.

Wright, J.V. 1972. *Ontario Prehistory.* National Museum of Man, Ottawa.

Wright, J.V. 1972. *The Shield Archaic.* National Museums of Canada, Publications in Archaeology no. 3, Ottawa.

Wright, J.V. 1979. *Quebec Prehistory.* National Museum of Man, Ottawa.

Chapter Six *The Plains*

Bryan (1991) provides a general overview of archaeology on the Plains. Useful provincial summaries are given in Vickers (1986) for Alberta, Dyck (1983) for Saskatchewan and Pettipas (1983) for Manitoba.

Among the ethnographic groups, the Blackfoot are the best documented. Important ethnographic sources are Wissler (1910, 1912, 1913), Ewers (1958) and Grinnell (1962). Dempsey (1986) gives a useful summary. Other major ethnographic works include Lowie (1909) on the Assiniboine, Mandelbaum (1979) on the Plains Cree and Jenness (1938) on the Sarcee. The Canadian Dakota are well covered in books by LaViolette (1944), Wallis (1947) and Howard (1984), and in articles by A. B. Kehoe (1970) and Stanley (1978).

Adams, Gary 1977. *The Estuary Pound Site in Southwestern Saskatchewan*. National Museum of Man Mercury Series, Archaeological Survey of Canada Paper no. 68, Ottawa.

Ahenakew, Edward 1973. *Voices of the Plains Cree*. McClelland & Stewart, Toronto.

Arthur, George W. 1975. *An Introduction to the Ecology of Early Historic Communal Bison Hunting Among the Northern Plains Indians*. National Museum of Man Mercury Series, Archaeological Survey of Canada Paper no. 37, Ottawa.

Barry, P. S. 1991. *Mystical Themes in Milk River Rock Art*. University of Alberta Press, Edmonton.

Brink, Jack 1979. *Excavations at Writing-On-Stone*. Occasional Paper no. 12, Archaeological Survey of Alberta, Edmonton.

Brink, Jack 1986. *Dog Days in Southern Alberta*. Occasional Paper no. 28, Archaeological Survey of Alberta, Edmonton.

Brumley, John H. 1975. *The Cactus Flower Site in Southeastern Alberta: 1972-1974 Excavations*. National Museum of Man Mercury Series, Archaeological Survey of Canada Paper no. 46, Ottawa.

Brumley, John H. 1976. *Ramillies: A Late Prehistoric Bison Kill and Campsite Located in Southeastern Alberta, Canada*. National Museum of Man Mercury Series, Archaeological Survey of Canada Paper no. 55, Ottawa.

Brumley, John H. 1985. The Ellis site (EcOp-4): A late prehistoric burial lodge/medicine wheel site in southeastern Alberta. In *Contributions to Plains Prehistory*, ed. David Burley, pp. 180-232. Occasional Paper no. 26, Archaeological Survey of Alberta, Edmonton.

Brumley, John H. 1988. *Medicine Wheels on the Northern Plains: A Summary and Appraisal*. Archaeological Survey of Alberta, Manuscript Series no. 12, Edmonton.

Bryan, Liz 1991. *The Buffalo People: Prehistoric Archaeology on the Canadian Plains*. University of Alberta Press, Edmonton.

Buckley, Helen 1992. *From Wooden Ploughs to Welfare: Why Indian Policy Failed in the Prairie Provinces*. McGill-Queen's University Press, Montreal and Kingston.

Byrne, William J. 1973. *The Archaeology and Prehistory of Southern Alberta as Reflected by Ceramics*. National Museum of Man Mercury Series, Archaeological Survey of Canada Paper no. 14, Ottawa.

Calder, James M. 1977. *The Majorville Cairn and Medicine Wheel Site, Alberta*. National Museum of Man Mercury Series, Archaeological Survey of Canada Paper no. 62, Ottawa.

Capes, Katherine H. 1963. *The W.B. Nickerson Survey and Excavations, 1912-15, of the Southern Manitoba Mounds Region*. Anthropology Papers no. 4, National Museum of Canada, Ottawa.

Carter, Sarah 1990. *Lost Harvests: Prairie Indian Reserve Farmers and Government Policy*. McGill-Queen's University Press, Montreal and Kingston.

Corrigan, Samuel W. 1970. The Plains Indian powwow: Cultural integration in Manitoba and Saskatchewan. *Anthropologica* 12: 253-277.

Curtis, Edward S. 1911. *The North American Indian* (vol. 6). Johnson Reprint, New York (1970).

Dempsey, Hugh A. 1972. *Crowfoot: Chief of the Blackfoot*. Hurtig, Edmonton.

Dempsey, Hugh A. 1980. *Red Crow: Warrior Chief*. Western Producer Prairie Books, Saskatoon.

Dempsey, Hugh A. 1986. The Blackfoot Indians. In *Native Peoples: The Canadian Experience*, ed. R. B. Morrison and C. R. Wilson, pp. 404-435. McClelland & Stewart, Toronto.

Dempsey, Hugh A. 1986. *Indian Tribes of Alberta* (2nd ed.). Glenbow Museum, Calgary.

Denig, Edwin T. 1961. *Five Indian Tribes of the Upper Missouri*. University of Oklahoma Press, Norman.

Dyck, Ian G. 1977. *The Harder Site: A Middle Period Bison Hunter's Campsite in the Northern Great Plains*. National Museum of Man Mercury Series, Archaeological Survey of Canada Paper no. 67, Ottawa.

Dyck, Ian G. 1983. The prehistory of southern Saskatchewan. In *Tracking Ancient Hunters*, ed. H. T. Epp and I. Dyck, pp. 63-139. Saskatchewan Archaeological Society, Regina.

Eddy, John A. 1974. Astronomical alignment of the Big Horn Medicine Wheel. *Science* 184(4141):1035-1043.

Eddy, John A. 1977. Medicine wheels and Plains Indian astronomy. In *Native American Astronomy*, ed. A. F. Aveni, pp. 147-169. University of Texas Press, Austin.

Elias, Peter D. 1988. *The Dakota of the Canadian Northwest: Lessons for Survival*. University of Manitoba Press, Winnipeg.

Epp, Henry (ed.) 1993. *Three Hundred Prairie Years: Henry Kelsey's "Inland Country of Good Report."* Canadian Plains Research Center, Regina.

Ewers, John C. 1958. *The Blackfoot: Raiders on the Northwestern Plains*. University of Oklahoma Press, Norman.

Ewers, John C. 1980. *The Horse in Blackfoot Indian Culture*. Smithsonian Institution Press, Washington, DC.

Finnigan, James T. 1982. *Tipi Rings and Plains Prehistory: A Reassessment of their Archaeological Potential*. National Museum of Man Mercury Series, Archaeolgical Survey of Canada Paper no. 108, Ottawa.

Fisher, A. D. 1986. Great Plains ethnology. In *Native Peoples: The Canadian Experience*, ed. R. B. Morrison and C. R. Wilson, pp. 358-375. McClelland & Stewart, Toronto.

Forbis, Richard G. 1962. The Old Women's buffalo Jump, Alberta. In *Contributions to Anthropology 1960*, pt. I, pp. 56-123. National Museum of Canada Bulletin no. 180, Ottawa.

Forbis, Richard G. 1970. *A Review of Alberta Archaeology to 1964*. National Museums of Canada Publications in Archaeology no. 1, Ottawa.

Forbis, Richard G. 1977. *Cluny: An Ancient Fortified Village in Alberta*. Occasional Papers no. 4, Department of Archaeology, University of Calgary.

Frison, George C. 1978. *Prehistoric Hunters of the High Plains*. Academic Press, New York.

Gordon, B. H. C. 1979. *Of Men and Herds in Canadian Plains Prehistory*. National Museum of Man Mercury Series, Archaeological Survey of Canada Paper no. 84, Ottawa.

Grinnell, George B. 1962. *Blackfoot Lodge Tales*. University of Nebraska Press, Lincoln.

Hanks, Lucien M. and J. R. Hanks 1950. *Tribe Under Trust: A Study of the Blackfoot Reserve of Alberta*. University of Toronto Press, Toronto.

Hanna, Margaret G. 1976. *The Moose Bay Burial Mound*. Anthropological Series no. 3, Saskatchewan Museum of Natural History, Regina.

Hind, Henry Y. 1971. *Narrative of the Canadian Red River Exploring Expedition of 1857 and of the Assiniboine and Saskatchewan Exploring Expedition of 1858*. Hurtig, Edmonton.

Hlady, Walter M. (ed.) 1970. *Ten Thousand Years: Archaeology in Manitoba*. Manitoba Archaeological Society, Winnipeg.

Howard, James H. 1961. The identity and demography of the Plains-Ojibwa. *Plains Anthropologist* 6:171-178.

Howard, James H. 1984. *The Canadian Sioux*. University of Nebraska Press, Lincoln.

Hungry Wolf, A. 1977. *The Blood People*. Harper & Row, New York.

Jenness, Diamond 1938. *The Sarcee Indians of Alberta*. National Museum of Canada Bulletin no. 90, Anthropological Series no. 23, Ottawa.

Kehoe, Alice B. 1968. The Ghost Dance religion in Saskatchewan, Canada. *Plains Anthropologist* 13:296-304.

Kehoe, Alice B. 1970. The Dakota in Saskatchewan. In *The Modern Sioux*, ed. E. Nurge, pp. 148-172. University of Nebraska Press, Lincoln.

Kehoe, Alice B. 1989. *The Ghost Dance: Ethnohistory and Revitalization*. Holt, Rinehart and Winston, New York.

Kehoe, Alice B. and T. F. Kehoe 1979. *Solstice-Aligned Boulder Configurations in Saskatchewan*. National Museum of Man Mercury Series, Canadian Ethnology Service Paper no. 48, Ottawa.

Kehoe, Thomas F. 1973. *The Gull Lake Site: A Prehistoric Bison Drive Site in Southwestern Saskatchewan*. Publications in Anthropology and History no. 1, Milwaukee Public Museum.

Kennedy, Dan (Ochankugahe) 1972. *Recollections of an Assiniboine Chief*. McClelland & Stewart, Toronto.

Keyser, James D. 1977. Writing-On-Stone: rock art on the northwestern Plains. *Canadian Journal of Archaeology* 1:15-80.

Kidd, Kenneth E. 1986. *Blackfoot Ethnography*. Archaeological Survey of Alberta, Manuscript Series no. 8, Edmonton.

Kroeber, A. L. 1908. Ethnology of the Gros Ventre. *Anthropological Papers of the American Museum of Natural History*, vol. 1, pt. 4, pp. 145-281.

LaViolette, Gontran 1944. *The Sioux Indians in Canada*. Marion Press, Regina.

Lewis, Oscar 1942. *The Effects of White Contact upon Blackfoot Culture with Special Reference to the Role of the Fur Trade.* University of Washington Press, Seattle.

Lowie, Robert H. 1909. The Assiniboine. *Anthropological Papers of the American Museum of Natural History,* vol. 4, pt. 1, pp. 1-270.

McClintock, Walter 1910. *The Old North Trail.* Macmillan, London.

MacEwen, Grant 1973. *Sitting Bull: The Years in Canada.* Hurtig, Edmonton.

Mandelbaum, David G. 1979. *The Plains Cree: An Ethnographic, Historical, and Comparative Study.* Canadian Plains Research Centre, University of Regina.

Millar, J. F. V. 1981. Mortuary practices of the Oxbow complex. *Canadian Journal of Archaeology* 5:103-117.

Milloy, John S. 1988. *The Plains Cree: Trade, Diplomacy and War, 1790 to 1870.* University of Manitoba Press, Winnipeg.

Moore, T. A. (ed.) 1981. *Alberta Archaeology: Prospect and Retrospect.* Archaeological Society of Alberta, Lethbridge.

Mountain Horse, Mike 1979. *My People The Bloods.* Glenbow-Alberta Institute and the Blood Tribal Council, Calgary.

Nicholson, B. A. 1990. Ceramic affiliations and the case for incipient horticulture in southwestern Manitoba. *Canadian Journal of Archaeology* 14:33-59.

Pettipas, Leo F. (ed.) 1983. *Introducing Manitoba Prehistory.* Papers in Manitoba Archaeology, Department of Culture, Heritage and Recreation, Winnipeg.

Pohorecky, Zenon 1970. *Saskatchewan Indian Heritage: the First 200 Centuries.* Extension Division, University of Saskatchewan, Saskatoon.

Ray, Arthur J. 1974. *Indians in the Fur Trade.* University of Toronto Press, Toronto.

Reeves, Brian O. K. 1978. Head-Smashed-In: 5500 years of bison jumping in the Alberta Plains. *Plains Anthropologist,* Memoir 14, pt. 2, pp. 151-174.

Reeves, Brian O. K. 1983. *Culture Change in the Northern Plains: 1000 B.C. - A.D. 1000.* Occasional Paper no. 20, Archaeological Survey of Alberta, Edmonton.

Reeves, Brian O. K. 1983. Six millenniums of buffalo kills. *Scientific American* 249(4):120-135.

Reeves, Brian O. K. 1990. Communal bison hunters of the Northern Plains. In *Hunters of the Recent Past,* ed. L. B. Davis and B. O. K. Reeves, pp. 168-194. Unwin Hyman, London.

Rodnick, David 1937. Political structure and status among the Assiniboine Indians. *American Anthropologist* 39:408-416.

Sharrock, Susan R. 1974. Crees, Cree-Assiniboines, and Assiniboines: interethnic social organization on the far northern Plains. *Ethnohistory* 21(2):95-122.

Skinner, Alanson 1914. Notes on the Plains Cree. *American Anthropologist* 16:68-87.

Skinner, Alanson 1914. The cultural position of the Plains Ojibwa. *American Anthropologist* 16:314-318.

Skinner, Alanson 1914. Political organization, cults, and ceremonies of the Plains-Ojibwa and Plains-Cree Indians. *Anthropological Papers of the American Museum of Natural History,* vol. 11, pt. 6, pp. 474-542.

Snow, Chief John 1977. *These Mountains Are Our Sacred Places.* Samuel Stevens, Toronto.

Stanley, George F. G. 1978. Displaced Red Men: The Sioux in Canada. In *One Century Later,* ed. I. A. L. Getty and D. B. Smith, pp. 55-81. University of British Columbia Press, Vancouver.

Syms, E. Leigh 1977. Cultural ecology and ecological dynamics of the ceramic period in southwestern Manitoba. *Plains Anthropologist,* Memoir 12, pt. 2.

Syms, E. Leigh 1979. The Devils Lake-Sourisford Burial Complex on the Northeastern Plains. *Plains Anthropologist* 24(86):283-308.

Tarasoff, Koozma J. 1980. *Persistent Ceremonialism: The Plains Cree and Saulteaux.* National Museum of Man Mercury Series, Canadian Ethnology Service Paper no. 69, Ottawa.

Verbicky-Todd, E. 1984. *Communal Buffalo Hunting among the Plains Indians.* Occasional Paper no. 24, Archaeological Survey of Alberta, Edmonton.

Vickers, J. R. 1986. *Alberta Plains Prehistory: A Review.* Occasional Paper no. 27, Archaeological Survey of Alberta, Edmonton.

Wallis, Wilson D. 1919. The Sun Dance of the Canadian Dakota. *Anthropological Papers of the American Museum of Natural History,* vol. 16, pp. 317-380.

Wallis, Wilson D. 1947. The Canadian Dakota. *Anthropological Papers of the American Museum of Natural History,* vol. 41, pt. 1.

Wissler, Clark 1910. Material culture of the Blackfoot Indians. *Anthropological Papers of the American Museum of Natural History,* vol. 4, pt. 1.

Wissler, Clark 1912. Social organization and ritualistic ceremonies of the Blackfoot Indians. *Anthropological Papers of the American Museum of Natural History*, vol. 7.

Wissler, Clark 1913. Societies and dance associations of the Blackfoot Indians. *Anthropological Papers of the American Museum of Natural History*, vol. 11, pt. 4.

Wissler, Clark 1914. The influence of the horse in the development of Plains culture. *American Anthropologist* 16:1-25.

Wissler, Clark and D. C. Duvall 1909. Mythology of the Blackfoot Indians. *Anthropological Papers of the American Museum of Natural History*, vol. 2, pt. 1.

Wormington, H. M. and R. G. Forbis 1965. *An Introduction to the Archaeology of Alberta, Canada.* Denver Museum of Natural History.

Chapter Seven *The Plateau*

By far the most important ethnographic sources for the Canadian Plateau are the works of James Teit (1900, 1906, 1909, 1930), particularly his detailed study of the Thompson (1900). The Kutenai are not well documented; Turney-High's rather late ethnography (1941) is the standard source. Ray (1939) provides a useful overview of the entire Plateau.

Canadian Plateau prehistory is summarized in two works by Fladmark (1982, 1986), which deal with all of British Columbia. An overview of late prehistory is given by Richards and Rousseau (1987).

Boas, Franz 1918. *Kutenai Tales.* Smithsonian Institution, Bureau of American Ethnology, Bulletin 59, Washington, DC.

Carstens, Peter 1991. *The Queen's People: A Study of Hegemony, Coercion and Accommodation among the Okanagan of Canada.* University of Toronto Press, Toronto.

Corner, John 1968. *Pictographs in the Interior of British Columbia.* Wayside Press, Vernon, BC.

Curtis, Edward S. 1911. *The North American Indian* (vol. 7). Johnson Reprint, New York.

Drake-Terry, Joanne 1989. *The Same as Yesterday: The Lillooet Chronicle the Theft of Their Lands and Resources.* Lillooet Tribal Council, Lillooet, BC.

Fisher, Robin 1977. *Contact and Conflict: Indian-European Relations in British Columbia, 1774-1890.* University of British Columbia Press, Vancouver.

Fladmark, K. R. 1982. An introduction to the prehistory of British Columbia. *Canadian Journal of Archaeology* 6:95-156.

Fladmark, K. R. 1986. *British Columbia Prehistory.* National Museums of Canada, Ottawa.

Fraser, Simon 1960. *The Letters and Journals of Simon Fraser, 1806-1808,* ed W. Kaye Lamb. Macmillan, Toronto.

Hayden, Brian (ed.) 1992. *A Complex Culture of the British Columbia Plateau: Traditional Stl'atl'imx Resource Use.* University of British Columbia Press, Vancouver.

Hayden, Brian, Morley Eldridge, Anne Eldridge and Aubrey Cannon 1985. Complex hunter-gatherers in interior British Columbia. In *Prehistoric Hunter-Gatherers*, ed. T. D. Price and J. A. Brown, pp. 181-199. Academic Press, New York.

Hayden, Brian and June M. Ryder 1991. Prehistoric cultural collapse in the Lillooet area. *American Antiquity* 56:50-65.

Hewlett, Edward S. 1973. The Chilcotin uprising of 1864. *BC Studies* 19:50-72.

Hudson, Douglas 1986. The Okanagan Indians. In *Native Peoples: The Canadian Experience.*, ed. R. B. Morrison and C. R. Wilson, pp. 445-466. McClelland & Stewart, Toronto.

Kane, Paul 1968. *Wanderings of an Artist.* Hurtig, Edmonton.

Kennedy, Dorothy I. D. and Randy Bouchard 1978. Fraser River Lillooet: An ethnographic summary. In *Reports of the Lillooet Archaeological Project*, ed. A. H. Stryd and S. Lawhead, pp. 22-55. National Museum of Man Mercury Series, Archaeological Survey of Canada Paper no. 73, Ottawa.

Keyser, James D. 1992. *Indian Rock Art of the Columbia Plateau.* University of Washington Press, Seattle.

Lane, Robert B. 1981. Chilcotin. In *Handbook of North American Indians*, vol. 6, *Subarctic*, ed. June Helm, pp. 402-412. Smithsonian Institution, Washington, DC.

Maud, Ralph (ed.) 1978. *The Salish People: The Local Contributions of Charles Hill-Tout* (vols. 1 and 2). Talonbooks, Vancouver.

Ray, Verne F. 1939. *Cultural Relations in the Plateau of Northwestern America.* Southwest Museum, Los Angeles.

Richards, Thomas H. and Michael K. Rousseau 1987. *Late Prehistoric Cultural Horizons on the*

Canadian Plateau. Publication no. 16, Department of Archaeology, Simon Fraser University, Burnaby, BC.

Rousseau, Mike K. 1993. Early prehistoric occupation of south-central British Columbia: a review of the evidence and recommendations for future research. *BC Studies* 99:140-183.

Sanger, David 1968. The Chase Burial Site EeQw:1, British Columbia. *Contributions to Anthropology 6: Archaeology*: pp. 86-185. National Museums of Canada, Bulletin 224, Ottawa.

Sanger, David 1970. The archaeology of the Lochnore-Nesikep locality, British Columbia. *Syesis* 3, suppl. 1. British Columbia Provincial Museum.

Stryd, Arnoud 1983. Prehistoric mobile art from the mid-Fraser and Thompson River areas. In *Indian Art Traditions of the Northwest Coast*, ed. R. L. Carlson, pp. 167-181. Archaeology Press, Simon Fraser University, Burnaby, BC.

Teit, James A. 1900. *The Thompson Indians of British Columbia*. American Museum of Natural History Memoir, vol. 1, pt. 4, pp. 163-392. (AMS Press reprint 1975).

Teit, James A. 1906. *The Lillooet Indians*. American Museum of Natural History Memoir, vol. 2, pt. 5, pp. 193-300. (AMS Press reprint 1975).

Teit, James A. 1909. *The Shuswap*. American Museum of Natural History Memoir, vol. 2, pt. 7, pp. 443-758. (AMS Press reprint 1975).

Teit, James A. 1912. *Mythology of the Thompson Indians*. American Museum of Natural History, Memoir, vol. 8, pp. 199-416. (AMS Press reprint 1975).

Teit, James A. 1930. *The Salishan Tribes of the Western Plateaus*. Bureau of American Ethnology, Annual Report 45, Washington, DC.

Turnbull, Christopher J. 1977. *Archaeology and Ethnohistory in the Arrow Lakes, Southeastern British Columbia*. National Museum of Man Mercury Series, Archaeological Survey of Canada Paper no. 65, Ottawa.

Turney-High, Harry H. 1941. *Ethnography of the Kutenai*. Memoir no. 56, American Anthropological Association, Menasha, WI.

Wilmeth, Roscoe 1978. *Anahim Lake Archaeology and the Early Historic Chilcotin Indians*. National Museum of Man Mercury Series, Archaeological Survey of Canada Paper no. 82, Ottawa.

Wilson, Robert L. and C. Carlson 1980. *The Archaeology of Kamloops*. Publication no. 7, Department of Archaeology, Simon Fraser University, Burnaby, BC.

York, Annie, Richard Daly and Chris Arnett 1993. *They Write Their Dreams on the Rock Forever: Rock Writings in the Stein River Valley of British Columbia*. Talonbooks, Vancouver.

Chapter Eight *The Northwest Coast*

An invaluable source, providing summary articles on all Northwest Coast groups, is the *Handbook of North American Indians*, vol. 7, *Northwest Coast* (Suttles 1990).

The major ethnographic sources are Swanton (1909) for the Haida; Emmons (1991), Krause (1956) and Oberg (1973) for the Tlingit; Boas (1897, 1909) for the Kwagiulth; Drucker (1951) and Arima (1983) for the Nuu-chah-nulth; McIlwraith (1948) for the Nuxalk and Barnett (1955) and Duff (1952) for the Coast Salish. Drucker (1965) provides a good general treatment.

Fladmark (1986) gives an excellent general account of B.C. prehistory. Historic overviews are provided by Duff (1964), Fisher (1977) and Gunther (1972).

Adams, John W. 1973. *The Gitksan Potlatch*. Holt, Rinehart and Winston, Toronto.

Ames, Kenneth M. 1981. The evolution of social ranking on the Northwest Coast of North America. *American Antiquity* 46:789-805.

Amoss, Pamela 1978. *Coast Salish Spirit Dancing*. University of Washington Press, Seattle.

Arima, Eugene Y. 1983. *The West Coast (Nootka) People*. British Columbia Provincial Museum, Victoria.

Assu, Harry with Joy Inglis 1989. *Assu of Cape Mudge: Recollections of a Coastal Indian Chief*. University of British Columbia Press, Vancouver.

Barbeau, Marius 1928. *The Downfall of Temlaham*. Hurtig, Edmonton.

Barbeau, Marius 1950. *Totem Poles* (2 vols.). National Museum of Canada, Bulletin no. 119, Ottawa.

Barbeau, Marius 1958. *Medicine Men on the North Pacific Coast*. National Museum of Canada, Bulletin no. 152, Ottawa.

Barnett, H. G. 1938. The nature of the potlatch. *American Anthropologist* 40:349-358.

Barnett, H. G. 1955. *The Coast Salish of British Columbia*. University of Oregon Press, Eugene.

Bernick, Kathryn 1983. *A Site Catchment Analysis of the Little Qualicum River Site, DiSc 1: A Wet Site on* the *East Coast of Vancouver Island, B.C.* National Museum of Man Mercury Series, Archaeological Survey of Canada Paper no. 118, Ottawa.

Boas, Franz 1897. *The Social Organization and the Secret Societies of the Kwakiutl Indians.* Johnson Reprint, New York (1970).

Boas, Franz 1909. *The Kwakiutl of Vancouver Island.* Memoir of the American Museum of Natural History, vol. 5.

Boas, Franz 1916. *Tsimshian Mythology.* U.S. Bureau of Ethnology, Washington (Johnson Reprint 1970).

Boas, Franz 1935. *Kwakiutl Culture as Reflected in Mythology.* American Folklore Society, New York.

Boas, Franz 1966. *Kwakiutl Ethnography* (ed. Helen Codere). University of Chicago Press, Chicago.

Boelscher, Marianne 1988. *The Curtain Within: Haida Social and Mythical Discourse.* University of British Columbia Press, Vancouver.

Borden, Charles E. 1975. *Origins and Development of Early Northwest Coast Culture to About 3000* B.C. National Museum of Man Mercury Series, Archaeological Survey of Canada Paper no. 45, Ottawa.

Borden, Charles E. 1979. Peopling and early cultures of the Pacific Northwest. *Science* 203:936-971.

Burley, David V. 1980. *Marpole: Anthropological Reconstructions of a Prehistoric Northwest Coast Culture Type.* Publication no. 8, Department of Archaeology, Simon Fraser University, Burnaby, BC.

Carlson, Roy L. (ed.) 1983. *Indian Art Traditions of the Northwest Coast.* Archaeology Press, Simon Fraser University, Burnaby, BC.

Clutesi, George 1969. *Potlatch.* Gray's, Sidney, BC.

Codere, Helen 1950. *Fighting With Property.* University of Washington Press, Seattle.

Cole, Douglas and Ira Chaikin 1990. *An Iron Hand Upon the People: The Law Against the Potlatch on the Northwest Coast.* Douglas & McIntyre, Vancouver.

Cook, Captain James 1784. *A Voyage to the Pacific Ocean.* W. and A. Strahan, London.

Croes, Dale R. (ed.) 1976. *The Excavation of Water-Saturated Archaeological Sites (Wet Sites) on the Northwest Coast of North America.* National Museum of Man Mercury Series, Archaeological Survey of Canada Paper no. 50, Ottawa.

Curtis, Edward S. 1915. *The North American Indian,* vol. 10, *Kwakiutl.* Johnson Reprint, New York (1970).

Curtis, Edward S. 1916. *The North American Indian,* vol. 11, *Nootka and Haida.* Johnson Reprint, New York (1970).

Dewhirst, John 1980. *The Yuquot Project,* Vol. 1, *The Indigenous Archaeology of Yuquot, a Nootkan Outside Village.* History and Archaeology 39, Parks Canada, Ottawa.

Drucker, Philip 1951. *The Northern and Central Nootkan Tribes.* Smithsonian Institution, Bureau of American Ethnology Bulletin 144, Washington, DC.

Drucker, Philip 1965. *Cultures of the North Pacific Coast.* Chandler, San Francisco.

Drucker, Philip and Robert F. Heizer 1967. *To Make My Name Good.* University of California Press, Berkeley and Los Angeles.

Duff, Wilson 1952. *The Upper Stalo Indians of the Fraser River of B.C.* Anthropology in British Columbia Memoir no. 1, British Columbia Provincial Museum, Victoria.

Duff, Wilson 1964. *The Indian History of British Columbia,* Vol. 1: *The Impact of the White Man.* Anthropology in British Columbia Memoir no. 5, British Columbia Provincial Museum, Victoria.

Duff, Wilson 1969. The Fort Victoria treaties. *BC Studies* 3:3-57.

Duff, Wilson 1975. *Images: Stone: B.C.* Hancock House, Surrey, BC.

Ellis, David W. and Luke Swan 1981. *Teachings of the Tides.* Theytus Books, Nanaimo, BC.

Emmons, George T. 1991. *The Tlingit Indians* (ed. F. de Laguna). Douglas & McIntyre, Vancouver and American Museum of Natural History, New York.

Fisher, Robin 1977. *Contact and Conflict: Indian-European Relations in British Columbia, 1774-1890.* University of British Columbia Press, Vancouver.

Fladmark, Knut R. 1975. *A Paleoecological Model for Northwest Coast Prehistory.* National Museum of Man Mercury Series, Archaeological Survey of Canada Paper no. 43, Ottawa.

Fladmark, Knut R. 1982. An introduction to the prehistory of British Columbia. *Canadian Journal of Archaeology* 6:95-156.

Fladmark, Knut R. 1986. *British Columbia Prehistory.* National Museum of Man, Ottawa.

Fraser, Simon 1960. *The Letters and Journals of Simon Fraser, 1806-1808.* ed. W. Kaye Lamb. Macmillan, Toronto.

Garfield, Viola E. and Paul S. Wingert 1966. *The Tsimshian Indians and Their Arts.* University of Washington Press, Seattle.

Gibson, James R. 1992. *Otter Skins, Boston Ships, and China Goods: The Maritime Fur Trade of the*

Northwest Coast, 1785-1841. McGill-Queen's University Press, Montreal and Kingston.

Glavin, Terry 1990. *A Death Feast in Dimlahamid.* New Star Books, Vancouver.

Goldman, Irving 1975. *The Mouth of Heaven: An Introduction to Kwakiutl Religious Thought.* Wiley, New York.

Gunther, Erna 1966. *Art in the Life of the Northwest Coast Indians.* Portland Art Museum.

Gunther, Erna 1972. *Indian Life on the Northwest Coast of North America as Seen by the Early Explorers and Fur Traders during the Last Decades of the Eighteenth Century.* University of Chicago Press, Chicago.

Gustafson, Paula 1980. *Salish Weaving.* Douglas & McIntyre, Vancouver.

Hawthorn, Audrey 1979. *Kwakiutl Art.* Douglas & McIntyre, Vancouver.

Hill, Beth and Ray Hill 1974. *Indian Petroglyphs of the Pacific Northwest.* Hancock House Publishers, Surrey, BC.

Holm, Bill 1965. *Northwest Coast Indian Art: An Analysis of Form.* University of Washington Press, Seattle.

Holm, Bill 1983. *Smoky-Top: The Art and Times of Willie Seaweed.* University of Washington Press, Seattle and Douglas & McIntyre, Vancouver.

Holm, Bill 1984. *The Box of Daylight: Northwest Coast Indian Art.* Seattle Art Museum, University of Washington Press, Seattle and Douglas & McIntyre, Vancouver.

Jenness, Diamond 1955. *The Faith of a Coast Salish Indian.* Anthropology in British Columbia Memoir no. 3, British Columbia Provincial Museum, Victoria.

Jilek, Wolfgang G. 1982. *Indian Healing: Shamanic Ceremonialism in the Pacific Northwest Today.* Hancock House Publishers, Surrey, BC.

Jonaitis, Aldona 1988. *From the Land of the Totem Poles: The Northwest Coast Indian Art Collection at the American Museum of Natural History.* American Museum of Natural History, New York and Douglas & McIntyre, Vancouver.

Jonaitis, Aldona (ed.) 1991. *Chiefly Feasts: The Enduring Kwakiutl Potlatch.* American Museum of Natural History, New York and Douglas & McIntyre, Vancouver.

Kenyon, Susan M. 1980. *The Kyuquot Way: A Study of a West Coast (Nootkan) Community.* National Museum of Man Mercury Series, Canadian Ethnology Service Paper no. 61, Ottawa.

Kirk, Ruth 1986. *Wisdom of the Elders: Native Traditions on the Northwest Coast.* Douglas & McIntyre, Vancouver.

Krause, Aurel 1956. *The Tlingit Indians.* University of Washington Press, Seattle.

LaViolette, F. E. 1973. *The Struggle for Survival: Indian Cultures and the Protestant Ethic in British Columbia.* University of Toronto Press, Toronto.

MacDonald, George F. 1983. *Haida Monumental Art.* University of British Columbia Press, Vancouver.

MacDonald, George F. and Richard Inglis 1975. *The Dig: An Archaeological Reconstruction of a West Coast Village.* National Museum of Man, Ottawa.

McFeat, Tom (ed.) 1966. *Indians of the North Pacific Coast.* Carleton Library no. 25. McClelland & Stewart, Toronto.

McIlwraith, T. F. 1948. *The Bella Coola Indians* (2 vols.). University of Toronto Press, Toronto.

McMillan, Alan D. and Denis E. St. Claire 1982. *Alberni Prehistory.* Theytus Books, Penticton, BC.

Macnair, Peter 1986. From Kwakiutl to Kwakwaka'wakw. In *Native Peoples: The Canadian Experience,* ed. R. B. Morrison and C. R. Wilson, pp. 501-520. McClelland & Stewart, Toronto.

Macnair, Peter L., Alan Hoover and Kevin Neary 1980. *The Legacy.* British Columbia Provincial Museum, Victoria.

Matson, R. G. (ed.) 1976. *The Glenrose Cannery Site.* National Museum of Man Mercury Series, Archaeological Survey of Canada Paper no. 52, Ottawa.

Maud, Ralph (ed.) 1978. *The Salish People: The Local Contributions of Charles Hill-Tout* (vols. 2-4). Talonbooks, Vancouver.

Mitchell, D. H. 1971. Archaeology of the Gulf of Georgia Area, a natural region and its culture types. *Syesis,* vol. 4, Suppl. 1. British Columbia Provincial Museum, Victoria.

Murray, Peter 1985. *The Devil and Mr. Duncan.* Sono Nis Press, Victoria.

Niblack, Albert P. 1890. *The Coast Indians of Southern Alaska and Northern British Columbia.* Johnson Reprint, New York (1970).

Oberg, Kalervo 1973. *The Social Organization of the Tlingit Indians.* University of Washington Press, Seattle.

Raunet, Daniel 1984. *Without Surrender, Without Consent: A History of the Nishga Land Claims.* Douglas & McIntyre, Vancouver.

Rohner, Ronald P. 1967. *The People of Gilford: A Contemporary Kwakiutl Village.* National Museum of

Canada Bulletin 225, Ottawa.

Rohner, Ronald P. and Evelyn C. Rohner 1970. *The Kwakiutl: Indians of British Columbia.* Holt, Rinehart and Winston, New York and Toronto.

Rosman, Abraham and Paula Rubel 1971. *Feasting With Mine Enemy.* Columbia University Press, New York.

Seguin, Margaret (ed.) 1984. *The Tsimshian: Images of the Past, Views for the Present.* University of British Columbia Press, Vancouver.

Shadbolt, Doris 1986. *Bill Reid.* Douglas & McIntyre, Vancouver.

Spradley, James P. (ed.) 1969. *Guests Never Leave Hungry: The Autobiography of James Sewid, a Kwakiutl Indian.* Yale University Press, New Haven, CT.

Sproat, Gilbert M. 1987. *The Nootka: Scenes and Studies of Savage Life.* Ed. C. Lillard. Sono Nis Press, Victoria.

Stearns, Mary Lee 1981. *Haida Culture in Custody.* University of Washington Press, Seattle.

Stewart, Hilary 1973. *Artifacts of the Northwest Coast Indians.* Hancock House, Surrey, BC.

Stewart, Hilary 1977. *Indian Fishing: Early Methods on the Northwest Coast.* Douglas & McIntyre, Vancouver.

Stewart, Hilary 1979. *Looking at Indian Art of the Northwest Coast.* Douglas & McIntyre, Vancouver.

Stewart, Hilary 1979. *Robert Davidson: Haida Printmaker.* Douglas & McIntyre, Vancouver.

Stewart, Hilary 1984. *Cedar.* Douglas & McIntyre, Vancouver.

Stewart, Hilary 1990. *Totem Poles.* Douglas & McIntyre, Vancouver.

Stott, Margaret A. 1975. *Bella Coola Ceremony and Art.* National Museum of Man Mercury Series, Canadian Ethnology Service Paper no. 21, Ottawa.

Suttles, Wayne 1955. *Katzie Ethnographic Notes.* Anthropology in British Columbia Memoir no. 2, British Columbia Provincial Museum, Victoria.

Suttles, Wayne 1974. *The Economic Life of the Coast Salish of Haro and Rosario Straits.* Garland, New York.

Suttles, Wayne 1987. *Coast Salish Essays.* Talonbooks, Vancouver.

Suttles, Wayne (ed.) 1990. *Handbook of North American Indians,* vol. 7, *Northwest Coast.* Smithsonian Institution, Washington, DC.

Swanton, John R. 1909. *Contributions to the Ethnology of the Haida.* Memoirs of the American Museum of Natural History vol. 5.

Tennant, Paul 1990. *Aboriginal Peoples and Politics: The Indian Land Question in British Columbia, 1849-1989.* University of British Columbia Press, Vancouver.

Thom, Ian (ed.) 1993. *Robert Davidson: Eagle of the Dawn.* Douglas & McIntyre, Vancouver.

Usher, Jean 1974. *William Duncan of Metlakatla.* National Museums of Canada, Publications in History no. 5, Ottawa.

Van Den Brink, J. H. 1974. *The Haida Indians.* E.J. Brill, Leiden.

Wolcott, Harry F. 1967. *A Kwakiutl Village and School.* Holt, Rinehart and Winston, New York.

Woodcock, George 1977. *Peoples of the Coast.* Hurtig, Edmonton.

Chapter Nine *The Western Subarctic*

An important source on all aspects of Subarctic Athapaskan life is the *Handbook of North American Indians,* vol. 6, *Subarctic* (Helm 1981). Standard ethnographic sources on traditional Athapaskan cultures are Birket-Smith (1930), Emmons (1911), P. E. Goddard (1916), Honigmann (1946, 1954), Jenness (1937, 1943), McClellan (1975), McKennan (1965), Morice (1893) and Osgood (1936, 1971). VanStone (1974) provides a general overview. D. W. Clark (1991) summarizes the archaeology of the Western Subarctic.

The late-eighteenth- century journals of Hearne (1971), Thompson (1962) and Mackenzie (1971) give early historic glimpses into Athapaskan life. A good summary of fur trade changes on Athapaskan cultures is given by Yerbury (1986).

For descriptions of recent and modern Athapaskan cultures see Hara (1980), Helm (1961), Savishinsky (1974), Slobodin (1962), D. M. Smith (1982) and VanStone (1965). In addition, both Brody (1981)and Ridington (1988) provide sensitive accounts of modern life among the Beaver.

Albright, Sylvia 1984. *Tahltan Ethnoarchaeology.* Publication no. 15, Department of Archaeology, Simon Fraser University, Burnaby, BC.

Asch, Michael 1986. The Slavey Indians: The relevance of ethnohistory to development. In *Native*

Peoples: The Canadian Experience, ed. R. B. Morrison and C. R. Wilson, pp. 271-296. McClelland & Stewart, Toronto.

Balikci, Asen 1963. *Vunta Kutchin Social Change*. Northern Co-ordination and Research Centre, Department of Northern Affairs and National Resources, Ottawa.

Berger, Thomas R. 1977. *Northern Frontier, Northern Homeland: The Report of the Mackenzie Valley Pipeline Inquiry* (2 vols.). Ministry of Supply and Services Canada, Ottawa.

Birket-Smith, Kaj 1930. *Contributions to Chipewyan Ethnology*. AMS Press, New York (1976).

Bone, Robert, Earl Shannon, and Stewart Raby 1973. *The Chipewyan of the Stony Rapids Region*. Institute for Northern Studies, University of Saskatchewan, Saskatoon.

Brody, Hugh 1981. *Maps and Dreams*. Douglas & McIntyre, Vancouver.

Canada, Indian and Northern Affairs 1992. *Gwich'in Comprehensive Land Claim Agreement*. Ottawa.

Canada, Indian and Northern Affairs 1993. *Sahtu Dene and Métis Comprehensive Land Claim Agreement*. Ottawa.

Canada, Indian and Northern Affairs 1993. *Umbrella Final Agreement: Council For Yukon Indians*. Ottawa.

Christian, Jane and P. M. Gardner 1977. *The Individual in Northern Dene Thought and Communication: A Study in Sharing and Diversity*. National Museum of Man Mercury Series, Canadian Ethnology Service Paper no. 35, Ottawa.

Clark, A. McFadyen 1974. *The Athapaskans: Strangers of the North*. National Museum of Man, Ottawa.

Clark, Donald W. 1976. Prehistory of the Western Subarctic. *Canadian Archaeological Association Bulletin* 7:76-95.

Clark, Donald W. 1991. *Western Subarctic Prehistory*. Canadian Museum of Civilization, Hull, PQ.

Clark, Donald W. and Richard E. Morlan 1982. Western Subarctic prehistory: Twenty years later. *Canadian Journal of Archaeology* 6:79-93.

Coates, Ken S. 1991. *Best Left as Indians: Native-White Relations in the Yukon Territory, 1840-1973*. McGill-Queen's University Press, Montreal and Kingston.

Cruikshank, Julie 1979. *Athapaskan Women: Lives and Legends*. National Museum of Man Mercury Series, Canadian Ethnology Service Paper no. 57, Ottawa.

Cruikshank, Julie 1990. *Life Lived Like a Story: Life Stories of Three Yukon Elders*. University of British Columbia Press, Vancouver.

Cruikshank, Julie 1991. *Reading Voices: Oral and Written Interpretations of the Yukon's Past*. Douglas & McIntyre, Vancouver.

Dene Nation 1984. *Denendeh: A Dene Celebration*. The Dene Nation, Yellowknife, NWT.

Duncan, Kate C. 1989. *Northern Athapaskan Art: A Beadwork Tradition*. Douglas & McIntyre, Vancouver.

Emmons, G. T. 1911. *The Tahltan Indians*. Anthropological Publications of the University of Pennsylvania Museum, vol. 4, no. 1.

Fumoleau, Rene 1973. *As Long as This Land Shall Last: A History of Treaty 8 and Treaty 11*. McClelland & Stewart, Toronto.

Gillespie, Beryl C. 1975. Territorial expansion of the Chipewyan in the 18th century. In *Proceedings: Northern Athapaskan Conference, 1971*, ed. A. McFadyen Clark, pp. 350-388. National Museum of Man Mercury Series, Canadian Ethnology Service Paper no. 27, Ottawa.

Goddard, John 1991. *Last Stand of the Lubicon Cree*. Douglas & McIntyre, Vancouver.

Goddard, Pliny Earle 1916. *The Beaver Indians*. Anthropological Papers of the American Museum of Natural History, vol. 10, pt. 4, pp. 203-293.

Goldman, Irving 1940. The Alkatcho Carrier of British Columbia. In *Acculturation in Seven American Indian Tribes*, ed. R. Linton, pp. 333-386. Peter Smith, Gloucester, MA.

Goldman, Irving 1941. The Alkatcho Carrier: Historical background of crest prerogatives. *AmericanAnthropologist* 43:396-418.

Gordon, Bryan H. C. 1976. *Migod—8,000 Years of Barrenland Prehistory*. National Museum of Man Mercury Series, Archaeological Survey of Canada Paper no. 56, Ottawa.

Hara, Sue Hiroko 1980. *The Hare Indians and Their World*. National Museum of Man Mercury Series, Canadian Ethnology Service Paper no. 63, Ottawa.

Hearne, Samuel 1971. *A Journey From Prince of Wales's Fort in Hudson's Bay to the Northern Ocean*. Hurtig, Edmonton.

Helm, June 1961. *The Lynx Point People: The Dynamics of a Northern Athapaskan Band*. National Museum of Canada, Bulletin no. 176, Ottawa.

Helm, June 1972. The Dogrib Indians. In *Hunters and Gatherers Today*, ed. M. G. Bicchieri, pp. 51-89. Holt, Rinehart and Winston, New York.

Helm, June (ed.) 1981. *Handbook of North American Indians*, vol. 6, *Subarctic*. Smithsonian Institution, Washington, DC.

Helm, June et al. 1975. The contact history of the Subarctic Athapaskans: An overview. In *Proceedings: Northern Athapaskan Conference, 1971*, ed. A. McFadyen Clark, pp. 302-349. National Museum of Man Mercury Series, Canadian Ethnology Service Paper no. 27, Ottawa.

Helmer, J. W., S. Van Dyke, and F. J. Kense (eds.) 1977. *Problems in the Prehistory of the North American Subarctic: The Athapaskan Question*. Department of Archaeology, University of Calgary.

Honigmann, John J. 1946. *Ethnography and Acculturation of the Fort Nelson Slave*. Yale University Publications in Anthropology no. 33, Yale University Press, New Haven, CT.

Honigmann, John J. 1954. *The Kaska Indians: An Ethnographic Reconstruction*. Yale University Publications in Anthropology no. 51, Yale University Press, New Haven, CT.

Ives, John W. 1990. *A Theory of Northern Athapaskan Prehistory*. Westview Press/University of Calgary Press, Boulder and Calgary.

Jenness, Diamond 1937. *The Sekani Indians of British Columbia*. National Museum of Canada, Bulletin no. 84, Ottawa.

Jenness, Diamond 1943. *The Carrier Indians of the Bulkley River: Their Social and Religious Life*. Bureau of American Ethnology Bulletin 133:469-586. Washington, DC.

Jones, T. E. H. 1981. *The Aboriginal Rock Paintings of the Churchill River*. Saskatchewan Museum of Natural History, Anthropological Series no. 4, Regina.

Krech, Shepard, III 1976. The Eastern Kutchin and the fur trade, 1800-1860. *Ethnohistory* 23(3):213-235.

Krech, Shepard, III 1978. Disease, starvation, and Northern Athapaskan social organization. *American Ethnologist* 5(4):710-732.

Krech, Shepard, III 1984. The trade of the Slavey and Dogrib at Fort Simpson in the early nineteenth century. In *The Subarctic Fur Trade: Native Social and Economic Adaptations*, ed. Shepard Krech III, pp. 99-146. The University of British Columbia Press, Vancouver.

Leechman, Douglas 1954. *The Vanta Kutchin*. Department of Northern Affairs and National Resources, Ottawa.

Legros, Dominique 1985. Wealth, poverty, and slavery among 19th-century Tutchone Athapaskans. *Research in Economic Anthropology* 7:37-64.

McClellan, Catherine 1975. *My Old People Say: An Ethnographic Survey of Southern Yukon Territory* (2 vols.). National Museums of Canada, Publications in Ethnology no. 6, Ottawa.

McClellan, Catherine 1975. Feuding and warfare among northwestern Athapaskans. In *Proceedings: Northern Athapaskan Conference, 1971*, ed. A. McFadyen Clark, pp. 181-258. National Museum of Man Mercury Series, Canadian Ethnology Service Paper no. 27, Ottawa.

McClellan, Catherine 1987. *Part of the Land, Part of the Water: A History of the Yukon Indians*. Douglas & McIntyre, Vancouver.

McKennan, Robert A. 1965. *The Chandalar Kutchin*. Arctic Institute of North America, Technical Paper no. 17.

Mackenzie, Alexander 1971. *Voyages from Montreal on the River St. Lawrence through the Continent of North America to the Frozen and Pacific Oceans in the Years 1789 and 1793*. Hurtig, Edmonton.

Mason, J. Alden 1946. *Notes on the Indians of the Great Slave Lake Area*. Yale University Publications in Anthropology no. 34, Yale University Press, New Haven, CT.

Meyer, David 1983. The prehistory of northern Saskatchewan. In *Tracking Ancient Hunters*, ed. H. T. Epp and I. Dyck, pp. 141-170. Saskatchewan Archaeological Society, Regina.

Morice, Rev. Father A. G. 1893. *Notes Archaeological, Industrial and Sociological on the Western Denes with an Ethnological Sketch of the Same*. Transactions of the Canadian Institute vol. 4, Toronto.

Morlan, Richard E. 1973. *The Later Prehistory of the Middle Porcupine Drainage, Northern Yukon Territory*. National Museum of Man Mercury Series, Archaeological Survey of Canada Paper no. 11, Ottawa.

Morrison, William R. 1992. Aboriginal land claims in the Canadian north. In *Aboriginal Land Claims in Canada*, ed. K. Coates, pp. 167-194. Copp Clark Pitman, Toronto.

Nash, Ronald J. 1975. *Archaeological Investigations in the Transitional Forest Zone: Northern Manitoba, Southern Keewatin, N.W.T.* Manitoba Museum of Man and Nature, Winnipeg.

Nelson, Richard K. 1973. *Hunters of the Northern Forest*. University of Chicago Press, Chicago.

Osgood, Cornelius 1932. The ethnography of the Great Bear Lake Indians. *National Museum of Canada Bulletin* 70:31-97.

Osgood, Cornelius 1936. *Contributions to the Ethnography of the Kutchin*. Yale University Publications in Anthropology no. 14, New Haven, CT.

Osgood, Cornelius 1936. The distribution of the Northern Athapaskan Indians. *Yale University Publications in Anthropology* 7:3-23.

Osgood, Cornelius 1971. *The Han Indians.* Yale University Publications in Anthropology no. 74, New Haven, CT.

Ridington, Robin 1968. The medicine fight: An instrument of political process among the Beaver Indians. *American Anthropologist* 70(6):1152-1160.

Ridington, Robin 1971. Beaver dreaming and singing. *Anthropologica* 13:115-128.

Ridington, Robin 1978. *Swan People: A Study of the Dunne-za Prophet Dance.* National Museum of Man Mercury Series, Canadian Ethnology Service Paper no. 38, Ottawa.

Ridington, Robin 1979. Changes of mind: Dunne-za resistance to empire. *BC Studies* 43:65-80.

Ridington, Robin 1988. *Trail to Heaven: Knowledge and Narrative in a Northern Native Community.* Douglas & McIntyre, Vancouver.

Rushforth, E. Scott 1986. The Bear Lake Indians. In *Native Peoples: The Canadian Experience*, ed. R. B. Morrison and C. R. Wilson, pp. 243-271. McClelland & Stewart, Toronto.

Russell, Dale R. 1991. *Eighteenth-Century Western Cree and Their Neighbours.* Canadian Museum of Civilization, Hull, PQ.

Savishinsky, Joel S. 1974. *The Trail of the Hare: Life and Stress in an Arctic Community.* Gordon and Breach, New York.

Slobodin, Richard 1960. Eastern Kutchin warfare. *Anthropologica* 2(1):76-94.

Slobodin, Richard 1962. *Band Organization of the Peel River Kutchin.* National Museum of Canada Bulletin no. 179, Ottawa.

Slobodin, Richard 1966. *Métis of the Mackenzie District.* Canadian Research Centre for Anthropology, Saint-Paul University, Ottawa.

Smith, David M. 1982. *Moose-Deer Island House People: A History of the Native People of Fort Resolution.* National Museum of Man Mercury Series, Canadian Ethnology Service Paper no. 81, Ottawa.

Smith, J. G .E. 1975. The ecological basis of Chipewyan socio-territorial organization. In *Proceedings: Northern Athapaskan Conference, 1971*, ed. A. McFadyen Clark, pp. 389-461. National Museum of Man Mercury Series, Canadian Ethnology Service Paper no. 27, Ottawa.

Smith, James G.E. (ed.) 1976. Chipewyan adaptations: Papers from a symposium on the Chipewyan of Subarctic Canada. *Arctic Anthropology* 13(1):1-83.

Teit, J. A. 1956. Field notes on the Tahltan and Kaska Indians: 1912-1915. *Anthropologica* 3:39-193.

Thompson, David 1962. *David Thompson's Narrative 1784-1812*, ed. Glover, Richard. Champlain Society, Toronto.

VanStone, James W. 1965. *The Changing Culture of the Snowdrift Chipewyan.* National Museum of Canada Bulletin 209, Ottawa.

VanStone, James W. 1974. *Athapaskan Adaptations.* Aldine, Chicago.

Watkins, Mel (ed.) 1977. *Dene Nation: The Colony Within.* University of Toronto Press, Toronto.

Workman, William B. 1974. The cultural significance of a volcanic ash which fell in the upper Yukon Basin about 1400 years ago. In *International Conference on the Prehistory and Paleoecology of Western North American Arctic and Subarctic*, ed. S. Raymond and P. Schledermann, pp. 239-261. Archaeological Association, University of Calgary.

Workman, William B. 1978. *Prehistory of the Aishihik-Kluane Area, Southwest Yukon Territory.* National Museum of Man Mercury Series, Archaeological Survey of Canada Paper no. 74, Ottawa.

Wright, J. V. 1975. *The Prehistory of Lake Athabasca: An Initial Statement.* National Museum of Man Mercury Series, Archaeological Survey of Canada Paper no. 29, Ottawa.

Yerbury, J. C. 1976. The post-contact Chipewyan: Trade rivalries and changing territorial boundaries. *Ethnohistory* 23(3):237-263.

Yerbury, J.C. 1980. Protohistoric Canadian Athapaskan populations: An ethnohistorical reconstruction. *Arctic Anthropology* 17(2):17-33.

Yerbury, J.C. 1986. *The Subarctic Indians and the Fur Trade, 1680-1860.* University of BritishColumbia Press, Vancouver.

Chapter Ten *The Arctic*

Summary articles on all Arctic peoples are provided in the *Handbook of North American Indians,* vol. 5, *Arctic* (Damas 1984).

Recommended sources on Arctic archaeology are by McGhee (1978) and Maxwell (1985).

General ethnographic treatments of the Inuit are given in Birket-Smith (1971) and Weyer (1932).

Detailed ethnographies of the Central Inuit include Balikci (1970), Boas (1901, 1964), Jenness (1922, 1946) and the publications of the Fifth Thule Expedition (Birket-Smith 1929; Mathiassen 1928; Rasmussen 1929, 1930, 1931, 1932). Other regions are less well documented. Hawkes (1916) is the standard source for the Labrador Inuit. For the western Arctic, Petitot (1981) gives important nineteenth-century observations and McGhee (1974) provides a useful summary.

An excellent historical overview, focusing on the relationship between government and the Inuit, is given by Jenness (1964). Studies of modern Arctic communities include those of Brody (1975), Honigmann and Honigmann (1970) and Vallee (1967). The historical events leading to Nunavut are well covered in Duffy (1988) and Purich (1992).

Arima, Eugene Y. 1975. *A Contextual Study of the Caribou Eskimo Kayak.* National Museum of Man Mercury Series, Canadian Ethnology Service Paper no. 25, Ottawa.

Arnold, Charles D. 1981. *The Lagoon Site (OjRl-3): Implications for Paleoeskimo Interactions.* National Museum of Man Mercury Series, Archaeological Survey of Canada Paper no. 107, Ottawa.

Arnold, Charles D. and C. Stimmel 1983. An analysis of Thule pottery. *Canadian Journal of Archaeology* 7(1):1-21.

Balikci, Asen 1970. *The Netsilik Eskimo.* The Natural History Press, New York.

Bielawski, E. 1988. Paleoeskimo variability: The early Arctic small-tool tradition in the central Canadian Arctic. *American Antiquity* 53(1):52-74.

Birket-Smith, K. 1929. *The Caribou Eskimos: Material and Social Life and Their Cultural Position.* Report of the Fifth Thule Expedition 1921-24, vol. V, pts. 1 and 2, Copenhagen. (AMS Press reprint 1976).

Birket-Smith 1971. *Eskimos.* Crown, New York.

Blodgett, Jean 1985. *Kenojuak.* Firefly Books, Toronto.

Boas, Franz 1901. *The Eskimo of Baffin Land and Hudson Bay.* Bulletin of the American Museum of Natural History, vol. 15. (AMS Press reprint).

Boas, Franz 1964. *The Central Eskimo.* University of Nebraska Press, Lincoln. (Orig. pub. 1888).

Brody, Hugh 1975. *The People's Land: Eskimos and Whites in the Eastern Arctic.* Penguin Books, Harmondsworth, England.

Burch, Ernest S., Jr. 1978. Caribou Eskimo origins: An old problem reconsidered. *Arctic Anthropology* 15(1):1-35.

Burch, Ernest S., Jr. 1986. The Caribou Inuit. In *Native Peoples: The Canadian Experience,* ed. R.B. Morrison and C. R. Wilson, pp. 106-133. McClelland & Stewart, Toronto.

Canada, Indian and Northern Affairs 1984. *The Western Arctic Claim: The Inuvialuit Final Agreement.* Ottawa.

Canada, Indian and Northern Affairs 1993. *Agreement Between the Inuit of the Nunavut Settlement Area and Her Majesty the Queen in Right of Canada.* Ottawa.

Clark, Brenda 1977. *The Development of Caribou Eskimo Culture.* National Museum of Man Mercury Series, Archaeological Survey of Canada Paper no. 59, Ottawa.

Damas, David 1963. *Igluligmiut Kinship and Local Groupings: A Structural Approach.* National Museum of Canada Bulletin no. 196, Ottawa.

Damas, David 1972. Central Eskimo systems of food sharing. *Ethnology* 11(3):220-240.

Damas, David 1972. The Copper Eskimo. In *Hunters and Gatherers Today,* ed. M.G. Bicchieri, pp. 3-50. Holt, Rinehart and Winston, New York.

Damas, David (ed.) 1984. *Handbook of North American Indians,* vol. 5, *Arctic.* Smithsonian Institution, Washington, DC.

Duffy, R. Q. 1988. *The Road to Nunavut: The Progress of the Eastern Arctic Inuit Since the Second World War.* McGill-Queen's University Press, Kingston and Montreal.

Dumond, Don E. 1977. *The Eskimos and Aleuts.* Thames and Hudson, London.

Finkler, Harold W. 1975. *Inuit and the Administration of Criminal Justice in the Northwest Territories: The Case of Frobisher Bay.* Indian and Northern Affairs, Ottawa.

Freeman, Milton M. R. (ed.) 1976. *Inuit Land Use and Occupancy Project* (3 vols.). Indian and Northern Affairs, Ottawa.

Harp, Elmer, Jr. 1964. *The Cultural Affinities of the Newfoundland Dorset Eskimo.* National Museum of Canada Bulletin no. 200, Ottawa.

Hawkes, E. W. 1916. *The Labrador Eskimo.* Department of Mines, Geological Survey Memoir 91, Ottawa.

Hickey, C. G. 1986. The archaeology of Arctic Canada. In *Native Peoples: The Canadian Experience,* ed. R. B. Morrison and C. R. Wilson, pp. 73-97. McClelland & Stewart, Toronto.

Honigmann, John J. and Irma Honigmann 1970. *Arctic Townsmen*. Canadian Research Centre for Anthropology, Saint-Paul University, Ottawa.

Houston, Alma (ed.) 1988. *Inuit Art: An Anthology*. Watson & Dwyer, Winnipeg.

Hughes, Charles C. 1965. Under four flags: Recent culture change among the Eskimos. *Current Anthropology* 6(1): 3-69.

Jenness, Diamond 1922. *The Life of the Copper Eskimos*. Report of the Canadian Arctic Expedition 1913-18, vol. 12, pt. A. (Johnson Reprint 1970).

Jenness, Diamond 1946. *Material Culture of the Copper Eskimo*. Report of the Canadian Arctic Expedition 1913-18, vol. 16, Ottawa.

Jenness, Diamond 1964. *Eskimo Administration: II. Canada*. Arctic Institute of North America, Technical Paper no. 14.

Jenness, Diamond 1965. *Eskimo Administration: III. Labrador*. Arctic Institute of North America, Technical Paper no. 16.

Linnamae, Urve 1975. *The Dorset Culture: A Comparative Study in Newfoundland and the Arctic*. Technical Papers of the Newfoundland Museum no. 1, St. John's.

McCartney, Allen P. 1977. *Thule Eskimo Prehistory along Northwestern Hudson Bay*. National Museum of Man Mercury Series, Archaeological Survey of Canada Paperno. 70, Ottawa.

McCartney, Allen P. (ed.) 1979. *Thule Eskimo Culture: An Anthropological Perspective*. National Museum of Man Mercury Series, Archaeological Survey of Canada Paper no. 88, Ottawa.

McCartney, Allen P. 1980. The nature of Thule Eskimo whale use. *Arctic* 33(3):517-541.

McCartney, A. P. and D. J. Mack 1973. Iron utilization by Thule Eskimos of central Canada. *American Antiquity* 38:328-339.

McCartney, Allen P. and James M. Savelle 1985. Thule whaling in the central Canadian Arctic. *Arctic Anthropology* 22(2):37-58.

McCullough, Karen M. 1989. *The Ruin Islanders: Early Thule Culture Pioneers in the Eastern High Arctic*. Archaeological Survey of Canada Mercury Series Paper 141, Canadian Museum of Civilization, Hull.

McGhee, Robert 1972. *Copper Eskimo Prehistory*. National Museums of Canada, Publications in Archaeology no. 2, Ottawa.

McGhee, Robert 1974. *Beluga Hunters: An Archaeological Reconstruction of the History and Culture of the Mackenzie Delta Kittegaryumiut*. Institute of Social and Economic Research, Memorial University of Newfoundland, St. John's.

McGhee, Robert 1978. *Canadian Arctic Prehistory*. National Museum of Man, Ottawa.

McGhee, Robert 1979. *The Paleoeskimo Occupations at Port Refuge, High Arctic Canada*. National Museum of Man Mercury Series, Archaeological Survey of Canada Paper no. 92, Ottawa.

McGhee, Robert 1981. *The Dorset Occupations in the Vicinity of Port Refuge, High Arctic Canada*. National Museum of Man Mercury Series, Archaeological Survey of Canada Paper no. 105, Ottawa.

McGhee, Robert 1981. *The Tuniit: First Explorers of the High Arctic*. National Museum of Man, Ottawa.

McGhee, Robert 1984. *The Thule Village at Brooman Point, High Arctic Canada*. National Museum of Man Mercury Series, Archaeological Survey of Canada Paper no. 125, Ottawa.

Mathiassen, Therkel 1927. *Archaeology of the Central Eskimos*. Report of the Fifth Thule Expedition 1921-24, vol. 4, pts. 1 and 2, Copenhagen. (AMS Press reprint 1976).

Mathiassen, Therkel 1928. *Material Culture of the Iglulik Eskimos*. Report of the Fifth Thule Expedition 1921-24, vol. 6, no. l, Copenhagen. (AMS Press reprint 1976).

Matthiasson, John S. 1992. *Living on the Land: Change among the Inuit of Baffin Island*. Broadview Press, Peterborough, ON.

Martijn, Charles A. 1964. Canadian Eskimo carving in historical perspective. *Anthropos* 59(3-4):545-596.

Maxwell, Moreau S. (ed.) 1976. *Eastern Arctic Prehistory: Paleoeskimo Problems*. Memoirs of the Society for American Archaeology no. 31.

Maxwell, Moreau S. 1985. *Prehistory of the Eastern Arctic*. Academic Press, New York.

Meyer, David A. 1977. *Pre-Dorset Settlements at the Seahorse Gully Site*. National Musuem of Man Mercury Series, Archaeological Survey of Canada Paper no. 57, Ottawa.

Morrison, David A. 1983. *Thule Culture in Western Coronation Gulf, N.W.T.* National Museum of Man Mercury Series, Archaeological Survey of Canada Paper no. 116, Ottawa.

Morrison, David A. 1983. Thule sea mammal hunting in the western central Arctic. *Arctic Anthropology* 20(2):61-78.

Mowat, Farley 1951. *People of the Deer*. McClelland & Stewart, Toronto.

Mowat, Farley 1959. *The Desperate People*. McClelland & Stewart, Toronto.

Nash, Ronald J. 1969. *The Arctic Small Tool Tradition in Manitoba.* University of Manitoba Press, Winnipeg.

Nelson, Richard K. 1969. *Hunters of the Northern Ice.* University of Chicago Press, Chicago.

Oswalt, Wendell H. 1979. *Eskimos and Explorers.* Chandler and Sharp, Novato, CA.

Park, Robert W. 1993. The Dorset-Thule succession in Arctic North America: assessing claims for culture contact. *American Antiquity* 58(2):203-234.

Patterson, Palmer 1982. *Inuit Peoples of Canada.* Grolier, Toronto.

Petitot, Father Emile 1981. *Among the Chiglit Eskimos.* Boreal Institute for Northern Studies, University of Alberta, Edmonton.

Purich, Donald 1992. *The Inuit and their Land: The Story of Nunavut.* James Lorimer, Toronto.

Rasmussen, Knud 1929. *Intellectual Culture of the Iglulik Eskimos.* Report of the Fifth Thule Expedition 1921-24, vol. 7, no. 1, Copenhagen. (AMS Press reprint 1976).

Rasmussen, Knud 1930. *Observations on the Intellectual Culture of the Caribou Eskimos.* Report of the Fifth Thule Expedition 1921-24, vol. 7, no. 2, Copenhagen. (AMS Press reprint 1976).

Rasmussen, Knud 1931. *The Netsilik Eskimos: Social Life and Spiritual Culture.* Report of the Fifth Thule Expedition 1921-24, vol. 8, no. 1-2, Copenhagen. (AMS Press reprint 1976).

Rasmussen, Knud 1932. *Intellectual Culture of the Copper Eskimos.* Report of the Fifth Thule Expedition 1921-24, vol. 9, Copenhagen. (AMS Press reprint 1976).

Rasmussen, Knud 1942. *The Mackenzie Eskimos* (ed. H. Ostermann). Report of the Fifth Thule Expedition 1921-24, vol. 10, no. 2, Copenhagen. (AMS Press reprint 1976).

Ross, W. Gillies 1975. *Whaling and Eskimos: Hudson Bay 1860-1915.* National Museums of Canada, Publications in Ethnology no. 10, Ottawa.

Savelle, James M. 1981. The nature of nineteenth century Inuit occupations of the High Arctic islands of Canada. *Études/Inuit/Studies* 5(2):109-123.

Schledermann, Peter 1975. *Thule Eskimo Prehistory of Cumberland Sound, Baffin Island, Canada.* National Museum of Man Mercury Series, Archaeological Survey of Canada Paper no. 38, Ottawa.

Schledermann, Peter 1978. Prehistoric demographic trends in the Canadian High Arctic. *Canadian Journal of Archaeology* 2:43-58.

Schledermann, Peter 1980. Notes on Norse finds from the east coast of Ellesmere Island, N.W.T. *Arctic* 33(3):454-463.

Schledermann, Peter 1981. Eskimo and Viking finds in the High Arctic. *National Geographic* 159(5):574-601.

Schledermann, Peter 1990. *Crossroads to Greenland: 3000 Years of Prehistory in the Eastern High Arctic.* Arctic Institute of North America, University of Calgary.

Stefansson, V. 1919. *The Stefansson-Anderson Arctic Expedition: Preliminary Ethnological Report.* Anthropological Papers vol. 14, American Museum of Natural History, New York. (AMS Press reprint 1978).

Swinton, George 1972. *Sculpture of the Inuit.* McClelland & Stewart, Toronto.

Taylor, J. Garth 1974. *Labrador Eskimo Settlements of the Early Contact Period.* National Museums of Canada, Publications in Ethnology no. 9, Ottawa.

Taylor, J. Garth 1985. The Arctic whale cult in Labrador. *Etudes/Inuit/Studies* 9(2):121-132.

Taylor, William E., Jr. 1968. *The Arnapik and Tyara Sites: An Archaeological Study of Dorset Culture Origins.* Memoirs of the Society for American Archaeology no. 22.

Taylor, William E., Jr. and G. Swinton 1967. Prehistoric Dorset art. *The Beaver* 298:32-47.

Tester, Frank J. and P. Kulchyski 1994. *Tammarniit (Mistakes): Inuit Relocation in the Eastern Arctic, 1939-63.* University of British Columbia Press, Vancouver.

Tuck, James A. 1976. *Newfoundland and Labrador Prehistory.* National Museum of Man, Ottawa.

Turner, Lucien M. 1979. *Indians and Eskimos in the Quebec-Labrador Peninsula.* Presses Comeditex, Quebec.

Usher, Peter 1971. The Canadian Western Arctic: A century of change. *Anthropologica* 13(1-2):169-183.

Valentine, Victor F. and F. G. Vallee (eds.) 1968. *Eskimo of the Canadian Arctic.* Carleton Library, McClelland & Stewart, Toronto.

Vallee, F. G. 1967. *Kabloona and Eskimo in the Central Keewatin.* The Canadian Research Centre for Anthropology, Saint Paul University, Ottawa.

Wenzel, G. 1991. *Animal Rights, Human Rights: Ecology, Economy and Ideology in the Canadian Arctic.* University of Toronto Press, Toronto.

Weyer, Edward M. 1932. *The Eskimos: Their Environment and Folkways.* Yale University Press, New Haven, CT.

Yorga, Brian W. D. 1980. *Washout: A Western Thule Site on Herschel Island, Yukon Territory*. National Museum of Man Mercury Series, Archaeological Survey of Canada Paper no. 98, Ottawa.

Chapter Eleven *The Métis*

The major historical source on the Métis is the massive two-volume work by Giraud (published in French in 1945, reprinted in English translation in 1986). A spate of more recent books has appeared on the Métis. Purich (1988), Harrison (1985) and Sealey and Lussier (1975) provide useful and readable summaries; see also the articles in Peterson and Brown (1985). The important role of women in the fur trade has been examined by Van Kirk (1980) and Brown (1980). A number of eyewitness accounts exist for the Red River colony and the buffalo hunt, but perhaps the best is given by Ross (1856), a prominent member of the colony. A number of Métis writers, such as Campbell (1973), Adams (1975) and Redbird (1980), provide their perspective on Métis culture and history.

Numerous studies on Riel and the rebellions exist. For somewhat different viewpoints see the works of Stanley (1960, 1963), Howard (1952) and Flanagan (1979, 1983). Woodcock (1975) provides a useful biography of Gabriel Dumont.

Adams, Howard 1975. *Prison of Grass: Canada from the Native Point of View*. General, Toronto.

Barron, F. Laurie and J. B. Waldram (eds.) 1986. *1885 and After: Native Society in Transition*. Canadian Plains Research Centre, University of Regina.

Brown, Jennifer S. H. 1980. *Strangers in Blood: Fur Trade Company Families in Indian Country*. University of British Columbia Press, Vancouver.

Burley, David V., G. A. Horsfall and J. D. Brandon 1992. *Structural Considerations of Métis Ethnicity: An Archaeological, Architectural, and Historical Study*. University of South Dakota Press, Vermillion.

Campbell, Maria 1973. *Halfbreed*. McClelland & Stewart, Toronto.

Chartrand, Paul L .A. H. 1991. *Manitoba's Métis Settlement Scheme of 1870*. Native Law Centre, University of Saskatchewan, Saskatoon.

Daniels, Harry W. 1979. *The Forgotten People: Métis and Non-Status Indian Land Claims*. Native Council of Canada, Ottawa.

Dempsey, Hugh A. 1984. *Big Bear: The End of Freedom*. Douglas & McIntyre, Vancouver.

Driben, Paul 1983. The nature of Métis claims. *Canadian Journal of Native Studies* 3(1):183-196.

Flanagan, Thomas 1979. *Louis "David" Riel: "Prophet of the New World."* University of Toronto Press, Toronto.

Flanagan, Thomas 1983. *Riel and the Rebellion: 1885 Reconsidered*. Western Producer Prairie Books, Saskatoon.

Flanagan, Thomas 1991. *Métis Lands in Manitoba*. University of Calgary Press, Calgary.

Foster, John E. 1986. The Plains Métis. In *Native Peoples: The Canadian Experience*, ed. R. B. Morrison and C. R. Wilson, pp. 375-404. McClelland & Stewart, Toronto.

Giraud, Marcel 1986. *The Métis in the Canadian West* (2 vols.). The University of Alberta Press, Edmonton.

Harrison, Julia D. 1985. *Metis*. Glenbow-Alberta Institute, with Douglas & McIntyre, Vancouver.

Howard, Joseph K. 1952. *Strange Empire: The Story of Louis Riel*. Swan, Toronto.

Lussier, A. S. (ed.) 1979. *Louis Riel and the Métis*. Pemmican, Winnipeg.

Lussier, Antoine S. and D. B. Sealey 1978. *The Other Natives: The Métis* (3 vols.). Manitoba Métis Federation Press, Winnipeg.

MacLeod, Margaret A. and W. L. Morton 1963. *Cuthbert Grant of Grantown*. McClelland & Stewart, Toronto.

Martin, Fred V. 1989. Federal and provincial responsibility in the Métis settlements of Alberta. In *Aboriginal Peoples and Government Responsibility*, ed. D .C. Hawkes, pp. 243-296. Carleton University Press, Ottawa.

Métis Association of Alberta, Joe Sawchuk, Patricia Sawchuk and Theresa Ferguson 1981. *Métis Land Rights in Alberta: A Political History*. Metis Association of Alberta, Edmonton.

Morton, W. L. (ed.) 1956. *Alexander Begg's Red River Journal and Other Papers Relative to the Red River Resistance of 1869-1870*. Champlain Society, Toronto.

Pannekoek, Frits 1991. *A Snug Little Flock: The Social Origins of the Riel Resistance of 1869-70*. Watson & Dwyer, Winnipeg.

Pelletier, Emile 1977. *A Social History of the Manitoba Métis*. Manitoba Métis Federation Press, Winnipeg.

Peterson, Jacqueline 1978. Prelude to Red River: a social portrait of the Great Lakes Métis. *Ethnohistory* 25(1):41-67.

Peterson, Jacqueline and Jennifer S. H. Brown (eds.) 1985. *The New Peoples: Being and Becoming Métis in North America*. University of Manitoba Press, Winnipeg.

Pocklington, T. C. 1991. *The Government and Politics of the Alberta Metis Settlements*. Canadian Plains Research Centre, University of Regina.

Purich, Donald 1988. *The Metis*. James Lorimer, Toronto.

Redbird, Duke 1980. *We Are Métis*. Ontario Métis and Non Status Indian Association, Willowdale, ON.

Ross, Alexander 1856. *The Red River Settlement: Its Rise, Progress, and Present State*. Smith, Elder, London.

Sawchuk, Joe 1978. *The Metis of Manitoba*. Peter Martin Associates, Toronto.

Sealey, D. Bruce and Antoine S. Lussier 1975. *The Métis: Canada's Forgotten People*. Manitoba Métis Federation Press, Winnipeg.

Sprague, D. N. 1988. *Canada and the Métis, 1869-1885*. Wilfrid Laurier University Press, Waterloo, ON.

Sprague, D. N. 1992. Métis land claims. In *Aboriginal Land Claims in Canada*, ed. K. Coates, pp. 195-213. Copp Clark Pitman, Toronto.

Spry, Irene M. (ed.) 1963. *The Palliser Expedition*. Macmillan, Toronto.

Stanley, George F. G. 1960. *The Birth of Western Canada: A History of the Riel Rebellions*. University of Toronto Press, Toronto.

Stanley, George F. G. 1963. *Louis Riel*. Ryerson Press, Toronto.

Taylor, John L. 1983. An historical introduction to Métis claims in Canada. *Canadian Journal of Native Studies* 3(1):151-181.

Tremaudan, A. H. de 1982. *Hold High Your Heads (History of the Métis Nation in Western Canada)*. Pemmican, Winnipeg.

Van Kirk, Sylvia 1980. *Many Tender Ties: Women in Fur-Trade Society in Western Canada, 1670-1870*. Watson & Dwyer, Winnipeg.

Verbicky-Todd, Eleanor 1984. *Communal Buffalo Hunting Among the Plains Indians*. Occasional Paper No. 24, Archaeological Survey of Alberta, Edmonton.

Woodcock, George 1975. *Gabriel Dumont*. Hurtig, Edmonton.

Chapter Twelve *Native Canadians: Major Contemporary Issues*

Frideres (1993) provides a useful overview on contemporary native issues in Canada. Aboriginal legal issues are extensively reviewed by Morse (1985) and Woodward (1989). Coates (1992) provides recent summaries on the state of land claims in Canada. The Royal Commission on Aboriginal Peoples (1993) has released the reports of several National Round Tables on modern issues. Perspectives of aboriginal politicians are given in Cardinal (1969, 1977), Manuel and Posluns (1974), Mercredi and Turpel (1993) and contributors to the volume edited by Richardson (1989).

Asch, Michael 1984. *Home and Native Land: Aboriginal Rights and the Canadian Constitution*. Methuen, Toronto.

Barman, Jean, Yvonne Hebert and D. McCaskill (eds.) 1987. *Indian Education in Canada* (vol. 2: *The Challenge*). University of British Columbia Press, Vancouver.

Bartlett, Richard H. 1990. *Indian Reserves and Aboriginal Lands in Canada: A Homeland*. University of Saskatchewan Native Law Centre, Saskatoon.

Boldt, Menno 1993. *Surviving as Indians: The Challenge of Self-Government*. University of Toronto Press, Toronto.

Boldt, Menno and J. A. Long (eds.) 1985. *The Quest for Justice: Aboriginal Peoples and Aboriginal Rights*. University of Toronto Press, Toronto.

Brody, Hugh 1971. *Indians on Skid Row*. Northern Science Research Group, Department of Indian Affairs and Northern Development, Ottawa.

Brown, George and Ron Maguire 1979. *Indian Treaties in Historical Perspective*. Research Branch, Department of Indian and Northern Affairs, Ottawa.

Canada, House of Commons 1983. *Indian Self-Government in Canada: Report of the Special Committee*. Ottawa.

Canada, Indian and Northern Affairs 1980. *Indian Conditions: A Survey*. Ottawa.

Canada, Indian and Northern Affairs 1985. *Living Treaties: Lasting Agreements: Report of the Task Force To Review Comprehensive Claims Policy*. Ottawa.

Canada, Indian and Northern Affairs 1985. *Task Force on Indian Economic Development*. Ottawa.

Canadian Education Association 1984. *Recent Developments in Native Education*. Toronto.

Cardinal, Harold 1969. *The Unjust Society: The Tragedy of Canada's Indians*. Hurtig, Edmonton.

Cardinal, Harold 1977. *The Rebirth of Canada's Indians*. Hurtig, Edmonton.

Cassidy, Frank (ed.) 1991. *Aboriginal Self-Determination*. Oolichan Books, Lantzville, BC.

Cassidy, Frank and Robert L. Bish 1989. *Indian Government: Its Meaning in Practice*. Oolichan Books, Lantzville, BC.

Coates, Ken (ed.) 1992. *Aboriginal Land Claims in Canada: A Regional Perspective*. Copp Clark Pitman, Toronto.

Comeau, Pauline 1993. *Elijah: No Ordinary Hero*. Douglas & McIntyre, Vancouver.

Comeau, Pauline and Aldo Santin 1990. *The First Canadians: A Profile of Canada's Native People Today*. James Lorimer, Toronto.

Corrigan, Samuel W. and Lawrence J. Barkwell (eds.) 1991. *The Struggle for Recognition: Canadian Justice and the Métis Nation*. Pemmican, Winnipeg.

Cumming, Peter A. and Neil H. Mickenberg (eds.) 1972. *Native Rights in Canada* (2nd ed.). General, Toronto.

Daniels, H. W. (Commissioner) 1981. *Native People and the Constitution of Canada* (The Report of the Métis and Non-Status Indian Constitutional Review Commission). Mutual Press, Ottawa.

Dosman, Edgar J. 1972. *Indians: The Urban Dilemma*. McClelland & Stewart, Toronto.

Dyck, Noel 1991. *What is the Indian "Problem": Tutelage and Resistance in Canadian Indian Administration*. Institute of Social and Economic Research, Memorial University of Newfoundland, St. John's.

Engelstad, Diane and John Bird (eds.) 1992. *Nation to Nation: Aboriginal Sovereignty and the Future of Canada*. House of Anansi Press, Concord, ON.

Frideres, James. S. 1993. *Native Peoples in Canada: Contemporary Conflicts* (4th ed). Prentice-Hall, Scarborough, ON.

Gaffney, R. E., G. P. Gould, and A. J. Semple 1984. *Broken Promises: The Aboriginal Constitutional Conferences*. New Brunswick Association of Métis and Non-Status Indians, Fredericton.

Hamilton, A. C. and C. M. Sinclair 1991. *Report of the Aboriginal Justice Inquiry of Manitoba*, Vol. 1: *The Justice System and Aboriginal People*. Queen's Printer, Winnipeg.

Hawkes, David C. (ed.) 1989. *Aboriginal Peoples and Government Responsibility: Exploring Federal and Provincial Roles*. Carleton University Press, Ottawa.

Hawley, Donna L. 1993. *The Annotated Indian Act 1993*. Carswell, Toronto.

Hawthorn, H. B. (ed.) 1966. *A Survey of the Contemporary Indians of Canada: Economic, Political, Educational Needs and Policies* (2 vols.). Indian Affairs Branch, Ottawa.

Jamieson, Kathleen 1978. *Indian Women and the Law in Canada: Citizens Minus*. Advisory Council on the Status of Women, Ottawa.

Johnston, Basil H. 1988. *Indian School Days*. Key Porter Books, Toronto.

Johnston, Patrick 1983. *Native Children and the Child Welfare System*. James Lorimer, Toronto.

Krotz, Larry 1980. *Urban Indians: The Strangers in Canada's Cities*. Hurtig, Edmonton.

Krotz, Larry 1990. *Indian Country: Inside Another Canada*. McClelland & Stewart, Toronto.

Kuhlen, Daniel J. and Anne Skarsgard 1985. *A Layperson's Guide to Treaty Rights in Canada*. University of Saskatchewan Native Law Centre, Saskatoon.

LaRoque, Emma 1975. *Defeathering the Indian*. Book Society of Canada, Agincourt, ON.

Little Bear, Leroy, Menno Boldt, and J. A. Long (eds.) 1984. *Pathways to Self-Determination: Canadian Indians and the Canadian State*. University of Toronto Press, Toronto.

McCullum, Hugh and Karmel McCullum 1975. *This Land is Not For Sale*. Anglican Book Centre, Toronto.

Manuel, George and Michael Posluns 1974. *The Fourth World: An Indian Reality*. Collier-Macmillan, Don Mills, ON.

Maracle, Brian 1993. *Crazywater: Native Voices on Addiction and Recovery*. Viking, Toronto.

Mercredi, Ovide and Mary Ellen Turpel 1993. *In the Rapids: Navigating the Future of First Nations*. Viking, Toronto.

Morse, Bradford W. (ed.) 1985. *Aboriginal Peoples and the Law: Indian, Metis and Inuit Rights in Canada*. Carleton University Press, Ottawa.

Naglcr, Mark 1970. *Indians in the City*. Canadian Research Centre for Anthropology, Saint Paul University, Ottawa.

Paquette, Jerry 1986. *Aboriginal Self-Government and Education in Canada*. Institute of Intergovernmental Relations, Kingston, ON.

Ponting, J. Rick (ed.) 1986. *Arduous Journey: Canadian Indians and Decolonization*. McClelland & Stewart, Toronto.

Ponting, J. Rick and Roger Gibbons 1980. *Out of Irrelevance: A Socio-Political Introduction to Indian Affairs in Canada*. Butterworths, Toronto.

Purich, Donald 1986. *Our Land: Native Rights in Canada*. James Lorimer, Toronto.

Richardson, Boyce (ed.) 1989. *Drum Beat: Anger and Renewal In Indian Country*. Assembly of First Nations and Summerhill Press, Toronto.

Richardson, Boyce 1993. *People of Terra Nullius: Betrayal and Rebirth in Aboriginal Canada*. Douglas & McIntyre, Vancouver.

Robertson, Heather 1970. *Reservations are for Indians*. James Lewis & Samuel, Toronto.

Royal Commission on Aboriginal Peoples 1993. *Aboriginal Peoples and the Justice System: Report of the National Round Table on Aboriginal Justice Issues*. Canada Communication Group, Ottawa.

Royal Commission on Aboriginal Peoples 1993. *Aboriginal Peoples in Urban Centres: Report of the National Round Table on Aboriginal Urban Issues*. Canada Communication Group, Ottawa.

Royal Commission on Aboriginal Peoples 1993. *Partners in Confederation: Aboriginal Peoples, Self-Government, and the Constitution*. Canada Communication Group, Ottawa.

Royal Commission on Aboriginal Peoples 1993. *The Path to Healing: Report of the National Round Table on Aboriginal Health and Social Issues*. Canada Communication Group, Ottawa.

Schmeiser, Douglas A. 1974. *The Native Offender and the Law*. Law Reform Commission of Canada.

Silverman, Robert A. and Marianne O. Nielsen (eds.) 1992. *Aboriginal Peoples and Canadian Criminal Justice*. Butterworths, Toronto.

Smith, Dan 1993. *The Seventh Fire: The Struggle for Aboriginal Government*. Key Porter Books, Toronto.

Stanbury, W. T. assisted by Jay H. Siegel 1975. *Success and Failure: Indians in Urban Society*. University of British Columbia Press, Vancouver.

Tanner, Adrian (ed.) 1983. *The Politics of Indianness: Case Studies of Native Ethnopolitics in Canada*. Institute of Social and Economic Research, Memorial University of Newfoundland, St. John's.

Tennant, Paul 1990. *Aboriginal Peoples and Politics: The Indian Land Question in British Columbia, 1849-1989*. University of British Columbia Press, Vancouver.

Waubageshig (ed.) 1970. *The Only Good Indian: Essays by Canadian Indians*. New Press, Toronto.

Weaver, Sally M. 1981. *Making Canadian Indian Policy: The Hidden Agenda 1968-70*. University of Toronto Press, Toronto.

Woodward, Jack 1989. *Native Law*. Carswell, Toronto.

Wotherspoon Terry and Vic Satzewich 1993. *First Nations: Race, Class, and Gender Relations*. Nelson Canada, Scarborough, ON.

York, Geoffrey 1989. *The Dispossessed: Life and Death in Native Canada*. Lester & Orpen Dennys, Toronto.

Index